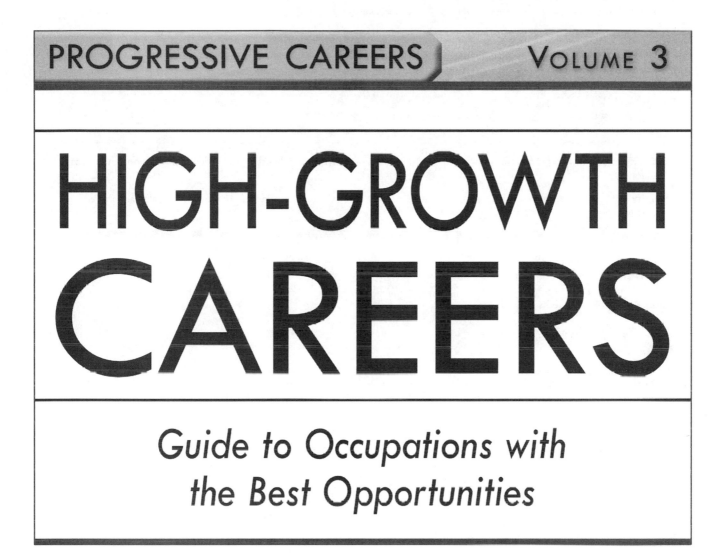

PROGRESSIVE CAREERS — VOLUME 3

HIGH-GROWTH CAREERS

Guide to Occupations with the Best Opportunities

The Editors @ JIST

jist Works
America's Career Publisher

PROGRESSIVE CAREERS, VOLUME 3

High-Growth Careers: Guide to Occupations with the Best Opportunities

© 2011 by JIST Publishing

Published by JIST Works, an imprint of JIST Publishing
7321 Shadeland Station, Suite 200
Indianapolis, IN 46256-3923
Phone: 800-648-JIST   Fax: 877-454-7839
E-mail: info@jist.com   Web site: www.jist.com

Visit our Web site at www.jist.com for information on JIST, tables of contents, sample pages, and ordering instructions for our many products.

Quantity discounts are available for JIST products. Please call 800-648-5478 or visit www.jist.com for a free catalog and more information.

Acquisitions Editor: Susan Pines
Writers/Researchers: Laurence Shatkin, Ph.D., and Dave Anderson
Designer: Aleata Halbig
Proofreaders: Paula Lowell, Jeanne Clark

Printed in the United States of America

15 14 13 12 11 10   9 8 7 6 5 4 3 2 1

Library of Congress Cataloging-in-Publication data appears in *Progressive Careers, Volume 1: Nontraditional Careers.*

We have been careful to provide accurate information throughout this book, but it is possible that errors and omissions have been introduced. Please consider this in making any career plans or other important decisions. Trust your own judgment above all else and in all things.

Trademarks: All brand names and product names used in this book are trade names, service marks, trademarks, or registered trademarks of their respective owners.

ISBN for four-volume set: 978-1-59357-768-1

ABOUT *PROGRESSIVE CAREERS*

Do you want to save the earth? Advance science? Create innovative technology? Forge a path for others to follow? Or do you want a job with the potential for growth and security? Pick the *Progressive Careers* volume that matches your motive and discover the kinds of careers that speak to you.

Each book in *Progressive Careers* consists of carefully chosen and well-researched job descriptions that represent growing, cutting-edge, or nontraditional ways of earning a living. It's a contemporary, relevant, and exciting way to approach career research and career choice.

Here's a brief description of each *Progressive Careers* volume:

- **Volume 1.** *Nontraditional Careers: Guide to Nontraditional Occupations for Women and for Men.* Describes jobs traditionally dominated by men or women.

- **Volume 2.** *STEM Careers: Guide to Occupations in Science, Technology, Engineering, and Mathematics.* Covers jobs focused on the study and application of science, technology, engineering, and mathematics.

- **Volume 3.** *High-Growth Careers: Guide to Occupations with the Best Opportunities.* Features jobs that are projected to need more workers in the future.

- **Volume 4.** *Green Careers: Guide to Occupations That Benefit the Environment.* Explains jobs that conserve resources and preserve our environment.

By carefully researching careers of interest, you will be better informed about all aspects of the jobs you are considering—from potential pay to job prospects, from the amount of education required to the daily working conditions. This information will help you make better education and career decisions. While the perseverance depends on you, *Progressive Careers* can help with planning an exciting future.

TABLE OF CONTENTS

Introduction

What Is a High-Growth Career?

A high-growth career certainly *sounds* good—and in general, it is better than one with little or no growth—but what does high-growth mean? When an occupation is growing, the size of its workforce is getting larger. Like everything in economics, this is the result of a combination of supply and demand. The demand for workers is produced by some economic need, such as the need for a certain kind of product or service. Consumers, businesses, or government agencies are willing to pay for the product or service, so employers can afford to pay their current workers and create job openings.

Of course, there must also be a supply of workers to hold these jobs, and this can happen for several reasons:

- Many young people may be preparing for and entering the career.

- Many mid-life career changers may be switching to this occupation.

- People *already* in the occupation may be staying instead of retiring or moving on to another career at the usual rates.

The economists at the U.S. Department of Labor monitor economic trends and, based on what they observe of supply and demand for workers in each occupation in our economy, they forecast the amount of growth (or shrinkage) that is likely to happen to the occupation. These forecasts enabled us to create this book. The *average* growth that the Department of Labor projects for all occupations in the 10-year period ending 2018 is 10.1 percent. We limited the book to 57 occupations for which the Department of Labor forecasts at least 20 percent growth, which is considered well above average.

Why Consider a High-Growth Career?

Occupations that are growing fast usually have a lot of job openings, which means that you will more likely have some choice about where you work. Later, if the particular position turns out to be unsuitable, you're more likely to have chances to jump to another employer. If the job is growing especially fast and the supply of qualified workers is low, you may find salaries increasing as employers compete for workers. Your stretches of unemployment will probably be few and brief.

One possible disadvantage to being in a high-growth career is if the need for the work is so great that you are expected to work long hours. But remember that these long hours are likely to earn you a good income, perhaps overtime pay.

1

Does "High-Growth" Equal "Guaranteed Job"?

Perhaps you've noticed that in the preceding paragraphs we use the words "likely" and "may" a lot, rather than "definitely" and "will." That's because the economic forecasts that are the basis of this book are like weather forecasts: They're the best projections that experts can make from present conditions.

Of course, conditions sometimes change in ways that economists don't foresee. For example, unexpected breakthroughs in technology can drastically change the way people do their jobs. The invention of the phonograph severely reduced the number of jobs for musicians, musical instrument makers, and music teachers because live performance no longer was the only way to listen to music. On the other hand, the new technology also created jobs. Record companies formed, and for decades every downtown business district or shopping mall had at least one record store, providing jobs that didn't exist before Thomas Edison's invention. Now we're seeing a drastic loss of jobs in the music distribution business because the way we obtain music has changed again, this time because of the Internet—a destroyer and creator of jobs in many fields. Perhaps in the next few years some other breakthrough technology will emerge and have as big an impact as the Internet, but there is no way to construct a forecast around an unknown factor.

The lesson to take away is that even if you aim for a high-growth job and its future seems promising, you should be prepared for changes in your career. Cultivate a range of skills so you can be flexible if conditions change. The most important skill of all is the *ability to learn,* and one of the most important work habits is a willingness to learn constantly. You'll need to learn new skills just to stay in the job you're in, but up-to-date skills will also be helpful when some new career opportunity comes along.

The Difference Between Job Growth and Job Openings

Another principle of economics to bear in mind is that job *growth* does not, by itself, guarantee a large number of job *openings.* For example, consider audiologists, the workers who assess and treat people with hearing disorders. This occupation is growing at the impressive rate of 25 percent, but it's a tiny occupation, with only around 13,000 workers. Therefore, despite its fast growth, it's expected to create only about 580 job openings each year. Now consider cashiers, which is growing at only 3.5 percent and therefore is not included in this book. It has a workforce of more than 3.5 million, and it is expected to create about 170,000 job openings each year.

When an occupation (like cashiers) has a huge workforce, a large number of workers are likely to leave the occupation each year because of retirement, illness, or job opportunities elsewhere—and as long as the occupation is not shrinking rapidly, this turnover means job openings for other workers. Turnover is particularly high in jobs (like cashiers) that are easy to obtain without a lot of education or training. Workers have not invested a lot in getting the job, and most such jobs don't pay very well, so the workers don't hesitate to leave it. Now go back to audiologists. To get their job, these workers need at least a master's degree, not to mention strong interpersonal and technology skills. After meeting these qualifications, passing the licensure exam, and landing their professional-level (and high-paying) job, they tend to stick around for many years rather than leave and create job openings.

So when you consider a high-growth career, be sure to look at the figure for projected job openings.

Consider the Competition

One final factor to consider is the amount of competition for job openings. The figures on job growth and openings don't tell you how many people will be competing with you to be hired, and that's an important issue that you should research for any tentative career goal. Profes sional athletes are the classic example of a highly competitive occupation, because only a few exceptionally talented and highly driven athletes can outcompete the thousands of players who enjoy the sport and dream of high salaries and lucrative product-endorsement contracts. For an example of the opposite, consider cost estimators. The occupation is not well known, and colleges do not offer a specific bachelor's degree program targeted for it. Therefore, anyone with a degree in a construction-related field or several years of experience in the industry should face little competition and have good opportunities.

Although the Department of Labor does not publish figures on the supply of job candidates competing for each job opening, many of the job descriptions in this book (and in the other volumes in *Progressive Careers*) provide informative statements under the "Job Prospects" heading.

To learn about the level of competition, you also should speak to people who educate or train tomorrow's workers. These educators have a good idea of how many graduates find rewarding employment and how quickly. People in the workforce can provide additional insights into this issue. Use your critical-thinking skills to evaluate what people tell you. For example, educators or trainers may be trying to recruit you, whereas people in the workforce may be trying to discourage you from competing. Get a variety of opinions to balance out possible biases.

Would a High-Growth Career Suit You?

The high-growth careers are found in many different industries, with different work conditions and different kinds and amounts of educational requirements. Therefore, before you decide on a career that might suit you, you need to know more about them (and about yourself) than simply the opportunities to be employed.

Probably the best place to start is with some self-exploration. Appendix A in the *Green Careers* volume can help you consider how your personality, interests, skills, and work preferences fit with your career options. The appendix includes information to help you set priorities, plus lists of high-growth jobs related to your results.

When you decide on a career goal, you will need to get the appropriate education or training to prepare for it. You should carefully consider all of your options for learning, from apprenticeships and military training to graduate and professional degrees. Appendix B in the *Green Careers* volume covers all the ways people get education and training. Read it to find the options that will work best for you.

While many people choose a high-growth career because of the nature of the work itself (think people who go into nursing because they want to help others), others choose a career precisely *because* it is growing (think people who go into nursing because they are confident there will be a job waiting for them when they finish their degree). Similarly, you will find some accountants who love what they do and other accountants who do what they do because the job offers security and a sizeable paycheck. As you research careers, it is important to try to balance all of your wants and needs and to consider the external and internal rewards of a job.

Another issue that will greatly affect your career choice is the kind and amount of education or training you're willing to undertake. You may not have thought about some options, such as apprenticeship and military training. Appendix B in the volume about *Green Careers* covers all the ways people get education and training. Read it to find the options that will work best for you.

What's Inside

Effective career research and planning requires having all the facts. *Progressive Careers* offers the latest information in an interesting, easy-to-read format. Each entry in this volume includes the following:

- The name of the occupation with a very brief summary.

- **Just the Facts.** At-a-glance information on median earnings, projected job growth through 2018, estimated number of annual job openings, and the minimal education and training required. In cases where the job is linked to multiple specializations with differing entry requirements, more than one level of education or training is listed.

- **While at Work.** An in-depth description of the job, including work tasks and job duties, alternative job titles, and working conditions.

- **Job Fit.** The skills and work styles required by the job as well as the personality types and career cluster interests the job is likely to satisfy.

- **What's Required.** The education and training required for getting and advancing on the job, including alternative education paths, certification and licensing requirements, postsecondary courses to consider, and high school courses necessary for preparation. You'll learn how workers move up in the career.

- **Employment.** Current and future job prospects and in-depth earnings information for the job. Bar charts depict job growth, annual job openings, beginning wages, and median wages. Related jobs are also listed.

- **How to Learn More.** Sources of additional information on the job, including Web sites.

- **Why It's Hot.** Learn why this career is growing, trends that are increasing demand, or what you can do to take advantage of new opportunities in the field.

In addition, throughout each job description you will find **Consider This** sections with numerous facts and figures. This material offers valuable insights into key aspects of the job.

The information for each career is presented so that you can quickly find the facts or data you need. However, we encourage you to read the entire description for the careers that interest you the most. For details on our data sources, see Appendix A in *Green Careers*.

Acknowledgement. Thank you to the Bureau of Labor Statistics, U.S. Department of Labor, for the occupational data and other information used in this book.

HIGH-GROWTH CAREERS

Accountants and Auditors

Accountants and auditors prepare, analyze, and verify financial documents in order to provide information to clients.

Just the Facts

Earnings: $59,430
Job Growth: 21.6%
Annual Openings: 49,750
Education and Training: Bachelor's degree

◼ While at Work

Accountants and auditors help to ensure that the nation's firms are run efficiently, its public records kept accurately, and its taxes paid properly and on time. They analyze and communicate financial information for companies, individuals, and governments. Many accountants also offer budget analysis, financial and investment planning, information technology consulting, and limited legal services.

Specific job duties vary widely among the four major fields of accounting and auditing: public, management, and government accounting and internal auditing.

Public accountants perform a broad range of accounting, auditing, tax, and consulting activities for their clients, which may be corporations, governments, nonprofit organizations, or individuals. For example, some public accountants concentrate on tax matters such as advising companies about the tax advantages and disadvantages of certain business decisions and preparing individual income tax returns. Others offer advice in areas such as compensation or employee health-care benefits or the selection of controls to safeguard assets. Still others audit clients' financial statements and inform investors and authorities that the statements have been correctly prepared and reported. These accountants are also referred to as *external auditors*. Public accountants, many of whom are Certified Public Accountants (CPAs), generally have their own businesses or work for public accounting firms.

Management accountants—also called *cost, managerial, industrial, corporate, or private accountants*—record and analyze the financial information of the companies for which they work. Among their other responsibilities are budgeting, performance evaluation, cost management,

and asset management. Usually, management accountants are involved in strategic planning or the development of new products. They analyze and interpret the financial information that corporate executives need in order to make sound business decisions. They also prepare financial reports for other groups, including stockholders, creditors, regulatory agencies, and tax authorities. Within accounting departments, management accountants may work in various areas, including financial analysis, planning and budgeting, and cost accounting.

Government accountants and auditors work in the public sector, maintaining and examining the records of government agencies and auditing private businesses and individuals whose activities are subject to government regulations or taxation. Accountants employed by federal, state, and local governments ensure that revenues are received and expenditures are made in accordance with laws and regulations. Those employed by the federal government may work as Internal Revenue Service agents or in financial management, financial institution examination, or budget analysis and administration.

Internal auditors verify the effectiveness of their organization's internal controls and check for mismanagement, waste, or fraud. They examine and evaluate their firms' financial and information systems and management procedures to ensure that records are accurate and controls are adequate. They also review company operations, evaluating their efficiency, effectiveness, and compliance with corporate policies and government regulations.

> ### CONSIDER THIS…
>
> In response to recent accounting scandals, new federal legislation restricts the nonauditing services that public accountants can provide to clients. If an accounting firm audits a client's financial statements, that same firm cannot provide advice on human resources, technology, investment banking, or legal matters, although accountants may still advise on tax issues.

> ### CONSIDER THIS…
>
> Computers enable accountants and auditors to be more mobile and to use their clients' computer systems to extract information more easily. As a result, a growing number of accountants and auditors with extensive computer skills specialize in correcting problems with software or in developing software to meet unique data management and analytical needs.

Internal auditors may also have specialty titles such as information technology auditors, environmental auditors, and compliance auditors.

Many accountants and auditors work in comfortable offices.

Technology is rapidly changing the nature of the work of most accountants and auditors. With the aid of special software packages, accountants summarize transactions in the standard formats of financial records and organize data in special formats employed in financial analysis. These accounting packages greatly reduce the tedious work associated with data management and recordkeeping. Accountants also are beginning to perform more technical duties such as implementing, controlling, and auditing computer systems and networks and developing a business's technology plans.

CONSIDER THIS...

Tax specialists often work long hours during the tax season. It's not unusual for accountants to work 60-hour weeks during the months of January through April.

Accountants also act as personal advisors. They not only provide clients with accounting and tax help, but also help them develop personal budgets, manage assets and investments, plan for retirement, and recognize and reduce their exposure to risks. This role is in response to clients' demands for a single trustworthy individual or firm to meet all of their financial needs. However, accountants are restricted from providing these services to clients whose financial statements they also prepare.

Also Known As

Forensic accountants investigate white-collar crimes such as securities fraud and embezzlement, bankruptcies and contract disputes, and other complex and possibly criminal financial transactions. Forensic accountants combine their knowledge of accounting and finance with law and investigative techniques to determine whether an activity is illegal. Many forensic accountants work closely with law enforcement personnel and lawyers during investigations, often appearing as expert witnesses during trials.

Job Fit

Personality Type
Conventional-Enterprising-Investigative

Career Clusters
04 Business, Management, and Administration
07 Government and Public Administration

Skills
Computer Programming
Mathematics
Management
Thought-Processing
Communications
Social Skills

Work Styles
Analytical Thinking
Integrity
Attention to Detail
Achievement/Effort
Persistence
Leadership
Stress Tolerance
Initiative

Working Conditions

Most accountants and auditors work in a typical office setting. Some may be able to do part of their work at home. Accountants and auditors employed by public accounting firms, government agencies, and organizations with multiple locations may travel frequently to perform audits at branches, clients' places of business, or government facilities.

Most accountants and auditors usually work a standard 40-hour week, but many work longer hours, particularly if they are self-employed and have numerous clients.

■ What's Required

Most accountants and auditors need at least a bachelor's degree in business, accounting, or a related field. Many accountants and auditors choose to obtain certification to help advance their careers, such as becoming a Certified Public Accountant (CPA).

Education and Training

Most accountant and auditor positions require at least a bachelor's degree in accounting or a related field. Some employers prefer applicants with a master's degree in accounting or with a master's degree in business administration with a concentration in accounting.

Some universities and colleges are now offering programs to prepare students to work in growing specialty professions such as internal auditing. In addition, many professional associations offer continuing professional education courses, conferences, and seminars.

> **CONSIDER THIS...**
> Some graduates of junior colleges or business or correspondence schools, as well as bookkeepers and accounting clerks who meet the education and experience requirements set by their employers, can obtain junior accounting positions and advance to accountant positions by demonstrating their accounting skills on the job.

Most beginning accountants and auditors work under supervision or closely with an experienced accountant or auditor before gaining more independence and responsibility.

Any accountant filing a report with the Securities and Exchange Commission (SEC) is required by law to be a Certified Public Accountant (CPA). CPAs are licensed by their State Board of Accountancy. Any accountant who passes a national exam and meets the other requirements of the state where they practice can become a CPA. The vast majority of states require CPA candidates to be college graduates, but a few states will substitute a number of years of public accounting experience for a college degree.

As of 2009, 47 states and the District of Columbia required CPA candidates to complete 150 semester hours of college coursework—an additional 30 hours beyond the usual 4-year bachelor's degree. In response to this trend, many schools offer master's degrees as part of the 150 hours. Prospective accounting majors should carefully research accounting curricula and the requirements of any states in which they hope to become licensed.

All states use the four-part Uniform CPA Examination prepared by the American Institute of Certified Public Accountants (AICPA). The CPA examination is rigorous, and less than one-half of those who take it each year pass every part on the first try. Candidates are not required to pass all four parts at once, but most states require candidates to pass all four sections within 18 months of passing their first section. Most states also require applicants for a CPA certificate to have some accounting experience; however, requirements vary by state or jurisdiction.

> **CONSIDER THIS...**
> The CPA exam is now computerized and is offered 2 months out of every quarter at various testing centers throughout the United States.

Nearly all states require CPAs and other public accountants to complete a certain number of hours of continuing professional education before their licenses can be renewed. The professional associations representing accountants sponsor numerous courses, seminars, group study programs, and other forms of continuing education.

Postsecondary Programs to Consider

- Accounting
- Accounting and business/management
- Accounting and computer science
- Accounting and finance
- Auditing
- Taxation

Additional Qualifications

Previous experience in accounting or auditing can help an applicant get a job. Many colleges offer students the opportunity to gain experience through summer or part-time internship programs conducted by public accounting or business firms. In addition, as many business processes are now automated, practical knowledge of computers and their applications is a great asset for jobseekers.

People planning a career in accounting and auditing should have an aptitude for mathematics and be able to analyze, compare, and interpret facts and figures quickly. They must be able to communicate the results of their work clearly to clients and managers. Accountants and auditors must be good at working with people, business sys-

> **CONSIDER THIS...**
> Because financial decisions are made on the basis of their statements and services, accountants and auditors should have high standards of integrity.

tems, and computers. At a minimum, accountants and auditors should be familiar with basic accounting and computer software packages.

School Subjects to Study

- Algebra
- Computer science
- English
- Geometry
- Pre-calculus and calculus
- Public speaking
- Trigonometry

Moving Up

Beginning public accountants often advance to positions with more responsibility in 1 or 2 years and to senior positions within another few years. Those who excel may become supervisors, managers, or partners; open their own public accounting firm; or transfer to executive positions in management accounting or internal auditing in private firms.

Management accountants often start as cost accountants, junior internal auditors, or trainees for other accounting positions. As they rise through the organization, they may advance to accounting manager, chief cost accountant, budget director, or manager of internal auditing. Some become controllers, treasurers, financial vice presidents, chief financial officers, or corporation presidents.

Professional recognition through certification, or a designation other than the CPA, provides a distinct advantage in the job market. Accountants and auditors can seek credentials from a wide variety of professional societies.

The Institute of Management Accountants confers the Certified Management Accountant (CMA) designation upon applicants who complete a bachelor's degree or who attain a minimum score or higher on specified graduate school entrance exams. Applicants must have worked at least 2 years in management accounting, pass a four-part examination, agree to meet continuing education requirements, and comply with standards of professional conduct.

The Institute of Internal Auditors offers the Certified Internal Auditor (CIA) designation to graduates from accredited colleges and universities who have worked for 2 years as internal auditors and have passed a four-part examination. The IIA also offers the designations of Certified in Control Self-Assessment (CCSA), Certified Government Auditing Professional (CGAP), and Certified Financial Services Auditor (CFSA) to those who pass the exams and meet educational and experience requirements.

The ISACA, formerly known as the Information Systems Audit and Control Association, confers the Certified Information Systems Auditor (CISA) designation upon candidates who pass an examination and have 5 years of experience auditing information systems.

The Accreditation Council for Accountancy and Taxation, a satellite organization of the National Society of Accountants, confers four designations—Accredited Business Accountant (ABA), Accredited Tax Advisor (ATA), Accredited Tax Preparer (ATP), and Elder Care Specialist (ECS)—on accountants specializing in tax preparation for small and medium-sized businesses. Candidates for the ABA must pass an exam; candidates for the other designations must complete the required coursework and in some cases pass an exam.

The Association of Certified Fraud Examiners offers the Certified Fraud Examiner (CFE) designation for forensic or public accountants involved in fraud prevention, detection, deterrence, and investigation. To obtain the designation, individuals must have a bachelor's degree and 2 years of relevant experience, pass a four-part examination, and abide by a code of professional ethics.

The Association of Government Accountants grants the Certified Government Financial Manager (CGFM) designation for accountants, auditors, and other government financial workers at the federal, state, and local levels. Candidates must have a minimum of a bachelor's degree, 24 hours of study in financial management, 2 years of experience in government, and passing scores on a series of three exams.

For those accountants with their CPA, the AICPA offers the option to receive any or all of the Accredited in Business Valuation (ABV), Certified Information Technology

Professional (CITP), and Personal Financial Specialist (PFS) designations. CPAs with these designations demonstrate a level of expertise in these areas in which accountants practice ever more frequently.

Employment

Accountants and auditors held about 1.3 million jobs in 2008. They worked throughout private industry and government, but 24 percent of accountants and auditors worked for accounting, tax preparation, bookkeeping, and payroll services firms. Approximately 8 percent of accountants and auditors were self-employed.

Most accountants and auditors work in urban areas, where public accounting firms and central or regional offices of businesses are concentrated.

Job Prospects

Employment of accountants and auditors is expected to grow by 22 percent in the 10-year period ending 2018, which is much faster than the average for all occupations. This occupation will have a very large number of new jobs arise, about 279,400 over the projections decade.

As businesses grow, the volume and complexity of information reviewed by accountants and auditors regarding costs, expenditures, taxes, and internal controls will expand as well. The globalization of business also has led to more demand for accounting expertise and services related to international trade and accounting rules and international mergers and acquisitions.

An increased need for accountants and auditors also will arise from changes in legislation related to taxes, financial reporting standards, business investments, mergers, and other financial events. These changes are expected to lead to increased scrutiny of company finances and accounting procedures. This should create opportunities for accountants and auditors, particularly CPAs, to audit financial records more thoroughly. Management accountants and internal auditors increasingly will also be needed to ensure that important processes and procedures are documented accurately and thoroughly. Also, efforts

> **CONSIDER THIS...**
> There is a growing movement towards International Financial Reporting Standards (IFRS), which uses a judgment-based system to determine the fair market value of assets and liabilities. This trend should increase demand for accountants and auditors because of their specialized expertise.

to make government agencies more efficient and accountable will increase demand for government accountants.

The increasing popularity of tax preparation firms and computer software will shift accountants away from tax preparation. As computer programs continue to simplify some accounting-related tasks, clerical staff will increasingly handle many routine calculations.

> **CONSIDER THIS...**
> Increased focus on financial crimes such as embezzlement, bribery, and securities fraud will increase the demand for forensic accountants to detect illegal financial activity. Computer technology has made these crimes easier to commit, and they are on the rise.

Some individuals with backgrounds in accounting and auditing are full-time college and university faculty; others teach part time while working as self-employed accountants or as accountants for private industry or government.

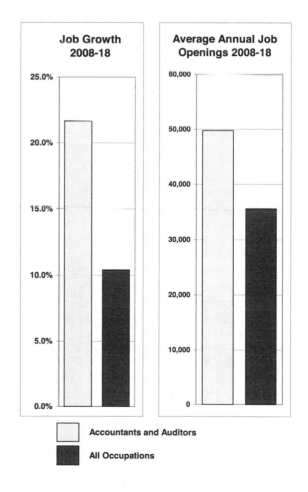

Overall, job opportunities for accountants and auditors should be favorable. Those who earn a CPA should have excellent job prospects. Regardless of specialty, accountants and auditors who have earned professional recognition through certification or licensure should have the best job prospects. Applicants with a master's degree in accounting or a master's degree in business administration with a concentration in accounting also will have an advantage.

Income

Median annual earnings of wage-and-salary accountants and auditors were $59,430 in May 2008. The middle half of the occupation earned between $45,900 and $78,210. The top 10 percent earned more than $102,380. Government jobs generally pay less than those in the private sector.

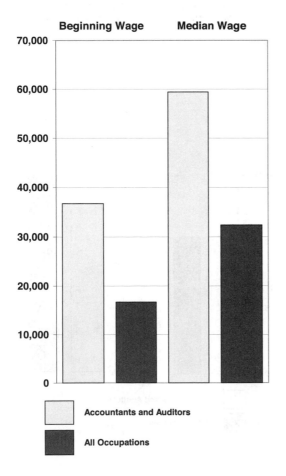

Beginning Wage   Median Wage

☐ Accountants and Auditors

■ All Occupations

According to a salary survey conducted by the National Association of Colleges and Employers, bachelor's degree candidates in accounting received starting offers averaging $48,993 a year in July 2009; master's degree candidates in accounting were offered $49,786 initially.

Wage-and-salary accountants and auditors usually receive standard benefits, including health and medical insurance, life insurance, a 401(k) plan, and paid annual leave. High-level senior accountants may receive additional benefits such as the use of a company car and an expense account.

Related Jobs

- Bill and account collectors
- Bookkeeping, accounting, and auditing clerks
- Budget analysts
- Cost estimators
- Personal financial advisors
- Loan officers
- Tax examiners, collectors, and revenue agents

■ How to Learn More

Information on accredited accounting programs can be obtained from

- AACSB International—Association to Advance Collegiate Schools of Business, 777 South Harbour Island Blvd., Suite 750, Tampa FL 33602-5730. Internet: www.aacsb.edu/accreditation/AccreditedMembers.asp

Information about careers in certified public accounting and CPA standards and examinations may be obtained from

- American Institute of Certified Public Accountants, 1211 Avenue of the Americas, New York, NY 10036. Internet: www.aicpa.org
- The Uniform CPA Examination, 1211 Avenue of the Americas, New York, NY 10036. Internet: www.cpa-exam.org

Information on CPA licensure requirements by state may be obtained from

- National Association of State Boards of Accountancy, 150 Fourth Ave. North, Suite 700, Nashville, TN 37219-2417. Internet: www.nasba.org

Information on careers in management accounting and the CMA designation may be obtained from

- Institute of Management Accountants, 10 Paragon Dr., Montvale, NJ 07645-1718. Internet: www.imanet.org

Information on the Accredited in Accountancy, Accredited Business Accountant, Accredited Tax Advisor, or Accredited Tax Preparer designation may be obtained from

- Accreditation Council for Accountancy and Taxation, 1010 N. Fairfax St., Alexandria, VA 22314-1574. Internet: www.acatcredentials.org

Information on the Certified Fraud Examiner designation may be obtained from

- Association of Certified Fraud Examiners, 716 West Ave., Austin, TX 78701-2727.

Information on careers in internal auditing and the CIA designation may be obtained from

- The Institute of Internal Auditors, 247 Maitland Ave., Altamonte Springs, FL 32701-4201. Internet: www.theiia.org

Information on careers in information systems auditing and the CISA designation may be obtained from

- ISACA, 3701 Algonquin Rd., Suite 1010, Rolling Meadows, IL 60008. Internet: www.isaca.org

Information on careers in government accounting and the CGFM designation may be obtained from

- Association of Government Accountability, 2208 Mount Vernon Ave., Alexandria, VA 22301. Internet: www.agacgfm.org

Information on obtaining positions as an accountant or auditor with the federal government is available at www.usajobs.opm.gov.

Why It's Hot

This job is growing so fast because of the increasing number of businesses, changing financial laws and corporate governance regulations, and increasing accountability for protecting an organization's stakeholders. As business grows more complex, transparency in business becomes more valuable. Accountants and auditors have the skills to generate understandable numbers describing what—and how well—a business is doing.

Actuaries

Actuaries use their knowledge of statistics, finance, and business to assess the risk of events occurring; they also help create policies that minimize risk and its financial impact on companies and clients.

Just the Facts

Earnings: $84,810

Job Growth: 21.4%

Annual Openings: 1,000

Education and Training: Bachelor's or higher degree, plus work experience

While at Work

Consumers and businesses all enjoy the peace of mind that comes from being insured against accidents, fires, thefts, and loss of health. But how do insurance companies achieve peace of mind? Their business depends on being able to foresee how often and how much they will need to pay out to policyholders. Based on that knowledge, they can determine a sufficient amount to charge for insurance coverage. Instead of using a crystal ball to predict the future, insurance companies hire actuaries.

Actuaries assemble and analyze data to estimate the probability and likely cost of an event such as death, sickness, injury, disability, or loss of property. Actuaries also address financial questions, including those involving the level of pension contributions required to produce a certain retirement income level and the way in which a company should invest resources to maximize return on investments in light of potential risk. Using their broad knowledge of statistics, finance, and business, actuaries help design insurance policies, pension plans, and other financial strategies in a manner that will help ensure that the plans are maintained on a sound financial basis.

Most actuaries are employed in the insurance industry, specializing in either life and health insurance or property and casualty insurance. They produce probability tables or use more sophisticated dynamic modeling techniques that determine the likelihood that a potential event will generate a claim. From these tables, they estimate the amount a company can expect to pay in claims. For example, *property and casualty actuaries* calculate the expected number of claims resulting from automobile accidents, which varies depending on the insured person's age, sex, driving history, type of car, and other factors. Actuaries ensure that the price, or premium, charged for such insurance will enable the company to cover claims and other expenses. This premium must be profitable, yet competitive with other insurance companies. Within the life and health insurance fields, actuaries help to develop long-term-care insurance and annuity policies, the latter a growing investment tool for many individuals.

Actuaries in other financial service industries manage credit and help price corporate security offerings. They also devise new investment tools to help their firms compete with other financial service companies. *Pension actuaries* work under the provisions of the Employee Retirement Income Security Act (ERISA) of 1974 to evaluate pension plans covered by that Act and report on the plans' financial soundness to participants, sponsors, and federal regulators. Actuaries working for the government help manage social programs such as Social Security and Medicare.

Actuaries may help determine company policy and may help companies develop plans to enter new lines of business or new geographic markets by forecasting demand in competitive settings.

Consulting actuaries provide advice to clients on a contract basis. The duties of most consulting actuaries are similar to those of other actuaries. For example, some may evaluate company pension plans by calculating the future value of employee and employer contributions and determining whether the amounts are sufficient to meet the future needs of retirees. Others help companies reduce their insurance costs by lowering the level of risk the companies take on. For example, they may provide advice on how to lessen the risk of injury on the job. Consulting actuaries sometimes testify in court regarding the value of potential lifetime earnings of a person who is disabled or killed in an accident, the current value of future pension benefits (in divorce cases), or other values arrived at by complex calculations.

Actuaries must have good math skills.

Also Known As

Reinsurance actuaries help one insurance company arrange to share a large prospective liability policy with another insurance company in exchange for a percentage of the premium.

Job Fit

Personality Type
Conventional-Investigative-Enterprising

Career Cluster
06 Finance

Skills
Computer Programming
Mathematics
Thought-Processing
Equipment/Technology Analysis
Science
Communications
Social Skills
Management

Work Styles
Analytical Thinking
Achievement/Effort
Integrity
Persistence
Initiative
Attention to Detail
Leadership
Dependability

Working Conditions

Actuaries have desk jobs, and their offices usually are comfortable and pleasant. They often work at least 40 hours a week. Some actuaries—particularly consulting actuaries—may travel to meet with clients. Consulting actuaries also may experience more erratic employment and be expected to work more than 40 hours per week.

■ What's Required

Actuaries need a strong foundation in mathematics, statistics, and general business. They generally have a bachelor's degree and are required to pass a series of exams in order to become certified.

Education and Training

Actuaries usually earn an undergraduate degree in mathematics, statistics, actuarial science, or a business-related field such as finance, economics, or business. While in college, students should complete coursework in economics, applied statistics and corporate finance, which is a requirement for professional certification. Furthermore, many students obtain internships to gain experience in the profession prior to graduation. About 100 colleges and universities offer an actuarial science program, and most offer a degree in mathematics, statistics, economics, or finance.

Some companies hire applicants without specifying a major, provided that the applicant has a working knowledge of mathematics—including calculus, probability, and statistics—and has demonstrated this knowledge by passing one or two actuarial exams required for professional designation. Companies increasingly prefer well-rounded individuals who, in addition to having acquired a strong technical background, have some training in business and liberal arts and possess strong communication skills.

Beginning actuaries often rotate among different jobs in an organization, such as marketing, underwriting, financial reporting, and product development, to learn various actuarial operations and phases of insurance work. At first, they prepare data for actuarial projects or perform other simple tasks. As they gain experience, actuaries may supervise clerks, prepare correspondence, draft reports, and conduct research. They may move from one company to another early in their careers as they advance to higher positions.

Two professional societies sponsor programs leading to full professional status in their specialty: the Society of Actuaries (SOA) and the Casualty Actuarial Society (CAS). The SOA certifies actuaries in the fields of life insurance, health benefits systems, retirement systems, and finance and investment. The CAS gives a series of examinations in the property and casualty field, which includes car, homeowners, medical malpractice, workers compensation, and personal injury liability.

Three of the first four exams in the SOA and CAS examination series are jointly sponsored by the two societies and cover the same material. For this reason, students do not need to commit themselves to a specialty until they have taken the initial examinations, which test an individual's competence in probability, statistics, and other branches of mathematics and finance. The first few examinations help students evaluate their potential as actuaries.

Many candidates find work as an actuary immediately after graduation and work through the certification process while gaining some experience in the field. In fact, many employers pay the examination fees and provide their employees time to study. As actuaries pass exams, they are often rewarded with a pay increase.

The process for gaining certification in the Casualty Actuarial Society is predominantly exam based. To reach the first level of certification, the Associate or ACAS level, a candidate must complete seven exams, attend one course on professionalism, and complete the coursework in applied statistics, corporate finance, and economics required by both the SOA and CAS. This process generally takes from 4 to 6 years. The next level, the Fellowship or FCAS level, requires passing two additional exams in advanced topics, including investment and assets and dynamic financial analysis and the valuation of insurance. Most actuaries reach the fellowship level 2 to 3 years after attaining Associate status.

The certification process of the Society of Actuaries blends exams with computer learning modules and coursework. After taking the initial exams, candidates must choose a specialty: group and health benefits, individual life and annuities, retirement benefits, pensions, investments, or finance/enterprise risk management. To reach the Associate or ASA level, a candidate must complete the initial four exams, the coursework in applied statistics, corporate finance and economics required by the SOA and CAS, eight computer modules with two corresponding assessments, and a course in professionalism. This process generally takes from 4 to 6 years. To attain the Fellowship or FSA level, a candidate must pass two additional exams within a chosen specialty and must complete three computer modules and a professionalism course. Attaining Fellowship status usually takes an additional 2 to 3 years after becoming an Associate.

Specific requirements apply to pension actuaries, who verify the financial status of defined-benefit pension plans for the federal government. These actuaries must be enrolled by the Joint Board of the U.S. Treasury Department and the U.S. Department of Labor for the Enrollment of Actuaries. To qualify for enrollment, applicants must meet certain experience and examination requirements, as stipulated by the Board.

- Actuarial science

Additional Qualifications

In addition to knowledge of mathematics, computer skills are becoming increasingly important. Actuaries should be able to develop and use spreadsheets and databases, as well as standard statistical analysis software. Knowledge of computer programming languages, such as Visual Basic for Applications, SAS, or SQL, is also useful.

To perform their duties effectively, actuaries must keep up with current economic and social trends and legislation, as well as with developments in health, business, and finance that could affect insurance or investment practices. Good communication and interpersonal skills also are important, particularly for prospective consulting actuaries.

School Subjects to Study

- Algebra
- Computer science
- English
- Geometry
- Pre-calculus and calculus
- Trigonometry

Moving Up

Advancement depends largely on job performance and the number of actuarial examinations passed. Actuaries with a broad knowledge of the insurance, pension, investment, or employee benefits fields can rise to administrative and executive positions in their companies. Actuaries with supervisory ability may advance to management positions in other areas, such as underwriting, accounting, data processing, marketing, and advertising. Increasingly, actuaries with knowledge of business are beginning to rise to high-level positions within their companies, such as Chief Risk Officer, Chief Financial Officer, or other executive level positions. These generally require that actuaries use their abilities for assessing risk and apply it to the entire company as a whole. Furthermore, some experienced actuaries move into consulting, often by opening their own consulting firm. Some actuaries transfer to college and university faculty positions.

Employment

Actuaries held about 19,700 jobs in 2008. About 55 percent of all actuaries were employed by insurance carriers. Approximately 16 percent work for management, scien-

tific, and technical consulting services. Others worked for insurance agents and brokers and in the management of companies and enterprises industry. A relatively small number of actuaries are employed by government agencies.

Job Prospects

Employment of actuaries is expected to increase by 21 percent over the 10-year period ending 2018, which is much faster than the average for all occupations. While employment in the insurance industry—the largest employer of actuaries—will experience some growth, greater job growth will occur in other industries, such as financial services and consulting.

Despite slower-than-average growth of the insurance industry, employment in this key sector is expected to increase during the projection period as actuaries will be needed to develop, price, and evaluate a variety of insurance products and calculate the costs of new risks. Natural disasters should continue to require the work of actuaries in property and casualty insurance while the growing popularity of annuities, a financial product offered primarily by life insurance companies, will also spur demand. Penetration among actuaries into non-traditional areas, such as the financial services sector, to help price corporate security offerings, for example, will also contribute to some employment growth.

Consulting firms should experience strong employment demand as an increasing number of industries utilize actuaries to assess risk. Increased regulation of managed health-care companies and drafting health-care legislation will also spur employment growth.

Nonetheless, growth may be, to a degree, offset by corporate downsizing and consolidation of the insurance industry—the largest employer of actuaries. Life insurance companies, for example, are expected to increasingly shed high-level actuarial positions as companies merge and streamline operations. Pension actuaries will also experience declining demand. This is largely due to the decline of defined benefit plans, which required review by an actuary, in favor of investment-based retirement funds, such as 401(k)s.

Job seekers are likely to face competition because the number of job openings is expected to be less than the number of qualified applicants. College graduates who have passed two of the initial exams and completed an internship should enjoy the best prospects. A solid foundation in mathematics, including the ability to compute complex probability and statistics, is essential. In addition to job growth, a small number of jobs will open up each year to replace actuaries who retire or transfer to new jobs.

The best employment opportunities should be in consulting firms. Companies that may not find it cost-effective to employ their own actuaries are increasingly hiring consulting actuaries to analyze various risks. Openings should also be available in the health-care field if changes take place in managed health care. The desire to contain health-care costs will provide job opportunities for actuaries who will be needed to evaluate the risks associated with new medical issues, such as the impact of new diseases.

Because actuarial skills are increasingly seen as useful to other industries that deal with risk, such as the airline and banking industries, additional job openings may be created in these industries.

Income

Median annual wages of actuaries were $84,810 in May 2008. The middle 50 percent earned between $62,020 and $119,110. The lowest 10 percent had wages less than $49,150, while the top 10 percent earned more than $160,780.

According to the National Association of Colleges and Employers, annual starting salaries for graduates with a bachelor's degree in actuarial science averaged $56,320 in July 2009.

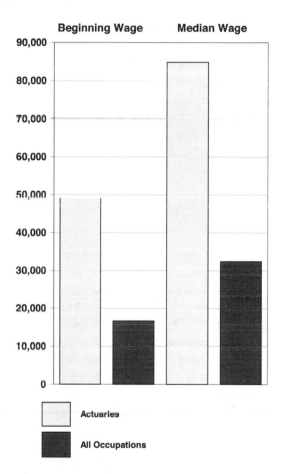

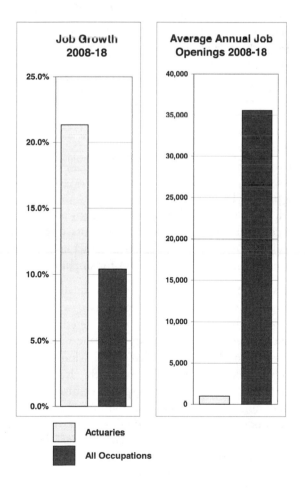

Related Jobs

- Accountants and auditors
- Budget analysts
- Economists
- Insurance underwriters
- Market and survey researchers
- Mathematicians
- Personal financial advisors
- Statisticians

How to Learn More

Career information on actuaries specializing in pensions is available from

- American Society of Pension Actuaries, 4245 N. Fairfax Dr., Suite 750, Arlington, VA 22203. Internet: www.aspa.org

For information about actuarial careers in life and health insurance, employee benefits and pensions, and finance and investments, contact

- Society of Actuaries (SOA), 475 N. Martingale Rd., Suite 600, Schaumburg, IL 60173-2226. Internet: www.soa.org

For information about actuarial careers in property and casualty insurance, contact

- Casualty Actuarial Society (CAS), 4350 N. Fairfax Dr., Suite 250 Arlington, VA 22203. Internet: www.casact.org

- The SOA and CAS jointly sponsor a Web site for those interested in pursuing an actuarial career. Internet: www.BeAnActuary.org

For general information on a career as an actuary, contact

- American Academy of Actuaries, 1100 17th St. NW, 7th Floor, Washington, DC 20036. Internet: www.actuary.org

Why It's Hot

Entry and advancement in this occupation depend on passing rigorous exams, which restrict the amount of competition for job openings. The largest employer, the insurance industry, seems likely to offer steady employment because there are always new risks that need to be quantified—for example, lately it's risks from terrorism or from natural disasters caused by global climate change.

Animal Care and Service Workers

Animal care and service workers train, feed, water, groom, bathe, and exercise animals and clean, disinfect, and repair their cages.

Just the Facts

Earnings: $19,940
Job Growth: 20.6%
Annual Openings: 9,260

Education and Training: Short-term on-the-job training

Moderate-term on-the-job training

While at Work

Many people like animals. But, as pet owners will admit, taking care of them is hard work. Animal care and service workers provide basic care for animals, train them, play with them, provide companionship, and observe behavioral changes that could indicate illness or injury. Boarding kennels, pet stores, animal shelters, rescue leagues, veterinary hospitals and clinics, stables, laboratories, aquariums and natural aquatic habitats, and zoological parks all house animals and employ animal care and service workers. These workers go by two occupational titles, *animal caretakers* and *animal trainers,* but their job titles and duties vary considerably by employment setting.

Kennel attendants care for pets while their owners are working or traveling out of town. Beginning attendants perform basic tasks, such as cleaning both the cages and the dog runs, filling food and water dishes, and exercising animals. Experienced attendants may provide basic animal health care, as well as bathe animals, trim nails, and attend to other grooming needs. Attendants who work in kennels also may sell pet food and supplies, assist in obedience training, or prepare animals for shipping.

> **CONSIDER THIS...**
>
> Mobile grooming services are growing rapidly because they offer convenience for pet owners, flexibility of schedules for groomers, and minimal trauma for pets resulting from their being in unfamiliar surroundings.

Groomers are animal caretakers who specialize in maintaining a pet's appearance. Most groom dogs; a few groom cats. Some groomers work in kennels, veterinary clinics, animal shelters, or pet supply stores. Others operate their own grooming business, typically at a salon or, increasingly, by making house calls. Groomers clean and sanitize equipment to prevent the spread of disease, as well as maintaining a clean and safe environment for the animals. Groomers also schedule appointments, discuss pets' grooming needs with clients, and collect general information on the pets' health and behavior. Groomers sometimes are the first to notice a medical problem, such as an ear or skin infection, that requires veterinary care.

Grooming the pet involves several steps: an initial brush-out is followed by a clipping of hair with combs and grooming shears; the groomer then cuts the animal's nails, cleans the ears, bathes and blow-dries the animal, and ends with a final trim and styling.

Animal caretakers in animal shelters work mainly with cats and dogs and perform a variety of duties typically determined by the worker's experience. In addition to attending to the basic needs of the animals, caretakers at shelters keep records of the animals, including information about any tests or treatments performed on them. Experienced caretakers may vaccinate newly admitted animals under the direction of a veterinarian or veterinary technician and euthanize (painlessly put to death) seriously ill, severely injured, or unwanted animals. Animal caretakers in animal shelters also interact with the public, answering telephone inquiries, screening applicants who wish to adopt an animal, or educating visitors on neutering and other animal health issues.

Pet sitters look after one or more animals when their owner is away. They do this by traveling to the pet owner's home to carry out the daily routine. (Pets that remain in their normal surroundings experience less trauma and can maintain their normal diet and exercise regimen.) Most pet sitters feed, walk, and play with the animal, but some more experienced sitters also may be required to bathe, train, or groom them. Most watch over dogs and cats.

In zoos, animal care and service workers, called *keepers*, prepare the diets and clean the enclosures of animals and sometimes assist in raising them when they are very young. They watch for any signs of illness or injury, monitor eating patterns or any changes in behavior and record their observations. Keepers also may answer questions and ensure that the visiting public behaves responsibly toward the exhibited animals. Depending on the zoo, keepers may be assigned to work with a broad group of animals, such as mammals, birds, or reptiles, or they may work with a limited collection of animals such as primates, large cats, or small mammals.

Animal trainers train animals for riding, security, performance, obedience, or assisting people with disabilities. Animal trainers do this by accustoming the animal to the human voice and human contact and teaching the animal to respond to commands. Trainers use several techniques to help them train animals. One technique, known as a bridge, is a stimulus that a trainer uses to communicate the precise moment an animal does something correctly. When the animal responds correctly, the trainer gives positive reinforcement in a variety of ways: offering food, toys, play, and rubdowns or speaking the word "good." Animal training takes place in small steps and often takes

months and even years of repetition. During the teaching process, trainers provide animals with mental stimulation, physical exercise, and husbandry. A relatively new form of training teaches animals to cooperate with workers giving medical care: animals learn "veterinary" behaviors, such as allowing for the collection of blood samples; physical, X-ray, ultrasonic, and dental exams; physical therapy; and the administration of medicines and replacement fluids.

Training also can be a good tool for facilitating the relocation of animals from one habitat to another, easing, for example, the process of loading horses onto trailers. Trainers often work in competitions or shows, such as circuses, marine parks, and aquariums; many others work in animal shelters, dog kennels and salons, or horse farms. Trainers in shows work to display the talent and ability of an animal, such as a dolphin, through interactive programs to educate and entertain the public.

In addition to their hands-on work with the animals, trainers often oversee other aspects of animals' care, such as preparing their diet and providing a safe and clean environment and habitat.

> ### CONSIDER THIS...
> The three most commonly trained animals are dogs; horses; and marine mammals, including dolphins and sea lions.

Animal care and service workers groom animals.

Also Known As

Grooms, or *caretakers*, care for horses in stables. They saddle and unsaddle horses, give them rubdowns, and walk them to cool them off after a ride. They also feed, groom, and exercise the horses; clean out stalls and replenish bedding; polish saddles; clean and organize the tack (harness, saddle, and bridle) room; and store supplies and feed. Experienced grooms may help train horses.

Job Fit

Personality Type

Realistic-Conventional

Career Cluster

01 Agriculture, Food, and Natural Resources

Skills

Management

Social Skills

Science

Equipment/Technology Analysis

Communications

Thought-Processing

Equipment Use/Maintenance

Computer Programming

Mathematics

Work Styles

Self-Control

Dependability

Independence

Stress Tolerance

Cooperation

Integrity

Social Skills Orientation

Concern for Others

Working Conditions

People who love animals get satisfaction from working with and helping them. However, some of the work may be unpleasant, physically or emotionally demanding, and, sometimes, dangerous. Data from the U.S. Bureau of Labor Statistics show that full-time animal care and service workers experienced a work-related injury and illness rate that was higher than the national average. Most animal care and service workers have to clean animal cages and

lift, hold, or restrain animals, risking exposure to bites or scratches. Their work often involves kneeling, crawling, repeated bending, and, occasionally, lifting heavy supplies such as bales of hay or bags of feed. Animal caretakers must take precautions when treating animals with germicides or insecticides. They may work outdoors in all kinds of weather, and the work setting can be noisy. Caretakers of show and sports animals travel to competitions.

Animal care and service workers often work irregular hours. Most animals are fed every day, so caretakers often work weekend and holiday shifts. In some animal hospitals, research facilities, and animal shelters, an attendant is on duty 24 hours a day, which means night shifts.

CONSIDER THIS...

Animal care and service workers who witness abused animals or who assist in euthanizing unwanted, aged, or hopelessly injured animals may experience emotional distress. Those working for private humane societies and municipal animal shelters often deal with the public, some of whom may be hostile. Such workers must maintain a calm and professional demeanor while helping to enforce the laws regarding animal care.

What's Required

On-the-job training is the most common way animal care and service workers learn their work; however, employers generally prefer to hire people who have experience with animals. Some jobs require formal education.

Education and Training

Animal trainers often need a high school diploma or GED equivalent. Some animal training jobs may require a bachelor's degree and additional skills. For example, marine mammal trainers usually need a bachelor's degree in biology, marine biology, animal science, psychology, or a related field. An animal health technician degree also may qualify trainers for some jobs.

Most equine trainers learn their trade by working as a groom at a stable. Some study at an accredited private training school.

Many dog trainers attend workshops and courses at community colleges and vocational schools. Topics include basic study of canines, learning theory of animals, teaching obedience cues, problem solving methods, and safety. Many such schools also offer business training.

Many zoos require their caretakers to have a bachelor's degree in biology, animal science, or a related field. Most require experience with animals, preferably as a volunteer or paid keeper in a zoo.

Pet groomers typically learn their trade by completing an informal apprenticeship, usually lasting 6 to 10 weeks, under the guidance of an experienced groomer. Prospective groomers also may attend one of the 50 state-licensed grooming schools throughout the country, with programs varying in length from 2 to 18 weeks. Beginning groomers often start by taking on one duty, such as bathing and drying the pet. They eventually assume responsibility for the entire grooming process, from the initial brush-out to the final clipping.

Animal caretakers in animal shelters are not required to have any specialized training, but training programs and workshops are available through the Humane Society of the United States, the American Humane Association, and the National Animal Control Association. Workshop topics include investigations of cruelty, appropriate methods of euthanasia for shelter animals, proper guidelines for capturing animals, techniques for preventing problems with wildlife, and dealing with the public.

Beginning animal caretakers in kennels learn on the job and usually start by cleaning cages and feeding animals.

Certifications are available in many animal service occupations. For dog trainers, certification by a professional association or one of the hundreds of private vocational or state-approved trade schools can be advantageous. The National Dog Groomers Association of America offers certification for master status as a groomer. To earn certification, applicants must demonstrate their practical skills and pass two exams. The National Association of Professional Pet Sitters offers a two-stage, home-study certification program for those who wish to become pet care professionals. Topics include business management, animal care, and animal health issues, and applicants must pass a written exam to earn certification. The Pet Care Services Association offers a three-stage, home-study program for individuals interested in pet care. Levels I and II focus on basic principles of animal care and customer service, while Level III spotlights management and professional aspects of the pet care business. Those who complete the third stage and pass oral and written examinations become Certified Kennel Operators (CKO).

> **CONSIDER THIS...**
>
> Pet sitters are not required to have any specific training, but knowledge of and some form of previous experience with animals often are recommended.

Postsecondary Programs to Consider

- Agricultural/Farm Supplies Retailing and Wholesaling
- Animal Training
- Dog/Pet/Animal Grooming
- Equestrian/Equine Studies

Additional Qualifications

All animal care and service workers need patience, sensitivity, and problem-solving ability. Those who work in shelters also need tact and communication skills, because they often deal with individuals who abandon their pets. The ability to handle emotional people is vital for workers at shelters.

Animal trainers especially need problem-solving skills and experience in animal obedience. Successful marine mammal trainers also should have good-public speaking skills, because presentations are a large part of the job. Usually four to five trainers work with a group of animals at one time; therefore, trainers should be able to work as part of a team. Marine mammal trainers must also be good swimmers; certification in SCUBA is a plus.

Most horse-training jobs have minimum weight requirements for candidates.

School Subjects to Study

- Algebra
- Biology
- Public speaking

Moving Up

With experience and additional training, caretakers in animal shelters may become adoption coordinators, animal control officers, emergency rescue drivers, assistant shelter managers, or shelter directors. Pet groomers who work in large retail establishments or kennels may, with experience, move into supervisory or managerial positions. Experienced groomers often choose to open their own salons or mobile grooming business. Advancement for kennel caretakers takes the form of promotion to kennel supervisor, assistant manager, and manager; those with enough capital and experience may open up their own kennels. Zookeepers may advance to senior keeper, assistant head keeper, head keeper, and assistant curator, but very few openings occur, especially for the higher-level positions.

Employment

Animal care and service workers held 220,400 jobs in 2008. Nearly four out of five worked as nonfarm animal caretakers; the remainder worked as animal trainers. Nonfarm animal caretakers often worked in boarding kennels, animal shelters, rescue leagues, stables, grooming shops, pet stores, animal hospitals, and veterinary offices. A significant number of caretakers worked for animal humane societies, racing stables, dog and horse racetrack operators, zoos, theme parks, circuses, and other amusement and recreation services.

Employment of animal trainers is concentrated in animal services that specialize in training and in commercial sports, where racehorses and dogs are trained. About 54 percent of animal trainers were self-employed.

Job Prospects

Employment of animal care and service workers is expected to grow 21 percent over the 10-year period ending 2018, much faster than the average for all occupations. The companion pet population, which drives employment of animal caretakers in kennels, grooming shops, animal shelters, and veterinary clinics and hospitals, is anticipated to increase. Pet owners—including a large number of baby boomers, whose disposable income is expected to increase as they age—are expected to increasingly purchase grooming services, daily and overnight boarding services, training services, and veterinary services, resulting in more jobs for animal care and service workers. As more pet owners consider their pets part of the family, demand for luxury animal services and the willingness to spend greater amounts of money on pets should continue to grow. Demand for marine mammal trainers, on the other hand, should grow slowly.

Demand for animal care and service workers in animal shelters is expected to grow as communities increasingly recognize the connection between animal abuse and abuse toward humans and continue to commit private funds to animal shelters, many of which are working hand in hand with social service agencies and law enforcement teams.

Due to employment growth and the need to replace workers who leave the occupation, job opportunities for most positions should be ex-cellent. The need to replace pet sitters, dog walkers, kennel attendants, and animal control and shelter workers leaving the field will create the overwhelming majority of job openings. Many animal caretaker jobs require little or no training and have flexible work schedules, making them suitable for people seeking a first job or for temporary or part-time work. Prospective groomers also will face excellent opportunities as the companion dog population is expected to grow and services such as mobile grooming continue to grow in popularity.

The outlook for caretakers in zoos and aquariums is not favorable, due to slow job growth and keen competition for the few positions. Prospective mammal trainers also will face keen competition as the number of applicants greatly exceeds the number of available positions. Prospective horse trainers should anticipate an equally challenging labor market because the number of entry-level positions is limited.

> **CONSIDER THIS...**
>
> Job opportunities for animal care and service workers may vary from year to year because the strength of the economy affects demand for these workers. Pet owners tend to spend more on animal services when the economy is strong.

> **CONSIDER THIS...**
>
> Dog trainers should experience good opportunities, driven by dog owners' desire to instill obedience in their pets. Opportunities should be best in large metropolitan areas.

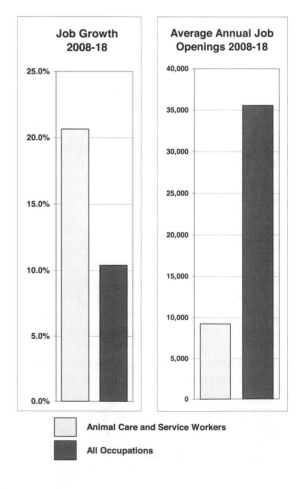

Job Growth 2008-18

Average Annual Job Openings 2008-18

Animal Care and Service Workers

All Occupations

Income

Wages are relatively low. Median annual wages of non-farm animal caretakers were $19,360 in May 2008. The middle 50 percent earned between $16,720 and $24,300. The bottom 10 percent earned less than $15,140, and the top 10 percent earned more than $31,590.

Median annual wages of animal trainers were $27,270 in May 2008. The middle 50 percent earned between $19,880 and $38,280. The lowest 10 percent earned less than $16,700, and the top 10 percent earned more than $51,400.

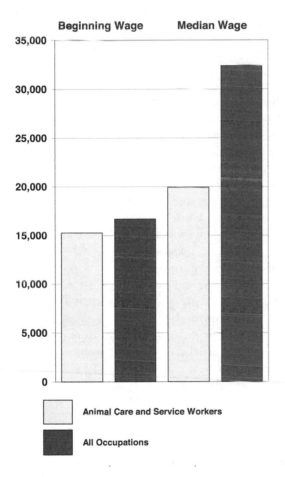

Beginning Wage   Median Wage

☐ Animal Care and Service Workers

■ All Occupations

Related Jobs

- Agricultural workers, other
- Animal control workers
- Biological scientists
- Farmers, ranchers, and agricultural managers
- Veterinarians
- Veterinary assistants and laboratory animal caretakers
- Veterinary technologists and technicians

How to Learn More

For career information and information on training, certification, and earnings of a related occupation—animal control officers—contact

- National Animal Control Association, P.O. Box 480851, Kansas City, MO 64148-0851. Internet: www.nacanet.org

For information on becoming an advanced pet care technician at a kennel, contact

- Pet Care Services Association, 2760 N. Academy Blvd., Suite 120, Colorado Springs, CO 80917. Internet: www.petcareservices.org

For general information on pet grooming careers, including workshops and certification information, contact

- National Dog Groomers Association of America, P.O. Box 101, Clark, PA 16113. Internet: www.nationaldoggroomers.com

For information on pet sitting, including certification information, contact

- National Association of Professional Pet Sitters, 15000 Commerce Parkway, Suite C, Mount Laurel, NJ 08054. Internet: www.petsitters.org

Why It's Hot

We have a two-sided attitude toward pets in the United States. Pets are treated like family members, so they need many services from animal care workers. At the same time, a shocking number of pets are also abandoned, creating a growing need for animal shelter workers. Both trends mean lots of job opportunities for people who enjoy working with animals.

Archivists, Curators, and Museum Technicians

Archivists, curators, and museum technicians work for museums, governments, zoos, colleges and universities, corporations, and other institutions that require experts to preserve important records and artifacts.

While at Work

Archivists, curators, and museum technicians preserve important objects and documents, including works of art, transcripts of meetings, photographs, coins and stamps, and historic objects.

Archivists and curators plan and oversee the arrangement, cataloguing, and exhibition of collections. They also maintain collections with technicians and conservators. They acquire and preserve important documents and other valuable items for permanent storage or display. They also describe, catalogue, and analyze, valuable objects for the benefit of researchers and the public.

CONSIDER THIS...

Although some duties of archivists and curators are similar, the types of items they deal with differ: Archivists mainly handle records and documents that are retained because of their importance and potential value, while curators usually handle objects with cultural, biological, or historical significance, such as sculptures, textiles, and paintings.

Archivists and curators may coordinate educational and public outreach programs, such as tours, workshops, lectures, and classes, and may work with the boards of institutions to administer plans and policies. They also may research topics or items relevant to their collections.

Archivists collect, organize, and maintain control over a wide range of information deemed important enough for permanent safekeeping. This information takes many forms: photographs, films, video and sound recordings, and electronic data files in a wide variety of formats, as well as more traditional paper records, letters, and documents.

In accordance with accepted standards and practices, archivists maintain records to ensure the long-term preservation and easy retrieval of documents and information. Records may be saved on any medium, including paper, film, videotape, audiotape, computer disk, or DVD. They also may be copied onto some other format to protect the original and to make the records more user accessible.

Generally, computers are used to generate and maintain archival records. Professional standards for the use of computers in handling archival records, especially electronic, are still evolving. However, computer capabilities will continue to expand and more records will be stored and exhibited electronically, providing both increased access and better protection for archived documents.

Archivists often specialize in an area of history so they can more accurately determine which records in that area qualify for retention and should become part of the archives. Archivists also may work with specialized forms of records, such as manuscripts, electronic records, Web sites, photographs, cartographic records, motion pictures, or sound recordings.

Curators administer museums, zoos, aquariums, botanical gardens, nature centers, and historic sites. The *museum director* often is a curator. Curators direct the acquisition, storage, and exhibition of collections, including negotiating and authorizing the purchase, sale, exchange, or loan of collections. They are also responsible for authenticating, evaluating, and categorizing the specimens in a collection. Curators often oversee and help conduct the institution's research projects and related educational programs. Today, an increasing part of a curator's duties involves fundraising and promotion, which may include the writing and reviewing of grant proposals, journal articles, and publicity materials, as well as attendance at meetings, conventions, and civic events.

CONSIDER THIS...

As various storage media evolve, archivists must keep abreast of technological advances in electronic information storage.

Most curators specialize in a particular field, such as botany, art, paleontology, or history. Those working in large institutions may be highly specialized. A large natural history museum, for example, would employ separate curators for its collections of birds, fishes, insects, and mammals. Some curators maintain their collections, others do research, and others perform administrative tasks. In small institutions with only one or a few curators, one curator may be responsible for a number of tasks, from maintaining collections to directing the affairs of the museum.

Conservators manage, care for, preserve, treat, and document works of art, artifacts, and specimens—work that may require substantial historical, scientific, and archaeological research. They use X-rays, chemical testing, microscopes, special lights, and other laboratory equipment and techniques to examine objects and determine their condition and the appropriate method for preserving them. Conservators document their findings and treat items to minimize their deterioration or to restore them to their original state. Conservators usually specialize in a particular material or group of objects, such as documents and books, paintings, decorative arts, textiles, metals, or architectural material. In addition to their conservation work, conservators participate in outreach programs, research topics in their area of specialty, and write articles for scholarly journals. They may be employed by museums or work on a freelance basis.

Curators oversee historic sites.

Also Known As

Museum technicians, commonly known as *registrars*, assist curators by performing various preparatory and maintenance tasks on museum items. Registrars may also answer public inquiries and assist curators and outside scholars in using collections. *Archives technicians* help archivists organize, maintain, and provide access to historical documentary materials.

Job Fit

Personality Type
Conventional-Realistic-Enterprising

Career Clusters
03 Arts, Audio/Video Technology, and Communications
15 Science, Technology, Engineering, and Mathematics

Skills
Management
Communications

Equipment/Technology Analysis
Thought-Processing
Social Skills
Mathematics
Computer Programming
Equipment Use/Maintenance
Science

Work Styles
Attention to Detail
Independence
Innovation
Cooperation
Initiative
Analytical Thinking
Dependability
Concern for Others

Working Conditions

The working conditions of archivists and curators vary. Some spend most of their time working with the public, providing reference assistance and educational services. Others perform research or process records, which reduces the opportunity to work with others. Those who restore and install exhibits or work with bulky, heavy record containers may lift objects, climb, or stretch. Those in zoos, botanical gardens, and other outdoor museums and historic sites frequently walk great distances. Conservators work in conservation laboratories. The size of the objects in the collection they are working with determines the amount of effort involved in lifting, reaching, and moving objects.

Curators who work in large institutions may travel extensively to evaluate potential additions to the collection, organize exhibitions, and conduct research in their area of expertise. However, travel is rare for curators employed in small institutions.

■ What's Required

Employment as an archivist, conservator, or curator usually requires graduate education and related work experience. While completing their formal education, many archivists and curators work in archives or museums to gain "hands-on" experience. Registrars often start work with a bachelor's degree.

Education and Training

Although archivists earn a variety of undergraduate degrees, a graduate degree in history or library science with courses in archival science is preferred by most employers. Many colleges and universities offer courses or practical training in archival techniques as part of their history, library science, or other curriculum. A few institutions offer master's degrees in archival studies. Some positions may require knowledge of the discipline related to the collection, such as computer science, business, or medicine. There are many archives that offer volunteer opportunities where students can gain experience.

For employment as a curator, most museums require a master's degree in an appropriate discipline of the museum's specialty—art, history, or archaeology—or in museum studies. Some employers prefer a doctoral degree, particularly for curators in natural history or science museums. In small museums, curatorial positions may be available to individuals with a bachelor's degree. Because curators, particularly those in small museums, may have administrative and managerial responsibilities, courses in business administration, public relations, marketing, and fundraising also are recommended. For some positions, an internship of full-time museum work supplemented by courses in museum practices is needed.

> **CONSIDER THIS...**
>
> Earning *two* graduate degrees—in museum studies (museology) and a specialized subject—may give a candidate a distinct advantage in a competitive job market for curators.

When hiring conservators, employers look for a master's degree in conservation or in a closely related field, together with substantial experience. There are only a few graduate programs in museum conservation techniques in the United States. Competition for entry to these programs is keen; to qualify, a student must have a background in chemistry, archaeology or studio art, and art history, as well as work experience. For some programs, knowledge of a foreign language also is helpful. Conservation apprenticeships or internships as an undergraduate can enhance one's admission prospects. Graduate programs last 2 to 4 years, the latter years of which include internship training. A few individuals enter conservation through apprenticeships

> **CONSIDER THIS...**
>
> Apprenticeship training, although accepted, is a more difficult and increasingly scarce route into the conservation profession.

with museums, nonprofit organizations, and conservators in private practice. Apprenticeships should be supplemented with courses in chemistry, studio art, and history.

Museum technicians usually need a bachelor's degree in an appropriate discipline of the museum's specialty, training in museum studies, or previous experience working in museums, particularly in the design of exhibits. Similarly, archives technicians usually need a bachelor's degree in library science or history, or relevant work experience. Relatively few schools grant a bachelor's degree in museum studies. More common are undergraduate minors or tracks of study that are part of an undergraduate degree in a related field, such as art history, history, or archaeology. Students interested in further study may obtain a master's degree in museum studies, offered in colleges and universities throughout the country. However, many employers feel that, while museum studies are helpful, a thorough knowledge of the museum's specialty and museum work experience are more important.

The Academy of Certified Archivists offers voluntary certification for archivists. The designation "Certified Archivist" can be obtained by those with at least a master's degree and a year of appropriate archival experience. The certification process requires candidates to pass a written examination, and they must renew their certification periodically.

Postsecondary Programs to Consider

- Art History, Criticism and Conservation
- Cultural Resource Management and Policy Analysis
- Historic Preservation and Conservation
- History, General
- Museology/Museum Studies
- Public/Applied History

Additional Qualifications

Archivists need research skills and analytical ability to understand the content of documents and the context in which they were created. They must also be able to decipher deteriorated or poor-quality printed matter, handwritten manuscripts, photographs, or films. A background in preservation management is often required of archivists because they are responsible for taking proper care of their records. Archivists also must be able to organize large amounts of information and write clear instructions for its retrieval and use. In addition, computer skills and the ability to work with electronic records and databases are very important. Because electronic records are becoming the prevalent form of recordkeeping, and archivists must create searchable databases, knowledge of Web technology may be required.

Curatorial positions often require knowledge in a number of fields. For historic and artistic conservation, courses in chemistry, physics, and art are desirable. Like archivists, curators need computer skills and the ability to work with electronic databases. Many curators are responsible for posting information on the Internet, so they also need to be familiar with digital imaging, scanning technology, and copyright law.

Curators must be flexible because of their wide variety of duties, including the design and presentation of exhibits. In small museums, curators need manual dexterity to build exhibits or restore objects. Leadership ability and business skills are important for museum directors, while marketing skills are valuable in increasing museum attendance and fundraising.

School Subjects to Study

- Algebra
- Art
- Chemistry
- Computer science
- English
- Foreign language
- Geometry
- History
- Public speaking

Moving Up

Continuing education is available through meetings, conferences, and workshops sponsored by archival, historical, and museum associations. Some larger organizations, such as the National Archives in Washington, D.C., offer such training in-house.

Many archives, including one-person shops, are very small and have limited opportunities for promotion. Archivists typically advance by transferring to a larger unit that has supervisory positions. A doctorate in history, library science, or a related field may be needed for some advanced positions, such as director of a state archive.

In large museums, curators may advance through several levels of responsibility, eventually becoming the museum director. Curators in smaller museums often advance to larger ones. Individual research and publications are important for advancement in larger institutions.

Employment

Archivists, curators, and museum technicians held about 29,100 jobs in 2008. About 39 percent were employed in museums, historical sites, and similar institutions and 18 percent worked for public and private educational services. Around 30 percent of archivists, curators, and museum technicians worked in federal, state, and local government, excluding educational institutions. Most federal archivists work for the National Archives and Records Administration; others manage military archives in the U.S. Department of Defense. Most federal government curators work at the Smithsonian Institution, in the military museums of the U.S. Department of Defense, and in archaeological and other museums and historic sites managed by the U.S. Department of the Interior. All state governments have archival or historical record sections employing archivists. State and local governments also have numerous historical museums, parks, libraries, and zoos employing curators.

Some large corporations that have archives or record centers employ archivists to manage the growing volume of records created or maintained as required by law or necessary to the firm's operations. Religious and fraternal organizations, professional associations, conservation organizations, major private collectors, and research firms also employ archivists and curators.

Conservators may work under contract to treat particular items, rather than as regular employees of a museum or other institution. These conservators may work on their own as private contractors, or they may work as an employee of a conservation laboratory or regional conservation center that contracts their services to museums. Most federal conservators work for the Smithsonian Institution, Library of Congress, and National Archives and Records Administration.

Job Prospects

Employment of archivists, curators, and museum technicians is expected to increase 20 percent over the 10-year period ending 2018, which is much faster than the average for all occupations. Jobs for archivists are expected to increase as public and private organizations require organization of and access to increasing volumes of records and information. Public interest in science, art, history, and technology will continue, creating opportunities for curators, conservators, and museum technicians. Museum attendance is expected to continue to be good. Many museums remain financially healthy and will schedule building and renovation projects as money is available.

Keen competition is expected for most jobs as archivists, curators, and museum technicians because qualified applicants generally outnumber job openings. Graduates with highly specialized training, such as master's degrees in both library science and history, with a concentration in archives or records management and extensive computer skills, should have the best opportunities for jobs as archivists.

Curator jobs, in particular, are attractive to many people, and many applicants have the necessary training and knowledge of the subject. But because there are relatively few openings, candidates may have to work part time, as an intern, or even as a volunteer assistant curator or research associate after completing their formal education. Substantial work experience in collection management, research, exhibit design, or restoration, as well as database management skills, will be necessary for permanent status.

Conservators also can expect competition for jobs. Competition is stiff for the limited number of openings in conservation graduate programs, and applicants need a technical background. Conservator program graduates with knowledge of a foreign language and a willingness to relocate will have better job opportunities.

CONSIDER THIS...

Museums and other cultural institutions can be subject to cuts in funding during recessions or periods of budget tightening, reducing demand for these workers.

Although the number of archivists and curators who move to other occupations is relatively low, the need to replace workers who retire or leave the occupation will create some job openings. However, workers in these occupations tend to work beyond the typical retirement age of workers in other occupations.

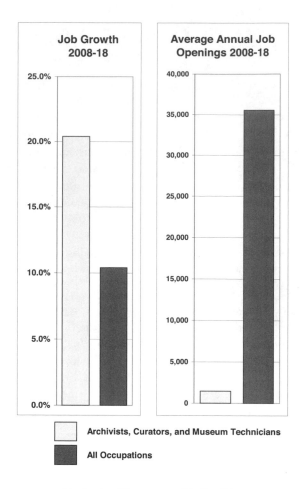

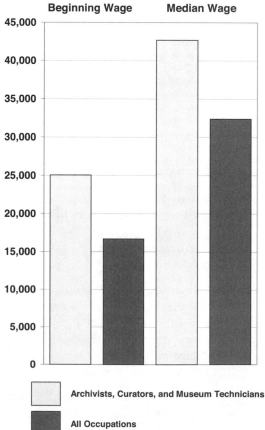

Income

Median annual wages of archivists in May 2008 were $45,020. The middle 50 percent earned between $34,050 and $60,150. The lowest 10 percent earned less than $26,600, and the highest 10 percent earned more than $76,790. Median annual wages of curators in May 2008 were $47,220. The middle 50 percent earned between $34,910 and $63,940. The lowest 10 percent earned less than $26,850, and the highest 10 percent earned more than $83,290. Median annual wages of museum technicians and conservators in May 2008 were $36,660. The middle 50 percent earned between $28,030 and $49,170. The lowest 10 percent earned less than $22,320, and the highest 10 percent earned more than $66,060.

In March 2009, the average annual salary for archivists in the federal government was $83,758; for museum curators, $90,205; for museum specialists and technicians, $62,520; and for archives technicians, $43,662.

Related Jobs

- Anthropologists
- Archeologists
- Artists and related workers
- Historians
- Librarians

How to Learn More

For information on archivists and on schools offering courses in archival studies, contact

- The Newspaper Association of America, 1921 Gallows Rd., Suite 600, Vienna, VA 22182. Internet: www.naa.org

For general information about careers as a curator and schools offering courses in museum studies, contact

- American Association of Museums, 1575 Eye St. NW, Suite 400, Washington, DC 20005. Internet: www.aam-us.org

For information about careers and education programs in conservation and preservation, contact

- American Institute for Conservation of Historic and Artistic Works, 1156 15th St. NW, Suite 320, Washington, DC 20005-1714. Internet: www.conservation-us.org

For information about archivists and archivist certification, contact

- Academy of Certified Archivists, 1450 Western Ave., Suite 101, Albany, NY 12203. Internet: www.certifiedarchivists.org

For information about government archivists, contact

- National Association of Government Archivists and Records Administrators, 1450 Western Ave., Suite 101, Albany, NY 12203. Internet: www.nagara.org

Information on obtaining positions as archivists, curators, and museum technicians with the federal government is available at www.usajobs.opm.gov.

Why It's Hot

Public interest in the past continues to grow. It's now common for newspapers, even in small cities, to put their complete archives on the Web. Museums also continue to attract visitors. Although job openings for archivists, curators, and museum technicians are growing fast, competition for these jobs will be intense.

Athletes, Coaches, Umpires, and Related Workers

Athletes, coaches, and sports officials compete in, train for, recruit for, coach in, or officiate at professional athletic events.

Just the Facts

Earnings: $28,881

Job Growth: 23.1%

Annual Openings: 10,900

Education and Training: Long-term on-the-job training

While at Work

Few people who dream of becoming paid professional athletes, coaches, or sports officials beat the odds and make a full-time living from professional athletics. Professional athletes often have short careers with little job security. Even though the chances of employment as a professional athlete are slim, there are many opportunities for at least a part-time job as a coach, instructor, referee, or umpire in amateur athletics or in high school, college, or university sports.

Athletes and *sports competitors* compete in organized, officiated sports events to entertain spectators. When playing a game, athletes are required to understand the strategies of their game while obeying the rules and regulations of the sport. The events in which they compete include both team sports, such as baseball, basketball, football, hockey, and soccer, and individual sports, such as golf, tennis, and bowling. The level of play varies from unpaid high school athletics to professional sports, in which the best from around the world compete in events broadcast on international television.

Being an athlete involves more than competing in athletic events. Athletes spend many hours each day practicing skills and improving teamwork under the guidance of a coach or a sports instructor. They view videotapes to critique their own performances and techniques and to learn their opponents' tendencies and weaknesses to gain a competitive advantage. Some athletes work regularly with strength trainers to gain muscle and stamina and to prevent injury. Many athletes push their bodies to the limit during both practice and play, so career-ending injury always is a risk; even minor injuries may put a player at risk of replacement.

Coaches organize amateur and professional athletes and teach them the fundamental skills of individual and team sports. (In individual sports, instructors sometimes may fill this role.) Coaches train athletes for competition by holding practice sessions to perform drills that improve the athletes' form, technique, skills, and stamina. Along with refining athletes' individual skills, coaches are responsible for instilling good sportsmanship, a competitive spirit, and teamwork and for managing their teams during both practice sessions and competitions. Before competition, coaches evaluate or scout the opposing team to determine game strategies and practice specific plays. During competition, coaches may call specific plays intended to surprise or overpower the oppo-

nent, and they may substitute players for optimum team chemistry and success. Coaches' additional tasks may include selecting, storing, issuing, and taking inventory of equipment, materials, and supplies.

Sports instructors teach professional and non-professional athletes individually. They organize, instruct, train, and lead athletes in indoor and outdoor sports such as bowling, tennis, golf, and swimming. Because activities are as diverse as weight lifting, gymnastics, scuba diving, and karate, instructors tend to specialize in one or a few activities. Like coaches, sports instructors also may hold daily practice sessions and be responsible for any needed equipment and supplies. Using their knowledge of their sport and of physiology, they determine the type and level of difficulty of exercises, prescribe specific drills, and correct athletes' techniques. Some instructors also teach and demonstrate the use of training apparatus, such as trampolines or weights, for correcting athletes' weaknesses and enhancing their conditioning. Like coaches, sports instructors evaluate the athlete and the athlete's opponents to devise a competitive game strategy.

Coaches and sports instructors sometimes differ in their approaches to athletes because of the focus of their work. For example, while coaches manage the team during a game to optimize its chance for victory, sports instructors—such as those who work for professional tennis players—often are not permitted to instruct their athletes during competition. Sports instructors spend more of their time with athletes working one-on-one, which permits them to design customized training programs for each individual.

Umpires, referees, and *other sports officials* officiate at competitive athletic and sporting events. They observe the play and impose penalties for infractions as established by the rules and regulations of the various sports. Umpires, referees, and sports officials anticipate play and position themselves to best see the action, assess the situation, and determine any violations. Some sports officials, such as boxing referees, may work independently, while others such as umpires work in groups. Regardless of the sport, the job is highly stressful because officials are often required to make a decision in a split second, sometimes resulting in strong disagreement among competitors, coaches, and spectators.

Coaches manage a team during games to maximize its chances of victory.

Also Known As

Professional scouts evaluate the skills of both amateur and professional athletes to determine talent and potential. As a sports intelligence agent, the scout's primary duty is to seek out top athletic candidates for the team he or she represents. At the professional level, scouts typically work for scouting organizations or as freelance scouts. In locating new talent, scouts perform their work in secrecy so as not to "tip off" their opponents about their interest in certain players. At the college level, the head scout often is an assistant coach, although freelance scouts may aid colleges by reporting to coaches about exceptional players. Scouts at this level seek talented high school athletes by reading newspapers, contacting high school coaches and alumni, attending high school games, and studying videotapes of prospects' performances. They also evaluate potential players' background and personal characteristics, such as motivation and discipline, by talking to the players' coaches, parents, and teachers.

Job Fit

Personality Type
Realistic-Enterprising-Social

Career Cluster
05 Education and Training

Skills
Social Skills
Management
Thought-Processing

Communications
Science
Equipment/Technology Analysis
Computer Programming
Equipment Use/Maintenance
Mathematics

Work Styles
Leadership
Social Skills Orientation
Persistence
Achievement/Effort
Innovation
Initiative
Concern for Others
Stress Tolerance

Working Conditions

Irregular work hours are common for athletes, coaches, umpires, referees, and other sports officials. They often work Saturdays, Sundays, evenings, and holidays. Athletes and full-time coaches usually work more than 40 hours a week for several months during the sports season, if not most of the year. High school coaches in educational institutions often coach more than one sport.

> **CONSIDER THIS...**
>
> Athletes and sports competitors had one of the highest rates of nonfatal on-the-job injuries. Coaches and sports officials also face the risk of injury, but the risk is not as great as that faced by athletes and sports competitors.

Athletes, coaches, and sports officials who participate in competitions that are held outdoors may be exposed to all weather conditions of the season. Athletes, coaches, and some sports officials frequently travel to sporting events. Scouts also travel extensively in locating talent. Athletes, coaches, and sports officials regularly encounter verbal abuse. Officials also face possible physical assault and, increasingly, lawsuits from injured athletes based on their officiating decisions.

What's Required

Education and training requirements for athletes, coaches, umpires, and related workers vary greatly by the level and type of sport. Regardless of the sport or occupation, these jobs require immense overall knowledge of the game, usually acquired through years of experience at lower levels.

Education and Training

Most athletes, coaches, umpires, and related workers get their training from having played in the sport at some level. All of these sports-related workers need to have an extensive knowledge of the way the sport is played, its rules and regulations, and strategies, which is often acquired by playing the sport in school or recreation center, but also with the help of instructors or coaches, or in a camp that teaches the fundamentals of the sport.

Athletes get their training in several ways. For most team sports, athletes gain experience by competing in high school and collegiate athletics or on club teams. Although a high school or college degree may not be required to enter the sport, most athletes who get their training this way are often required to maintain specific academic standards to remain eligible to play, which often results in earning a degree. Other athletes, in gymnastics or tennis for example, learn their sport by taking private or group lessons.

Although there may not be a specific education requirement, head coaches at public secondary schools and sports instructors at all levels usually must have a bachelor's degree. For high school coaching and sports instructor jobs, schools usually prefer and may have to hire teachers willing to take on these part-time jobs. If no suitable teacher is found, schools hire someone from outside. College coaches also usually are required to have a bachelor's degree. Degree programs specifically related to coaching include exercise and sports science, physiology, kinesiology, nutrition and fitness, physical education, and sports medicine.

> ### CONSIDER THIS...
> Some entry-level positions for coaches or instructors require only experience derived as a participant in the sport or activity.

Each sport has specific requirements for umpires, referees, and other sports officials; some require these officials to pass a test of their knowledge of the sport. Umpires, referees, and other sports officials often begin their careers and gain needed experience by volunteering for intramural, community, and recreational league competitions. They are often required to attend some form of training course or academy.

Scouting jobs often requires experience playing a sport at the college or professional level that makes it possible to spot young players who possess athletic ability and skills.

Most beginning scouting jobs are as part-time talent spotters in a particular area or region.

The need for athletes, coaches, umpires, and related workers to be licensed or certified to practice varies by sport and by locality. For example, in drag racing, drivers need to graduate from approved schools in order to be licensed to compete in the various drag racing series. The governing body of the sport may revoke licenses and suspend players who do not meet the required performance, education, or training. In addition, athletes may have their licenses or certification suspended for inappropriate activity.

Most public high school coaches need to meet state requirements for certification to become a head coach. Certification, however, may not be required for coaching and sports instructor jobs in private schools. College coaches may be required to be certified. For those interested in becoming scuba, tennis, golf, karate, or other kind of instructor, certification is highly desirable and may be required. There are many certifying organizations specific to the various sports, and their requirements vary. Coaches' certification often requires that one must be at least 18 years old and certified in cardiopulmonary resuscitation (CPR). Participation in a clinic, camp, or school also usually is required for certification. Part-time workers and those in smaller facilities are less likely to need formal education or training and may not need certification.

To officiate at high school athletic events, umpires, referees, and other officials must register with the state agency that oversees high school athletics and pass an exam on the rules of the particular game. For college refereeing, candidates must be certified by an officiating school and be evaluated during a probationary period.

> ### CONSIDER THIS...
> Some larger college sports conferences require officials to have certification and other qualifications, such as residence in or near the conference boundaries, along with several years of experience officiating at high school, community college, or other college conference games.

Postsecondary Programs to Consider

- Health and physical education, general
- Physical education teaching and coaching
- Sport and fitness administration/management
- Sports and exercise

Additional Qualifications

Athletes, coaches, umpires, and related workers often direct teams or compete on them. Thus these workers must relate well to others and possess good communication and leadership skills. They may need to pass a background check and applicable drug tests. Athletes who seek to compete professionally must have extraordinary talent, desire, and dedication to training. Coaches must be resourceful and flexible to successfully instruct and motivate individuals and groups of athletes. Officials need good vision, reflexes, and the ability to make decisions quickly.

School Subjects to Study

- Algebra
- Biology
- Chemistry
- English
- Geometry
- Physics
- Public speaking

Moving Up

For most athletes, turning professional is the biggest advancement. They often begin to compete immediately, although some may spend more time "on the bench," as a reserve, to gain experience. In some sports, such as baseball, athletes may begin their professional career on a minor league team before moving up to the major leagues. Professional athletes generally advance in their sport by winning and achieving accolades and earning a higher salary.

Many coaches begin their careers as assistant coaches to gain the knowledge and experience needed to become a head coach. Head coaches at large schools and colleges that strive to compete at the highest levels of a sport require substantial experience as a head coach at another school or as an assistant coach. To reach the ranks of professional coaching, a person usually needs years of coaching experience and a winning record in the lower ranks or experience as an athlete in that sport.

Standards for umpires and other officials become more stringent as the level of competition advances. A local or state academy may be required to referee a school baseball game. Those seeking to officiate at minor or major league games must attend a professional umpire training school. To advance to umpiring in Major League Baseball, umpires usually need 7 to 10 years of experience in various minor leagues before being considered for major league jobs.

Finding talented players is essential for scouts to advance. Hard work and a record of success often lead to full-time jobs and responsibility for scouting in more areas. Some scouts advance to scouting director jobs or various administrative positions in sports.

▉ Employment

Athletes, coaches, umpires, and related workers held about 258,100 jobs in 2008. Coaches and scouts held 225,700 jobs; athletes and sports competitors, 16,500; and umpires, referees, and other sports officials, 15,900. About half of all athletes, coaches, umpires, and related workers worked part time or maintained variable schedules.

Among those employed in wage-and-salary jobs, 52 percent held jobs in public and private educational services. About 13 percent worked in amusement, gambling, and recreation industries, including golf and tennis clubs, gymnasiums, health clubs, judo and karate schools, riding stables, swim clubs, and other sports and recreation facilities. Another 6 percent worked in the spectator sports industry.

About 16 percent of workers in this occupation were self-employed, earning prize money or fees for lessons, scouting, or officiating assignments.

Job Prospects

Employment of athletes, coaches, umpires, and related workers is expected to increase by 23 percent in the 10-year period ending 2018, which is much faster than the average for all occupations. A larger population overall that will continue to participate in organized sports for entertainment, recreation, and physical conditioning will boost demand for these workers, particularly for coaches, umpires, sports instructors, and other related workers. Job growth also will be driven by the increasing number of retirees who are expected to participate more in leisure activities such as golf and tennis, which require instruction. Additionally, the demand for private sports instruction is expected to grow among young athletes as parents try to

> ### CONSIDER THIS...
>
> Many sports officials and coaches receive such small and irregular payments for their services—occasional officiating at club games, for example—that they may not consider themselves employed in these occupations, even part time. Many others, although technically not self-employed, have such irregular or tenuous working arrangements that their working conditions resemble those of self-employment.

help their children reach their full potential. Future expansion of new professional teams and leagues may create additional openings for all of these workers.

Additional coaches and instructors are expected to be needed as school and college athletic programs expand. Population growth is expected to cause the construction of additional schools, but funding for athletic programs often is cut first when budgets become tight. Still, the popularity of team sports often enables shortfalls to be offset with the assistance from fundraisers, booster clubs, and parents. In colleges, most of the expansion is expected to be in women's sports.

Competition for professional athlete jobs will continue to be extremely keen. In major sports, such as basketball and football, only about 1 in 5,000 high school athletes becomes professional in these sports. The expansion of non-traditional sports may create some additional opportunities. Because most professional athletes' careers last only a few years due to debilitating injuries and age, annual replacement needs for these jobs is high, creating some job opportunities. However, the talented young men and women who dream of becoming sports superstars greatly outnumber the number of openings.

Opportunities should be best for persons seeking part-time umpire, referee, and other sports official jobs at the high school level. Coaches in girls' and women's sports may have better opportunities and face less competition for positions. Competition is expected for higher-paying jobs at the college level and will be even greater for jobs in professional sports. Competition should be keen for paying jobs as scouts, particularly for professional teams, because the number of available positions is limited.

Income

Median annual wages of athletes and sports competitors were $40,480 in May 2008. The middle 50 percent earned between $21,760 and $93,710. The highest paid professional athletes earn much more.

Median annual wages of umpires and related workers were $23,730 in May 2008. The middle 50 percent earned between $17,410 and $33,150. The lowest-paid 10 percent earned less than $15,450, and the highest-paid 10 percent earned more than $48,310.

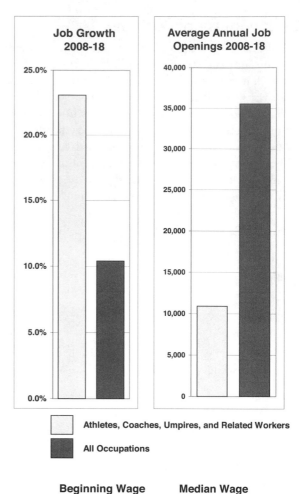

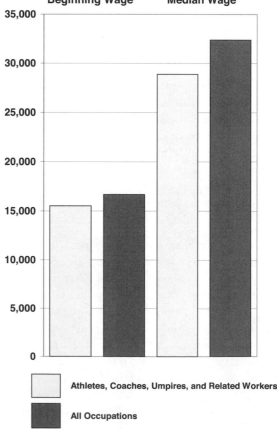

In May 2008, median annual wages of coaches and scouts were $28,340. The middle 50 percent earned between $18,220 and $43,440. The lowest-paid 10 percent earned less than $15,530, and the highest-paid 10 percent earned more than $62,660. However, the highest-paid professional coaches earn much more.

Wages vary by level of education, certification, and geographic region. Some instructors and coaches are paid a salary, while others may be paid by the hour, per session, or based on the number of participants.

Related Jobs

- Dietitians and nutritionists
- Fitness workers
- Physical therapists
- Recreation workers
- Recreational therapists
- Teachers—kindergarten, elementary, middle, and secondary

How to Learn More

For information about sports officiating for team and individual sports, contact

- National Association of Sports Officials, 2017 Lathrop Ave., Racine, WI 53405. Internet: www.naso.org

For additional information related to individual sports, refer to the organization that represents the sport.

Why It's Hot

We Americans love sports, both as participants and as fans. Professional leagues continue to grow, women's sports are gaining support, parents are nurturing their little sluggers, and retirees are looking forward to leisurely sports activities. All of these forces are creating demand for workers, although competition is often keen, especially for the high-paying players' jobs.

Athletic Trainers

Athletic trainers evaluate, advise, and treat athletes to assist recovery from injury, avoid injury, or maintain peak physical fitness.

Just the Facts

Earnings: $39,640

Job Growth: 36.9%

Annual Openings: 1,150

Education and Training: Bachelor's degree

While at Work

Athletic trainers help prevent and treat injuries for people of all ages. Their clients include everyone from professional athletes to industrial workers. Recognized by the American Medical Association as allied health professionals, athletic trainers specialize in the prevention, assessment, treatment, and rehabilitation of musculoskeletal injuries. Athletic trainers often are one of the first heath-care providers on the scene when injuries occur, and therefore they must be able to recognize, evaluate, and assess injuries and provide immediate care when needed. They also are heavily involved in the rehabilitation and reconditioning of injuries.

Athletic trainers often help prevent injuries by advising on the proper use of equipment and applying protective or injury-preventive devices such as tape, bandages, and braces. Injury prevention also often includes educating people on what they should do to avoid putting themselves at risk for injuries.

> CONSIDER THIS...
>
> Athletic trainers should not be confused with fitness trainers or personal trainers, who are not health-care workers, but rather train people to become physically fit.

Athletic trainers work under the supervision of a licensed physician, and in cooperation with other health-care providers. The level of medical supervision varies, depending upon the setting. Some athletic trainers meet with the team physician or consulting physician once or twice a week; others interact with a physician every day. The extent of the supervision ranges from discussing specific injuries and treatment options with a physician to performing evaluations and treatments as directed by a physician.

Athletic trainers often have administrative responsibilities. These may include regular meetings with an athletic director or other administrative officer to deal with budgets, purchasing, policy implementation, and other business-related issues.

Athletic trainers help prevent and treat sports injuries.

Also Known As

Some athletic trainers prefer the title *sports medicine trainers* because it emphasizes the health-care aspect of their work, which distinguishes them from fitness trainers.

Athletic trainers who join the military are classified as *health educators* or *training specialists*.

Job Fit

Personality Type
Social-Realistic-Investigative

Career Cluster
08 Health Science

Skills
Science
Management
Communications
Social Skills
Thought-Processing
Equipment/Technology Analysis
Equipment Use/Maintenance
Computer Programming
Mathematics

Work Styles
Concern for Others
Social Skills Orientation
Adaptability/Flexibility
Leadership
Analytical Thinking
Initiative
Innovation
Dependability

Working Conditions

The work of athletic trainers requires frequent interaction with others. This includes consulting with physicians as well as frequent contact with athletes and patients to discuss and administer treatments, rehabilitation programs, injury-preventive practices, and other health-related issues. Many athletic trainers work indoors most of the time; others, especially those in some sports-related jobs, spend much of their time working outdoors. The job also might require standing for long periods, working with medical equipment or machinery, and being able to walk, run, kneel, crouch, stoop, or crawl. Travel may be required.

Schedules vary by work setting. Athletic trainers in nonsports settings generally have an established schedule—usually about 40 to 50 hours per week—with nights and weekends off. Athletic trainers working in hospitals and clinics may spend part of their time working at other locations doing outreach. Most commonly, these outreach programs include conducting athletic training services and speaking at high schools, colleges, and commercial businesses.

> **CONSIDER THIS...**
>
> There is some stress involved with being an athletic trainer, as there is with most health-related occupations. Athletic trainers are responsible for their clients' health and sometimes have to make quick decisions that could affect the health or career of their clients. Athletics trainers also can be affected by the pressure to win that is typical of competitive sports teams.

Athletic trainers in sports settings have schedules that are longer and more variable. These athletic trainers must be present for team practices and games, which often are on evenings and weekends, and their schedules can change on short notice when games and practices have to be rescheduled. As a result, athletic trainers in sports settings may regularly work 6 or 7 days per week, including late hours.

In high schools, athletic trainers who also teach may work 60 to 70 hours a week, or more. In National Collegiate Athletic Association Division I colleges and universities, athletic trainers generally work with one team; when that team's sport is in season, working at least 50 to 60 hours a week is common. Athletic trainers in smaller colleges and universities often work with several teams and have teaching responsibilities. During the off-season, a 40-hour to 50-hour work week may be normal in most settings. Athletic trainers for professional sports teams generally work the most hours per week. During training camps, practices, and competitions, they may be required to work up to 12 hours a day.

What's Required

A bachelor's degree is usually the minimum requirement to work as an athletic trainer, but many athletic trainers hold a master's or doctoral degree. Licensure or some form of registration is also likely to be required.

Education and Training

A bachelor's degree from an accredited college or university is required for almost all jobs as an athletic trainer. In 2009, there were about 350 accredited undergraduate programs nationwide. Students in these programs are educated both in the classroom and in clinical settings. Formal education includes many science and health-related courses, such as human anatomy, physiology, nutrition, and biomechanics.

According to the National Athletic Trainers' Association, almost 70 percent of athletic trainers have a master's degree or higher. Athletic trainers may need a master's or higher degree to be eligible for some positions, especially those in colleges and universities, and to increase their advancement opportunities.

In 2009, 47 states required athletic trainers to be licensed or registered; this requires certification from the Board of Certification, Inc. (BOC). For BOC certification, athletic trainers need a bachelor's or master's degree from an accredited athletic training program and must pass a rigorous examination. To retain certification, credential holders must continue taking medical-related courses and adhere to the BOC standards of practice. In Alaska, California, West Virginia, and the District of Columbia where licensure is not required, certification is voluntary but may be helpful for those seeking jobs and advancement.

> ### CONSIDER THIS...
> Because some positions in high schools involve teaching along with athletic trainer responsibilities, a teaching certificate or license could be required for those jobs.

Postsecondary Program to Consider

- Athletic training/trainer training

Additional Qualifications

Because all athletic trainers deal directly with a variety of people, they need good social and communication skills. They should be able to manage difficult situations and the stress associated with them, such as when disagreements arise with coaches, clients, or parents regarding suggested treatment. Athletic trainers also should be organized, be able to manage time wisely, be inquisitive, and have a strong desire to help people.

School Subjects to Study

- Algebra
- Biology
- Chemistry
- English
- Geometry
- Physics
- Trigonometry

Moving Up

There are a number ways for athletic trainers to advance or move into related positions. Assistant athletic trainers may become head athletic trainers and, eventually, athletic directors. Athletic trainers also might enter a physician group practice and assume a management role. Some athletic trainers move into sales and marketing positions, using their athletic trainer expertise to sell medical and athletic equipment.

Employment

Athletic trainers held about 16,300 jobs in 2008 and are found in every part of the country. Most athletic trainer jobs are related to sports, although an increasing number also work in nonsports settings. About 39 percent were found in public and private educational services, primarily in colleges, universities, and high schools. Another 38 percent of athletic trainers worked in health care, including jobs in hospitals, offices of physicians, and offices of other health practitioners. About 13 percent worked in fitness and recreational sports centers. Around 5 percent work in spectator sports.

Job Prospects

Employment of athletic trainers is projected to grow 37 percent in the 10-year period ending 2018, much faster than the average for all occupations, because of their role in preventing injuries and reducing health-care costs. Job growth will be concentrated in the health-care industry, including hospitals and offices of health practitioners. Fitness and recreation sports centers also will provide new jobs, as these estab-lishments grow and con-tinue to need additional athletic trainers to pro-vide support for their clients. Growth in posi-tions with sports teams will be somewhat slower, however, as most profes-sional sports clubs and colleges and universities already have complete athletic training staffs.

The demand for health care, with an emphasis on preven-tive care, should grow as the population ages and as a way to reduce health-care costs. Athletic trainers will benefit from this expansion because they provide a cost-effective way to increase the number of health professionals in an office or other setting.

In some states, there are efforts underway to have an ath-letic trainer in every high school to work with student-athletes, which may lead to growth in the number of ath-letic trainers employed in high schools. In addition, as more young athletes specialize in certain sports, there is increasing demand for athletic trainers to deal with repet-itive stress injuries.

As athletic trainers continue to expand their services, more employers are expected to use these workers to re-duce health-care costs by preventing work-related injuries. Athletic trainers can help prevent injuries and provide im-mediate treatment for many injuries that do occur. For ex-ample, some athletic trainers may be hired to increase the fitness and performance of police and firefighters.

Job prospects should be good for athletic trainers in the health-care indus-try and in high schools. Those looking for a posi-tion with a professional or college sports team may face competition.

Because of relatively low turnover, the settings with the best job pros-pects will be the ones that are expected to have the most job growth, primarily positions in the health-care and fitness and recreational sports centers industries.

Additional job opportunities may arise in elementary and secondary schools as more positions are created. Some of these positions also will require teaching responsibilities.

There are relatively few positions for professional and col-legiate sports teams in comparison to the number of appli-cants. Turnover among professional sports team athletic trainers is also limited. Many athletic trainers prefer to continue to work with the same coaches, administrators, and players when a good working relationship already ex-ists.

There also are opportunities for athletic trainers to join the military, although they would not be classified as an athletic trainer. Enlisted soldiers and officers who are ath-letic trainers are usually placed in another program, such as health educator or training specialist, in which their skills are useful.

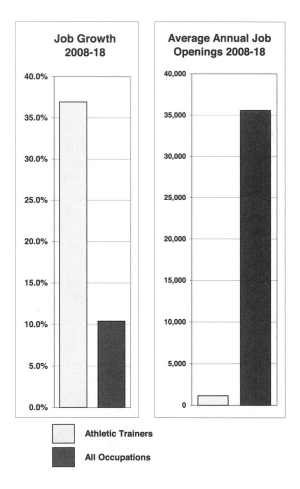

Athletic Trainers

All Occupations

Income

Most athletic trainers work in full-time positions, and typically receive benefits. The salary of an athletic trainer depends on experience and job responsibilities, and var-ies by job setting. Median annual earnings of wage-and-salary athletic trainers were $39,640 in May 2008. The middle 50 percent earned between $32,070 and $49,250. The lowest 10 percent earned less than $23,450, while the top 10 percent earned more than $60,960.

Many employers pay for some of the continuing education required for athletic trainers to remain certified, although the amount covered varies from employer to employer.

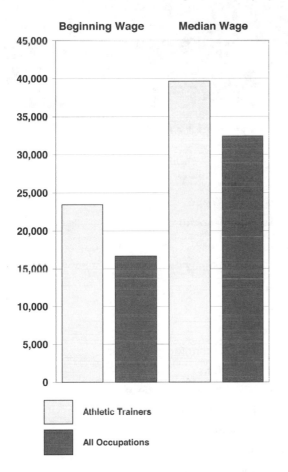

Beginning Wage   **Median Wage**

☐ Athletic Trainers

■ All Occupations

Related Jobs

- Chiropractors
- Emergency medical technicians and paramedics
- Licensed practical and licensed vocational nurses
- Massage therapists
- Occupational therapists
- Physical therapists
- Physician assistants
- Podiatrists
- Recreational therapists
- Registered nurses
- Respiratory therapists

How to Learn More

For further information on careers in athletic training, contact

- National Athletic Trainers Association, 2952 Stemmons Freeway, Dallas, TX 75247. Internet: www.nata.org

For further information on certification, contact

- Board of Certification, Inc., 1415 Harney St., Suite 200, Omaha, NE 68102. Internet: www.bocatc.org

Why It's Hot

Employment is projected to grow much faster than average. Although competition is expected for positions with sports teams, job prospects should be good in the health-care industry. People want to stay active and involved in sports much longer than they used to, and as this population ages, athletic trainers will be needed to keep them healthy.

Audiologists

Audiologists assess and treat persons with hearing and related disorders.

Just the Facts

Earnings: $62,030

Job Growth: 25.0%

Annual Openings: 580

Education and Training: First professional degree

While at Work

Audiologists work with people who have hearing, balance, and related ear problems. They examine individuals of all ages and identify those with the symptoms of hearing loss and other auditory, balance, and related sensory and neural problems. They then assess the nature and extent of the problems and help the individuals manage them. Using audiometers, computers, and other testing devices, they measure the loudness at which a person begins to hear sounds, the ability to distinguish between sounds, and the impact of hearing loss on an individual's daily life. In addition, audiologists use computer equipment to evaluate and diagnose balance disorders. Audiologists interpret these results and may coordinate them with medical, educational, and psychological information to make a diagnosis and determine a course of treatment.

Hearing disorders can result from a variety of causes including trauma at birth, viral infections, genetic disorders, exposure to loud noise, certain medications, or aging. Treatment may include examining and cleaning the ear canal, fitting and dispensing hearing aids, and fitting and programming cochlear implants. Audiologic treatment also includes counseling on adjusting to hearing loss, training on the use of hearing instruments, and teaching communication strategies for use in a variety of environments. For example, they may provide instruction in listening strategies. Audiologists also may recommend, fit, and dispense personal or large-area amplification systems and alerting devices.

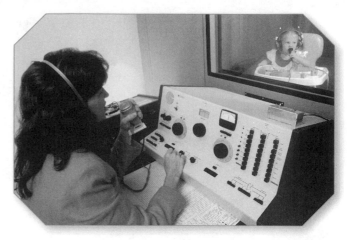
Audiologists check the hearing of patients of all ages.

> **CONSIDER THIS...**
> Audiologists who work in private practice also manage the business aspects of running an office, such as developing a patient base, hiring employees, keeping records, and ordering equipment and supplies.

In audiology clinics, audiologists may independently develop and carry out treatment programs. They keep records on the initial evaluation, progress, and discharge of patients. In other settings, audiologists may work with other health and education providers as part of a team in planning and implementing services for children and adults. Audiologists who diagnose and treat balance disorders often work in collaboration with physicians, and physical and occupational therapists.

Some audiologists specialize in work with the elderly, children, or hearing-impaired individuals who need special treatment programs. Others develop and implement ways to protect workers' hearing from on-the-job injuries. They measure noise levels in workplaces and conduct hearing protection programs in factories and in schools and communities.

Some audiologists conduct research on types of, and treatment for, hearing, balance, and related disorders. Others design and develop equipment or techniques for diagnosing and treating these disorders.

Also Known As

Some audiologist have job titles that reflect specializations, such as *dispensing audiologists, educational audiologists, infant hearing screening managers,* or *pediatric cochlear implant audiologists.*

Job Fit

Personality Type
Investigative-Social

Career Cluster
08 Health Science

Skills
Science
Social Skills
Equipment/Technology Analysis
Communications
Equipment Use/Maintenance
Thought-Processing
Management
Computer Programming
Mathematics

Work Styles
Concern for Others
Social Skills Orientation
Integrity
Self-Control
Stress Tolerance
Cooperation
Initiative
Analytical Thinking

Working Conditions

Audiologists usually work at a desk or table in clean, comfortable surroundings. The job is not physically demanding but does require attention to detail and intense concentration. The emotional needs of patients and their families may be demanding. Most full-time audiologists work about 40 hours per week, which may include weekends and evenings to meet the needs of patients. Those who work on a contract basis may spend a substantial amount of time traveling between facilities.

What's Required

All states regulate licensure of audiologists; requirements vary by state. At least a master's degree in audiology is required, but a doctoral degree is increasingly necessary.

Education and Training

Individuals pursuing a career will need to earn a doctoral degree. In 2009, 18 states required a doctoral degree or its equivalent for new applicants to practice audiology. The doctoral degree in audiology is a graduate program typically lasting 4 years and resulting in the Au.D. designation.

The Council on Academic Accreditation (CAA) is an entity of the American Speech-Language-Hearing Association (ASHA) that accredits education programs in audiology. In 2009, the CAA accredited 70 doctoral programs in audiology. Graduation from an accredited program may be required to obtain a license in some states and professional credentialing.

Requirements for admission to programs in audiology include courses in English, mathematics, physics, chemistry, biology, psychology, and communication. Graduate coursework in audiology includes anatomy; physiology; physics; genetics; normal and abnormal communication development; auditory, balance, and neural systems assessment and treatment; diagnosis and treatment; pharmacology; and ethics. Graduate curriculums also include supervised clinical practicum and externships.

Audiologists are regulated by licensure in all 50 states. Eighteen of those states require a doctoral degree for licensure. Many states require that audiologists complete continuing education for license renewal. Eligibility requirements, hearing aid dispensing requirements, and continuing education requirements vary from state to state. For specific requirements, contact your state's medical or health board.

CONSIDER THIS... Some states regulate the practice of audiology and the dispensing of hearing aids separately, meaning that some states require an additional license called a Hearing Aid Dispenser license.

Audiologists can earn the Certificate of Clinical Competence in Audiology (CCC-A) offered by the American Speech-Language-Hearing Association; they may also be credentialed through the American Board of Audiology. Professional credentialing may satisfy some or all of the requirements for state licensure.

CONSIDER THIS... It is important for audiologists to be aware of new diagnostic and treatment technologies. Most audiologists participate in continuing education courses to learn new methods and technologies.

Postsecondary Programs to Consider

- Audiology/Audiologist
- Audiology/Audiologist and Speech-Language Pathology/Pathologist
- Communication Disorders, General
- Communication Sciences and Disorders, General

Additional Qualifications

Audiologists should be able to communicate diagnostic test results, diagnoses, and proposed treatments in a manner that is effective and easily understood by their patients. They must be able to approach problems objectively and provide support to patients and their families. Because a patient's progress may be slow, patience, compassion, and good listening skills are necessary.

School Subjects to Study

- Algebra
- Biology
- Computer science
- English
- Geometry
- Physics
- Pre-calculus and calculus
- Trigonometry

Moving Up

With experience, audiologists can advance to open their own private practice. Audiologists working in hospitals and clinics can advance to management or supervisory positions.

Employment

Audiologists held about 12,800 jobs in 2008. About 64 percent of all jobs were in health-care facilities—offices of physicians or other health practitioners, including audiologists; hospitals; and outpatient care centers. About 14 percent of jobs were in educational services. Other jobs for audiologists were in health and personal care stores and in state and local governments.

Job Prospects

Employment of audiologists is expected to grow 25 percent in the 10-year period ending 2018, much faster than average for all occupations. Hearing loss is strongly associated with aging, so increased growth in older population groups will cause the number of people with hearing and balance impairments to increase markedly.

Medical advances also are improving the survival rate of premature infants and trauma victims, who then need assessment and sometimes treatment. Greater awareness of the importance of early identification and diagnosis of hearing disorders in infants also will increase employment. In addition to medical advances, technological advances in hearing aids may drive demand. Digital hearing aids have become smaller in size and also have quality-improving technologies like reducing feedback. Demand may be spurred by those who switch from analog to digital hearing aids, as well as those who will desire new or first-time hearing aids because they are becoming less visible.

> ### CONSIDER THIS...
>
> Growth in employment of audiologists will be moderated by limitations on reimbursements made by third-party payers for the tests and services they provide.

Employment in educational services will increase along with growth in elementary and secondary school enrollments, including enrollment of special education students.

Job prospects will be favorable for those possessing the Au.D. degree. Only a few job openings for audiologists will arise from the need to replace those who leave the occupation, because the occupation is relatively small and workers tend to stay in this occupation until they retire. Demand may be greater in areas with large numbers of retirees, so audiologists who are willing to relocate may have the best job prospects.

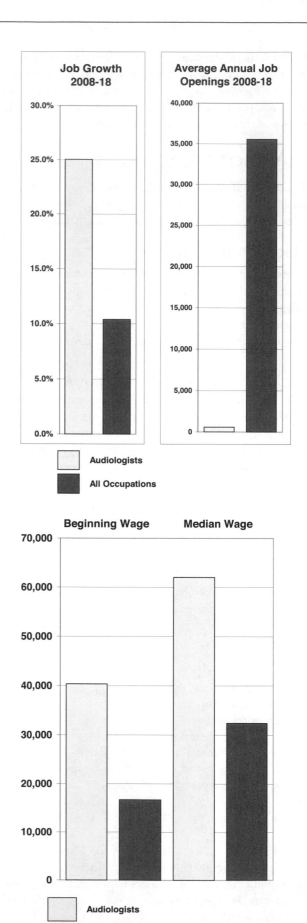

Income

Median annual wages of audiologists were $62,030 in May 2008. The middle 50 percent earned between $50,470 and $78,380. The lowest 10 percent earned less than $40,360, and the highest 10 percent earned more than $98,880. Some employers may pay for continuing education courses. About 15 percent of audiologists were union members or covered under union contracts in 2008.

Related Jobs

- Occupational therapists
- Optometrists
- Physical therapists
- Psychologists
- Speech-language pathologists

How to Learn More

State licensing boards can provide information on licensure requirements. State departments of education can supply information on certification requirements for those who wish to work in public schools.

For information on the specific requirements of your state, contact that state's licensing board. Career information, a description of the CCC-A credential, and information on state licensure is available from

- American Speech-Language-Hearing Association, 2200 Research Blvd., Rockville, MD 20850. Internet: www.asha.org

For information on the Au.D. degree, contact

- Audiology Foundation of America, 8 N. 3rd St., Suite 301, Lafayette, IN 47901. Internet: www.audfound.org

Why It's Hot

As the American population ages, the number of people with hearing disabilities continues to increase. The loud music enjoyed lifelong by baby boomers may worsen the natural aging process of their hearing. Meanwhile, new technologies are improving the performance of hearing aids, making them smaller and therefore increasing their appeal to users.

Barbers, Cosmetologists, and Other Personal Appearance Workers

Barbers, cosmetologists, and other personal appearance workers provide a wide range of services that help clients look and feel their best.

Just the Facts

Earnings: $22,893

Job Growth: 20.1%

Annual Openings: 28,580

Education and Training: Short-term on-the-job training

Postsecondary vocational training

While at Work

Most people want to look their best, and sometimes that requires the services of a professional. *Barbers* and *cosmetologists* focus on providing hair care services. Other personal appearance workers, such as *manicurists* and *pedicurists, shampooers, theatrical and performance makeup artists,* and *skin care specialists* provide more specialized beauty services.

Barbers cut, trim, shampoo, and style hair mostly for male clients. They also may fit hairpieces and offer scalp treatments and facial shaving. In many states, barbers are licensed to color, bleach, or highlight hair and to offer permanent-wave services. Barbers also may provide skin care and nail treatments.

Hairdressers, hairstylists, and *cosmetologists* offer a wide range of beauty services, such as shampooing, cutting, coloring, and styling of hair. They may advise clients on how to care for their hair at home. In addition, cosme-

CONSIDER THIS...

While barbers *tend* to be men and cosmetologists *tend* to be women, the difference is usually in the customer. Barbers cater to male clients, providing services such as beard trimming that aren't (usually) required for female clients. On the other hand, cosmetologists tend to serve more women than men. The line between the two occupations is growing thinner, however, as most businesses offer a "unisex" approach to personal grooming.

CONSIDER THIS...

In larger salons, workers may specialize in shampooing and conditioning hair, making that the sole focus of their job.

tologists may be trained to give manicures, pedicures, and scalp and facial treatments; provide makeup analysis; and clean and style wigs and hairpieces.

A number of workers offer specialized services. Manicurists and pedicurists, called nail technicians in some states, work exclusively on nails and provide manicures, pedicures, polishing, and nail extensions to clients. Theatrical and performance makeup artists, apply makeup to enhance performing artists' appearance for movie, television, or stage performances.

In addition to working with clients, personal appearance workers may keep records of hair color or skin care regimens used by their regular clients. A growing number actively sell hair, skin, and nail care products. Barbers, cosmetologists, and other personal appearance workers who operate their own salons have managerial duties that may include hiring, supervising, and firing workers, as well as keeping business and inventory records, ordering supplies, and arranging for advertising.

Also Known As

Skin care specialists, or estheticians, cleanse and beautify the skin by giving facials, full-body treatments, and head and neck massages as well as apply makeup. They also may remove hair through waxing or, if properly trained, laser treatments.

Job Fit

Personality Type
Artistic-Enterprising-Realistic

Career Cluster
10 Human Services

Skills
Science
Management
Equipment/Technology Analysis
Thought-Processing
Social Skills
Communications
Computer Programming

Work Styles
Social Skills Orientation
Innovation
Concern for Others
Self-Control
Cooperation
Achievement/Effort
Independence
Integrity

Barbers, cosmetologists, and other personal appearance workers must enjoy working with people.

Working Conditions

Most full-time barbers, cosmetologists, and other personal appearance workers put in a 40-hour week, but longer hours are common, especially among self-employed workers. Work schedules may include evenings and weekends, the times when beauty salons and barbershops are busiest.

In 2008, about 29 percent of barbers, hairstylists and cosmetologists worked part time, and 14 percent had variable schedules.

Barbers, cosmetologists, and other personal appearance workers usually work in clean, pleasant surroundings with good lighting and ventilation. Good health and stamina are important, because these workers are on their feet for most of their shift. Prolonged exposure to some hair and nail chemicals may cause irritation, so protective clothing, such as plastic gloves or aprons, may be worn.

What's Required

All states require barbers, cosmetologists, and other personal appearance workers to be licensed. To qualify for a license, most job seekers are required to graduate from a state-licensed barber or cosmetology school.

Education and Training

A high school diploma or GED is required for some personal appearance workers in some states. In addition, most states require that barbers and cosmetologists complete a program in a state-licensed barber or cosmetology school. Programs in hairstyling, skin care, and other personal appearance services can be found in both high schools and in public or private postsecondary vocational schools.

Full-time programs in barbering and cosmetology usually last 9 months and may lead to an associate degree, but training for manicurists and pedicurists and skin care specialists requires significantly less time. Makeup artists can attend schools that specialize in this subject, but it is not required.

During their first weeks on the job, new workers may be given relatively simple tasks. Once they have demonstrated their skills, they are gradually

permitted to perform more complicated procedures, such as coloring hair. As they continue to work in the field, more training usually is required to help workers learn the techniques particular to each salon and to build on the basics learned in cosmetology school.

All states require barbers, cosmetologists, and other personal appearance workers to be licensed, with the exceptions of shampooers and makeup artists. Qualifications for a license vary by state, but generally a person must have a high school diploma or GED, be at least 16 years old, and have graduated from a state-licensed barber or cosmetology school. After graduating from a state approved training program, students take a state licensing examination. The exam consists of a written test and, in some cases, a practical test of styling skills or an oral examination. In many states, cosmetology training may be credited toward a barbering license, and vice versa, and a few states combine the two licenses. Most states require separate licensing examinations for manicurists, pedicurists, and skin care specialists.

Postsecondary Programs to Consider

- Barbering/barber
- Cosmetology, barber/styling, and nail instructor
- Cosmetology/cosmetologist training, general
- Electrolysis/electrology and electrolysis technician training
- Facial treatment specialist/facialist training
- Hair styling/stylist and hair design
- Make-up artist/specialist training
- Nail technician/specialist and manicurist training
- Permanent cosmetics/makeup and tattooing
- Salon/beauty salon management

Additional Qualifications

Successful personal appearance workers should have an understanding of fashion, art, and technical design. They also must keep a neat personal appearance and a clean work area. Interpersonal skills, image, and attitude play an important role in career success. The ability to be an effective salesperson is vital for salon workers. Some cosmetology schools consider "people skills" to be such an integral part of the job that they require coursework in that area. Business skills are important for those who plan to operate their own salons.

School Subjects to Study

- Art
- Distributive education
- Public speaking

Moving Up

Advancement usually takes the form of higher earnings as barbers and cosmetologists gain experience and build a steady clientele. Some barbers and cosmetologists manage salons, lease booth space in salons, or open their own salons after several years of experience. Others teach in barber or cosmetology schools or provide training through vocational schools. Still others advance to become sales representatives, image or fashion consultants, or examiners for state licensing boards.

■ Employment

Barbers, cosmetologists, and other personal appearance workers held about 821,900 jobs in 2008. Of these, barbers and cosmetologists held 684,200 jobs, manicurists and pedicurists 76,000, skin care specialists 38,800, and shampooers 22,900.

Most of these workers are employed in personal care services establishments, such as beauty salons, barber shops, nail salons, day and resort spas. Others were employed in nursing and other residential care homes. Nearly every town has a barbershop or beauty salon, but employment in this occupation is concentrated in the most populous cities and States.

Job Prospects

Personal appearance workers will grow by 20 percent in the 10-year period ending 2018, which is much faster than the average for all occupations.

Consider This...

About 44 percent of all barbers, cosmetologists, and other personal appearance workers are self-employed. Many of these workers own their own salon, but a growing number of the self-employed lease booth space or a chair from the salon's owner. In this case, workers provide their own supplies and are responsible for paying their own taxes and benefits. They may pay a monthly or weekly fee to the salon owner, who is responsible for utilities and maintenance of the building.

Employment trends are expected to vary among the different occupational specialties. Employment of hairdressers, hairstylists, and cosmetologists will increase by about 20 percent, much faster than average, while the number of barbers will increase by 12 percent, about as fast as average. This growth will primarily come from an increasing population, which will lead to greater demand for basic hair services. Additionally, the demand for hair coloring and other advanced hair treatments has increased in recent years, particularly among baby boomers and young people. This trend is expected to continue, leading to a favorable outlook for hairdressers, hairstylists, and cosmetologists.

Continued growth in the number full-service spas and nail salons will also generate numerous job openings for manicurists, pedicurists, and skin care specialists. Estheticians and other skin care specialists will see large gains in employment, and are expected to grow almost 38 percent, much faster than average, primarily due to the popularity of skin treatments for relaxation and medical well-being. Manicurists and pedicurists meanwhile will grow by 19 percent, faster than average.

Job opportunities generally should be good, particularly for licensed personal appearance workers seeking entry-level positions. A large number of job openings will come about from the need to replace workers who transfer to other occupations, retire, or leave the labor force for other reasons. However, workers can expect keen competition for jobs and clients at higher-paying salons, as these positions are relatively few and require applicants to compete with a large pool of licensed and experienced cosmetologists. Opportunities will generally be best for those with previous experience and for those licensed to provide a broad range of services.

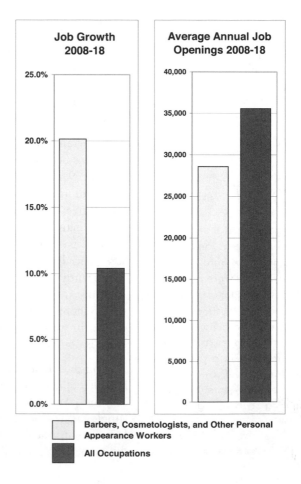

Job Growth 2008-18

Average Annual Job Openings 2008-18

□ Barbers, Cosmetologists, and Other Personal Appearance Workers

■ All Occupations

Income

Median hourly wages in May 2008 for hairdressers, hairstylists, and cosmetologists, including tips and commission, were $11.13. The middle 50 percent earned between $8.57 and $15.03. The lowest 10 percent earned less than $7.47, and the highest 10 percent earned more than $20.41.

Median hourly wages in May 2008 for barbers, including tips, were $11.56. The middle 50 percent earned between $8.93 and $14.69. The lowest 10 percent earned less than $7.56, and the highest 10 percent earned more than $19.51.

Among skin care specialists, median hourly wages, including tips, were $13.81, for manicurists and pedicurists $9.46, and for shampooers $8.32.

While earnings for entry-level workers usually are low, earnings can be considerably higher for those with experience. A number of factors, such as the size and location of the salon, determine the total income of personal appearance workers. They may receive commissions based on the price of the service, or a salary based on the number of hours worked, and many receive commissions on the products they sell. In addition, some salons pay bonuses to employees who bring in new business.

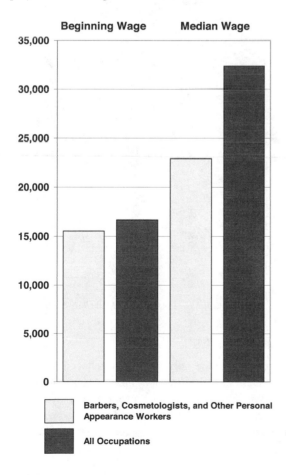

Beginning Wage   **Median Wage**

- ☐ Barbers, Cosmetologists, and Other Personal Appearance Workers
- ■ All Occupations

Although some salons offer paid vacations and medical benefits, many self-employed and part-time workers in this occupation do not enjoy such benefits. Some personal appearance workers receive free trial products from manufacturers in the hope that they will recommend the products to clients.

Related Jobs

- Fitness workers
- Massage therapists

How to Learn More

For details on state licensing requirements and approved barber or cosmetology schools, contact your state boards of barber or cosmetology examiners.

State licensing board requirements and a list of licensed training schools for cosmetologists may be obtained from

- National Accrediting Commission of Cosmetology Arts and Sciences, 4401 Ford Ave., Suite 1300, Alexandria, VA 22302. Internet: www.naccas.org

Information about a career in cosmetology is available from

- National Cosmetology Association, 401 N. Michigan Ave., 22nd Floor, Chicago, IL 60611. Internet: www.ncacares.org

For information on a career as a barber, contact

- National Association of Barber Boards of America, 2703 Pine Street, Arkadelphia, AR 71923. Internet: www.nationalbarberboards.com

An additional list of private schools for several different types of personal appearance workers is available from

- Beauty Schools Directory. Internet: www.beautyschoolsdirectory.com

Why It's Hot

As the population grows, there will be more heads growing hair and more hands growing nails. The aging boomers and young people in search of makeovers will need more hair coloring. Even though the occupation does not require a lot of education, there should be plenty of job openings for those entering the field.

Bill and Account Collectors

Bill and account collectors locate and notify customers of delinquent accounts by mail, telephone, or personal visit to solicit payment.

Just the Facts

Earnings: $30,630

Job Growth: 19.3%

Annual Openings: 15,690

Education and Training: Short-term on-the-job training

While at Work

Bill and account collectors, often called simply *collectors*, keep track of accounts that are overdue and attempt to collect payment on them. Some are employed by third-party collection agencies, while others—known as *in-house collectors*—work directly for the original creditors, such as department stores, hospitals, or banks.

The duties of bill and account collectors are similar across the many different organizations in which they work. First, collectors are called upon to locate and notify customers of delinquent accounts, usually over the telephone, but sometimes by letter. When customers move without leaving a forwarding address, collectors may check with the post office, telephone companies, credit bureaus, or former neighbors to obtain the new address. The attempt to find the new address is called "skip tracing." New computer systems assist in tracing by automatically tracking when customers change their address or contact information on any of their open accounts.

CONSIDER THIS...

Collectors use computers and a variety of automated systems to keep track of overdue accounts. In sophisticated predictive dialer systems, a computer dials the telephone automatically and the collector speaks only when a connection has been made. Such systems eliminate time spent calling busy or nonanswering numbers. Many collectors use regular telephones, but others wear headsets like those used by telephone operators.

Once collectors find the debtor, they inform him or her of the overdue account and solicit payment. If necessary, they review the terms of the sale, service, or credit contract with the customer. Collectors also may attempt to learn the cause of the delay in payment. Where feasible, they offer the customer advice on how to pay off the debts, such as taking out a bill consolidation loan. However, the collector's prime objective is always to ensure that the customer pays the debt in question.

If a customer agrees to pay, collectors record this commitment and check later to verify that the payment was made. Collectors may have authority to grant an extension of time if customers ask for one. If a customer fails to pay, collectors prepare a statement indicating the customer's action for the credit department of the establishment. In more extreme cases, collectors may initiate repossession proceedings, disconnect the customer's service, or hand the account over to an attorney for legal action. Most collectors handle other administrative functions for the accounts assigned to them, including recording changes of address and purging the records of the deceased.

Bill and account collectors spend a lot of time on the phone.

Also Known As

Some collectors have job titles that reflect their specialization, such as *insurance collectors, medical collectors,* or *rent collectors.* Others have titles that downplay their bill-collecting function, such as *account service representatives, credit coordinators,* or *patient account representatives.*

Job Fit

Personality Type
Conventional-Enterprising

Career Cluster
06 Finance

Skills
Computer Programming
Management
Mathematics
Communications
Social Skills
Thought-Processing
Equipment/Technology Analysis
Equipment Use/Maintenance

Work Styles
Stress Tolerance
Achievement/Effort
Self-Control
Persistence
Independence

Working Conditions

In-house bill and account collectors typically are employed in an office environment, and those who work for third-party collection agencies may work in a call-center environment. Workers spend most of their time on the phone tracking down and contacting people with debts.

Bill and account collectors often have to work evenings and weekends, when it is easier to reach people. Many collectors work part time or on flexible work schedules, though the majority work 40 hours per week.

What's Required

Most employers require collectors to have at a least a high school diploma and prefer some customer service experience. Employers usually provide on-the-job training to new employees.

Education and Training

A college degree is not needed, but employers prefer workers who have completed some college or who have experience in other occupations that involve contact with the public.

Once hired, workers usually receive on-the-job training. Under the guidance of a supervisor or some other senior worker, new employees learn company procedures. Some formal classroom training also may be necessary, such as training in specific computer software. Additional training topics usually include telephone techniques and negotiation skills. Workers are also instructed in the laws governing the collection of debt as mandated by the Fair Debt Collection Practices Act, which applies to all third-party and some in-house collectors.

CONSIDER THIS...
The work can be stressful because some customers are confrontational when pressed about their debts. Still, others appreciate assistance in resolving their outstanding debt. Collectors may also feel pressured to meet targets for debt recovered in a certain period.

Postsecondary Program to Consider

- Banking and financial support services

Additional Qualifications

Workers should have good communication and people skills, because they are constantly speaking to customers, some of whom may be in stressful financial situations. In addition, collectors should be computer literate, and experience with advanced telecommunications equipment is also useful.

School Subjects to Study

- Algebra
- Computer science
- English

Moving Up

Collectors most often advance by taking on more complex cases. Some might become team leaders or supervisors. Workers who acquire additional skills, experience, and training improve their advancement opportunities.

Employment

Bill and account collectors held about 411,000 jobs in 2008. About one quarter of collectors worked in business support services. Another 19 percent worked in finance and insurance, and 18 percent worked for health-care and social assistance providers.

Job Prospects

Employment of bill and account collectors is projected to grow by about 19 percent over the 10-year period ending 2018, which is faster than average for all occupations. New jobs should be created in key industries such as health-care and financial services, which often have delinquent accounts. In-house bill collectors will take on some of these collections, while others will be sold to third-party collection agencies. In both cases, bill and account collectors will be responsible for recovering these debts, causing the occupation to grow.

CONSIDER THIS...

Job growth will be tempered somewhat by continued outsourcing of collections work to offshore call centers. In recent years, many companies have chosen to use these call centers for some of their debt recovery efforts. Nevertheless, creditors will continue to hire collectors in the United States, as domestic workers tend to have greater success in negotiating with clients.

The occupation should see large growth in the health-care industry. The rapid growth projected in this industry, in combination with increasing prices, should result in many collections opportunities. This will affect both collectors who work in the health-care industry itself and those who work for collections agencies that accept accounts from health-care providers.

Opportunities for job seekers who are looking for bill and account collector jobs should be favorable due to continued job growth and the need to replace workers who leave the occupation. Those who have experience in a related occupation should have the best prospects. Companies prefer to hire workers who have worked in a call center before, or in another job that requires regular phone-based negotiations.

Unlike most occupations, the number of collections jobs tends to remain stable and even grow during economic downturns. When the economy suffers, individuals and businesses struggle to meet their financial obligations. While this increases the number of debts that must be collected, it also means that fewer people are able to pay their outstanding debt. Companies decide how many collectors to hire based on expected success rates. As a result, the number of collectors does not necessarily increase proportionally to the number of delinquent accounts. Nevertheless, the number of collections jobs tends to remain stable during downturns, although prospective employees may face increased competition for these jobs.

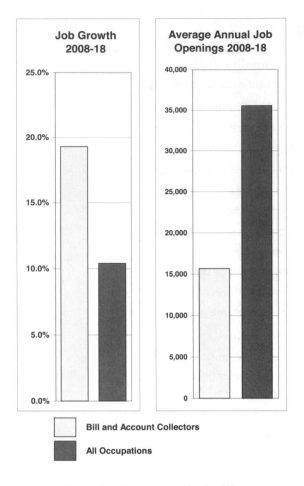

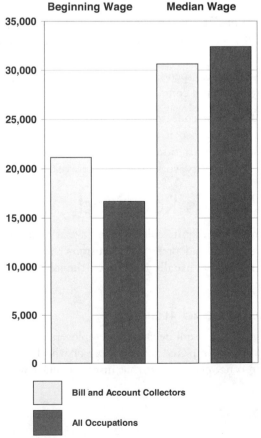

Income

Median hourly earnings of bill and account collectors were $14.73 in May 2008. The middle 50 percent earned between $12.14 and $18.12. The lowest 10 percent earned less than $10.17, and the highest 10 percent earned more than $22.07. Many bill and account collectors earn commissions based on the amount of debt they recover.

Related Jobs

- Credit authorizers, checkers, and clerks
- Interviewers
- Loan officers

How to Learn More

Career information on bill and account collectors is available from

- ACA International, The Association of Credit and Collection Professionals, P.O. Box 390106, Minneapolis, MN 55439. Internet: www.acainternational.org

Why It's Hot

Insurance reimbursements to hospitals and physicians' offices are not keeping up with cost increases, so these establishments are seeking to recover more money from patients. Government agencies also are making more use of collectors to collect on everything from parking tickets to child-support payments and past-due taxes. In addition, the Internal Revenue Service has begun outsourcing the collection of overdue federal taxes to third-party collection agencies, adding to the need for workers in this occupation.

Biological Scientists

Biological scientists study living organisms and their relationship to the environment. They perform research to gain a better understanding of fundamental life processes or apply that understanding to developing new products or processes.

Just the Facts

Earnings: $67,569

Job Growth: 21.0%

Annual Openings: 4,860

Education and Training: Bachelor's degree

Doctoral degree

While at Work

From the pets in our homes to the microbes that live inside our bodies, we interact every day with other living beings. Our economy depends on crops and domestic animals, and our survival depends on our understanding what we and other living things need. Biological scientists are essential for expanding this knowledge.

Many biological scientists work in research and development. Some conduct basic research to advance our knowledge of living organisms, including bacteria and other infectious agents, so we can develop solutions to human health problems and improve the natural environment. These biological scientists mostly work in government, university, or private industry laboratories, often exploring new areas of research. Many expand on specialized research they started in graduate school.

Biological scientists who work in applied research or product development use knowledge gained by basic research to develop new drugs, treatments, and medical diagnostic tests; increase crop yields; and develop new biofuels. They usually have less freedom than basic researchers do to choose the emphasis of their research, and they spend more time working on marketable treatments to meet the business goals of their employers. Biological scientists doing applied research and product development in private industry may be required to describe their research plans or results to nonscientists who are in a position to veto or approve their ideas. These scientists must consider the business effects of their work. Scientists often work in teams, interacting with engineers, scientists of other disciplines, business managers, and technicians. Some biological scientists also work with customers or suppliers and manage budgets.

Scientists usually conduct research in laboratories using a wide variety of equipment. Some conduct experiments involving animals or plants. This is particularly true of botanists, physiologists, and zoologists. Some biological research also takes place outside the laboratory. For example, a botanist might do field research in tropical rain forests to see which plants grow there, or an ecologist might study how a forest area recovers after a fire. Some marine biologists also work outdoors, often on research vessels from which they study fish, plankton, or other marine organisms.

Most biological scientists specialize in the study of a certain type of organism or in a specific activity, although recent advances have blurred some traditional classifications.

Aquatic biologists study micro-organisms, plants, and animals living in water. *Marine biologists* study saltwater organisms, and *limnologists* study freshwater organisms. Much of the work of marine biology centers on molecular biology, the study of the biochemical processes that take place inside living cells.

Biochemists study the chemical composition of living things. They analyze the complex chemical combinations and reactions involved in metabolism, reproduction, and growth. Biochemists do most of their work in biotechnology, which involves understanding the complex chemistry of life.

Botanists study plants and their environments. Some study all aspects of plant life, including algae, fungi, lichens, mosses, ferns, conifers, and flowering plants; others specialize in areas such as identification and classification of plants, the structure and function of plant parts, the biochemistry of plant processes, the causes and cures of plant diseases, the interaction of plants with other organisms and the environment, and the geological record of plants.

Microbiologists investigate the growth and characteristics of microscopic organisms such as bacteria, algae, or fungi. Most microbiologists specialize in environmental, food, agricultural, or industrial microbiology; virology (the study of viruses); immunology (the study of mechanisms that fight infections); or bioinformatics (the use of computers to handle or characterize biological information, usually at the molecular level). Many microbiologists use biotechnology to advance knowledge of cell reproduction and human disease.

Zoologists and *wildlife biologists* study animals and wildlife—their origin, behavior, diseases, and life processes. Some experiment with live animals in controlled or natural surroundings, while others dissect dead animals to study their structure. Zoologists and wildlife biologists also may collect and analyze biological data to determine the environmental effects of current and potential uses of land and water areas. Zoologists usually are identified by the animal group they study—*ornithologists* study birds, for example, *mammalogists* study mammals, *herpetologists* study reptiles, and *ichthyologists* study fish.

Ecologists investigate the relationships among organisms and between organisms and their environments, examining the effects of population size, pollutants, rainfall, temperature, and altitude. Using knowledge of various scientific disciplines, ecologists may collect, study, and report data on the quality of air, food, soil, and water.

Biological scientists conduct research in university, private industry, and government laboratories.

Also Known As

Physiologists study life functions of plants and animals, both in the whole organism and at the cellular or molecular level, under normal and abnormal conditions. Physiologists often specialize in functions such as growth, reproduction, photosynthesis, respiration, or movement, or in the physiology of a certain area or system of the organism.

Biophysicists study how physics, such as electrical and mechanical energy and related phenomena, relates to living cells and organisms. They perform research in fields such as neuroscience or bioinformatics.

Consider This...

Today, many biological scientists are involved in biotechnology. Those working on various genome (chromosomes with their associated genes) projects isolate genes and determine their function. This work continues to lead to the discovery of genes associated with specific diseases and inherited health risks, such as sickle cell anemia. Advances in biotechnology have created research opportunities in almost all areas of biology, with commercial applications in areas such as medicine, agriculture, and environmental remediation.

Job Fit

Personality Type

Investigative-Realistic

Career Clusters

01 Agriculture, Food, and Natural Resources

08 Health Science

15 Science, Technology, Engineering, and Mathematics

Skills

Science

Mathematics

Communications

Thought-Processing

Equipment/Technology Analysis

Management

Social Skills

Computer Programming

Equipment Use/Maintenance

Work Styles

Analytical Thinking

Persistence

Leadership

Innovation

Achievement/Effort

Initiative

Independence

Integrity

Working Conditions

Biological scientists usually are not exposed to unsafe or unhealthy conditions. Those who work with dangerous organisms or toxic substances in the laboratory must follow strict safety procedures to avoid contamination. Many biological scientists, such as botanists, ecologists, and zoologists, do field studies that involve strenuous physical activity and primitive living conditions. Biological scientists in the field may work in warm or cold climates, in all kinds of weather.

Marine biologists encounter a variety of working conditions. Some work in laboratories; others work on research ships, and those who work underwater must practice safe diving while working around sharp coral reefs and hazardous marine life. Although some marine biologists obtain their specimens from the sea, many still spend a good deal of their time in laboratories and offices, conducting tests, running experiments, recording results, and compiling data.

Many biological scientists depend on grant money to support their research. They may be under pressure to meet deadlines and to conform to rigid grant-writing specifications when preparing proposals to seek new or extended funding.

Biological scientists typically work regular hours. While the 40-hour work week is common, longer hours are not uncommon. Researchers may be required to work odd hours in laboratories or other locations (especially while in the field), depending on the nature of their research.

> **CONSIDER THIS...**
>
> Many research scientists must submit grant proposals to colleges and universities, private industry, and federal government agencies in order to obtain funding for their projects. Funding from grants is not guaranteed, so these workers are not as secure as those doing applied research or product development for an employer. On the other hand, researchers supported by grants often have more freedom to choose what topics they want to explore.

What's Required

Most biological scientists need a Ph.D. degree in biology or one of its subfields to work in research or development positions. A period of postdoctoral work in the laboratory of a senior researcher has become common for biological scientists who intend to conduct research or teach at the university level.

Education and Training

A Ph.D. degree usually is necessary for independent research, industrial research, and college teaching, as well as for advancement to administrative positions. A master's degree is sufficient for some jobs in applied research, product development, management, or inspection; it also may qualify one to work as a research technician or a teacher. The bachelor's degree is adequate for some nonresearch jobs. For example, graduates with a bachelor's degree may start as biological scientists in testing and inspection or may work in jobs related to biological science, such as technical sales or service representatives. Some work as research assistants, laboratory technicians, or high school biology teachers.

CONSIDER THIS...

Biological scientists with a Ph.D. often take temporary postdoctoral research positions that provide specialized research experience. Postdoctoral positions may offer the opportunity to publish research findings. A solid record of published research is essential in obtaining a permanent position involving basic research, especially for those seeking a permanent college or university faculty position.

In addition to required courses in chemistry and biology, undergraduate biological science majors usually study allied disciplines such as mathematics, physics, engineering, and computer science. Computer courses are beneficial for modeling and simulating biological processes, operating some laboratory equipment, and performing research in the emerging field of bioinformatics. Those interested in studying the environment also should take courses in environmental studies and become familiar with applicable legislation and regulations. Prospective biological scientists who hope to work as marine biologists should have at least a bachelor's degree in a biological or marine science. However, students should not overspecialize in undergraduate study, as knowledge of marine biology often is acquired in graduate study.

Most colleges and universities offer bachelor's degrees in biological science, and many offer advanced degrees. Advanced degree programs often emphasize a subfield such as microbiology or botany, but not all universities offer curricula in all subfields. Larger universities frequently have separate departments specializing in different areas of biological science. For example, a program in botany might cover agronomy, horticulture, or plant pathology. Advanced degree programs typically include classroom and fieldwork, laboratory research, and a thesis or dissertation.

Postsecondary Programs to Consider

- Anatomy
- Biochemistry/biophysics and molecular biology
- Biology/biological sciences, general
- Biostatistics
- Botany
- Cell biology and anatomy
- Developmental biology and embryology
- Ecology
- Endocrinology
- Entomology
- Environmental biology

- Epidemiology
- Genetics
- Marine biology
- Microbiology, general
- Plant physiology
- Soil chemistry and physics
- Virology
- Wildlife biology
- Zoology/animal biology

Additional Qualifications

Biological scientists should be able to work independently or as part of a team and be able to communicate clearly and concisely, both orally and in writing. Those in private industry, especially those who aspire to management or administrative positions, should possess strong business and communication skills and be familiar with regulatory issues and marketing and management techniques. Those doing field research in remote areas must have physical stamina. Biological scientists also must have patience and self-discipline to conduct long and detailed research projects.

School Subjects to Study

- Algebra
- Biology
- Chemistry
- Computer science
- English
- Geometry
- Physics
- Pre-calculus
- Trigonometry

Moving Up

As they gain experience, biological scientists typically gain greater control over their research and may advance to become lead researchers directing a team of scientists and technicians. Some work as consultants to businesses or to government agencies. However, those dependent on research grants are still constrained by funding agencies, and they may spend much of their time writing grant proposals. Others choose to move into managerial positions and become natural science managers. They may plan and administer programs for testing foods and drugs, for example, or direct activities at zoos or botanical gardens. Those who pursue management careers spend much of their time preparing budgets and schedules. Some leave biology for nontechnical managerial, administrative, or sales jobs.

Employment

Biological scientists held about 91,300 jobs in 2008. In addition, many biological scientists held biology faculty positions in colleges and universities but are not included in these numbers. Those whose primary work involves teaching and research are considered postsecondary teachers.

About 40 percent of all biological scientists were employed by federal, state, and local governments. Federal biological scientists worked mainly for the U.S. Departments of Agriculture, Interior, and Defense and for the National Institutes of Health. Most of the rest worked in scientific research and testing laboratories, the pharmaceutical and medicine manufacturing industry, or colleges and universities.

Job Prospects

Employment of biological scientists is projected to grow 21 percent over the 10-year period ending 2018, much faster than the average for all occupations, as biotechnological research and development continues to drive job growth. The federal government funds much basic research and development, including many areas of medical research that relate to biological science.

Biological scientists enjoyed very rapid employment gains over the past few decades—reflecting, in part, the growth of the biotechnology industry. Employment growth will moderate somewhat as the biotechnology industry matures, with fewer new firms being founded and existing firms merging or being absorbed by larger biotechnology or pharmaceutical firms. However, much of the basic biological research done in recent years has resulted in new knowledge, including the isolation and identification of genes. Biological scientists will be needed to take this knowledge to the next stage, understanding how certain genes function within an entire organism, so that medical treatments can be developed to treat various diseases.

In addition, efforts to discover new and improved ways to clean up and preserve the environment will continue to add to job growth. More biological scientists will be needed to determine the environmental impact of industry and government actions and to prevent or correct environmental problems, such as the negative effects of pesticide use. Some biological scientists will find opportunities in environmental regulatory agencies, while others will use their expertise to advise lawmakers on legislation to save environmentally sensitive areas. New industrial applications of biotechnology, such as new methods for producing biofuels, also will spur demand for biological scientists.

> **CONSIDER THIS...**
> Even pharmaceutical and other firms not solely engaged in biotechnology use biotechnology techniques extensively, spurring employment for biological scientists. For example, biological scientists are continuing to help farmers increase crop yields by pinpointing genes that can help crops such as wheat grow in more extreme climate conditions.

> **CONSIDER THIS...**
> Biological scientists are less likely to lose their jobs during recessions than are those in many other occupations because many are employed on long-term research projects. However, an economic downturn could influence the amount of money allocated to new research and development efforts, particularly in areas of risky or innovative research. An economic downturn also could limit the possibility of extension or renewal of existing projects.

The federal government is a major source of funding for basic research and development, including many areas of medical research that relate to biological science. Large budget increases at the National Institutes of Health in the early part of the decade led to increases in federal basic research and development expenditures, with research grants growing both in number and dollar amount. However, the increase in expenditures slowed substantially in recent years. Going forward, the level of federal funding will continue to impact competition for winning and renewing research grants.

There will continue to be demand for biological scientists specializing in botany, zoology, and marine biology, but opportunities will be limited because of the small size of these fields. Marine biology, despite its attractiveness as a career, is a very small specialty within biological science.

Doctoral degree holders are expected to face competition for basic research positions. Furthermore, should the number of advanced degrees awarded continue to grow, applicants for research grants are likely to face even more competition. Currently, about one in four grant proposals are approved for long-term research projects. In addition, applied research positions in private industry may become more difficult to obtain if increasing numbers of scientists seek jobs in private industry because of the competitive job market for independent research positions in universities and for college and university faculty.

Prospective marine biology students should be aware that those who would like to enter this specialty far outnumber the very few openings that occur each year for the type of glamorous research jobs that many would like to obtain. Almost all marine biologists who do basic research have a Ph.D.

People with bachelor's and master's degrees are expected to have more opportunities in nonscientist jobs related to biology. The number of science-related jobs in sales, marketing, and research management is expected to exceed the number of independent research positions. Non-Ph.D.s also may fill positions as science or engineering technicians or as medical health technologists and technicians. Some become high school biology teachers.

and $87,040. The lowest 10 percent earned less than $48,330, and the highest 10 percent earned more than $111,300.

Median annual earnings of zoologists and wildlife biologists were $55,290 in 2008. The middle 50 percent earned between $43,060 and $70,500. The lowest 10 percent earned less than $33,550, and the highest 10 percent earned more than $90,850.

According to the National Association of Colleges and Employers, beginning salary offers in 2007 averaged $34,953 a year for bachelor's degree recipients in biological and life sciences.

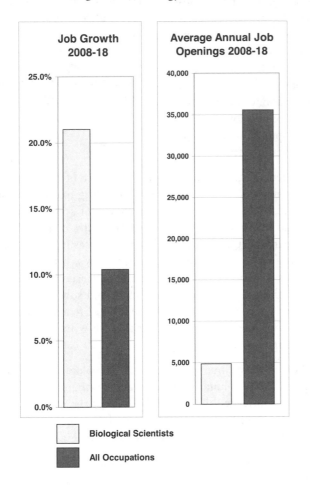

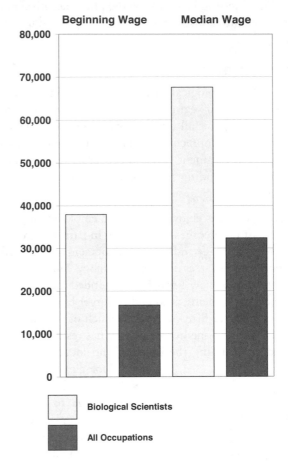

Income

Median annual earnings of biochemists and biophysicists were $82,840 in 2008. The middle 50 percent earned between $59,260 and $108,950. The lowest 10 percent earned less than $44,320, and the highest 10 percent earned more than $139,440. Median annual earnings of biochemists and biophysicists employed in scientific research and development services were $85,870 in 2008.

Median annual earnings of microbiologists were $64,350 in 2008. The middle 50 percent earned between $48,330

Related Jobs

- Agricultural and food scientists
- Conservation scientists and foresters
- Dentists
- Engineering and natural sciences managers
- Medical scientists
- Physicians and surgeons
- Veterinarians

How to Learn More

For information on careers in the biological sciences, contact

- American Institute of Biological Sciences, 1444 I St. NW, Suite 200, Washington, DC 20005. Internet: www.aibs.org

For information on careers in biochemistry or biological sciences, contact

- Federation of American Societies for Experimental Biology, 9650 Rockville Pike, Bethesda, MD 20814. Internet: www. faseb.org
- American Society for Biochemistry and Molecular Biology, 9650 Rockville Pike, Bethesda, MD 20814. Internet: www. asbmb.org

For information on careers in botany, contact

- The Botanical Society of America, 4475 Castleman Ave., P.O. Box 299, St. Louis, MO 63166. Internet: www.botany.org

For information on careers in cell biology, contact

- American Society for Cell Biology, 8120 Woodmont Ave, Suite 750, Bethesda, MD 20814. Internet: www.ascb.org

For information on careers in ecology, contact

- Ecological Society of America, 1990 M St. NW, Suite 700, Washington, DC 20036. Internet: www.esa.org

For information on careers in microbiology, contact

- American Society for Microbiology, Career Information— Education Department, 1752 N St. NW, Washington, DC 20036. Internet: www.asm.org

For information on careers in physiology, contact

- American Physiology Society, 9650 Rockville Pike, Bethesda, MD 20814. Internet: www.the-aps.org

Information on obtaining a biological scientist position with the federal government is available at www.usajobs.opm.gov.

Why It's Hot

Driven by research in genetics, biotechnology has become a huge industry that is spurring further research. Biological scientists can manipulate the genetic material of animals and plants to make them more productive or resistant to disease. Research on biotechnological processes, such as re-combining DNA, has led to the wide-scale production of human insulin and growth hormone. Genetic screening is helping doctors diagnose and treat patients for potentially devastating diseases. In the future, scientists hope that gene therapy can be used to treat or cure diseases such as AIDS or cancer. New industrial applications of biotechnology, such as new methods for making ethanol for transportation fuel, also will require the work of biological scientists.

Cardiovascular Technologists and Technicians

Cardiovascular technologists and technicians assist physicians in diagnosing and treating cardiac (heart) and peripheral vascular (blood vessel) ailments.

Just the Facts

Earnings: $47,010

Job Growth: 24.1%

Annual Openings: 1,910

Education and Training: Associate degree

While at Work

Cardiovascular technologists and technicians schedule appointments, perform ultrasound or cardiovascular procedures, review doctors' interpretations and patient files, and monitor patients' heart rates. They also operate and care for testing equipment, explain test procedures, and compare findings to a standard to identify problems. Other day-to-day activities vary significantly between specialties.

Cardiovascular technologists may specialize in any of three areas of practice: invasive cardiology, echocardiography, or vascular technology.

Invasive cardiology. Cardiovascular technologists specializing in invasive procedures are called *cardiology technologists*. They assist physicians with cardiac catheterization procedures, in which a small tube, or catheter, is threaded through a patient's artery from a spot on the patient's groin to the heart. The procedure can determine whether a blockage exists in the blood vessels that supply the heart muscle. The procedure also can help to diagnose other problems. Part of the procedure may involve balloon angioplasty, which can be used to treat blockages of blood vessels or heart valves without the need for heart surgery. Cardiology technologists assist physicians as they insert a catheter with a balloon on the end to the point of the obstruction. Another procedure using the catheter is electrophysiology testing, which helps locate the specific areas of heart tissue that give rise to the abnormal electrical impulses that cause arrhythmias.

Technologists prepare patients for cardiac catheterization by first positioning them on an examining table and then shaving, cleaning, and administering anesthesia to the top of their leg near the groin. During the procedures, they monitor patients' blood pressure and heart rate with EKG equipment and notify the physician if something appears to be wrong. Technologists also may prepare and monitor patients during open-heart surgery and during the insertion of pacemakers and stents that open up blockages in arteries to the heart and major blood vessels.

Noninvasive technology. Some technologists specialize in performing tests using equipment that is called "noninvasive" because it does not require the insertion of probes or other instruments into the patient's body. For example, procedures such as Doppler ultrasound transmit high-frequency sound waves into areas of the patient's body and then process reflected echoes of the sound waves to form an image. Technologists view the ultrasound image on a screen and may record the image on videotape or photograph it for interpretation and diagnosis by a physician. As the technologist uses the instrument to perform scans and record images, technologists check the image on the screen for subtle differences between healthy and diseased areas, decide which images to include in the report to the physician, and judge whether the images are satisfactory for diagnostic purposes. They also explain the procedure to patients, record any additional medical history the patient relates, select appropriate equipment settings, and change the patient's position as necessary.

Vascular technology. Technicians who assist physicians in the diagnosis of disorders affecting the circulation are known as *vascular technologists* or *vascular sonographers*. Vascular technologists complete patients' medical histories; evaluate pulses and assess blood flow in arteries and veins by listening to the vascular flow sounds for abnormalities; and assure the appropriate vascular test has been ordered. Then they perform a noninvasive procedure using ultrasound instruments to record vascular information such as vascular blood flow, blood pressure, oxygen saturation, cerebral circulation, peripheral circulation, and abdominal circulation. Many of these tests are performed during or immediately after surgery. Vascular technologists then provide a summary of findings to the physician to aid in patient diagnosis and management.

Echocardiography. This area of practice includes giving electrocardiograms (EKGs) and sonograms of the heart. Cardiovascular technicians who specialize in EKGs, stress testing, and performing Holter monitor procedures are known as *cardiographic* or *electrocardiograph* (or *EKG*) *technicians*.

To take a basic EKG, which traces electrical impulses transmitted by the heart, technicians attach electrodes to the patient's chest, arms, and legs, and then manipulate switches on an EKG machine to obtain a reading. An EKG is printed out for interpretation by the physician. This test is done before most kinds of surgery or as part of a routine physical examination, especially on persons who have reached middle age or who have a history of cardiovascular problems.

EKG technicians with advanced training perform Holter monitor and stress testing. For Holter monitoring, technicians place electrodes on the patient's chest and attach a portable EKG monitor to the patient's belt. Following 24 or more hours of normal activity by the patient, the technician removes a tape from the monitor and places it in a scanner. After checking the quality of the recorded impulses on an electronic screen, the technician usually prints the information from the tape for analysis by a physician. Physicians use the output from the scanner to diagnose heart ailments, such as heart rhythm abnormalities or problems with pacemakers.

For a treadmill stress test, EKG technicians document the patient's medical history, explain the procedure, connect the patient to an EKG monitor, and obtain a baseline reading and resting blood pressure. Next, they monitor the heart's performance while the patient is walking on a treadmill, gradually increasing the treadmill's speed to observe the effect of increased exertion. Like vascular technologists and cardiac sonographers, cardiographic technicians who perform EKG, Holter monitor, and stress tests are known as "noninvasive" technicians.

Technologists who use ultrasound to examine the heart chambers, valves, and vessels are referred to as *cardiac sonographers*, or *echocardiographers*. They use ultrasound instrumentation to create images called echocardiograms. An echocardiogram may be performed while the patient is either resting or physically active. Technologists may administer medication to physically active patients to assess their heart function.

> **CONSIDER THIS...**
>
> For a really close-up view of how the heart is functioning, cardiac sonographers may assist physicians in performing transesophageal echocardiography, which involves placing a tube in the patient's esophagus to obtain ultrasound images.

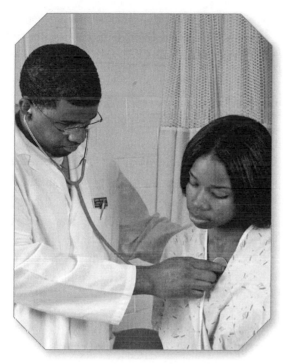

Cardiovascular technologists assist physicians in diagnosing and treating cardiac and vascular problems.

Also Known As

Some workers also conduct tests of the pulmonary system and have job titles that reflect these duties: *cardiopulmonary technicians, cardiopulmonary technologists, pulmonary function technicians,* or *pulmonary function technologists.*

Job Fit

Personality Type
Investigative-Social-Realistic

Career Cluster
08 Health Science

Skills
Communications
Equipment Use/Maintenance
Computer Programming
Social Skills
Thought-Processing

Work Styles
Concern for Others
Social Skills Orientation
Stress Tolerance
Integrity
Independence
Persistence
Self-Control
Cooperation

Working Conditions

Cardiovascular technologists and technicians spend a lot of time walking and standing. Heavy lifting may be involved to move equipment or transfer patients. These workers wear heavy protective aprons while conducting some procedures.

Some cardiovascular technologists and technicians may have the potential for radiation exposure, which is kept to a minimum by strict adherence to radiation safety guidelines. In addition, those who use sonography can be at an increased risk for musculoskeletal disorders such as carpal tunnel syndrome, neck and back strain, and eye strain. However, greater use of ergonomic equipment and an increasing awareness will continue to minimize such risks.

> **CONSIDER THIS...**
>
> Those who work in catheterization laboratories may face stressful working conditions because they are in close contact with patients with serious heart ailments. For example, some patients may encounter complications that have life-or-death implications.

Technologists and technicians generally work a 5-day, 40-hour week that may include weekends. Those in catheterization laboratories tend to work longer hours and may work evenings. They also may be on call during the night and on weekends.

■ What's Required

The most common level of education completed by cardiovascular technologists and technicians is an associate degree. Certification, although not required in all cases, is available.

Education and Training

Although a few cardiovascular technologists, vascular technologists, and cardiac sonographers are currently trained on the job, most receive training in 2- to 4-year programs. The majority of technologists complete a 2-year junior or community college program, but 4-year programs are increasingly available. The first year is dedicated to core courses and is followed by a year of specialized instruction in either invasive, noninvasive cardiovascular, or noninvasive vascular technology.

The Joint Review Committee on Education in Cardiovascular Technology reviews education programs seeking accreditation. The Commission on Accreditation of Allied Health Professionals (CAAHEP) accredits these education programs; as of 2009, there were 34 programs accredited in cardiovascular technology in the United States. Similarly, those who want to study echocardiography or vascular sonography may also attend CAAHEP accredited programs in diagnostic medical sonography. In 2009, there were 168 diagnostic medical sonography programs accredited by CAAHEP. Those who attend these accredited programs are eligible to obtain professional certification.

Unlike most other cardiovascular technologists and technicians, most EKG technicians are trained on the job by an EKG supervisor or a cardiologist. On-the-job training usually lasts about 8 to 16 weeks. Most employers prefer to train people already in the health-care field—nursing aides, for example. Some EKG technicians are students enrolled in 2-year programs to become technologists, working part time to gain experience and make contact with employers. One-year certification programs exist for basic EKGs, Holter monitoring, and stress testing.

Some states require workers in this occupation to be licensed. For information on a particular state, contact that state's medical board. Certification is available from two organizations: Cardiovascular Credentialing International (CCI) and the American Registry of Diagnostic Medical Sonographers (ARDMS). The CCI offers four certifications—Certified Cardiographic Technician (CCT), Registered Cardiac Sonographer (RCS), Registered Vascular Specialist (RVS), and Registered Cardiovascular Invasive Specialist (RCIS). The ARDMS offers Registered Diag-

nostic Cardiac Sonographer (RDCS) and Registered Vascular Technologist (RVT) credentials. Some states require certification as part of licensure. In other states, certification is not required, but many employers prefer it.

Postsecondary Programs to Consider

- Cardiopulmonary technology/technologist training
- Cardiovascular technology/technologist training
- Electrocardiograph technology/technician training
- Perfusion technology/perfusionist training

Additional Qualifications

Cardiovascular technologists and technicians must be reliable, have mechanical aptitude, and be able to follow detailed instructions. A pleasant, relaxed manner for putting patients at ease is an asset. They must be articulate, because they must communicate technically with physicians and also explain procedures simply to patients.

School Subjects to Study

- Algebra
- Biology
- Computer science
- Electronics shop
- English
- Geometry
- Physics
- Trigonometry

Moving Up

Technologists and technicians can advance to higher levels of the profession as many institutions structure the occupation with multiple levels, each having an increasing amount of responsibility. Technologists and technicians also can advance into supervisory or management positions. Other common possibilities include working in an educational setting or conducting laboratory work.

Employment

Cardiovascular technologists and technicians held about 49,500 jobs in 2008. About 77 percent of jobs were in hospitals (public and private), primarily in cardiology departments. The remaining jobs were mostly in offices of physicians, including cardiologists, or in medical and diagnostic laboratories, including diagnostic imaging centers.

Job Prospects

Employment of cardiovascular technologists and technicians is expected to increase 24 percent in the 10-year period ending 2018, much faster than the average for all occupations. Demand will stem from the prevalence of heart disease and the aging population.

Employment of vascular technologists and echocardiographers will grow as advances in vascular technology and sonography reduce the need for more costly and invasive procedures. However, fewer EKG technicians will be needed, as hospitals train nursing aides and others to perform basic EKG procedures. Individuals trained in Holter monitoring and stress testing are expected to have more favorable job prospects than those who can perform only a basic EKG.

The rules governing reimbursement by Medicare and Medicaid for medical procedures will affect the frequency of their use and demand for imaging technologists.

In addition to job growth, job openings for cardiovascular technologists and technicians will arise from replacement needs as individuals transfer to other jobs or leave the labor force. Job prospects will be best for those with multiple professional credentials, trained to perform a wide range of procedures. Those willing to relocate or work irregular hours also will have better job opportunities.

It is not uncommon for cardiovascular technologists and technicians to move between the specialties within the occupation by obtaining certification in more than one specialty. Technologists with multiple credentials will be the most marketable to employers.

Income

Median annual earnings of cardiovascular technologists and technicians were $47,010 in May 2008. The middle 50 percent earned between $32,800 and $61,580. The lowest 10 percent earned less than $25,510, and the highest 10 percent earned more than $74,760. Median annual earnings of cardiovascular technologists and technicians in 2008 were $48,590 in offices of physicians and $46,670 in general medical and surgical hospitals.

Related Jobs

- Diagnostic medical sonographers
- Nuclear medicine technologists
- Radiation therapists, radiologic technologists and technicians
- Respiratory therapists

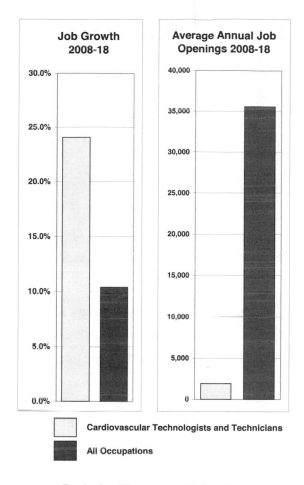

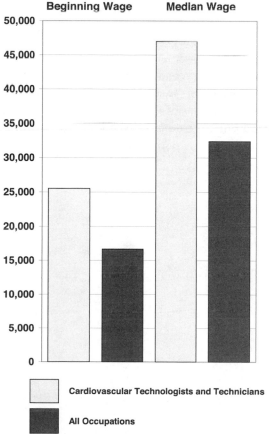

◼ How to Learn More

For general information about a career in cardiovascular technology, contact

- Alliance of Cardiovascular Professionals, Thalia Landing Offices, Bldg. 2, 4356 Bonney Rd., Suite 103, Virginia Beach, VA 23452-1200. Internet: www.acp-online.org

For a list of accredited programs in cardiovascular technology, contact

- Committee on Accreditation for Allied Health Education Programs, 1361 Park St, Clearwater, FL 33756. Internet: www.caahep.org
- Society for Vascular Ultrasound, 4601 Presidents Dr., Suite 260, Lanham, MD 20706-4381. Internet: www.svunet.org

For information on echocardiography, contact

- American Society of Echocardiography, 1500 Sunday Dr., Suite 102, Raleigh, NC 27607. Internet: www.asecho.org

For information regarding registration and certification, contact

- Cardiovascular Credentialing International, 1500 Sunday Dr., Suite 102, Raleigh, NC 27607. Internet: www.cci-online.org
- American Registry of Diagnostic Medical Sonographers, 51 Monroe St., Plaza East One, Rockville, MD 20850-2400. Internet: www.ardms.org

Why It's Hot

Employment is expected to grow much faster than average. Growth will occur as the population ages. Procedures such as ultrasound are being performed more often as a replacement for more expensive and more invasive procedures. Due to advances in medicine and greater public awareness, signs of vascular disease can be detected earlier, creating demand for cardiovascular technologists and technicians to perform various procedures.

Cargo and Freight Agents

Cargo and freight agents help transportation companies manage incoming and outgoing shipments in airline, train, or trucking terminals or on shipping docks.

Just the Facts

Earnings: $37,270

Job Growth: 23.9%

Annual Openings: 4,030

Education and Training: Moderate-term on-the-job training

◼ While at Work

Across the country, trucks, trains, and airplanes are in constant motion, shipping cargo from one business to another or from a business to a consumer. Cargo and freight agents expedite shipments by determining a route, preparing all necessary documents, and arranging for the pickup of freight or cargo and its delivery to loading platforms. They may also keep records of the cargo, including its amount, type, weight, dimensions, destination, and time of shipment. They also keep a tally of missing items and record the condition of damaged items.

Cargo and freight agents arrange cargo according to destination. They also determine any shipping rates and other applicable charges. For imported or exported freight, they verify that the proper customs paperwork is in order. Cargo and freight agents often track shipments electronically, using bar codes, and answer customers' questions about the status of their shipments.

CONSIDER THIS...

Bar codes and radio frequency identification (RFID) tags have changed the shipping industry. Packages and even boxcars are now scanned at each stage of their journey from sender to receiver, and their status is immediately updated in a database that is accessible via the Internet. This enables sellers, buyers, and shippers to check the progress of the merchandise at any time.

Cargo and freight agents are responsible for shipping goods all around the world.

Also Known As

Some job titles for these workers reflect the kind of shipping they use—for example, *air export logistics managers* or *ship brokers*.

Job Fit

Personality Type
Conventional-Enterprising

Career Cluster
04 Business, Management, and Administration

Skills
Social Skills
Communications
Thought-Processing
Mathematics
Computer Programming

Work Styles
Independence
Persistence

Working Conditions

Cargo and freight agents work in a wide variety of environments. Some work in warehouses, stockrooms, or shipping and receiving rooms that may not be temperature controlled. Others may spend time in cold storage rooms or outside on loading platforms, where they are exposed to the weather.

Most jobs for cargo and freight agents involve frequent standing, bending, walking, and stretching. Some lifting and carrying of small items may be involved. Although automated devices have lessened the physical demands of this occupation, not every employer has these devices. The work still can be strenuous, even though mechanical material-handling equipment is used to move heavy items.

The typical workweek is Monday through Friday. However, evening and weekend hours are common in jobs involving large shipments.

> **CONSIDER THIS...**
> The work is sometimes stressful because of the pressure of tight time schedules. This most often tends to happen during seasons such as Christmas, when companies receive rush orders.

> **CONSIDER THIS...**
> One place to get training is the armed forces, where supplies and equipment to support troops are shipped and exchanged regularly. For example, in the Army these workers are known as Cargo Specialists and get eight weeks of training beyond basic training. This military job, however, involves loading and unloading, not just clerical duties.

▓ What's Required

Cargo and freight agents need no more than a high school diploma and learn their duties informally on the job.

Education and Training

Many jobs are entry level and most require a high school diploma. Cargo and freight agents undergo informal on-the-job training. For example, they may start out by checking items to be shipped and making sure that addresses are correct.

Postsecondary Program to Consider

- General office occupations and clerical services

Additional Qualifications

Employers prefer to hire people who are comfortable using computers. Typing, filing, recordkeeping, and other clerical skills also are important.

School Subjects to Study

- Algebra
- Computer science
- English
- Office practices

Moving Up

Advancement opportunities for cargo and freight agents are usually limited, but some agents may become team leaders or use their experience to switch to other clerical occupations in the businesses where they work. Some may move to higher-paying transportation industry jobs, such as freight brokering.

■ Employment

Cargo and freight agents held about 85,900 jobs in 2008. Most agents were employed in transportation. Approximately 52 percent worked for firms engaged in support activities for the transportation industry, 19 percent were in the air transportation industry, 8 percent worked for courier businesses, and 7 percent were in the truck transportation industry.

Job Prospects

Employment of cargo and freight agents is expected to increase by 24 percent during the 10-year period ending 2018, which is much faster than the average for all occupations. As the overall economy continues to grow, more agents will be needed to handle the growing number of shipments resulting from increases in cargo traffic. Additionally, as shipments require multiple modes of transportation to reach their final destinations, such as freight trucking and air, a greater number of agents will be needed to manage the process.

CONSIDER THIS...
Some of these workers—for example, those who work in a UPS store—interact with the public and need good interpersonal skills.

The growing popularity of online shopping and same-day delivery may also spur employment growth.

A combination of job growth and turnover are expected to result in good job prospects for cargo and freight agents. However, employment of cargo and freight agents is sensitive to the fluctuations of the economy, and workers may experience high levels of unemployment when the overall level of economic activity falls.

CONSIDER THIS...
Frederick W. Smith, who invented the idea of overnight parcel delivery and founded FedEx, first outlined his plan in a paper for a college economics class in 1962. It took many years until computers allowed his concept to be turned into a business.

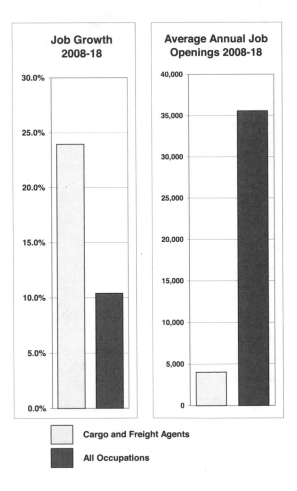

Job Growth 2008-18 / Average Annual Job Openings 2008-18

- Cargo and Freight Agents
- All Occupations

Income

Median hourly wages of cargo and freight agents in May 2008 were $17.92. The middle 50 percent earned between $13.67 and $22.92. The lowest 10 percent earned less than $10.65, and the highest 10 percent earned more than $27.70.

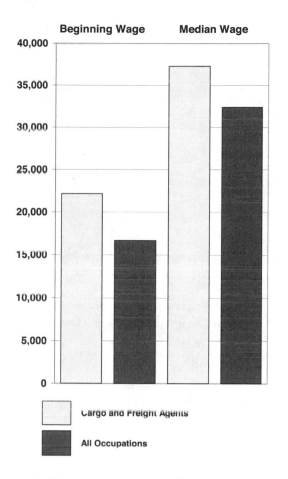

Beginning Wage **Median Wage**

Cargo and Freight Agents

All Occupations

These workers usually receive the same benefits as most other workers. If uniforms are required, employers generally provide them or offer an allowance to purchase them.

Related Jobs

- Postal service clerks
- Postal service mail sorters, processors, and processing machine operators
- Shipping, receiving, and traffic clerks
- Weighers, measurers, checkers, and samplers, recordkeeping

How to Learn More

Information about the freight and cargo industry, including training opportunities, is available from

- Transportation Intermediaries Association (TIA), 1625 Prince St., Suite 200, Alexandria, VA 22314. Internet: www.tianet.org

Why It's Hot

Business now depends on just-in-time manufacturing to keep inventories low and to respond quickly to changes in customer demand. Consumers expect to be able to order products online and receive them in a day or two. These trends, along with overall economic growth, keep the shipping industry busy and create a need for efficient transportation and accurate records of shipments.

Computer Network, Systems, and Database Administrators

Computer network, systems, and database administrators help individuals and organizations share and store information through computer networks and systems, the Internet, and computer databases.

Just the Facts

Earnings: $70,001

Job Growth: 29.8%

Annual Openings: 46,080

Education and Training: Associate degree

Bachelor's degree

While at Work

Though we still have libraries full of bound books and file cabinets full of paper, today most information is analyzed, stored, protected, processed, and transmitted using computers and computer technology. Information Technology (IT) has become an integral part of modern life. The workers described next all help individuals and organizations share and store information through computer networks and systems, the Internet, and computer databases.

Network architects or *network engineers* design computer networks. They set up, test, and evaluate systems such as local area networks (LANs), wide area networks (WANs), the Internet, intranets, and other data communications systems. Systems are configured in many ways and can range from a connection between two offices in the same building to globally distributed networks, voice mail, and e-mail systems of a multinational organization. Network architects and engineers perform network modeling, analysis, and planning, which often require both hardware and software solutions. These workers may also research related products and make necessary hardware and software recommendations, as well as address information security issues.

Network and computer systems administrators design, install, and support an organization's computer systems. They are responsible for LANs, WANs, network segments, and Internet and intranet systems. They install and maintain network hardware and software, analyze problems, and monitor networks to ensure their availability to users. These workers gather data to evaluate a system's performance, identify user needs, and determine system and network requirements.

Database administrators work with database management software and determine ways to store, organize, analyze, use, and present data. They identify user needs and set up new computer databases. In many cases, database administrators must integrate data from old systems into a new system. They also test and coordinate modifications to the system when needed, and troubleshoot problems when they occur.

Computer security specialists plan, coordinate, and maintain an organization's information security. These workers educate users about computer security, install security software, monitor networks for security breaches, respond to cyber attacks, and, in some cases, gather data and evidence to be used in prosecuting cyber crime. The responsibilities of computer security specialists have increased in recent years as cyber attacks have become more sophisticated.

Telecommunications specialists focus on the interaction between computer and communications equipment. These workers design voice, video, and data-communication systems, supervise the installation of the systems, and provide maintenance and other services to clients after the systems

are installed. They also test lines, oversee equipment repair, and may compile and maintain system records.

Computer network, systems, and database administrators help organizations share and store information.

Also Known As

The growth of the Internet and the expansion of the World Wide Web (the graphical portion of the Internet) have generated a variety of occupations related to the design, development, and maintenance of Web sites and their servers. For example, *Web masters* are responsible for all technical aspects of a Web site, including performance issues such as speed of access, and for approving the content of the site. *Internet developers* or *Web developers*, also called *Web designers*, are responsible for day-to-day site creation and design.

Job Fit

Personality Type
Investigative-Conventional-Realistic

Career Clusters
04 Business, Management, and Administration

11 Information Technology

Skills
Computer Programming

Equipment/Technology Analysis

Equipment Use/Maintenance

Management

Thought-Processing

Communications

Mathematics

Social Skills

Science

Work Styles

Analytical Thinking

Adaptability/Flexibility

Integrity

Persistence

Initiative

Attention to Detail

Stress Tolerance

Achievement/Effort

Working Conditions

Computer network, systems, and database administrators normally work in well-lighted, comfortable offices or computer laboratories. Most work about 40 hours a week. However, about 15 percent worked more than 50 hours per week in 2008. In addition, some of these workers may be required to be "on call" outside of normal business hours in order to resolve system failures or other problems.

Like other workers who spend long periods in front of a computer terminal typing on a keyboard, computer network, systems, and database administrators are susceptible to eyestrain, back discomfort, and hand and wrist problems such as carpal tunnel syndrome.

> **CONSIDER THIS...**
>
> Telecommuting is increasingly common for many computer professionals as networks expand, allowing more work to be done from remote locations through modems, laptops, electronic mail, and the Internet. However, some work still must be done in the office for security or other reasons.

■ What's Required

Rapidly changing technology requires an increasing level of skill and education on the part of workers in these occupations. Employers look for professionals with an ever-broader background and range of skills, including technical knowledge, as well as communication and other interpersonal skills.

Education and Training

Network and computer systems administrators often are required to have a bachelor's degree, although an associate degree or professional certification, along with related work experience, may be adequate for some positions. Most of these workers begin as computer support specialists before advancing into network or systems administration positions. Common majors for network and systems administrators are computer science, information science, and management information systems (MIS), but a degree in any field, supplemented with computer courses and experience, may be adequate.

For network architect and database administrator positions, a bachelor's degree in a computer-related field generally is required, although some employers prefer applicants with a master's degree in business administration (MBA) with a concentration in information systems. MBA programs usually require 2 years of study beyond the undergraduate degree, and, like undergraduate business programs, include courses on finance, marketing, accounting, and management, as well as database management, electronic business, and systems management and design. In addition to formal education, network architects may be required to have several years of relevant work experience.

For Webmasters, an associate degree or certification is sufficient; although more advanced positions might require a computer-related bachelor's degree. For telecommunications specialists, employers prefer applicants with an associate degree in electronics or a related field, but for some positions, experience may substitute for formal education. Applicants for security

> **CONSIDER THIS...**
>
> Management information systems (MIS) usually are part of the business school of a college and differ considerably from computer science programs, emphasizing business and management-oriented coursework and business computing courses.

> **CONSIDER THIS...**
>
> Despite employers' preference for those with technical degrees, individuals with postsecondary degrees in a variety of other subjects may find employment in these occupations. Generally speaking, some coursework in computer science combined with an undergraduate degree are sufficient qualifications, especially if the applicant has a reasonable amount of experience.

specialist and Web developer positions generally need a bachelor's degree in a computer-related field, but for some positions, related experience and certification may be adequate.

Postsecondary Programs to Consider

- Computer and Information Sciences
- Computer and Information Systems Security/ Information Assurance
- Computer Engineering
- Computer Science
- Computer Software Engineering
- Computer Systems Analysis/Analyst
- Computer Systems Networking and Telecommunications
- Data Modeling/Warehousing and Database Administration
- E-Commerce/Electronic Commerce
- Information Science/Studies
- Information Technology
- Management Information Systems
- Network and System Administration/Administrator
- System, Networking, and LAN/WAN Management/Manager
- Web Page, Digital/Multimedia and Information Resources Design
- Web/Multimedia Management and Webmaster Training

Additional Qualifications

Workers in these occupations must have strong problem-solving, analytical, and communication skills. Because they often deal with a number of tasks simultaneously, the ability to concentrate and pay close attention to detail also is important. Although these workers sometimes work independently, they frequently work in teams on large projects. As a result, they must be able to communicate effectively with others.

Jobseekers can enhance their employment opportunities by earning certifications, most of which are offered through private companies, with many related to specific products. Many employers regard these certifications as the industry standard. For example, one method of acquiring enough knowledge to get a job as a database administrator is to become certified in database management with a certain software package. Voluntary certification also is available through various organizations associated with computer specialists. Professional certification may afford a jobseeker a competitive advantage.

Consider This...

Because technology is so closely connected to the functioning of businesses, many workers in these occupations come from elsewhere in the business or industry to become computer specialists. This background helps them to better understand how their networking and database tools are being used within the organization.

School Subjects to Study

- Algebra
- Computer science
- English
- Geometry
- Physics
- Pre-calculus and calculus
- Trigonometry

Moving Up

Entry-level network and computer systems administrators are involved in routine maintenance and monitoring of computer systems. After gaining experience and expertise, they are often able to advance to more senior-level positions. They may also advance to supervisory positions.

Database administrators and network architects may advance into managerial positions, such as chief technology officer, on the basis of their experience. Computer specialists with work experience and considerable expertise in a particular area may find opportunities as independent consultants.

Computer security specialists can advance into supervisory positions, or may move into other occupations, such as computer systems analysts.

▇ Employment

Computer network, systems, and database administrators held about 961,200 jobs in 2008. Of these, 339,500 were network and computer systems administrators, 120,400 were database administrators, and 292,000 were network and data communications analysts.

These workers were employed in a wide range of industries. About 14 percent of all computer network, systems, and database administrators were in computer systems design and related services. Substantial numbers of these workers were also employed in telecommunications companies, financial firms and insurance providers, business management organizations, schools, and government agencies. About 7 percent were self-employed.

Job Prospects

Overall employment of computer network, systems, and database administrators is projected to increase by 30 percent in the 10-year period ending 2018, much faster than the average for all occupations. In addition, this occupation will add 286,600 new jobs over that period.

Job growth will vary by specialty. Employment of network and computer systems administrators is expected to increase by 23 percent. Computer networks are an integral part of business, and demand for these workers will increase as firms continue to invest in new technologies to communicate with employees, clients, and consumers. Growth will also be driven by the increasing need for information security. As cyber attacks become more sophisticated, demand will increase for workers with security skills.

Employment of database administrators is expected to grow by 20 percent. Demand for these workers is expected to increase as organizations need to store, organize, and analyze increasing amounts of data. In addition, as more databases are connected to the Internet, and as data security becomes increasingly important, a growing number of these workers will be needed to protect databases from attack.

Employment of network systems and data communications analysts is projected to increase by 53 percent, placing it among the fastest growing of all occupations. This category includes network architects and engineers, as well as Web administrators and developers. Demand for network architects and engineers will increase as organizations continue to upgrade their IT capacity and incorporate the newest technologies. The growing reliance on wireless networks will result in a need for many more of these workers. Workers with knowledge of information security also will be in demand, as computer networks transmit an increasing amount of sensitive data.

Demand for Web administrators and Web developers will also be strong. More of these workers will be needed to accommodate the increasing amount of data sent over the Internet, as well as the growing number of Internet users. In addition, as the number of services provided over the Internet expands, Web administrators and developers will continue to see employment increases.

Growth in computer network, systems, and database administrators will be rapid in the computer systems design, data processing and hosting, software publishing, and technical consulting industries, though such growth may be tempered by offshore outsourcing and the consolidation of IT services.

In general, applicants with a college degree and certification will have the best opportunities. However, for some of these occupations, opportunities will be available for applicants with related work experience. Job openings in these occupations will be the result of strong employment growth, as well as the need to replace workers who transfer to other occupations or leave the labor force.

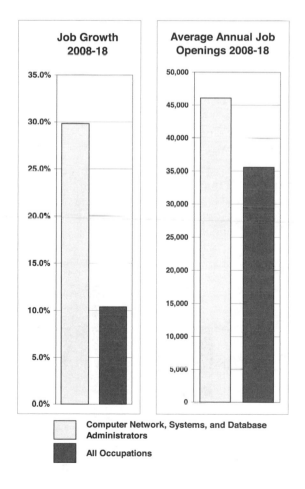

Income

Median annual wages of network and computer systems administrators were $66,310 in May 2008. The middle 50 percent earned between $51,690 and $84,110. The lowest 10 percent earned less than $41,000, and the highest 10 percent earned more than $104,070.

Median annual wages of database administrators were $69,740 in May 2008. The middle 50 percent earned between $52,340 and $91,850. The lowest 10 percent earned less than $39,900, and the highest 10 percent earned more than $111,950. In May 2008, median annual wages of database administrators employed in computer systems design and related services were $78,510, and for those in management of companies and enterprises, wages were $74,730.

Median annual wages of network systems and data communication analysts were $71,100 in May 2008. The middle 50 percent earned between $54,330 and $90,740. The lowest 10 percent earned less than $41,660, and the highest 10 percent earned more than $110,920. These wages include network architects, telecommunications specialists, Webmasters, and Web developers.

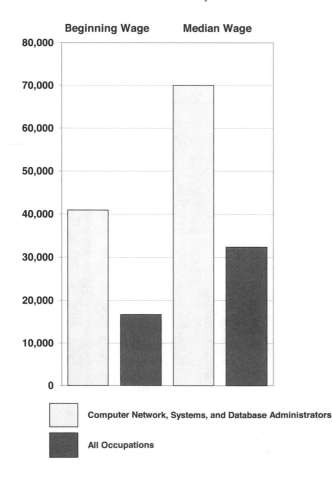

Beginning Wage   Median Wage

- ☐ Computer Network, Systems, and Database Administrators
- ■ All Occupations

- Computer and information systems managers
- Computer scientists
- Computer software engineers
- Computer support specialists
- Computer systems analysts

How to Learn More

For additional information about a career as a computer network, systems, or database administrator, contact

- The League of Professional System Administrators, 15000 Commerce Pkwy., Suite C, Mount Laurel, NJ 08054. Internet: www.lopsa.org
- Data Management International, 19239 N. Dale Mabry Hwy. #132, Lutz, FL 33548. Internet: www.dama.org

Additional information on a career in information technology is available from the following organizations:

- Association for Computing Machinery (ACM), 2 Penn Plaza, Suite 701, New York, NY 10121-0701. Internet: http://computingcareers.acm.org
- Institute of Electrical and Electronics Engineers Computer Society, Headquarters Office, 2001 L St. NW, Suite 700 Washington, DC 20036-4910. Internet: www.computer.org
- National Workforce Center for Emerging Technologies, 3000 Landerholm Circle SE, Bellevue, WA 98007. Internet: www.nwcet.org
- University of Washington Computer Science and Engineering Department, AC101 Paul G. Allen Center, Box 352350, 185 Stevens Way, Seattle, WA 98195-2350. Internet: www.cs.washington.edu/WhyCSE
- National Center for Women and Information Technology, University of Colorado, Campus Box 322 UCB, Boulder, CO 80309-0322. Internet: www.ncwit.org

Why It's Hot

Computer networks have become as vital for businesses as almost every kind of business information is organized into databases. Consumers are also using networks and databases in their homes. The job market for specialists who can work with these technologies will remain excellent. In fact, one of the fastest-growing occupations in our economy is network systems and data communications analysts.

Computer Scientists

Computer scientists conduct research and develop theoretical concepts to improve computer systems and the way they store and retrieve information.

Just the Facts

Earnings: $97,970
Job Growth: 24.2%
Annual Openings: 1,320
Education and Training: Doctoral degree

While at Work

Most innovations in computer technology are imagined first by computer scientists. By designing, creating, and inventing new technology, or finding alternative uses for existing resources, these scientists solve complex business, scientific, and general computing problems. Some computer scientists work on multidisciplinary projects, collaborating with electrical engineers, mechanical engineers, and other specialists.

Computer scientists conduct research on a wide array of topics. Examples include computer hardware architecture, virtual reality, and robotics. Scientists who research hardware architecture discover new ways for computers to process and transmit information. They design computer chips and processors, using new materials and techniques to make them work faster and give them more computing power. When working with virtual reality, scientists use technology to create life-like situations. For example, scientists may invent video games that make users feel like they are actually in the game.

Consider This...

Computer scientists working with robotics try to create machines that can perform tasks on their own—without people controlling them. Robots perform many tasks, such as sweeping floors in people's homes, assembling cars on factory production lines, and "auto-piloting" airplanes.

Also Known As

Computer science researchers are often employed by academic institutions and have job functions that are similar in many ways to those employed by other organizations. In general, researchers in academic settings have more flexibility to focus on pure theory, while those working in business or scientific organizations, covered here, usually focus on projects that have the possibility of producing patents and profits. However, those working in academic settings are also expected to teach as well.

Job Fit

Personality Type
Investigative-Realistic-Conventional

Career Clusters
08 Health Science
11 Information Technology

Skills
Computer Programming
Science
Equipment/Technology Analysis
Mathematics
Thought-Processing
Management
Communications
Social Skills
Equipment Use/Maintenance

Work Styles
Initiative
Persistence
Achievement/Effort
Independence
Innovation
Adaptability/Flexibility
Analytical Thinking
Leadership

Working Conditions

Computer scientists normally work in offices or laboratories in comfortable surroundings. Like other workers who spend long periods in front of a computer terminal typing on a keyboard, computer scientists are susceptible to eyestrain, back discomfort, and hand and wrist problems such as carpal tunnel syndrome.

Computer scientists work on innovative research projects.

What's Required

A Ph.D. is required for most jobs as computer scientists, and an aptitude for math is important.

Education and Training

Most computer scientists are required to possess a Ph.D. in computer science, computer engineering, or a closely related discipline. For some positions in the federal government, a bachelor's degree in a computer-related field may be adequate.

To be admitted to a Ph.D. program, applicants generally are required to obtain a bachelor's degree with a strong computer science or computer engineering component. Popular undergraduate majors for Ph.D. program applicants include computer science, computer engineering, software engineering, information systems, and information technology. A bachelor's degree generally takes 4 years to complete. A Ph.D. generally requires at least 5 years of study beyond the bachelor's degree. Ph.D. students usually spend the first 2 years taking classes on advanced topics, including computer and software systems, artificial intelligence, digital communication, and microprocessors. Students spend the remaining years conducting research on topics in computer science or computer engineering.

Postsecondary Programs to Consider

- Artificial Intelligence
- Computer and Information Sciences
- Computer Science
- Computer Systems Analysis/Analyst
- Information science/studies
- Medical informatics

Additional Qualifications

Computer scientists must be able to think logically and creatively. They must possess a strong aptitude for math and other technical topics, as these are critical to the computing field. Because they often deal with a number of tasks simultaneously, the ability to concentrate and pay close attention to detail also is important.

Although computer scientists sometimes work independently, they frequently work in teams on large projects. As a result, they must be able to communicate effectively with computer personnel, such as programmers and managers, as well as with users or other staff who may have no technical computer background.

CONSIDER THIS...

Technological advances come so rapidly in the computer field that continuous study is necessary to keep one's skills up to date. Employers, hardware and software vendors, colleges and universities, and private training institutions offer continuing education. Additional training may come from professional development seminars offered by professional computing societies.

School Subjects to Study

- Algebra
- Computer science
- English
- Geometry
- Physics
- Pre-calculus and calculus
- Trigonometry

Moving Up

Computer scientists may advance into managerial or project leadership positions. Many having advanced degrees choose to leave private industry for academic positions.

Employment

Computer scientists held about 28,900 jobs in 2008. Although they are increasingly employed in every sector of the economy, the greatest concentration of these workers, about 23 percent, was in the computer systems design and related services industry. Many computer scientists were also employed by software publishing firms, scientific research and development organizations, and in education.

Job Prospects

Employment of computer scientists is expected to grow by 24 percent in the 10-year period ending 2018, which is much faster than the average for all occupations. Employment of these computer specialists is expected to grow as individuals and organizations continue to demand increasingly sophisticated technologies. Job increases will be driven, in part, by very rapid growth in computer systems design and related services industry, as well as the software publishing industry, which are projected to be among the fastest-growing industries in the U.S. economy.

Computer scientists should enjoy excellent job prospects. Graduates from Ph.D. programs in computer science and engineering are in high demand, and many companies report difficulties finding sufficient numbers of these highly skilled workers.

> **CONSIDER THIS...**
>
> Computer scientists develop the theories that allow many new technologies to be developed. The demand for increasing efficiency in areas such as networking technology, computing speeds, software performance, and embedded systems will lead to employment growth. In addition, the growing emphasis on information security will lead to new jobs.

Income

Median annual earnings of computer and information scientists were $97,970 in May 2008. The middle 50 percent earned between $75,340 and $124,370. The lowest 10 percent earned less than $57,480, and the highest 10 percent earned more than $151,250. Median annual earnings of computer and information scientists employed in computer systems design and related services in May 2008 were $99,900.

Related Jobs

- Computer and information systems managers
- Computer network, systems, and database administrators
- Computer programmers
- Computer software engineers
- Computer support specialists

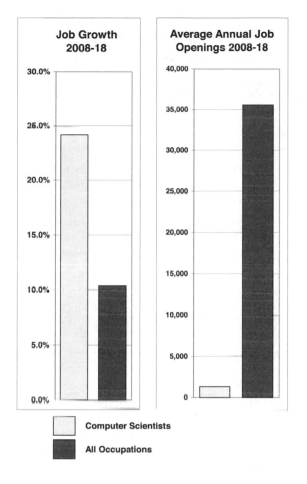

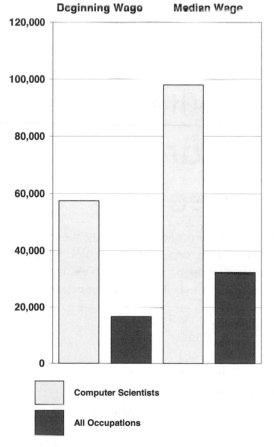

How to Learn More

Further information about computer careers is available from

- Association for Computing Machinery (ACM), 1515 Broadway, New York, NY 10036. Internet: www.acm.org

- Institute of Electrical and Electronics Engineers Computer Society, Headquarters Office, 1730 Massachusetts Ave. NW, Washington, DC 20036-1992. Internet: www.computer.org

- National Center for Women and Information Technology, University of Colorado, Campus Box 322 UCB, Boulder, CO 80309-0322. Internet: www.ncwit.org

- National Workforce Center for Emerging Technologies, 3000 Landerholm Circle SE, Bellevue, WA 98007. Internet: www.nwcet.org

- University of Washington Computer Science and Engineering Department, AC101 Paul G. Allen Center, Box 352350, 185 Stevens Way, Seattle, WA 98195-2350. Internet: www.cs.washington.edu/WhyCSE

Why It's Hot

All industries are finding uses for computers, which creates a constant demand for innovative computer software products and techniques. As a result, computer scientists are projected to have excellent growth over the next decade. Strong employment growth combined with a limited supply of qualified workers will result in excellent employment prospects for this occupation and a high demand for their skills.

Computer Software Engineers

Computer software engineers apply the principles of computer science and mathematical analysis to the design, development, testing, and evaluation of the software and systems that make computers work.

Just the Facts

Earnings: $88,481
Job Growth: 32.5%
Annual Openings: 37,170
Education and Training: Bachelor's degree

While at Work

The tasks that computer software engineers perform are constantly evolving, reflecting new areas of specialization or changes in technology, as well as the preferences and practices of employers. Software engineers can be involved in the design and development of many types of software, including computer games, word processing and business applications, operating systems and network distribution, and compilers, which convert programs to machine language for execution on a computer.

Computer software engineers begin by analyzing users' needs and then design, test, and develop software to meet those needs. During this process they create the detailed sets of instructions, called algorithms, that tell the computer what to do. They also may be responsible for converting these instructions into a computer language, a process called programming or coding, but this usually is the responsibility of computer programmers.

Computer applications software engineers analyze users' needs and design, construct, and maintain general computer applications software or specialized utility programs. These workers use different programming languages, depending on the purpose of the program. The programming languages most often used are C, C++, and Java, with Fortran and COBOL used less commonly. Some software engineers develop both packaged systems and systems software or create customized applications.

Computer systems software engineers coordinate the construction, maintenance, and expansion of an organization's computer systems. Working with the organization, they coordinate each department's computer needs—ordering, inventory, billing, and payroll recordkeeping, for example—and make suggestions about its technical direction. They also might set up the organization's intranets—networks that link computers within the organization and ease communication among various departments.

Systems software engineers also work for companies that configure, implement, and install the computer systems of other organizations. These workers may be members of the marketing or sales staff, serving as the primary technical resource for sales workers. They also may help with sales and provide customers with techni-

Consider This...

Computer software engineers often work as part of a team that designs new hardware, software, and systems. A core team may comprise engineering, marketing, manufacturing, and design people who work together to release a product.

cal support. Since the selling of complex computer systems often requires substantial customization to meet the needs of the purchaser, software engineers help to identify and explain needed changes. In addition, systems software engineers are responsible for ensuring security across the systems they are configuring.

Computer software engineers develop software to meet users' needs.

Also Known As

Many computer software engineers have job titles that reflect a specialization, such as *artificial intelligence specialists, bioinformatics specialists, certified Novell engineers (CNE), data warehouse architects, game developers, Lotus Notes developers, operating systems specialists, usability engineers,* or *wide area network engineers.*

Job Fit

Personality Type

Investigative-Conventional-Realistic

Career Clusters

11 Information Technology

15 Science, Technology, Engineering, and Mathematics

Skills

Computer Programming

Equipment/Technology Analysis

Science

Mathematics

Thought-Processing

Equipment Use/Maintenance

Communications

Social Skills

Management

Work Styles

Analytical Thinking

Innovation

Achievement/Effort

Persistence

Adaptability/Flexibility

Initiative

Cooperation

Working Conditions

Computer software engineers normally work in clean, comfortable offices or in laboratories in which computer equipment is located. Software engineers who work for software vendors and consulting firms frequently travel overnight to meet with customers. Telecommuting is also becoming more common, allowing workers to do their jobs from remote locations.

Most software engineers work at least 40 hours a week, but about 17 percent work more than 50 hours a week. Software engineers also may have to work evenings or weekends to meet deadlines or solve unexpected technical problems.

Like other workers who spend long hours typing at a computer, software engineers are susceptible to eyestrain, back discomfort, and hand and wrist problems such as carpal tunnel syndrome.

■ What's Required

Most employers prefer applicants who have at least a bachelor's degree and experience with a variety of computer systems and technologies. In order to remain competitive, computer software engineers must continually strive to acquire the latest technical skills. Advancement opportunities are good for those with relevant experience.

Education and Training

The usual college major for applications software engineers is computer science or software engineering. Systems software engineers often study computer science or computer information systems. Graduate degrees are preferred for some of the more complex jobs. In 2008, about 82 percent of workers had a bachelor's degree or higher.

Academic programs in software engineering may offer the program as a degree option or in conjunction with computer science degrees. Because of increasing emphasis on computer security, software engineers with advanced degrees in areas such as mathematics and systems design will be sought after by software developers, government agencies, and consulting firms.

Students seeking software engineering jobs enhance their employment opportunities by participating in internships or co-ops. These experiences provide students with broad knowledge and experience, making them more attractive to employers. Inexperienced college graduates may be hired by large computer and consulting firms that train new employees in intensive, company-based programs.

Postsecondary Programs to Consider

- Artificial intelligence and robotics
- Bioinformatics
- Computer engineering technologies/technician training, other
- Computer engineering, general
- Computer science
- Computer software engineering
- Information science/studies
- Information technology
- Medical illustration and informatics, other
- Medical informatics
- System, networking, and LAN/WAN management/manager training

Additional Qualifications

People interested in jobs as computer software engineers must have strong problem-solving and analytical skills. They also must be able to communicate effectively with team members, other staff, and the customers they meet. Because they often deal with a number of tasks simultaneously, they must be able to concentrate and pay close attention to detail.

As technology advances, employers will need workers with the latest skills. Computer software engineers must continually strive to acquire new skills if they wish to remain in this dynamic field. To help keep up with changing technology, workers may take continuing education and professional development seminars offered by employers, software vendors, colleges and universities, private training institutions, and professional computing societies.

School Subjects to Study

- Algebra
- Computer science
- English
- Geometry
- Physics
- Pre-calculus and calculus
- Trigonometry

Moving Up

As with most occupations, advancement opportunities for computer software engineers increase with experience. Entry-level computer software engineers are likely to test designs. As they become more experienced, engineers may begin helping to design and develop software. Eventually, they may advance to become a project manager, manager of information systems, or chief information officer, especially if they have business skills and training. Some computer software engineers with several years of experience or expertise find lucrative opportunities working as systems designers or independent consultants.

Employment

Computer software engineers held about 910,000 jobs in 2008. Approximately 515,000 were computer applications software engineers and about 395,000 were computer systems software engineers. Although they are employed in most industries, the largest concentration of computer software engineers—more than 32 percent—is in computer systems design and related services. Many computer software engineers also work for establishments in other industries, such as software publishers, government agencies, manufacturers of computers and related electronic equipment, financial institutions, insurance providers, and management of companies and enterprises.

An increasing number of computer software engineers work as independent consultants on a temporary or contract basis, many of whom are self-employed. About 25,000 computer software engineers were self-employed in 2008.

Job Prospects

Employment of computer software engineers is projected to increase by 32 percent during the 10-year period ending 2018, which is much faster than the average for all occupations. This occupation will generate about 372,000 new jobs over the projections decade, one of the largest employment increases of any occupation.

Demand for computer software engineers will increase as businesses adopt new computer technologies, including networking. For example, expanding Internet technologies have spurred demand for computer software engineers who can develop Internet, Intranet, and World Wide Web applications. Likewise, electronic data-processing systems in business, telecommunications, government, and other settings continue to become more sophisticated and complex. Implementing, safeguarding, and updating computer systems and resolving problems will fuel the demand for growing numbers of systems software engineers.

New growth areas will also continue to arise from rapidly evolving technologies. The increasing uses of the Internet, the proliferation of Web sites, and mobile technology such as wireless Internet have created a demand for a wide variety of new products. As individuals and businesses rely more on hand-held computers and wireless networks, it will be necessary to integrate current computer systems with this new, more mobile technology.

In addition, information security concerns have given rise to new software needs. Concerns over "cyber security" should result in businesses and government continuing to invest heavily in software that protects their networks and vital electronic infrastructure from attack. The expansion of this technology in the next 10 years will lead to an increased need for computer engineers to design and develop the software and systems to run these new applications and integrate them into older systems.

As a result of rapid employment growth over the 10-year period ending 2018, job prospects for computer software engineers should be excellent. Those with practical experience and at least a bachelor's degree in computer engineering or computer science should have the best opportunities. Employers will continue to seek computer professionals with strong programming, systems analysis, interpersonal, and business skills. In addition to jobs created through employment growth, many job openings will result from the need to replace workers who move into managerial positions, transfer to other occupations, or leave the labor force. Consulting opportunities for computer software engineers also should continue to grow as businesses seek help to manage, upgrade, and customize their increasingly complicated computer systems.

CONSIDER THIS...

As with other information technology jobs, outsourcing of software development to other countries may temper somewhat the employment growth of computer software engineers. Firms may look to cut costs by shifting operations to foreign countries with lower prevailing wages and highly educated workers. Jobs in software engineering are less prone to being offshored than are jobs in other computer specialties, however, because software engineering requires innovation and intense research and development.

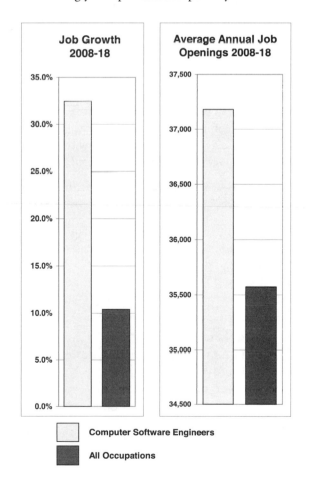

Income

In May 2008, median annual earnings of wage-and-salary computer applications software engineers were $85,430. The middle 50 percent earned between $67,790 and $104,870. The lowest 10 percent earned less than $53,720, and the highest 10 percent earned more than $128,870. The May 2008 earnings in the industries employing the largest numbers of computer applications software engineers were $84,610 in computer systems design and related services, $87,710 in software publishers, $85,990 in management of companies and enterprises, $80,370 in insurance carriers, and $93,740 in professional and commercial equipment and supplies merchant wholesalers.

In May 2008, median annual earnings of wage-and-salary computer systems software engineers were $92,430. The middle 50 percent earned between $73,200 and $113,960. The lowest 10 percent earned less than $57,810, and the highest 10 percent earned more than $135,780. The May 2008 earnings in the industries employing the largest numbers of computer systems software engineers were $91,610 in computer systems design and related services, $93,590 in software publishers, $101,270 in computer and peripheral equipment manufacturing, $102,090 in scientific research and development services, and $91,720 in navigational, measuring, electromedical, control instruments manufacturing, and $87,730 in data processing, hosting, and related services.

According to the National Association of Colleges and Employers, starting salary offers for graduates with a bachelor's degree in computer engineering averaged $56,201 in 2007. Starting salary offers for graduates with a bachelor's degree in computer science averaged $53,396.

According to Robert Half Technology, starting salaries for software engineers in software development ranged from $66,500 to $99,750 in 2007. For network engineers, starting salaries ranged from $65,750 to $90,250.

Related Jobs

- Actuaries
- Commercial and industrial designers
- Computer hardware engineers
- Computer network, systems, and database administrators
- Computer programmers
- Computer support specialists and systems administrators
- Computer systems analysts
- Engineers
- Mathematicians
- Statisticians

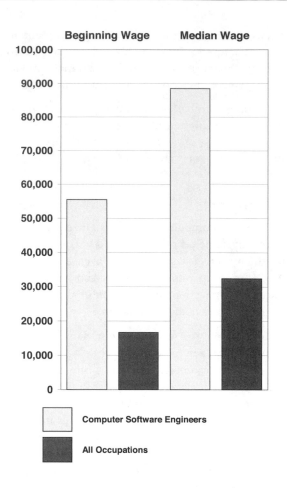

Computer Software Engineers

All Occupations

How to Learn More

Additional information on a career in computer software engineering is available from the following organizations:

- Association for Computing Machinery (ACM), 2 Penn Plaza, Suite 701, NY 10121-0701. Internet: www.acm.org

- Institute of Electronics and Electrical Engineers Computer Society, Headquarters Office, 1730 Massachusetts Ave. NW, Washington, DC 20036-1992. Internet: www.computer.org

- National Workforce Center for Emerging Technologies, 3000 Landerholm Circle SE, Bellevue, WA 98007. Internet: www.nwcet.org

- University of Washington Computer Science and Engineering Department, AC101 Paul G. Allen Center, Box 352350, 185 Stevens Way, Seattle, WA 98195-2350. Internet: www.cs.washington.edu/WhyCSE

Why It's Hot

Employment growth will result as businesses and other organizations adopt and integrate new technologies and seek to maximize the efficiency of their computer systems. Competition among businesses will continue to create incentives for sophisticated technological innovations, and organizations will need more computer software engineers to implement these changes. Job prospects should be excellent, as computer software engineers are expected to be among the fastest-growing occupations through 2018.

Computer Systems Analysts

Computer systems analysts analyze data processing problems in science, engineering, and business and devise ways to automate or improve existing systems.

Just the Facts

Earnings: $75,500

Job Growth: 20.3%

Annual Openings: 22,280

Education and Training: Bachelor's degree

While at Work

All organizations rely on computer and information technology to conduct business and operate efficiently. Computer systems analysts help organizations to use the technology effectively and to incorporate rapidly changing technologies into their existing systems. The work of computer systems analysts evolves rapidly, reflecting new areas of specialization and changes in technology.

Computer systems analysts solve computer problems and use computer technology to meet the needs of an organization. They may design and develop new computer systems by choosing and configuring hardware and software. They may also devise ways to apply existing systems' resources to additional tasks. Most systems analysts work with specific types of computer systems—for example, business, accounting, or financial systems or scientific and engineering systems—that vary with the kind of organization.

To begin an assignment, systems analysts consult managers and users to define the goals of the system. Analysts then design a system to meet those goals. They specify the inputs that the system will access, decide how the inputs will be processed, and format the output to meet

users' needs. Analysts use techniques such as structured analysis, data modeling, information engineering, mathematical model building, sampling, and cost accounting to make sure their plans are efficient and complete. They also may prepare cost-benefit and return-on-investment analyses to help management decide whether implementing the proposed technology would be financially feasible.

When a system is approved, systems analysts determine what computer hardware and software will be needed to set it up. They coordinate tests and observe the initial use of the system to ensure that it performs as planned. They prepare specifications, flow charts, and process diagrams for computer programmers to follow; then they work with programmers to "debug," or eliminate errors, from the system. Systems analysts who do more in-depth testing may be called *software quality assurance analysts*. In addition to running tests, these workers diagnose problems, recommend solutions, and determine whether program requirements have been met.

In some organizations, *programmer-analysts* design and update the software that runs a computer. They also create custom applications tailored to their organization's tasks. Because they are responsible for both programming and systems analysis, these workers must be proficient in both areas. As this dual proficiency becomes more common, analysts are increasingly working with databases, object-oriented programming languages, client–server applications, and multimedia and Internet technology.

Also Known As

Analysts who specialize in helping an organization select the proper system software and infrastructure are often called *system architects*. Analysts who specialize in developing and fine-tuning systems often are known as *systems designers*.

> #### CONSIDER THIS...
>
> One challenge created by expanding computer use is the need for different computer systems to communicate with each other. Systems analysts work to make the computer systems within an organization, or across organizations, compatible so that information can be shared. Many systems analysts are involved with these "networking" tasks, connecting all the computers internally—in an individual office, department, or establishment—or externally, as when setting up e-commerce networks to facilitate business among companies.

Computer systems analysts consult managers and users to define the goals of the system.

Job Fit

Personality Type
Investigative-Conventional

Career Cluster
11 Information Technology

Skills
Computer Programming
Equipment/Technology Analysis
Equipment Use/Maintenance
Thought-Processing
Mathematics
Social Skills
Management
Communications
Science

Work Styles
Analytical Thinking
Innovation
Adaptability/Flexibility
Initiative
Persistence
Attention to Detail
Achievement/Effort
Stress Tolerance

Working Conditions

Computer systems analysts work in offices or laboratories in comfortable surroundings. They usually work about 40 hours a week—about the same as many other professional or office workers. Evening or weekend work may be necessary, however, to meet deadlines or solve specific problems. Many analysts telecommute, using computers to work from remote locations.

Like other workers who spend long periods typing on a computer, computer systems analysts are susceptible to eyestrain, back discomfort, and hand and wrist problems such as carpal tunnel syndrome or cumulative trauma disorder.

■ What's Required

Training requirements for computer systems analysts vary depending on the job, but many employers prefer applicants who have a bachelor's degree. Relevant work experience also is very important. Advancement opportunities are good for those with the necessary skills and experience.

Education and Training

Although the bachelor's degree is a common entry route, people with graduate degrees are preferred for more technically complex jobs.

The level and type of education that employers require reflects changes in technology. Employers often scramble to find workers capable of implementing the newest technologies. Workers with formal education or experience in information security, for example, are currently in demand because of the growing use of computer networks, which must be protected from threats.

For jobs in a technical or scientific environment, employers often seek applicants who have at least a bachelor's degree in a technical field, such as computer science, information science, applied mathematics, engineering, or the physical sciences. For jobs in a business environment, employers often seek applicants with at least a bachelor's degree in a business-related field such as management information systems (MIS). Increasingly, employers are seeking individuals who have a master's degree in business administration (MBA) with a concentration in information systems.

Despite the preference for technical degrees, however, people who have degrees in other majors may find employment as systems analysts if they also have technical skills. Courses in computer science or related subjects combined with practical experience can qualify people for some jobs in the occupation.

Technological advances come so rapidly in the computer field that continuous study is necessary to remain competitive. Employers, hardware and software vendors, colleges and universities, and private training institutions offer continuing education to help workers attain the latest skills. Additional training may come from professional development seminars offered by professional computing societies.

Postsecondary Programs to Consider

- Computer and information sciences, general
- Computer systems analysis/analyst training
- Information technology
- Web/multimedia management and webmaster training

Additional Qualifications

Employers usually look for people who have broad knowledge and experience related to computer systems and technologies, strong problem-solving and analytical skills, and the ability to think logically. In addition, because they often deal with a number of tasks simultaneously, the ability to concentrate and pay close attention to detail is important. Although these workers sometimes work independently, they frequently work in teams on large projects. Therefore, they must have good interpersonal skills and be able to communicate effectively with computer personnel, users, and other staff who may have no technical background.

School Subjects to Study

- Algebra
- Computer science
- English
- Geometry
- Pre-calculus and calculus
- Trigonometry

Moving Up

With experience, systems analysts may be promoted to senior or lead systems analyst. Those who possess leadership ability and good business skills also can become computer and information systems managers or can advance into other management positions such as manager of information systems or chief information officer. Those with work experience and considerable expertise in a particular subject or application may find lucrative opportunities as independent consultants or may choose to start their own computer consulting firms.

Employment

Computer systems analysts held about 532,200 jobs in 2008. Although they are employed in many industries, 24 percent of these workers were in the computer systems design and related services industry. Computer systems analysts also were employed by governments, insurance companies, financial institutions, and business management firms. About 30,300 computer systems analysts were self-employed in 2008.

Job Prospects

Employment of computer systems analysts is expected to grow by 20 percent in the 10-year period ending 2018, which is much faster than the average for all occupations. Demand for these workers will increase as organizations continue to adopt and integrate increasingly sophisticated technologies and as the need for information security grows.

As information technology becomes an increasingly important aspect of the business environment, the demand for computer networking, Internet, and intranet functions will drive demand for computer systems analysts. The increasing adoption of the wireless Internet, known as WiFi, and of personal mobile computers has created a need for new systems that can integrate these technologies into existing networks. Explosive growth in these areas is expected to fuel demand for analysts who are knowledgeable about systems development and integration. In addition, as sensitive data continues to be transmitted and stored electronically, the need for information security specialists is expected to grow rapidly.

Job prospects should be excellent. Job openings will occur as a result of strong job growth and from the need to replace workers who move into other occupations or who leave the labor force.

Income

Median annual earnings of wage-and-salary computer systems analysts were $75,500 in May 2008. The middle 50 percent earned between $58,460 and $95,810 a year. The lowest 10 percent earned less than $45,390, and the highest 10 percent earned more than $118,440. Broken down by the industries with largest employment, median annual earnings in May 2008 were $78,680 in computer systems design and related services, $76,070 in management of companies and enterprises, $74,610 in insurance carriers, $89,670 in professional and commercial equipment and supplies merchant wholesalers, and $78,010 in data processing, hosting, and related services.

According to Robert Half Technology, starting salaries for systems analysts ranged from $64,000 to $87,000 in 2007. Starting salaries for business systems analysts ranged from $61,250 to $86,500. Starting salaries for developer/programmer analysts ranged from $55,250 to $90,250.

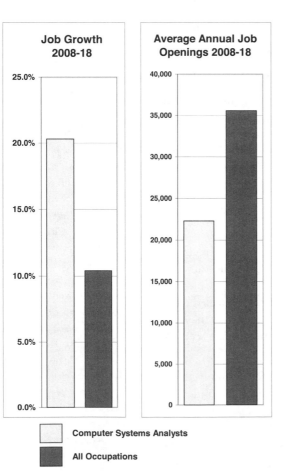

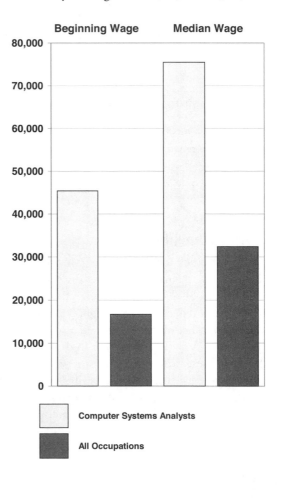

Related Jobs

- Actuaries
- Computer and information systems managers
- Computer programmers
- Computer software engineers
- Engineers
- Management analysts
- Mathematicians
- Operations research analysts
- Statisticians

How to Learn More

Further information about computer careers is available from

- Association for Computing Machinery (ACM), 2 Penn Plaza, Suite 701, New York, NY 10121-0701. Internet: www.acm.org

- Institute of Electrical and Electronics Engineers Computer Society, Headquarters Office, 1730 Massachusetts Ave. NW, Washington, DC 20036-1992. Internet: www.computer.org

- National Workforce Center for Emerging Technologies, 3000 Landerholm Circle SE, Bellevue, WA 98007. Internet: www.nwcet.org

- University of Washington Computer Science and Engineering Department, AC101 Paul G. Allen Center, Box 352350, 185 Stevens Way, Seattle, WA 98195-2350. Internet: www.cs.washington.edu/WhyCSE

- National Center for Women and Information Technology, University of Colorado, Campus Box 322 UCB, Boulder, CO 80309-0322. Internet: www.ncwit.org

Why It's Hot

The growth of electronic commerce and the integration of Internet technologies into business have resulted in a growing need for specialists who can develop and support Internet and intranet applications. Moreover, falling prices of computer hardware and software should continue to induce more businesses to expand their computerized operations and incorporate new technologies.

Construction Laborers

Construction laborers perform tasks involving physical labor at building, highway, and heavy construction projects, tunnel and shaft excavations, and demolition sites.

Just the Facts

Earnings: $28,520
Job Growth: 20.5%
Annual Openings: 33,940
Education and Training: Moderate-term on-the-job training

While at Work

Construction laborers can be found on almost all construction sites, performing a wide range of tasks from the very easy to the hazardous. Many of the jobs they perform require physical strength, training, and experience. Other jobs require little skill and can be learned quickly. Although most construction laborers specialize in a type of construction, such as highway or tunnel construction, some are generalists who perform many different tasks during all stages of construction.

Construction laborers clean and prepare construction sites. They remove trees and debris; tend pumps, compressors, and generators; and erect and disassemble scaffolding and other temporary structures. They load, unload, identify, and distribute building materials to the appropriate location according to project plans and specifications. Laborers also tend machines; for example, they may use a portable mixer to mix concrete or tend a machine that pumps concrete, grout, cement, sand, plaster, or stucco through a spray gun for application to ceilings and walls. They often help other craftworkers, including carpenters, plasterers, operating engineers, and masons.

> **CONSIDER THIS...**
> Construction laborers who work in underground construction, such as in tunnels, or in demolition are more likely to specialize in only those areas.

Construction laborers are responsible for the installation and maintenance of traffic control devices and patterns. At highway construction sites, this work may include clearing and preparing highway work zones and rights-of-way; installing traffic barricades, cones, and markers; and controlling traffic passing near, in, and around work zones. Construction laborers also dig trenches; install sewer, water, and storm drainpipes; and place concrete and asphalt on roads. Other highly specialized tasks include operating laser guidance equipment to place pipes; operating air, electric, and pneumatic drills; and transporting and setting explosives for the construction of tunnels, shafts, and roads.

Construction laborers operate a variety of equipment, including pavement breakers; jackhammers; earth tampers; concrete, mortar, and plaster mixers; electric and hydraulic boring machines; torches; small mechanical hoists; laser beam equipment; and surveying and measuring equipment. They may use computers and other high-tech input devices to control robotic pipe cutters and cleaners. To perform their jobs effectively, construction laborers must be familiar with the duties of other craftworkers and with the materials, tools, and machinery they use, as all of these workers work as part of a team, jointly carrying out assigned construction tasks.

Construction laborers work with many kinds of tools.

Also Known As

Many job titles indicate the kind of tools that construction laborers work with—for example, *air drill operators, demolition hammer operators, dredge pipe operators, jackhammer operators,* or *plaster machine tenders.* Other job titles refer to specialized tasks, such as *asphalt tampers, cement finishers, culvert installers, mortar carrier,* or *wall steamers.*

Job Fit

Personality Type
Realistic-Conventional

Career Cluster
02 Architecture and Construction

Skills
Equipment Use/Maintenance
Mathematics
Management

Work Styles
Leadership
Achievement/Effort
Social Skills Orientation
Self-Control
Attention to Detail
Stress Tolerance
Concern for Others
Cooperation

Working Conditions

Most construction laborers do physically demanding work. Some work at great heights or outdoors in all weather conditions. Some jobs expose workers to harmful materials or chemicals, fumes, odors, loud noises, or dangerous machinery. Some laborers may be exposed to lead-based paint, asbestos, or other hazardous substances during their work, especially when they work in confined spaces. To avoid injury, workers in these jobs wear safety clothing, such as gloves, hardhats, protective chemical suits, and devices to protect their eyes, respiratory system, or hearing. While working underground, construction laborers must be especially alert in order to follow procedures safely and must deal with a variety of hazards.

A standard 40-hour work week is the most common work week for construction laborers. About 1 in 7 has a variable schedule, as overnight work may be required in highway work. In some parts of the country, construction laborers may work only during certain seasons. They also may experience weather-related work stoppages at any time of the year.

What's Required

Many construction laborer jobs require a variety of basic skills, but others require specialized training and experience. Most construction laborers learn on the job, but formal apprenticeship programs provide the most thorough preparation.

Education and Training

Although some construction laborer jobs have no specific educational qualifications or entry-level training, apprenticeships for laborers usually require a high school diploma or the equivalent.

Most workers start by getting a job with a contractor who provides on-the-job training. Entry-level workers generally help more experienced workers, by performing routine tasks such as cleaning and preparing the worksite and unloading materials. When the opportunity arises, they learn from experienced construction trades workers how to do more difficult tasks, such as operating tools and equipment. Construction laborers also may choose or be required to attend a trade or vocational school, association training class, or community college to receive further trade-related training.

> **CONSIDER THIS...**
>
> Increasingly, construction laborers are finding work through temporary-help agencies that send laborers to construction sites for short-term work.

Some laborers receive more formal training in the form of an apprenticeship. These programs include between 2 and 4 years of classroom and on-the-job training. In the first 200 hours, workers learn basic construction skills, such as blueprint reading, the correct use of tools and equipment, and safety and health procedures. The remainder of the curriculum consists of specialized skills training in three of

> **CONSIDER THIS...**
>
> Training in "green" energy-efficient construction, an area of growth in the construction industry, is now available and can help workers find employment.

the largest segments of the construction industry: building construction, heavy and highway construction, and environmental remediation, such as lead or asbestos abatement and mold or hazardous waste remediation.

Workers who use dangerous equipment or handle toxic chemicals usually receive specialized safety training. Laborers who remove hazardous materials are required to take union- or employer-sponsored Occupational Safety and Health Administration safety training.

Apprenticeship applicants usually must be at least 18 years old and meet local requirements. Because the number of apprenticeship programs is limited, however, only a small proportion of laborers learn their trade in this way.

Laborers may earn certifications in welding, scaffold erecting, and concrete finishing. These certifications help workers prove that they have the knowledge to perform more complex tasks.

Postsecondary Program to Consider

- Construction trades, other

Additional Qualifications

Laborers need manual dexterity, eye-hand coordination, good physical fitness, a good sense of balance, and an ability to work as a member of a team. The ability to solve arithmetic problems quickly and accurately may be required. In addition, military service or a good work history is viewed favorably by contractors.

School Subjects to Study

- Algebra
- Blueprint reading
- English
- Industrial arts
- Mechanical drawing
- Physics
- Welding

Moving Up

Through training and experience, laborers can move into other construction occupations. Laborers may also advance to become construction supervisors or general contractors. For those who would like to advance, it is increasingly important to be able to communicate in both English and Spanish in order to relay instructions and safety precautions to workers with limited understanding of English; Spanish-speaking workers make up a large part of the construction workforce in many areas. Supervisors and contractors need good communication skills to deal with clients and subcontractors.

In addition, supervisors and contractors should be able to identify and estimate the quantity of materials needed to complete a job and accurately estimate how long a job will take to complete and what it will cost. Computer skills also are important for advancement as construction becomes increasingly mechanized and computerized.

Employment

Construction laborers held about 1.2 million jobs in 2008. They worked throughout the country but, like the general population, were concentrated in metropolitan areas. About 62 percent of construction laborers worked in the construction industry, including 27 percent who worked for specialty trade contractors. About 21 percent were self-employed in 2008.

Job Prospects

Employment of construction laborers is expected to grow by 20 percent over the 10-year period ending 2018, much faster than the average for all occupations. Because of the large variety of tasks that laborers perform, demand for laborers will mirror the level of overall construction activity. However, some jobs may be adversely affected by automation as they are replaced by new machinery and equipment that improves productivity and quality.

> **CONSIDER THIS...**
>
> Some laborers—about 14 percent—belong to a union, mainly the Laborers' International Union of North America.

Increasing job prospects for construction laborers, however, is the expected additional government funding for the repair and reconstruction of the nation's infrastructure, such as roads, bridges, public buildings, and water lines. The occupation should experience an increase in demand because laborers make up a significant portion of workers on these types of projects.

> **CONSIDER THIS...**
>
> Overall opportunities will be best for those with experience and specialized skills and for those who can relocate to areas with new construction projects. Opportunities also will be better for laborers specializing in road construction.

New emphasis on green construction also should help lead to better employment prospects as many green practices require more labor on construction sites. For example, in green construction projects, work-ers are needed to separate materials that can be used again from those that cannot. In addition, workers will be needed for the construction of any new projects to harness wind or solar power.

In many geographic areas, construction laborers—especially for those with limited skills—will experience competition because of a plentiful supply of workers who are willing to work as day laborers.

Employment of construction laborers, like that of many other construction workers, is sensitive to the fluctuations of the economy. On the one hand, workers in these trades may experience periods of unemployment when the overall level of construction falls. On the other hand, shortages of these workers may occur in some areas during peak periods of building activity.

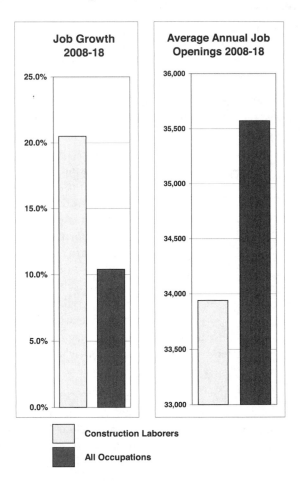

Income

Median hourly wages of wage-and-salary construction laborers in May 2008 were $13.71. The middle 50 percent earned between $10.74 and $18.57. The lowest 10 percent earned less than $8.67, and the highest 10 percent earned more than $25.98.

Earnings for construction laborers can be reduced by poor weather or by downturns in construction activity, which sometimes result in layoffs. Apprentices or helpers usually start out earning about 60 percent of the wage paid to experienced workers. Pay increases as apprentices gain experience and learn new skills.

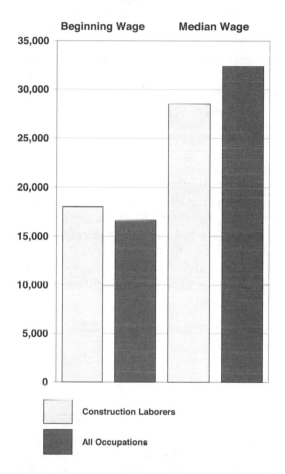

Beginning Wage   Median Wage

- Construction Laborers
- All Occupations

Related Jobs

- Assemblers and fabricators
- Brickmasons, blockmasons, and stonemasons
- Forest and conservation workers
- Grounds maintenance workers
- Highway maintenance workers
- Logging workers
- Material moving occupations
- Refractory materials repairers, except brickmasons
- Roustabouts, oil and gas

How to Learn More

For information about jobs as a construction laborer, contact local building or construction contractors, local joint labor-management apprenticeship committees, apprenticeship agencies, or the local office of your State Employment Service. You also can find information on the registered apprenticeships, together with links to state apprenticeship programs, on the U.S. Department of Labor's Web site: www.doleta.gov/OA/eta_default.cfm.

For general information on apprenticeships and how to get them, see the Occupational Outlook Quarterly article "Apprenticeships: Career training, credentials—and a paycheck in your pocket," online at www.bls.gov/opub/ooq/2002/summer/art01.pdf and in print at many libraries and career centers.

For information on education programs for laborers, contact

- Laborers-AGC Education and Training Fund, 37 Deerfield Rd., P.O. Box 37, Pomfret Center, CT 06258-0037.

- National Center for Construction Education and Research, 3600 NW 43rd St., Bldg. G, Gainesville, FL 32606. Internet: www.nccer.org

Why It's Hot

Economists expect America to undergo a spurt of construction activity over the next decade, including work to patch up and expand our infrastructure of roads, bridges, power grids, and levees. Construction laborers, especially those who can move to where they're needed, will find many jobs in these projects.

Cost Estimators

Cost estimators develop the cost information that business owners and managers need to make decisions on projects and products.

Just the Facts

Earnings: $56,510

Job Growth: 25.3%

Annual Openings: 10,360

Education and Training: Bachelor's degree

While at Work

Business managers must always assess the risks and costs associated with any new product or venture. Accurately forecasting the cost, size, and duration of future projects is the job of cost estimators. The information they provide helps businesses decide on the profitability of a proposed new project or product.

Job duties vary widely depending on the type and size of the project. Regardless of the industry in which they work, however, estimators collect and analyze data on all of the factors that can affect costs, such as materials, labor, location, duration of the project, and special machinery requirements, including computer hardware and software.

The methods for estimating costs can also differ greatly by industry. On a large construction project, for example, the estimating process begins with the decision to submit a bid. After reviewing various preliminary drawings and specifications, the estimator visits the site of the proposed project to gather important information, such as the availability of electricity, water, and other services. After the site visit, the estimator determines the quantity of materials and the labor required to complete the firm's part of the project. The estimator must make decisions concerning equipment needs, the sequence of operations, the size of the crew required, and physical constraints at the site. Allowances for wasted materials, inclement weather, shipping delays, and other factors that may increase costs also must be incorporated in the estimate. After completing the quantity surveys, the estimator prepares a cost summary for the entire project, which includes the costs of labor, equipment, materials, subcontractors, overhead, taxes, insurance, markup, and any additional costs that may affect the project. The chief estimator then prepares the bid proposal for submission to the owner.

> **CONSIDER THIS...**
>
> On large construction projects, there may be several estimators, each specializing in one area, such as electrical work or excavation, concrete, and forms.

Construction cost estimators also may be employed by the project's architect, engineering firm, or owner to help establish a budget, manage and control project costs, and to track actual costs relative to bid specifications as the project develops. During construction, estimators may be employed to manage the cost of change orders and negotiate and settle and extra costs or mitigate potential claims. Estimators may also be called upon as expert witness on cost in a construction dispute case.

In manufacturing, cost estimators usually are assigned to the engineering, cost, or pricing department. The estimator's goal is to accurately estimate the costs associated with developing and producing products. The job may begin when management requests an estimate of the costs associated with a major redesign of an existing product or the development of a new product or production process. For example, when estimating the cost of manufacturing a new product, the estimator works with engineers, first reviewing blueprints or conceptual drawings to determine the machining operations, tools, gauges, and materials that will be required. The estimator then prepares a parts list and determines whether it would be more efficient to produce or to purchase the parts.

The cost estimator then prepares "cost reduction" curves and calculates the standard labor hours necessary to produce a specified number of units. Standard labor hours are then converted to dollar values, to which are added factors for waste, overhead, and profit to yield the unit cost in dollars. The estimator compares the cost of purchasing parts with the firm's estimated cost of manufacturing them to determine which is less expensive.

Operations research, production control, cost, and price analysts who work for government agencies may do significant amounts of cost estimating in the course of their usual duties.

> **CONSIDER THIS...**
>
> Some high-technology products require a considerable amount of computer programming during the design phase. The cost of software development is one of the fastest-growing and most difficult activities to estimate. As a result, some cost estimators now specialize in estimating only computer software development and related costs.

Cost estimators develop information that managers need to determine the potential profitability of a new product.

Also Known As

Software cost estimators make accurate predictions of the effort and cost involved in creating or adapting computer software to solve a particular problem or meet a particular need. This is becoming more and more important as businesses in nearly every industry try to harness the power of new computer technology without incurring too much cost.

Job Fit

Personality Type
Conventional-Enterprising

Career Clusters
02 Architecture and Construction

04 Business, Management, and Administration

13 Manufacturing

15 Science, Technology, Engineering, and Mathematics

Skills
Mathematics

Computer Programming

Management

Communications

Thought-Processing

Social Skills

Work Styles
Analytical Thinking

Attention to Detail

Stress Tolerance

Persistence

Integrity

Achievement/Effort

Dependability

Initiative

Working Conditions

Although estimators spend most of their time in a comfortable office, construction estimators also visit worksites that can be dusty, dirty, and occasionally hazardous. Likewise, estimators in manufacturing spend time on the factory floor, where it also can be noisy and dirty. In some industries, frequent travel between a firm's headquarters and its subsidiaries or subcontractors may be required.

Estimators normally work a 40-hour week, but overtime is common. Cost estimators often work under pressure and stress, especially when facing bid deadlines. Inaccurate estimating can cause a firm to lose a bid or to lose money on a job that was not accurately estimated.

◼ What's Required

Job entry requirements for cost estimators vary by industry. In the construction industry, employers increasingly prefer to hire cost estimators with a bachelor's degree in construction science, construction management, or building science, although it is also possible for experienced construction workers to become cost estimators. Employers in manufacturing usually prefer someone with a bachelor's degree in mathematics, statistics, or engineering.

Education and Training

In addition to a bachelor's degree, most construction estimators also have considerable construction experience, gained through work in the industry, internships, or cooperative education programs. Applicants can achieve a competitive edge by acquiring a thorough knowledge of construction materials, costs, and procedures in areas ranging from heavy construction to electrical work, plumbing systems, or masonry work.

In manufacturing industries, employers prefer to hire individuals with a degree in engineering, physical science, operations research, mathematics, statistics, accounting, finance, business, economics, or a related subject. In most industries, experience in quantitative techniques is important.

Many colleges and universities include cost estimating as part of bachelor's and associate degree curriculums in civil engineering, industrial engineering, and construction management or construction engineering technology. In addition, cost estimating is often part of master's degree programs in construction science or construction management. Specialized courses and programs in cost-estimating techniques and procedures also are offered by many technical schools, community colleges, and universities.

Estimators also receive much training on the job because every com-

Consider This...
Organizations representing cost estimators, such as the Association for the Advancement of Cost Engineering (AACE International) and the Society of Cost Estimating and Analysis (SCEA), sponsor educational and professional development programs. These programs help students, estimators-in-training, and experienced estimators learn about changes affecting the profession.

pany has its own way of handling estimates. Working with an experienced estimator, newcomers become familiar with each step in the process. Those with no experience reading construction specifications or blueprints first learn that aspect of the work. Then they may accompany an experienced estimator to the construction site or shop floor, where they observe the work being done, take measurements, or perform other routine tasks. As they become more knowledgeable, estimators learn how to tabulate quantities and dimensions from drawings and how to select the appropriate prices for materials.

Postsecondary Programs to Consider

- Business administration and management
- Construction engineering
- Construction engineering technology/technician
- Manufacturing engineering
- Materials engineering
- Mechanical engineering

Additional Qualifications

Cost estimators should have an aptitude for mathematics; be able to quickly analyze, compare, and interpret detailed but sometimes poorly defined information; and be able to make sound and accurate judgments based on this information. Assertiveness and self-confidence in presenting and supporting conclusions are also important, as are strong communications and interpersonal skills, because estimators may work as part of a team alongside managers, owners, engineers, and design professionals.

Cost estimators also need knowledge of computers, including word-processing and spreadsheet packages. In some instances, familiarity with special estimation software or programming skills also may be required.

School Subjects to Study

- Algebra
- Computer science
- English
- Geometry
- Physics
- Pre-calculus and calculus
- Trigonometry

Moving Up

Voluntary certification can be valuable to cost estimators because it provides professional recognition of the estimator's competence and experience. In some instances, individual employers may even require professional certification for employment. Both AACE International and SCEA administer certification programs. To become certified, estimators usually must have between 2 and 8 years of estimating experience and must pass an examination. In addition, certification requirements may include the publication of at least one article or paper in the field.

For most estimators, advancement takes the form of higher pay and prestige. Some move into management positions, such as project manager for a construction firm or manager of the industrial engineering department for a manufacturer. Others may go into business for themselves as consultants, providing estimating services for a fee to government or to construction or manufacturing firms.

Employment

Cost estimators held about 217,800 jobs in 2008. About 59 percent of estimators were in the construction industry and another 15 percent were employed in manufacturing. The remainder worked in a wide range of other industries.

Cost estimators work throughout the country, usually in or near major industrial, commercial, and government centers and in cities and suburban areas experiencing rapid change or development.

Job Prospects

Employment of cost estimators is expected to grow by 25 percent in the 10-year period ending 2018, much faster than average for all occupations. Growth in the construction industry will account for most new jobs in this occupation. In particular, construction and repair of highways, streets, bridges, subway systems, airports, water and sewage systems, and electric power plants and transmission lines will stimulate the need for more cost estimators.

An increasing population will result in more construction of residential homes, hospitals, schools, restaurants, and other structures that require cost estimators. As the population ages, the demand for nursing and extended-care facilities will also increase. The growing complexity of construction projects will also boost demand for cost estimators as more workers specialize in a particular area of construction.

Because there are no formal bachelor's degree programs in cost estimating, some employers have difficulty recruiting qualified cost estimators, resulting in good employment opportunities. Job prospects in construction should be best for those who have a degree in construction science, construction management, or building science or have years of practical experience in the various phases of construction or in a specialty craft area. Knowledge of Building Information Modeling software would also be helpful.

For cost estimating jobs in manufacturing, those who have degrees in mathematics, statistics, engineering, accounting, business administration, or economics, and who are familiar with cost estimation software should have the best job prospects.

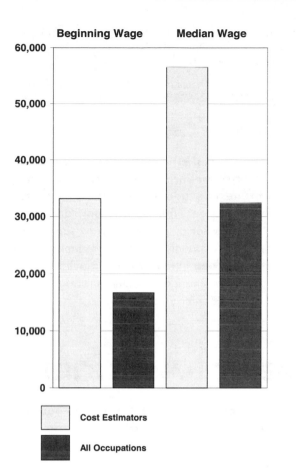

Cost Estimators

All Occupations

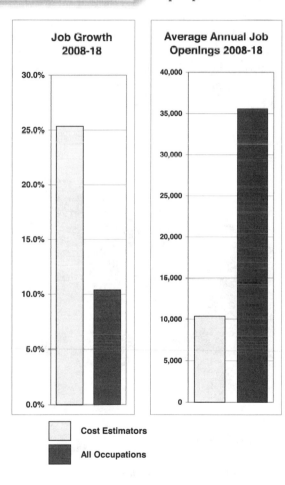

Cost Estimators

All Occupations

Income

Salaries of cost estimators vary widely by experience, education, size of firm, and industry. Median annual wages of wage-and-salary cost estimators in May 2008 were $56,510. The middle 50 percent earned between $42,720 and $74,320. The lowest 10 percent earned less than $33,150, and the highest 10 percent earned more than $94,470.

Related Jobs

- Accountants and auditors
- Budget analysts
- Claims adjusters, appraisers, examiners, and investigators
- Construction managers
- Economists
- Industrial production managers
- Insurance underwriters
- Loan officers
- Market and survey researchers
- Operations research analysts
- Personal financial advisors

▆ How to Learn More

Information about career opportunities, certification, educational programs, and cost-estimating techniques may be obtained from the following organizations:

- Association for the Advancement of Cost Engineering (AACE International), 209 Prairie Ave., Suite 100, Morgantown, WV 26501. Internet: www.aacei.org

- American Society of Professional Estimators (ASPE), 2525 Perimeter Place Drive, Suite 103, Nashville, TN 37214. Internet: www.aspenational.org

- Society of Cost Estimating and Analysis, 527 Maple Ave. East, Suite 301, Vienna, VA 22180. Internet: www.sceaonline.net

Why It's Hot

Over half of cost estimators work in the construction industry, which is expected to grow rapidly over the next decade. The national infrastructure of roads, bridges, rail lines, levees, and power lines needs a lot of patching up to support the 21st century economy. The smaller number of estimators working in manufacturing will be in demand to help American manufacturers keep pace with overseas competitors.

Dental Assistants

Dental assistants help a dentist, setting up patients and equipment and keeping records.

Just the Facts

Earnings: $32,380

Job Growth: 35.7%

Annual Openings: 16,100

Education and Training: Moderate-term on-the-job training

While at Work

Dental assistants work closely with, and under the supervision of, dentists. Assistants perform a variety of patient care, office, and laboratory duties.

> **CONSIDER THIS...**
>
> Some states are expanding dental assistants' duties to include tasks such as coronal polishing and restorative dentistry functions for those assistants who meet specific training and experience requirements.

Dental assistants sterilize and disinfect instruments and equipment, prepare and lay out the instruments and materials required to treat each patient, and obtain patients' dental records. Assistants make patients as comfortable as possible in the dental chair and prepare them for treatment. During dental procedures, assistants work alongside the dentist to provide assistance. They hand instruments and materials to dentists and keep patients' mouths dry and clear by using suction or other devices. They also instruct patients on postoperative and general oral health care.

Dental assistants may prepare materials for impressions and restorations, take dental X-rays, and process X-ray film as directed by a dentist. They also may remove sutures, apply topical anesthetics to gums or cavity-preventive agents to teeth, remove excess cement used in the filling process, and place rubber dams on the teeth to isolate them for individual treatment.

Dental assistants with laboratory duties make casts of the teeth and mouth from impressions, clean and polish removable appliances, and make temporary crowns. Those with office duties schedule and confirm appointments, receive patients, keep treatment records, send bills, receive payments, and order dental supplies and materials.

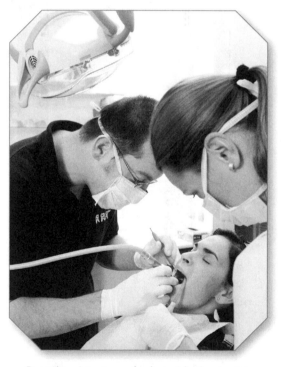

Dental assistants work alongside the dentist.

Also Known As

Dental assistants should not be confused with *dental hygienists,* who are licensed to perform different clinical tasks.

Job Fit

Personality Type

Conventional-Realistic-Social

Career Cluster

08 Health Science

Skills

Equipment Use/Maintenance

Social Skills

Equipment/Technology Analysis

Communications

Science

Management

Thought-Processing

Computer Programming

Work Styles

Social Skills Orientation

Concern for Others

Self-Control

Cooperation

Attention to Detail

Adaptability/Flexibility

Initiative

Dependability

Working Conditions

Dental assistants work in a well-lighted, clean environment. Their work area usually is near the dental chair so that they can arrange instruments, materials, and medication and hand them to the dentist when needed. Dental assistants must wear gloves, masks, eyewear, and protective clothing to protect themselves and their patients from infectious diseases. Assistants also follow safety procedures to minimize the risks associated with the use of X-ray machines.

About half of dental assistants have a 35- to 40-hour work week. Most of the rest work part-time or have variable schedules. Depending on the hours of the dental office where they work, assistants may have to work on Saturdays or evenings. Some dental assistants hold multiple jobs by working at dental offices that are open on different days or scheduling their work at a second office around the hours they work at their primary office.

What's Required

Many assistants learn their skills on the job, although an increasing number are trained in dental-assisting programs offered by community and junior colleges, trade schools, technical institutes, or the Armed Forces.

Education and Training

For students wishing to pursue postsecondary education, the Commission on Dental Accreditation within the American Dental Association (ADA) approved 283 dental-assisting training programs in 2009. Programs include classroom, laboratory, and preclinical instruction in dental-assisting skills and related theory. In addition, students gain practical experience in dental schools, clinics, or dental offices. Most programs take 1 year or less to complete and lead to a certificate or diploma. Two-year programs offered in community and junior colleges lead to an associate degree. All programs require a high school diploma or its equivalent, and some require science or computer-related courses for admission.

A large number of dental assistants learn through on-the-job training. In these situations, the employing dentist or other dental assistants in the dental office teach the new assistant dental terminology, the names of the instruments, how to perform daily duties, how to interact with patients, and other things necessary to help keep the dental office running smoothly. While some things can be picked up easily, it may be a few months before new dental assistants are completely knowledgeable about their duties and comfortable doing all of their tasks without assistance.

A period of on-the-job training is often required even for those who have completed a dental-assisting program or have some previous experience. Different dentists may have their own styles of doing things that need to be learned before an assistant can be comfortable working with them. Office-specific information, such as where files are kept, need to be learned at each new job. Also, as dental technology changes, dental assistants need to stay familiar with the tools and procedures that they will be using or helping dentists to use. On-the-job training is often sufficient to keep assistants up-to-date on these matters.

CONSIDER THIS...

Several private vocational schools offer 4- to 6-month courses in dental assisting, but the Commission on Dental Accreditation does not accredit these programs.

Most states regulate the duties that dental assistants are allowed to perform. Some states require licensure or registration, which may include passing a written or practical examination. Various schools offer courses—approximately 10 to 12 months in length—that meet their state's requirements. Other states require dental assistants to complete state-approved education courses of 4 to 12 hours in length. Some states offer registration or other dental assisting credentials with little or no education required. Some states require continuing education to maintain licensure or registration. A few states allow dental assistants to perform any function delegated to them by the dentist.

Individual states have adopted different standards for dental assistants who perform certain advanced duties. In some states, for example, dental assistants who perform radiological procedures must complete additional training. Completion of the Radiation Health and Safety examination offered by Dental Assisting National Board (DANB) meets the standards in more than 30 states. Some states require completion of a state-approved course in radiology as well.

Certification is available through the Dental Assisting National Board (DANB) and is recognized or required in more than 30 states. Certification is an acknowledgment of an assistant's qualifications and professional competence and may be an asset when one is seeking employment. Candidates may qualify to take the DANB certification examination by graduating from an ADA-accredited dental assisting education program or by having 2 years of full-time, or 4 years of part-time, experience as a dental assistant. In addition, applicants must have current certification in cardiopulmonary resuscitation. For annual recertification, individuals must earn continuing education credits. Other organizations offer registration, most often at the state level.

Postsecondary Program to Consider

• Dental assisting/assistant training

Additional Qualifications

Dental assistants must be a second pair of hands for a dentist; therefore, dentists look for people who are reliable, work well with others, and have good manual dexterity.

School Subjects to Study

• Algebra
• Biology
• Chemistry
• English
• Keyboarding

Moving Up

Without further education, advancement opportunities are limited. Some dental assistants become office managers, dental-assisting instructors, dental product sales representatives, or insurance claims processors for dental insurance companies. Others go back to school to become dental hygienists.

Employment

Dental assistants held about 295,300 jobs in 2008. About 93 percent of all jobs for dental assistants were in offices of dentists. A small number of jobs were in the federal, state, and local governments or in offices of physicians.

Job Prospects

Employment is expected to grow 36 percent in the 10-year period ending 2018, which is much faster than the average for all occupations. In fact, dental assistants are expected to be among the fastest-growing occupations over the 10-year projection period. Population growth, greater retention of natural teeth by middle-aged and older people, and an increased focus on preventative dental care for younger generations will fuel demand for dental services.

CONSIDER THIS...

For many, this entry-level occupation provides basic training and experience and serves as a stepping stone to more highly skilled and higher-paying jobs.

Job prospects should be excellent, as dentists continue to need the aid of qualified dental assistants. There will be many opportunities for entry-level positions, but some dentists prefer to hire experienced assistants, those who have completed a dental-assisting program, or have met state requirements to take on expanded functions within the office.

In addition to job openings due to employment growth, some job openings will arise out of the need to replace assistants who transfer to other occupations, retire, or leave for other reasons.

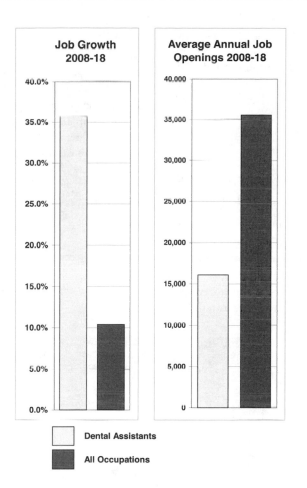

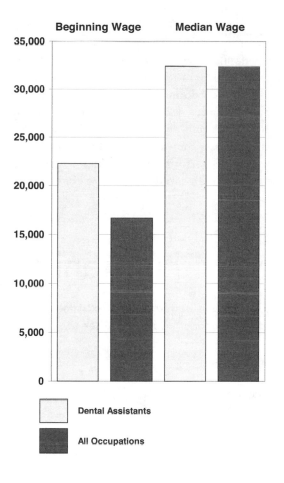

Income

Median hourly earnings of dental assistants were $15.57 in May 2008. The middle 50 percent earned between $12.97 and $18.73 an hour. The lowest 10 percent earned less than $10.71, and the highest 10 percent earned more than $22.19 an hour.

Benefits vary substantially by practice setting and may be contingent upon full-time employment. According to the American Dental Association, 87 percent of dentists offer reimbursement for continuing education courses taken by their assistants.

Related Jobs

- Dental hygienists
- Medical assistants
- Occupational therapist assistants and aides
- Pharmacy aides
- Pharmacy technicians and aides
- Physical therapist assistants and aides
- Surgical technologists

How to Learn More

Information about career opportunities and accredited dental assistant programs is available from

- Commission on Dental Accreditation, American Dental Association, 211 East Chicago Ave., Suite 1814, Chicago, IL 60611. Internet: www.ada.org

For information on becoming a Certified Dental Assistant and a list of state boards of dentistry, contact

- Dental Assisting National Board, Inc., 676 N. Saint Clair St., Suite 1880, Chicago, IL 60611. Internet: www.danb.org

For more information on a career as a dental assistant and general information about continuing education, contact

- American Dental Assistants Association, 35 E. Wacker Dr., Suite 1730, Chicago, IL 60601. Internet: www.dentalassistant.org

For more information about continuing education courses, contact

- National Association of Dental Assistants, 900 S. Washington St., Suite G-13, Falls Church, VA 22046.

Why It's Hot

Older dentists, who have been less likely to employ assistants or have employed fewer, are leaving the occupation and will be replaced by recent graduates, who are more likely to use one or more assistants. In addition, as dentists' workloads increase, they are expected to hire more assistants to perform routine tasks so that they may devote their own time to more complex procedures.

Dental Hygienists

Dental hygienists clean teeth and examine oral areas, head, and neck for signs of oral disease.

Just the Facts

Earnings: $66,570

Job Growth: 36.1%

Annual Openings: 9,840

Education and Training: Associate degree

While at Work

Dental hygienists remove soft and hard deposits from teeth, teach patients how to practice good oral hygiene, and provide other preventive dental care. They examine patients' teeth and gums, recording the presence of diseases or abnormalities.

Dental hygienists use an assortment of different tools to complete their tasks. Hand and rotary instruments and ultrasonic devices are used to clean and polish teeth, including removing calculus, stains, and plaque. Hygienists use X-ray machines to take dental pictures; sometimes they develop the film. They may use models of teeth to explain oral hygiene, perform root planning as a periodontal therapy, or apply cavity-preventative agents such as fluorides and pit and fissure sealants. In some states, hygienists are allowed to administer local anesthetics using syringes. Some states also allow hygienists to place and carve filling materials, temporary fillings, and periodontal dressings; remove sutures; and smooth and polish metal restorations.

Dental hygienists also help patients develop and maintain good oral health. For example, they may explain the relationship between diet and oral health or inform patients how to select toothbrushes and show them how to brush and floss their teeth.

Hygienists sometimes make a diagnosis and other times may prepare clinical and laboratory diagnostic tests for the dentist to interpret. Hygienists sometimes work chair-side with the dentist during treatment.

Consider This...

Dental hygienists sometimes visit elementary and secondary schools to educate young people about taking care of their teeth. They may demonstrate proper brushing and flossing techniques and stress the importance of checkups.

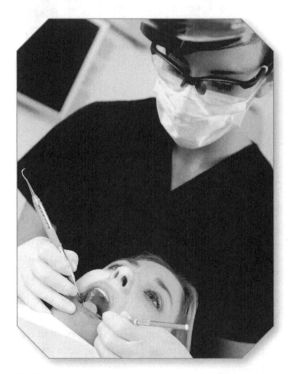

Dental hygienists examine patients' teeth and gums.

Also Known As

Dental hygienists should not be confused with *dental assistants,* who are licensed to perform different clinical tasks.

Job Fit

Personality Type
Social-Realistic-Conventional

Career Cluster
08 Health Science

Skills

Science

Communications

Social Skills

Thought-Processing

Equipment Use/Maintenance

Equipment/Technology Analysis

Management

Work Styles

Concern for Others

Social Skills Orientation

Cooperation

Independence

Achievement/Effort

Dependability

Stress Tolerance

Self-Control

Working Conditions

Dental hygienists work in clean, well-lighted offices. Important health safeguards include strict adherence to proper radiological procedures and the use of appropriate protective devices when administering anesthetic gas. Dental hygienists also wear safety glasses, surgical masks, and gloves to protect themselves and patients from infectious diseases.

▮ What's Required

Prospective dental hygienists must become licensed in the state in which they wish to practice. A degree from an accredited dental hygiene school is usually required, along with licensure examinations.

Education and Training

A high school diploma and college entrance test scores are usually required for admission to a dental hygiene program. Also, some dental hygiene programs require applicants to have completed at least 1 year of college. Specific entrance requirements vary from one school to another.

In 2009, there were 311 dental hygiene programs accredited by the Commission on Dental Accreditation. Most dental hygiene programs grant an associate degree, although some also offer a certificate, a bachelor's degree, or a master's degree. A minimum of an associate degree

or certificate in dental hygiene is generally required for practice in a private dental office. A bachelor's or master's degree usually is required for research, teaching, or clinical practice in public or school health programs.

Schools offer laboratory, clinical, and classroom instruction in subjects such as anatomy, physiology, chemistry, microbiology, pharmacology, nutrition, radiography, histology (the study of tissue structure), periodontology (the study of gum diseases), pathology, dental materials, clinical dental hygiene, and social and behavioral sciences.

Dental hygienists must be licensed by the state in which they practice. Nearly all states require candidates to graduate from an accredited dental hygiene school and pass both a written and clinical examination. The American Dental Association's Joint Commission on National Dental Examinations administers the written examination, which is accepted by all states and the District of Columbia. State or regional testing agencies administer the clinical examination. In addition, most states require an examination on the legal aspects of dental hygiene practice.

Postsecondary Program to Consider

• Dental hygiene/hygienist training

Additional Qualifications

Dental hygienists should work well with others, because they work closely with dentists and dental assistants as well as dealing directly with patients. Hygienists also need good manual dexterity, because they use dental instruments within a patient's mouth, with little room for error.

CONSIDER THIS...

Flexible scheduling is a distinctive feature of this job. Full-time, part-time, evening, and weekend schedules are widely available. Dentists frequently hire hygienists to work only 2 or 3 days a week, so hygienists may hold jobs in more than one dental office. More than half of all dental hygienists worked part time—less than 35 hours a week.

CONSIDER THIS...

Unlike all other states, Alabama allows candidates to take its licensing examinations if they have been trained through a state-regulated on-the-job program in a dentist's office.

- Algebra
- Biology
- Chemistry
- English
- Geometry
- Trigonometry

Moving Up

Advancement opportunities are limited without additional education; mostly they consist of higher wages. In a few large clinical settings, supervisory positions may be available. Some dental hygienists become dental hygiene instructors, dental product sales representatives, or insurance claims processors for dental insurance companies.

Employment

Dental hygienists held about 174,100 jobs in 2008. Because multiple job holding is common in this field, the number of jobs exceeds the number of hygienists. About 51 percent of dental hygienists worked part time. Almost all jobs for dental hygienists—about 96 percent—were in offices of dentists. A very small number worked for employment services, in physicians' offices, or in other industries.

Job Prospects

Employment of dental hygienists is expected to grow 36 percent through 2018, which is much faster than the average for all occupations. This projected growth ranks dental hygienists among the fastest growing occupations, in response to increasing demand for dental care and more use of hygienists.

The demand for dental services will grow because of population growth, older people increasingly retaining more teeth, and a growing emphasis on preventative dental care. To help meet this demand, facilities that provide dental care, particularly dentists' offices, will increasingly employ dental hygienists, often to perform services that have been performed by dentists in the past. Ongoing research indicating a link between oral health and general health also will spur the demand for preventative dental services, which are typically provided by dental hygienists.

Job prospects are expected to be favorable in most areas, but will vary by geographical location. Because graduates are permitted to practice only in the state in which they are licensed, hygienists wishing to practice in areas that have an abundance of dental hygiene programs may experience strong competition for jobs.

Older dentists, who have been less likely to employ dental hygienists, are leaving the occupation and will be replaced by recent graduates, who are more likely to employ one or more hygienists. In addition, as dentists' workloads increase, they are expected to hire more hygienists to perform preventive dental care, such as cleaning, so that they may devote their own time to more complex procedures.

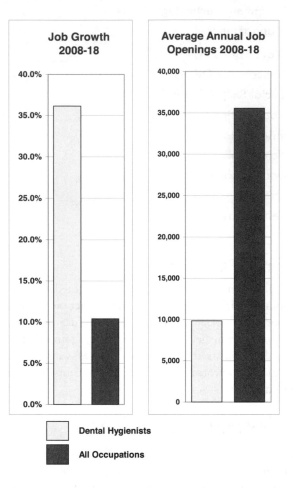

Income

Median hourly earnings of dental hygienists were $32.00 in May 2008. The middle 50 percent earned between $26.55 and $37.98 an hour. The lowest 10 percent earned less than $21.24, and the highest 10 percent earned more than $43.98 an hour.

Earnings vary by geographic location, employment setting, and years of experience. Dental hygienists may be paid on an hourly, daily, salary, or commission basis.

Benefits vary substantially by practice setting and may be contingent upon full-time employment. According to the American Dental Association, 86 percent of hygienists receive hospital and medical benefits.

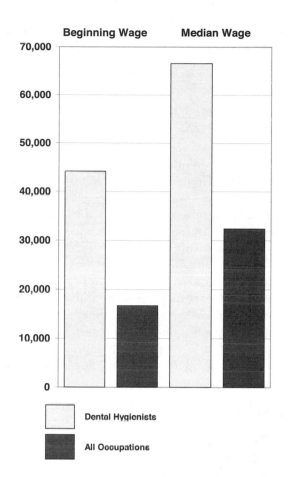

Beginning Wage **Median Wage**

Legend:
- Dental Hygienists
- All Occupations

Related Jobs

- Dental assistants
- Medical assistants
- Occupational therapist assistants and aides
- Physical therapist assistants and aides
- Physician assistants
- Radiation therapists
- Registered nurses

How to Learn More

For information on a career in dental hygiene, including educational requirements, contact

- Division of Education, American Dental Hygienists Association, 444 N. Michigan Ave., Suite 3400, Chicago, IL 60611. Internet: www.adha.org

For information about accredited programs and educational requirements, contact

- Commission on Dental Accreditation, American Dental Association, 211 E. Chicago Ave., Suite 1814, Chicago, IL 60611. Internet: www.ada.org

The State Board of Dental Examiners in each state can supply information on licensing requirements.

Why It's Hot

Dental hygienists rank among the fastest-growing occupations. The demand for dental services will increase because of population growth, older people retaining more teeth, and a focus on preventative dental care. To meet this demand, facilities that provide dental care, particularly dentists' offices, will increasingly employ dental hygienists—and more hygienists per office—to perform services that have been performed by dentists in the past.

Environmental Scientists and Hydrologists

Environmental scientists and hydrologists use their knowledge of the physical makeup and history of the Earth to protect the environment, study the properties of underground and surface waters, locate water and energy resources, predict water-related geologic hazards, and provide environmental site assessments and advice on indoor air quality and hazardous-waste-site remediation.

Just the Facts

Earnings: $60,762
Job Growth: 27.0%
Annual Openings: 5,220
Education and Training: Master's degree

While at Work

Environmental scientists conduct research to identify, abate, and eliminate hazards that affect people, wildlife, and their environments. These workers analyze measurements or observations of air, food, water, and soil to determine the way to clean and preserve the environment. Understanding the issues involved in protecting the environment—degradation, conservation, recycling, and replenishment—is central to the work of environmental scientists. They often use this understanding to design and monitor waste disposal sites, preserve water supplies, and reclaim contaminated land and water to comply with federal environmental regulations. They also write risk assessments, describing the likely effects of construction and other environmental changes; write technical proposals; and give presentations to managers and regulators.

Hydrologists study the quantity, distribution, circulation, and physical properties of bodies of water. Often, they specialize in either underground water or surface water. They examine the form and intensity of precipitation, its rate of infiltration into the soil, its movement through the Earth, and its return to the ocean and atmosphere. Hydrologists use sophisticated techniques and instruments. For example, they may use remote sensing technology, data assimilation, and numerical modeling to monitor the change in regional and global water cycles. Some surface-water hydrologists use sensitive stream-measuring devices to assess flow rates and water quality.

Many environmental scientists and hydrologists work at consulting firms, helping businesses and government agencies comply with environmental policy, particularly with regard to ground-water decontamination and flood control. They are usually hired to solve problems. Most consulting firms fall into two categories: large multidisciplinary engineering companies, the largest of which may employ thousands of workers, and small niche firms that may employ only a few workers. When looking for jobs, environmental scientists and hydrologists should consider the type of firm and the scope of the projects it undertakes. In larger firms, environmental scientists are more likely to engage in large, long-term projects in which they will work with people in other scientific disciplines. In smaller specialty firms, how-

ever, they work more often with business professionals and clients in government and the private sector.

Some environmental scientists work in managerial positions, usually after spending some time performing research or learning about environmental laws and regulations.

Many environmental scientists do work and have training that is similar to other physical or life scientists, but they focus on environmental issues. Many specialize in subfields such as environmental ecology and conservation, environmental chemistry, environmental biology, or fisheries science. Specialties affect the specific activities that environmental scientists perform, although recent understandings of the interconnectedness of life processes have blurred some traditional classifications. For example, *environmental ecologists* study the relationships between organisms and their environments and the effects on both of factors such as population size, pollutants, rainfall, temperature, and altitude. They may collect, study, and report data on air, soil, and water, using their knowledge of various scientific disciplines.

Environmental scientists analyze observations of air, food, water, and soil to determine how to clean and preserve the environment.

Also Known As

Ecological modelers study ecosystems, pollution control, and resource management, using mathematical modeling, systems analysis, thermodynamics, and computer techniques. *Environmental chemists* study the toxicity of various chemicals—that is, how those chemicals affect plants, animals, and people. *Climate change analysts* research and analyze policy developments related to climate change. They climate-related recommendations for actions such as legislation, awareness campaigns, or fundraising approaches.

Job Fit

Personality Type
Investigative-Realistic-Conventional

Career Clusters
01 Agriculture, Food, and Natural Resources
15 Science, Technology, Engineering, and Mathematics

Skills
Science
Computer Programming
Mathematics
Communications
Thought-Processing
Management
Social Skills

Work Styles
Analytical Thinking
Achievement/Effort
Cooperation
Integrity
Leadership
Independence
Attention to Detail
Innovation

Working Conditions

Most entry-level environmental scientists and hydrologists spend the majority of their time in the field, while more experienced workers generally devote more time to office or laboratory work. Many beginning hydrologists and some environmental scientists, such as environmental ecologists and environmental chemists, often take field trips that involve physical activity. Environmental scientists and hydrologists in the field may work in warm or cold climates, in all kinds of weather. In their research, they may dig or chip with a hammer, scoop with a net, come in contact with water, and carry equipment. Travel often is required to meet with prospective clients or investors.

CONSIDER THIS...
Researchers and consultants may face stress when looking for funding. Occasionally, those who write technical reports to business clients and regulators may be under pressure to meet deadlines and thus have to work long hours.

■ What's Required

Most environmental scientists and hydrologists need a master's degree. A Ph.D. is usually necessary for jobs in college teaching or research.

Education and Training

A bachelor's degree in an earth science is adequate for a few entry-level positions, but environmental scientists increasingly need a master's degree in environmental science, hydrology, or a related natural science. A master's degree also is the minimum educational requirement for most entry-level applied research positions in private industry, in state and federal agencies, and at state geological surveys. A doctoral degree generally is necessary for college teaching and most research positions.

Some environmental scientists have a degree in environmental science. Many, however, earn degrees in life science, chemistry, geology, geophysics, atmospheric science, or physics, and then apply their education to the environment. They often need research or work experience related to environmental science.

A bachelor's degree in environmental science offers an interdisciplinary approach to the natural sciences, with an emphasis on biology, chemistry, and geology. Undergraduate environmental science majors typically focus on data analysis and physical geography, which are particularly useful in studying pollution abatement, water resources, or ecosystem protection, restoration, and management. Understanding the geochemistry of inorganic compounds is becoming increasingly important in developing remediation goals. Students interested in working in the environmental or regulatory fields, either in environmental consulting firms or for federal or state governments, should take courses in hydrology, hazardous-waste management, environmental legislation, chemistry, fluid mechanics, and geologic logging, which is the gathering of geologic data. An understanding of environmental regulations and government permit issues also is valuable for those planning to work in mining and oil and gas extraction.

Students interested in hydrology should take courses in the physical sciences, geophysics, chemistry, engineering science, soil science, mathematics, aquatic biology, atmospheric science, geology, oceanography, hydrogeology, and the management or conservation of water resources. In some cases, a bachelor's degree in a hydrologic science is sufficient for positions consulting about water quality or wastewater treatment.

- Environmental science
- Environmental studies
- Geology/Earth science, general
- Hydrology and water resources science
- Oceanography, chemical and physical

Additional Qualifications

Computer skills are essential for prospective environmental scientists and hydrologists. Students who have some experience with computer modeling, data analysis and integration, digital mapping, remote sensing, and Geographic Information Systems (GIS) will be the most prepared to enter the job market. Familiarity with the Global Positioning System (GPS)—a locator system that uses satellites—is vital.

Environmental scientists and hydrologists must have good interpersonal skills, because they usually work as part of a team with other scientists, engineers, and technicians. Strong oral and written communication skills also are essential because writing technical reports and research proposals and communicating results to company managers, regulators, and the public are important aspects of the work. Because international work is becoming more common, knowledge of a second language can be an advantage. Those involved in fieldwork must have physical stamina.

CONSIDER THIS...

For environmental scientists and hydrologists who consult, courses in business, finance, marketing, or economics may be useful. In addition, combining environmental science training with other disciplines, such as engineering or business, qualifies these scientists for the widest range of jobs.

School Subjects to Study

- Algebra
- Biology
- Chemistry
- Computer science
- Earth science
- English
- Foreign language
- Geometry
- Physics
- Pre-calculus and calculus
- Trigonometry

Moving Up

Environmental scientists and hydrologists often begin their careers in field exploration or, occasionally, as research assistants or technicians in laboratories or offices. They are given more difficult assignments as they gain experience. Eventually, they may be promoted to project leader, program manager, or some other management and research position.

The American Institute of Hydrology offers certification programs in professional hydrology. Certification may be beneficial for those seeking advancement.

Employment

Environmental scientists and hydrologists held about 94,000 jobs in 2008. Jobs for hydrologists accounted for only 9 percent of the total. Many more individuals held environmental science faculty positions in colleges and universities, but they are classified as postsecondary teachers.

About 37 percent of environmental scientists were employed in state and local governments; 21 percent in management, scientific, and technical consulting services; 15 percent in architectural, engineering and related services; and 7 percent in the federal government. About 2 percent were self-employed.

Among hydrologists, 26 percent were employed in architectural, engineering, and related services, and 19 percent worked for management, scientific, and technical consulting services. In 2008, the federal government employed about 27 percent of hydrologists, mostly within the U.S. Department of the Interior for the U.S. Geological Survey (USGS) and within the U.S. Department of Defense. Another 21 percent worked for state agencies, such as state geological surveys and state departments of conservation. About 2 percent of hydrologists were self-employed, most as consultants to industry or government.

Job Prospects

Employment of environmental scientists is expected to increase by 28 percent in the 10-year period ending 2018, much faster than the average for all occupations. Over the same period, employment of hydrologists should increase by 18 percent, also much faster than the average. Job growth for environmental scientists and hydrologists should be strongest in private-sector consulting firms. Growth in employment of environmental scientists and hydrologists will be spurred largely by the increasing demands placed on the environment and water resources by population growth. Further demand should result from the need to comply with complex environmental laws and regulations, particularly those regarding ground-water decontamination, clean air, and flood control.

As people increasingly migrate toward environmentally sensitive locations, such as coastal regions, hydrologists will be needed to assess building sites for potential geologic hazards and to mitigate the effects of natural hazards such as floods, landslides, and hurricanes. Hydrologists also will be needed to study hazardous-waste sites and determine the effect of pollutants on soil and ground water so that engineers can design remediation systems. Increased government regulations, such as those regarding the management of storm water, and issues related to water conservation, deteriorating coastal environments, and rising sea levels also will stimulate employment growth for these workers.

Many environmental scientists and hydrologists work in consulting. Consulting firms have hired these scientists to help businesses and government address issues related to underground tanks, land disposal areas, and other hazardous-waste-management facilities. Currently, environmental consulting is evolving from investigations to creating remediation and engineering solutions. At the same time, the regulatory climate is moving from a rigid structure to a more flexible risk-based approach. These factors, coupled with new federal and state initiatives that integrate environmental activities into the business process itself, will result in a greater focus on waste minimization, resource recovery, pollution prevention, and the consideration of environmental effects during product development. This shift in focus to preventive management will provide many new opportunities for environmental scientists and hydrologists in consulting roles.

In addition to job openings due to growth, there will be additional demand for new environmental scientists and hydrologists to replace those who retire, advance to management positions, or change careers. Job prospects for hydrologists should be favorable, particularly for those with field experience. Demand for hydrologists who understand both the scientific and engineering aspects of waste remediation should be

strong. Few colleges and universities offer programs in hydrology, so the number of qualified workers may be limited.

Job prospects for environmental scientists also will be good, but less favorable than for hydrologists because of the larger number of workers seeking to enter the field.

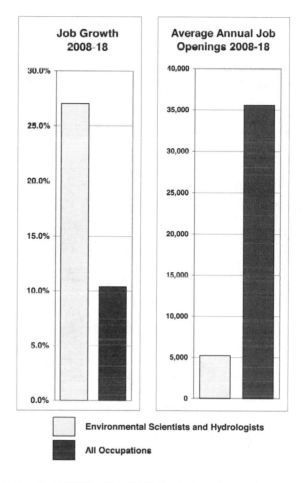

Income

Median annual earnings of environmental scientists were $59,750 in May 2008. The middle 50 percent earned between $45,340 and $78,980. The lowest 10 percent earned less than $36,310, and the highest 10 percent earned more than $102,610.

Median annual earnings of hydrologists were $71,450 in 2008, with the middle 50 percent earning between $54,910 and $89,200, the lowest 10 percent earning less than $44,410, and the highest 10 percent earning more than $105,010.

The industries employing the largest number of environmental scientists reported the following levels of pay in 2008: $57,970 in federal, state, and local government; $61,330 in professional, scientific, and technical services; $57,170 in educational services; and $83,440 in utilities.

For hydrologists, the earnings in the industries with the largest employment were $70,710 in federal, state, and local government; $72,120 in professional, scientific, and technical services; and $58,700 in educational services.

In March 2009, the federal government's average salary for hydrologists was $89,404.

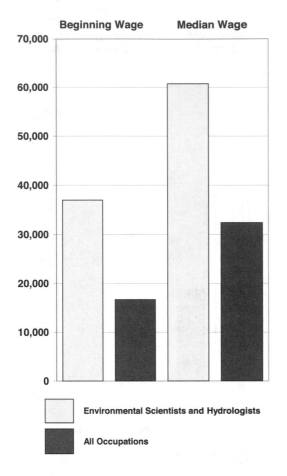

Beginning Wage   **Median Wage**

☐ Environmental Scientists and Hydrologists

■ All Occupations

Related Jobs

- Atmospheric scientists
- Biological scientists
- Chemists
- Computer network, systems, and database administrators
- Computer systems analysts
- Conservation scientists and foresters
- Engineering technicians
- Engineers
- Geoscientists
- Mathematicians
- Physicists
- Science technicians
- Surveyors, cartographers, photogrammetrists, and surveying technicians

How to Learn More

Information on training and career opportunities for environmental scientists is available from

- American Geological Institute, 4220 King St., Alexandria, VA 22302. Internet: www.agiweb.org

For information on careers in hydrology, contact

- American Institute of Hydrology, 300 Village Green Circle, Suite #201, Smyrna, GA 30080. Internet: www.aihydro.org

Information on obtaining a position as a hydrologist or an environmental protection specialist with the federal government is available at www.usajobs.opm.gov.

Why It's Hot

Environmental scientists and hydrologists will be in demand because of the need to monitor the quality of the environment, to interpret the impact of human actions on terrestrial and aquatic ecosystems, and to develop strategies for restoring ecosystems. In addition, environmental scientists will be needed to help planners develop and construct buildings, transportation corridors, and utilities that protect water resources and reflect efficient and beneficial land use.

Fitness Workers

Fitness workers lead, instruct, and motivate individuals or groups in exercise activities, including cardiovascular exercise, strength training, and stretching.

Just the Facts

Earnings: $29,210

Job Growth: 29.4%

Annual Openings: 12,380

Education and Training: Postsecondary vocational training

While at Work

Fitness workers work in health clubs, country clubs, hospitals, universities, yoga and Pilates studios, resorts, and clients' homes. Increasingly, fitness workers also are found in workplaces, where they organize and direct health and fitness programs for employees of all ages. Although gyms and health clubs offer a variety of exercise activities such as weightlifting, yoga, cardiovascular training, and karate, fitness workers typically specialize in only a few areas.

Personal trainers work one-on-one with clients either in a gym or in the client's home. They help clients assess their level of physical fitness and set and reach fitness goals. Trainers also demonstrate various exercises and help clients improve their exercise techniques. They may keep records of their clients' exercise sessions to monitor clients' progress toward physical fitness. They may also advise their clients on how to modify their lifestyle outside of the gym to improve their fitness.

Group exercise instructors conduct group exercise sessions that usually include aerobic exercise, stretching, and muscle conditioning. Cardiovascular conditioning classes are often set to music. Instructors choose and mix the music and choreograph a corresponding exercise sequence. Two increasingly popular conditioning methods taught in exercise classes are Pilates and yoga. In these classes, instructors demonstrate the different moves and positions of the particular method; they also observe students and correct those who are doing the exercises improperly. Group exercise instructors are responsible for ensuring that their classes are motivating, safe, and challenging, yet not too difficult for the participants.

> ## CONSIDER THIS...
>
> Some fitness workers may combine the duties of group exercise instructors and personal trainers, and in smaller facilities, the fitness director may teach classes and do personal training.

Fitness directors oversee the fitness-related aspects of a health club or fitness center. They create and oversee programs that meet the needs of the club's members, including new member orientations, fitness assessments, and workout incentive programs. They also select fitness equipment; coordinate personal training and group exercise programs; hire, train, and supervise fitness staff; and carry out administrative duties.

Fitness workers in smaller facilities with few employees may perform a variety of functions in addition to their fitness duties, such as tending the front desk, signing up new members, giving tours of the fitness center, writing newsletter articles, creating posters and flyers, and supervising the weight training and cardiovascular equipment areas. In larger commercial facilities, personal trainers are often required to sell their services to members and to make a specified number of sales.

Fitness instructors teach a variety of classes.

Also Known As

Many fitness instructors have job titles that reflect the specialized routine that they lead, such as *indoor cycling instructors*, *karate instructors*, *Pilates instructors*, *weight training instructors*, or *yoga instructors*. Others have more general job titles, such as *aerobics instructors*, *fitness teachers*, or *wellness coaches*.

Job Fit

Personality Type
Social-Realistic-Enterprising

Career Cluster
05 Education and Training

Skills
Social Skills

Science

Thought-Processing

Equipment/Technology Analysis

Management

Equipment Use/Maintenance

Computer Programming

Communications

Work Styles
Social Skills Orientation

Leadership

Concern for Others

Dependability

Integrity

Innovation

Self-Control

Adaptability/Flexibility

Working Conditions

Most fitness workers spend their time indoors at fitness centers and health clubs. Fitness directors and supervisors, however, typically spend most of their time in an office. Those in smaller fitness centers may split their time among office work, personal training, and teaching classes. Directors and supervisors generally engage in less physical activity than do lower-level fitness workers. Nevertheless, workers at all levels risk suffering injuries during physical activities.

Since most fitness centers are open long hours, fitness workers often work nights and weekends and even occasional holidays. Some may travel from place to place throughout the day, to different gyms or to clients' homes, to maintain a full work schedule.

Fitness workers generally enjoy a lot of autonomy. Group exercise instructors choreograph or plan their own classes, and personal trainers have the freedom to design and implement their clients' workout routines.

What's Required

For most fitness workers, certification is critical. Personal trainers usually must have certification to begin working with clients or with members of a fitness facility. Group fitness instructors may begin without a certification, but they are often encouraged or required by their employers to become certified.

Education and Training

Fitness workers usually do not receive much on-the-job training; they are expected to know how to do their jobs when they are hired. Workers may receive some organizational training to learn about the operations of their new employer. They occasionally receive specialized training if they are expected to teach or lead a specific method of exercise or focus on a particular age or ability group.

The education and training required depends on the specific type of fitness work: personal training, group fitness, or a specialization such as Pilates or yoga each need different preparation. Personal trainers often start out by taking classes to become certified. They then may begin by working alongside an experienced trainer before being allowed to train clients alone.

CONSIDER THIS...

Because the requirements vary from employer to employer, it may be helpful to contact your local fitness centers or other potential employers to find out what background they prefer before pursuing training.

Group fitness instructors often get started by participating in exercise classes until they are ready to successfully audition as instructors and begin teaching class. They also may improve their skills by taking training courses or attending fitness conventions. Most employers require instructors to work toward becoming certified.

Training for Pilates and yoga instructors is changing. Because interest in these forms of exercise has exploded in recent years, the demand for teachers has grown faster than the ability to train them properly. However, because inexperienced teachers have contributed to student injuries, there has been a push toward more standardized, rigorous requirements for teacher training.

Pilates and yoga teachers need specialized training in their particular method of exercise. For Pilates, training options range from weekend-long workshops to year-long programs, but the trend is toward requiring more training. The Pilates Method Alliance has established training standards that recommend at least 200 hours of training; the group also has standards for training schools and maintains a list of training schools that meet the requirements. However, some Pilates teachers are certified group exercise instructors who attend short Pilates workshops; currently, many fitness centers hire people with minimal Pilates training if the applicants have a fitness certification and group fitness experience.

Training requirements for yoga teachers are similar to those for Pilates teachers. Training programs range from a few days to more than 2 years. Many people get their start by taking yoga; eventually, their teachers may consider them ready to assist or to substitute teach. Some students may begin teaching their own classes when their yoga teachers think they are ready; the teachers may even provide letters of recommendation. Those who wish to pursue teaching more seriously usually pursue formal teacher training.

Currently, there are many training programs through the yoga community as well as programs through the fitness industry. The Yoga Alliance has established training standards requiring at least 200 training hours, with a specified number of hours in areas including techniques, teaching methodology, anatomy, physiology, and philosophy. The Yoga Alliance also registers schools that train students to its standards. Because some schools may meet the standards but not be registered, prospective students should check the requirements and decide if particular schools meet them.

An increasing number of employers require fitness workers to have a bachelor's degree in a field related to health or fitness, such as exercise science or physical education. Some employers allow workers to substitute a college degree for certification, but most employers who require a bachelor's degree also require certification.

Most personal trainers must obtain certification in the fitness field to gain employment. Group fitness instructors do not necessarily need certification to begin working. The most important characteristic that an employer looks for in a new fitness instructor is the ability to plan and lead a class that is motivating and safe. However, most organizations encourage their group instructors to become certified over time, and many require it.

In the fitness field, there are many organizations that offer certification. Becoming certified by one of the top certification organizations is increasingly important, especially for personal trainers.

Most certifying organizations require candidates to have a high school diploma, be certified in cardiopulmonary resuscitation (CPR), and pass an exam. All certification exams have a written component, and some also have a practical component. The exams measure knowledge of human physiology, proper exercise techniques, assessment of client fitness levels, and development of appropriate exercise programs. There is no particular training program required for certifications; candidates may prepare however they prefer. Certifying organizations do offer study materials, including books, CD-ROMs, other audio and visual materials, and exam preparation workshops and seminars, but exam candidates are not required to purchase materials to take exams.

Certification generally is good for 2 years, after which workers must become recertified by attending continuing education classes or conferences, writing articles, or giving presentations. Some organizations offer more advanced certification, requiring an associate or bachelor's degree in an exercise-related subject for individuals interested in training athletes, working with people who are injured or ill, or advising clients on general health.

Pilates and yoga instructors usually do not need group exercise certifications to maintain employment. It is more important that they have specialized training in their particular method of exercise. However, the Pilates Method Alliance does offer certification.

Postsecondary Programs to Consider

- Health and physical education, general
- Physical education teaching and coaching
- Sport and fitness administration/management

Additional Qualifications

People planning fitness careers should be outgoing, excellent communicators, good at motivating people, and sensitive to the needs of others. Excellent health and physical fitness are important due to the physical nature of the job. Those who wish to be personal trainers in a large commercial fitness center should have strong sales skills. All personal trainers should have the personality and motivation to attract and retain clients.

School Subjects to Study

- Algebra
- Biology
- English
- Public speaking

Moving Up

A bachelor's degree in exercise science, physical education, kinesiology (the study of muscles, especially the mechanics of human motion), or a related area, along with experience, usually is required to advance to management positions in a health club or fitness center. Some organizations require a master's degree. As in other occupations, managerial skills are also needed to advance to supervisory or managerial positions. College courses in management, business administration, accounting, and personnel management may be helpful, but many fitness companies have corporate universities in which they train employees for management positions.

Personal trainers may advance to head trainer, with responsibility for hiring and overseeing the personal training staff and for bringing in new personal training clients. Group fitness instructors may be promoted to group exercise director, responsible for hiring instructors and coordinating exercise classes. Later, a worker might become the fitness director, who manages the fitness budget and staff. Workers might also become the general manager, whose main focus is the financial aspects of an organization, particularly setting and achieving sales goals; in a small fitness center, however, the general manager is usually involved with all aspects of running the facility. Some workers go into business for themselves and open their own fitness centers.

Employment

Fitness workers held about 261,100, jobs in 2008. About 61 percent of all personal trainers and group exercise instructors worked in fitness and recreational sports centers, including health clubs. Another 13 percent worked in civic and social organizations. About 9 percent of fitness workers were self-employed; many of these were personal trainers, while others were group fitness instructors working on a contract basis with fitness centers. Many fitness jobs are part time, and many workers hold multiple jobs, teaching or doing personal training at several different fitness centers and at clients' homes.

Job Prospects

Employment of fitness workers is expected to increase 29 percent in the 10-year period ending 2018, which is much faster than the average for all occupations.

Aging baby boomers, one group that increasingly is becoming concerned with staying healthy and physically fit, will be the main driver of employment growth in fitness workers. An additional factor is the combination of a reduction in the number of physical education programs in schools with parents' growing concern about childhood obesity. This factor will increase the need for fitness workers to work with children in nonschool settings, such as health clubs. Increasingly, parents also are hiring personal trainers for their children, and the number of weight-training gyms for children is expected to continue to grow. Health club membership among young adults has grown steadily as well, driven by concern with physical fitness and by rising incomes.

CONSIDER THIS...

Part-time fitness jobs will be easier to find than full-time jobs.

As health clubs strive to provide more personalized service to keep their members motivated, they will continue to offer personal training and a wide variety of group exercise classes. Participation in yoga and Pilates is expected to continue to increase, driven partly by the aging population, which demands low-impact forms of exercise and seeks relief from arthritis and other ailments.

Opportunities are expected to be good for fitness workers because demand for these workers is expected to remain strong in health clubs, fitness facilities, and other settings in which fitness workers are concentrated. In addition, many job openings will stem from the need to replace the large numbers of workers who leave these occupations each year. People with degrees in fitness-related subjects will have better opportunities because clients prefer to work with people they perceive as higher quality trainers. Trainers who incorporate new technology and wellness issues as part of their services may be in more demand.

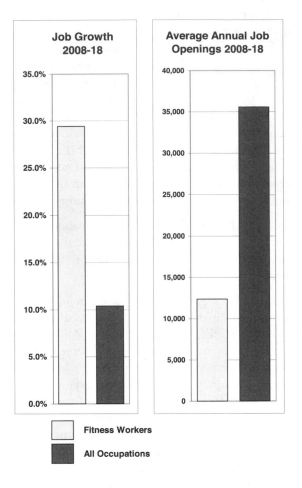

Income

Median annual earnings of fitness trainers and aerobics instructors in May 2008 were $29,210. The middle 50 percent earned between $19,610 and $44,420. The bottom 10 percent earned less than $16,120, while the top 10 percent earned $60,760 or more. These figures do not include the earnings of the self-employed. Earnings of successful self-employed personal trainers can be much higher. In the industries employing the largest numbers of fitness workers, the 2008 median annual earnings were $32,140 in other general medical and surgical hospitals, $30,610 in fitness and recreational sports centers, $30,200 in local government, $25,110 in civic and social organizations, and $24,230 in other schools and instruction.

Because many fitness workers work part time, they often do not receive benefits such as health insurance or retirement plans from their employers. They are able to use fitness facilities at no cost, however.

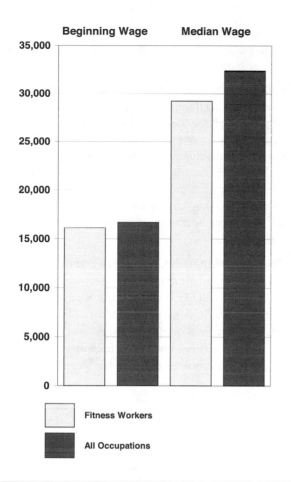

Beginning Wage   **Median Wage**

☐ Fitness Workers

■ All Occupations

Related Jobs

- Athletes, coaches, umpires, and related workers
- Dietitians and nutritionists
- Physical therapists
- Recreation workers

How to Learn More

For more information about fitness careers and universities and other institutions offering programs in health and fitness, contact

- IDEA Health and Fitness Association, 10455 Pacific Center Court., San Diego, CA 92121-4339.

- National Strength and Conditioning Association, 1885 Bob Johnson Drive, Colorado Springs, CO 80906. Internet: www.nsca-lift.org

For information about personal trainer and group fitness instructor certifications, contact

- American College of Sports Medicine, P.O. Box 1440, Indianapolis, IN 46206-1440. Internet: www.acsm.org

- American Council on Exercise, 4851 Paramount Dr., San Diego, CA 92123. Internet: www.acefitness.org

- National Academy of Sports Medicine, 26632 Agoura Rd., Calabasas, CA 91302. Internet: www.nasm.org

- NSCA Certification Commission, 3333 Landmark Circle, Lincoln, NE 68504. Internet: www.nsca-cc.org

For information about Pilates certification and training programs, contact

- Pilates Method Alliance, P.O. Box 370906, Miami, FL 33137-0906. Internet: www.pilatesmethodalliance.org

For information on yoga teacher training programs, contact

- Yoga Alliance, 7801 Old Branch Ave., Suite 400, Clinton, MD 20735. Internet: www.yogaalliance.org

To find accredited fitness certification programs, contact

- National Commission for Certifying Agencies, 2025 M St. NW, Suite 800, Washington, DC 20036. Internet: www.noca.org/ncca/accredorg.htm

For information about health clubs and sports clubs, contact

- International Health, Racquet, and Sportsclub Association, 263 Summer St., Boston, MA 02210. Internet: www.ihrsa.org

Why It's Hot

Fitness workers are expected to gain jobs because an increasing number of people are spending time and money on fitness and more businesses are recognizing the benefits of health and fitness programs for their employees.

Heating, Air-Conditioning, and Refrigeration Mechanics and Installers

Heating, air-conditioning, and refrigeration mechanics and installers set up or repair heating, central air conditioning, or refrigeration systems.

Just the Facts

Earnings: $39,680

Job Growth: 28.1%

Annual Openings: 13,620

Education and Training: Long-term on-the-job training

While at Work

Heating and air-conditioning systems control the temperature, humidity, and the total air quality in residential, commercial, industrial, and other buildings. Refrigeration systems make it possible to store and transport food, medicine, and other perishable items. Heating, air-conditioning, and refrigeration mechanics and installers install these systems and keep them working. Because heating, ventilation, air-conditioning, and refrigeration systems often are referred to as HVACR systems, these workers also may be called *HVACR technicians*.

These technicians must work on many mechanical, electrical, and electronic components, such as motors, compressors, pumps, fans, ducts, pipes, thermostats, and switches. Technicians must be able to maintain, diagnose, and correct problems throughout the entire system. To do this, they adjust system controls to recommended settings and test the performance of the system using special tools and test equipment.

Technicians often specialize in either installation or maintenance and repair, although they are trained to do both. They also may specialize in doing heating work or air-conditioning or refrigeration work. Some specialize in one type of equipment—for example, hydronics (water-based heating systems), solar panels, or commercial refrigeration.

Some technicians also sell service contracts to their clients. Service contracts provide for regular maintenance of the heating and cooling systems and they help to reduce the seasonal fluctuations of this type of work. This aspect of the job requires technicians to have good people skills.

Technicians follow blueprints or other specifications to install oil, gas, electric, solid-fuel, and multiple-fuel heating systems and air-conditioning systems. After putting the equipment in place, they install fuel and water supply lines, air ducts and vents, pumps, and other components. They may connect electrical wiring and controls and check the unit for proper operation.

After a furnace or air-conditioning unit has been installed, technicians often perform routine maintenance and repair work to keep the systems operating efficiently. They may adjust burners and blowers and check for leaks. If the system is not operating properly, they check the thermostat, burner nozzles, controls or other parts to diagnose and correct the problem.

During the summer, when heating systems are not being used, *heating equipment technicians* do maintenance work, such as replacing filters, ducts, and other parts of the system that may accumulate dust and impurities during the operating season. During the winter, *air-conditioning mechanics* inspect the systems and do required maintenance, such as overhauling compressors.

Refrigeration mechanics install, service, and repair industrial and commercial refrigerating systems and a variety of refrigeration equipment. They follow blueprints, and manufacturers' instructions to install motors, compressors, condensing units, evaporators, piping, and other components. They connect this equipment to the ductwork, refrigerant lines, and electrical power source. After making the connections, they charge the system with refrigerant, check it for proper operation and leaks, and program control systems.

Heating, air-conditioning, and refrigeration mechanics and installers are adept at using a variety of tools, including hammers, wrenches, electric drills, pipe cutters, measurement gauges, and acetylene torches. They use voltmeters, thermometers, pressure gauges, and other testing devices to check airflow, refrigerant pressure, electrical circuits, burners, and other components.

Heating, air-conditioning, and refrigeration mechanics maintain systems.

Also Known As

Solar thermal installers and technicians set up and maintain equipment that soaks up sunrays to heat water or indoor spaces. They need many of the same skills as technicians who work with gas, oil, and electric heat, plus knowledge of how to size and install systems that can draw sufficient heat from the sun.

Some geothermal technicians install and service heat-pump equipment that extracts and concentrates warmth from groundwater or the soil. Usually these installations reverse the process in summertime and provide air conditioning.

Job Fit

Personality Type
Realistic-Conventional

Career Cluster
02 Architecture and Construction

Skills
Equipment Use/Maintenance
Science
Mathematics
Equipment/Technology Analysis
Social Skills
Management
Thought-Processing
Communications
Computer Programming

Work Styles
Leadership
Independence
Persistence
Initiative
Cooperation
Self-Control
Dependability
Stress Tolerance

Working Conditions

Heating, air-conditioning, and refrigeration mechanics and installers work anywhere there is climate-control equipment that needs to be installed, repaired, or serviced. They may be assigned to specific job sites at the beginning of each day or may be dispatched to a variety of locations if they are making service calls.

Technicians may work outside in cold or hot weather or in buildings that are uncomfortable because the air-conditioning or heating equipment is broken. In addition, technicians might work in awkward or cramped po-

sitions and sometimes are required to work in high places. Hazards include electrical shock, burns, muscle strains, and other injuries from handling heavy equipment.

The majority of mechanics and installers work at least a 40-hour week. During peak seasons, they often work overtime or irregular hours. Maintenance workers, including those who provide maintenance services under contract, often work evening or weekend shifts and are on call. Most employers try to provide a full work week year-round by scheduling both installation and maintenance work, and many manufacturers and contractors now provide or even require year-round service contracts.

CONSIDER THIS...
The release of refrigerants can be harmful to the environment. When servicing equipment, technicians must use care to conserve, recover, and recycle the refrigerants used in air-conditioning and refrigeration systems. They must recycle it for reuse or dispose of it properly according to codes and standards.

CONSIDER THIS...
Inhalation of refrigerants when working in confined spaces is a possible hazard. Appropriate safety equipment is necessary when handling refrigerants because contact can cause skin damage, frostbite, or blindness.

What's Required

Because of the increasing sophistication of heating, air-conditioning, and refrigeration systems, employers prefer to hire those who have completed technical school training or a formal apprenticeship. Some mechanics and installers, however, still learn the trade informally on the job.

Education and Training

Many secondary and postsecondary technical and trade schools, junior and community colleges, and the U.S. Armed Forces offer 6-month to 2-year programs in heating, air-conditioning, and refrigeration. Students study theory of temperature control, equipment design and construction, and electronics. They also learn the basics of installation, maintenance, and repair. Three accrediting agencies have set academic standards for HVACR programs: HVAC Excellence, the National Center for Construction Education and Research, and the Partnership for Air-Conditioning, Heating, and Refrigeration Accreditation. After completing these programs, new technicians generally need between an additional 6 months and 2 years of field experience before they are considered proficient.

Many technicians train through apprenticeships. Apprenticeship programs frequently are run by joint committees representing local chapters of the Air-Conditioning Contractors of America, the Mechanical Contractors Association of America, Plumbing-Heating-Cooling Contractors—National Association, and locals of the sheet metal workers' International Association or the United Association of Journeymen and Apprentices of the Plumbing and Pipefitting Industry of the United States and Canada. Local chapters of the Associated Builders and Contractors and the National Association of Home Builders sponsor other apprenticeship programs.

Formal apprenticeship programs normally last 3 to 5 years and combine paid on-the-job training with classroom instruction. Classes include subjects such as the use and care of tools, safety practices, blueprint reading, and the theory and design of heating, ventilation, air-conditioning, and refrigeration systems. In addition to understanding how systems work, technicians must learn about refrigerant products and the legislation and regulations that govern their use.

Those who acquire their skills on the job usually begin by assisting experienced technicians. They may begin by performing simple tasks such as carrying materials, insulating refrigerant lines, or cleaning furnaces. In time, they move on to more difficult tasks, such as cutting and soldering pipes and sheet metal and checking electrical and electronic circuits.

Heating, air-conditioning, and refrigeration mechanics and installers are required to be licensed by some states and localities. Requirements for licensure vary greatly, but all states or localities that require a license have a test that must be passed.

In addition, all technicians who purchase or work with refrigerants must be certified in their proper handling. To become certified to purchase and handle refrigerants, technicians must pass a written examination specific to the type of work in which they specialize. The three possible areas of certification are: Type I—servicing small appliances; Type II—high-pressure refrigerants; and Type III—low-pressure refrigerants. Exams are administered by organizations approved by the U.S. Environmental Protection Agency.

Postsecondary Programs to Consider

- Heating, air conditioning, ventilation, and refrigeration technology/technician training (ACH/ACR/ACHR/HRAC/HVAC)
- Solar energy technology/technician training

Additional Qualifications

Some knowledge of plumbing or electrical work is helpful. A basic understanding of electronics is becoming more important because of the increasing use of electronics in equipment controls. Because technicians frequently deal directly with the public, they should be courteous and tactful, especially when dealing with an aggravated customer. They also should be in good physical condition because they sometimes have to lift and move heavy equipment.

School Subjects to Study

- Blueprint reading
- Chemistry
- Computer science
- Electronics
- English
- Geometry
- Mechanical drawing
- Physics
- Shop math
- Trigonometry

Moving Up

Throughout the learning process, technicians may have to take a number of tests that measure their skills. For those with relevant coursework and less than 1 year of experience, the industry has developed a series of exams to test basic competency in residential heating and cooling, light commercial heating and cooling, and commercial refrigeration. These are referred to as "entry-level" certification exams and are commonly conducted at both secondary and postsecondary technical and trade schools.

HVACR technicians who have at least 1 year of experience performing installations and 2 years of experience performing maintenance and repair can take a number of different tests to certify their competency in working with spe-

CONSIDER THIS...

cific types of equipment. These tests are offered through the Refrigeration Service Engineers Society, HVAC Excellence, Carbon Monoxide Safety Association, Air Conditioning and Refrigeration Safety Coalition, and North American Technician Excellence, Inc., among others. Employers increasingly recommend taking and passing these tests and obtaining certification; doing so may increase advancement opportunities.

Advancement usually takes the form of higher wages. Some technicians, however, may advance to positions as supervisor or service manager. Others may move into sales and marketing. Still others may become building superintendents, cost estimators, system test and balance specialists, or, with the necessary certification, teachers. Those with sufficient money and managerial skill can open their own contracting business.

Employment

Heating, air-conditioning, and refrigeration mechanics and installers held about 308,200 jobs in 2008; about 54 percent worked for plumbing, heating, and air-conditioning contractors. The rest were employed in a variety of industries throughout the country, reflecting a widespread dependence on climate-control systems. Some worked for refrigeration and air-conditioning service and repair shops, schools, and stores that sell heating and air-conditioning systems. Local governments, the federal government, hospitals, office buildings, and other organizations that operate large air-conditioning, refrigeration, or heating systems also employed these workers. About 16 percent of these workers were self-employed.

Job Prospects

Employment of heating, air-conditioning, and refrigeration mechanics and installers is projected to increase 28 percent in the 10-year period ending 2018, much faster than the average for all occupations. As the population and stock of buildings grows, so does the demand for residential, commercial, and industrial climate-control systems. Residential HVACR systems generally need replacement after 10 to 15 years; the large number of homes built in recent years will enter this replacement timeframe by 2018. The increased complexity of HVACR systems, which increases the possibility that equipment may malfunction, also will create opportunities for service technicians. A growing focus on improving indoor air quality and the increasing use of refrigerated equipment by a rising number of stores and gasoline stations that sell food should also create more jobs for heating, air-conditioning, and refrigeration technicians.

Concern for the environment and the need to reduce energy consumption overall has prompted the development of new energy-saving heating and air-conditioning systems. This emphasis on better energy management is expected to lead to the replacement of older systems and the installation of newer, more efficient systems in existing homes and buildings. Also, demand for maintenance and service work should rise as businesses and homeowners strive to keep increasingly complex systems operating at peak efficiency. Regulations prohibiting the discharge and production of older types of refrigerants that pollute the atmosphere should continue to result in the need to replace many existing air conditioning systems or to modify them to use new environmentally safe refrigerants. The pace of replacement in the commercial and indus-

CONSIDER THIS...

One form of heating that is often forgotten is wood-burning stoves. Some workers specialize in installing and maintaining these heaters. Woodstoves used to be inefficient and emit large quantities of particulate matter, but recent technologies have gained the approval of the Environmental Protection Agency. Wood also has the advantage of being a renewable resource that, while growing, absorbs as much carbon dioxide gas as it produces in combustion. Some of the most efficient stoves burn pellets made from sawdust, a waste material. Because woodstoves have hot exteriors and are usually located in living quarters, rather than in the basement, technicians need to be trained in installation procedures that reduce fire hazards.

trial sectors will quicken if Congress or individual states change tax rules designed to encourage companies to buy new HVACR equipment.

Job prospects for heating, air-conditioning, and refrigeration mechanics and installers are expected to be excellent, particularly for those who have completed training from an accredited technical school or a formal apprenticeship. A growing number of retirements of highly skilled technicians are expected to generate many more job openings. Many contractors have reported problems finding enough workers to meet the demand for service and installation of HVACR systems.

Technicians who specialize in installation work may experience periods of unemployment when the level of new construction activity declines, but maintenance and repair work usually remains relatively stable. People and businesses depend on their climate-control or refrigeration systems and must keep them in good working order, regardless of economic conditions.

In light of the complexity of new computer-controlled HVACR systems in modern high-rise buildings, prospects should be best for those who can acquire and demonstrate computer competency. Training in new techniques that improve energy efficiency will also make it much easier to enter the occupation.

Income

Median wage-and-salary earnings of heating, air-conditioning, and refrigeration mechanics and installers were $19.08 per hour in May 2008. The middle 50 percent earned between $14.94 and $24.84 an hour. The lowest 10 percent earned less than $12.19, and the top 10 percent earned more than $30.59. Broken down by industry, median hourly earnings for heating, air-conditioning, and refrigeration mechanics and installers were $22.18 in hardware, and plumbing and heating equipment and supplies merchant wholesalers; $20.98 in commercial and industrial machinery and equipment (except automotive and electronic) repair and maintenance; $20.03 in direct selling establishments; and 18.23 in plumbing, heating, and air-conditioning contractors.

About 15 percent of heating, air-conditioning, and refrigeration mechanics and installers are members of a union. The unions to which the greatest numbers of mechanics and installers belong are the Sheet Metal Workers International Association and the United Association of Journeymen and Apprentices of the Plumbing and Pipefitting Industry of the United States and Canada.

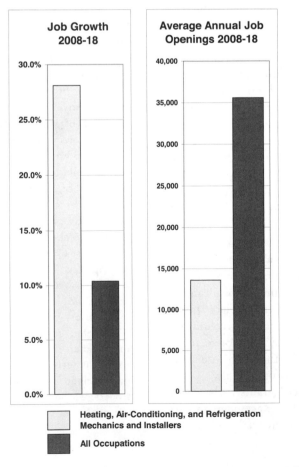

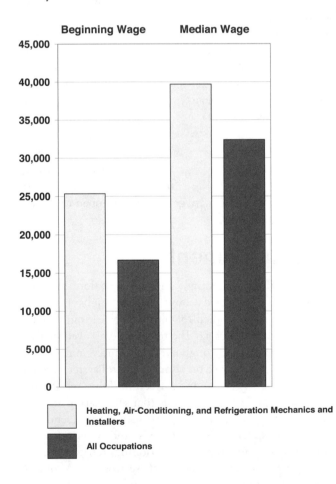

Related Jobs

- Boilermakers
- Electricians
- Energy conservation workers
- Home appliance repairers
- Pipelayers, plumbers, pipefitters, and steamfitters
- Sheet metal workers

How to Learn More

For more information about opportunities for training, certification, and employment in this trade, contact local vocational and technical schools; local heating, air-conditioning, and refrigeration contractors; a local office of the unions or organizations previously mentioned; a local joint union-management apprenticeship committee; or the nearest office of the state employment service or apprenticeship agency.

For information on career opportunities, training, and technician certification, contact the following:

- Air-Conditioning Contractors of America, 2800 Shirlington Rd., Suite 300, Arlington, VA 22206. Internet: www.acca.org
- Air-Conditioning and Refrigeration Institute, 4100 North Fairfax Dr., Suite 200, Arlington, VA 22203. Internet: www. coolcareers.org and www.ari.org
- Associated Builders and Contractors, Workforce Development Department, 4250 North Fairfax Dr., 9th Floor, Arlington, VA 22203. Internet: www.trytools.org
- Carbon Monoxide Safety Association, P.O. Box 669, Eastlake, CO 80614. Internet: www.cosafety.org
- Home Builders Institute, National Association of Home Builders, 1201 15th St. NW, 6th Floor, Washington, DC 20005. Internet: www.hbi.org
- HVAC Excellence, P.O. Box 491, Mt. Prospect, IL 60056. Internet: www.hvacexcellence.org
- Mechanical Contractors Association of America, Mechanical Service Contractors of America, 1385 Piccard Dr., Rockville, MD 20850. Internet: www.mcaa.org and www.mcaa.org/msca
- National Center for Construction Education and Research, P.O. Box 141104, Gainesville, FL 32601. Internet: www. nccer.org
- National Occupational Competency Testing Institute. Internet: www.nocti.org
- North American Technician Excellence, 4100 North Fairfax Dr., Suite 210, Arlington, VA 22203. Internet: www.natex.org
- Plumbing-Heating-Cooling Contractors, 180 S. Washington, St., P.O. Box 6808, Falls Church, VA 22046. Internet: www. phccweb.org org
- Refrigeration Service Engineers Society, 1666 Rand Rd., Des Plaines, IL 60016. Internet: www.rses.org

- Sheet Metal and Air-Conditioning Contractors National Association, 4201 Lafayette Center Dr., Chantilly, VA 20151. Internet: www.smacna.org
- United Association of Journeymen and Apprentices of the Plumbing and Pipefitting Industry, 901 Massachusetts Ave. NW, Washington, DC 20001. Internet: www.ua.org

Why It's Hot

As old heating and air-conditioning units wear out and new technologies promise greater efficiency, homeowners will be hiring these technicians to install the latest equipment. In commercial settings, managers are becoming aware of the cost savings from high-efficiency heating and cooling systems. These units are now so complex that do-it-yourself repairs are no longer an option; trained service technicians will have steady work.

Home Health Aides and Personal and Home Care Aides

Home health aides and personal and home care aides assist elderly or disabled adults with daily living activities at the person's home or in a daytime nonresidential facility.

Just the Facts

Earnings: $19,938

Job Growth: 48.1%

Annual Openings: 103,050

Education and Training: Short-term on-the-job training

While at Work

Many elderly adults and people who are disabled, chronically ill, or cognitively impaired need assistance with daily living tasks and with routine health care. Home health aides and personal and home care aides assist these people, assist people in hospices and day programs, and help individuals with disabilities go to work and remain engaged in their communities.

Aides provide light housekeeping and homemaking tasks such as laundry, change bed linens, shop for food, plan and prepare meals. Aides also may help clients get out of bed, bathe, dress, and groom. Some accompany clients to doctors' appointments or on other errands.

Aides' daily routine may vary. They may go to the same home every day or week for months or even years and often visit four or five clients on the same day. However, some aides may work solely with one client who is in need of more care and attention. In some situations, this may involve working with other aides in shifts so that the client has an aide throughout the day and night. Aides also work with clients, particularly younger adults at schools or at the client's work site.

In general, home health aides and personal and home care aides have similar job duties. However, there are some small differences.

Home health aides typically work for certified home health or hospice agencies that receive government funding and therefore must comply with regulations to receive funding. This means that they must work under the direct supervision of a medical professional, usually a nurse. These aides keep records of services performed and of clients' condition and progress. They report changes in the client's condition to the supervisor or case manager. Aides also work with therapists and other medical staff.

Home health aides may provide some basic health-related services, such as checking patients' pulse rate, temperature, and respiration rate. They also may help with simple prescribed exercises and assist with medications administration. Occasionally, they change simple dressings, give massage, provide skin care, or assist with braces and artificial limbs. With special training, experienced home health aides also may assist with medical equipment such as ventilators, which help patients breathe.

Personal and home care aides—also called *homemakers, caregivers, companions,* and *personal attendants*—work for various public and private agencies that provide home care services. In these agencies, caregivers are likely supervised by a licensed nurse, social worker, or other nonmedical managers. Aides receive detailed instructions explaining when to visit clients and what services to perform for them. However, personal and home care aides work independently, with only periodic visits by their supervisors. These caregivers may work with only one client each day or five or six clients once a day every week or every 2 weeks.

Some aides are hired directly by the patient or the patient's family. In these situations, personal and home care aides are supervised and assigned tasks directly by the patient or the patient's family.

Aides may also work with individuals who are developmentally or intellectually disabled. These workers are often called *direct support professionals* and they may assist in implementing a behavior plan, teaching self-care skills and providing employment support, as well as providing a range of other personal assistance services.

Home health aides provide basic health-related services to patients.

Also Known As

Some job titles for these workers indicate a level of certification, such as *Certified Nursing Assistant* (CNA), *licensed nursing assistant,* or *State Tested Nursing Assistant* (STNA).

Job Fit

Personality Type
Social-Realistic

Career Clusters
08 Health Science
10 Human Services

Skills
Social Skills
Communications
Computer Programming
Thought-Processing
Science

Work Styles
Concern for Others
Self-Control

Working Conditions

Work as an aide can be physically demanding. Aides must guard against back injury because they may have to move patients into and out of bed or help them to stand or walk. Aides also may face hazards from minor infections and exposure to communicable diseases, such as hepatitis, but can avoid infections by following proper procedures. Because mechanical lifting devices available in institutional settings are not as frequently available in patients' homes, home health aides must take extra care to avoid injuries resulting from overexertion when they assist patients. These workers experienced a larger-than-average number of work-related injuries or illnesses.

Most aides work with a number of different patients, each job lasting a few hours, days, or weeks. They often visit multiple patients on the same day. Surroundings differ by case. Some homes are neat and pleasant, whereas others are untidy and depressing. Some clients are pleasant and cooperative; others are angry, abusive, depressed, or otherwise difficult.

CONSIDER THIS...

Aides often perform tasks that some may consider unpleasant, such as emptying bedpans and changing soiled bed linens. The patients they care for may be disoriented, irritable, or uncooperative. Although their work can be emotionally demanding, many aides gain satisfaction from assisting those in need.

Home health aides and personal and home care aides generally work alone, with periodic visits from their supervisor. They receive detailed instructions explaining when to visit patients and what services to perform. Aides are responsible for getting to patients' homes, and they may spend a good portion of the work day traveling from one patient to another.

What's Required

Home health aides must receive formal training and pass a competency test to work for certified home health or hospice agencies that receive reimbursement from Medicare or Medicaid. Personal and home care aides, however, face a wide range of requirements, which vary from state to state.

Education and Training

In their training, aides are instructed on how to cook for a client, including on special diets. Furthermore, they may be trained in basic housekeeping tasks, such as making a bed and keeping the home sanitary and safe for the client. Generally, they are taught how to respond to an emergency, learning basic safety techniques. Employers also may train aides to conduct themselves in a professional and courteous manner while in a client's home. Some clients prefer that tasks are done a certain way and will teach the aide. A competency evaluation may be required to ensure that the aide can perform the required tasks.

Home health aides who work for agencies that receive reimbursement from Medicare or Medicaid must receive a minimum level of training. They must complete both a training program consisting of a minimum of 75 hours and a competency evaluation or state certification program. Training includes information regarding personal hygiene, safe transfer techniques, reading and recording vital signs, infection control, and basic nutrition. Aides may take a competency exam to become certified without taking any of the training. At a minimum, 16 hours of supervised practical training are required before an aide has direct contact with a resident. These certification requirements represent the minimum, as outlined by the federal government. Some states may require additional hours of training to become certified.

CONSIDER THIS...

Home health aides are generally not required to have a high school diploma. They usually are trained on the job by registered nurses, licensed practical nurses, or experienced aides.

Personal and home care aides are not required to be certified, but the National Association for Home Care and Hospice (NAHC) offers national certification, a demonstration that the aide has met industry standards. Certification requires the completion of 75 hours of training; observation and documentation of 17 skills for competency, assessed by a registered nurse; and the passing of a written exam developed by NAHC.

Postsecondary Programs to Consider

- Health aide training
- Home health aide/home attendant training
- Nurse/nursing assistant/aide and patient care assistant
- Psychiatric/mental health services technician

Additional Qualifications

Aides should have a desire to help people. They should be responsible, compassionate, patient, emotionally stable, and cheerful. In addition, aides should be tactful, honest, and discreet, because they work in private homes. Aides also must be in good health. A physical examination, including state-mandated tests for tuberculosis and other diseases, may be required. A criminal background check and a good driving record also may be required for employment.

School Subjects to Study

- Algebra
- Biology
- Chemistry
- Computer science
- English
- Foreign language
- Geometry
- Public speaking
- Trigonometry

Moving Up

Advancement for home health aides and personal and home care aides is limited. In some agencies, workers start out performing homemaker duties, such as cleaning. With experience and training, they may take on more personal care duties. Some aides choose to receive additional training to become nursing aides, licensed practical nurses, or registered nurses. Some may start their own home care agency or work as a self-employed aide. Self-employed aides have no agency affiliation or supervision and accept clients, set fees, and arrange work schedules on their own.

Employment

Home health aides and personal and home care aides held about 1.7 million jobs in 2008. The majority of jobs were in home health-care services, individual and family services, residential care facilities, and private households.

Job Prospects

Employment of home health aides is projected to grow by 50 percent in the 10-year period ending 2018, which is much faster than the average for all occupations. Employment of personal and home care aides is expected to grow by 46 percent in the 10-year period ending in 2018, which is much faster than the average for all occupations. For both occupations, the expected growth is due, in large part, to the projected rise in the number of elderly people, an age group that often has mounting health problems and that needs some assistance with daily activities. The elderly and other clients, such as the mentally disabled, increasingly rely on home care.

This trend reflects several developments. Inpatient care in hospitals and nursing homes can be extremely expensive, so more patients return to their homes from these facilities as quickly as possible in order to contain costs. Patients who need assistance with everyday tasks and household chores rather than medical care can reduce medical expenses by returning to their homes. Furthermore, most patients—particularly the elderly—prefer care in their homes rather than in nursing homes or other in-patient facilities. This development is aided by the realization that treatment can be more effective in familiar surroundings.

In addition to job openings created by the increased demand for these workers, replacement needs are expected to lead to many openings. The relatively low skill requirements, low pay, and high emotional demands of the work result in high replacement needs. For these same reasons, many people are reluctant to seek jobs in the occupation. Therefore, persons who are interested in and suited for this work—particularly those with experience or training as personal care, home health, or nursing aides—should have excellent job prospects.

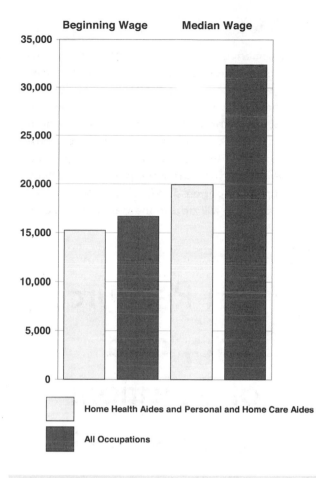

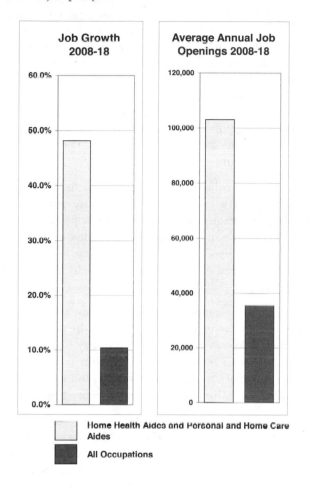

Income

Median hourly wages of wage-and-salary personal and home care aides were $9.22 in May 2008. The middle 50 percent earned between $7.81 and $10.98 an hour. The lowest 10 percent earned less than $6.84, and the highest 10 percent earned more than $12.33 an hour.

Median hourly wages of home health aides were $9.84 in May 2008. The middle 50 percent earned between $8.52 and $11.69 an hour. The lowest 10 percent earned less than $7.65, and the highest 10 percent earned more than $13.93 an hour.

Related Jobs

- Child care workers
- Licensed practical and licensed vocational nurses
- Medical assistants
- Nursing and psychiatric aides
- Occupational therapist assistants and aides
- Personal and home care aides
- Physical therapist assistants and aides
- Radiation therapists
- Registered nurses

How to Learn More

Information on licensing requirements for nursing and home health aides, as well as lists of state-approved nursing aide programs, are available from state departments of public health, departments of occupational licensing, boards of nursing, and home care associations.

For information about voluntary credentials for personal and home care aides, contact

- National Association for Home Care and Hospice, 228 7th St. SE., Washington, DC 20003. Internet: www.nahc.org

Why It's Hot

This is America's hottest career. Nowadays, hospitals often follow a practice that people sometimes call "24 and Out the Door." Patients are sent home as quickly as possible; many are treated as outpatients and never come near a hospital bed. As a result, most health care now takes place in the home, creating a huge need for workers to look after people in that setting. The rapid expansion of the elderly segment of the population will add to the demand for home care aides.

Human Resources, Training, and Labor Relations Managers and Specialists

Human resources, training, and labor relations managers and specialists plan, direct, or coordinate activities and staff of an organization to deal with policies and practices for compensation, benefits, training, and development within the organization.

Just the Facts

Earnings: $57,303

Job Growth: 21.8%

Annual Openings: 42,730

Education and Training: Bachelor's degree

Bachelor's or higher degree, plus work experience

▉ While at Work

Every organization wants to attract, motivate, and retain the most qualified employees and match them to jobs for which they are best suited. Human resources, training, and labor relations managers and specialists provide this connection. In the past, these workers performed the administrative function of an organization, such as handling employee benefits questions or recruiting, interviewing, and hiring new staff in accordance with policies established by top management. Today's human resources workers manage these tasks, but increasingly they consult with top executives regarding strategic planning. They have moved from behind-the-scenes staff work to leading the company in suggesting and changing policies.

> **CONSIDER THIS...**
> Although some jobs in the human resources field require only limited contact with people outside the human resources office, dealing with people is an important part of the job.

In an effort to enhance morale and productivity, limit job turnover, and help organizations increase performance and improve results, these workers also help their companies effectively use employee skills, provide training and development opportunities to improve those skills, and increase employees' satisfaction with their jobs and working conditions.

There are many types of human resources, training, and labor relations managers and specialists. In a small organization, a *human resources generalist* may handle all aspects of human resources work and thus require an extensive range of knowledge. The responsibilities of human resources generalists can vary widely, depending on their employer's needs.

In a large corporation, the *director of human resources* may supervise several departments, each headed by an experienced manager who most likely specializes in one human resources activity, such as employment and placement, compensation and benefits, training and development, or labor relations. The director may report to a top human resources executive.

Employment and placement managers supervise the recruitment, hiring, and separation of employees. They also supervise employment, recruitment, and placement specialists, including employment interviewers. *Employment, recruitment, and placement specialists* recruit and place workers.

Recruitment specialists maintain contacts within the community and may travel considerably, often to job fairs and college campuses, to search for promising job applicants. Recruiters screen, interview, and occasionally test applicants. They also may check references and extend job offers. These workers must be thoroughly familiar with their organization, the work that is done, and the human resources policies of their company in order to discuss wages, working conditions, and advancement opportunities with prospective employees. They also must stay informed about equal employment opportunity (EEO) and affirmative action guidelines and laws, such as the Americans with Disabilities Act.

Employment interviewers—whose many job titles include *human resources consultants*, *human resources development specialists*, and *human resources coordinators*—help to match employers with qualified jobseekers. Similarly, *employer relations representatives*, who usually work in government agencies or college career centers, maintain working relationships with prospective employers and promote the use of public employment programs and services.

Compensation, benefits, and job analysis specialists administer compensation programs for employers and may specialize in specific areas such as pensions or position classifications. For example, *job analysts*, occasionally called *position classifiers*, collect and examine detailed information about job duties in order to prepare job descriptions. These descriptions explain the duties, training, and skills that each job requires. Whenever a large organization introduces a new job or reviews existing jobs, it calls upon the expert knowledge of job analysts.

Occupational analysts research occupational classification systems and study the effects of industry and occupational trends on worker relationships. They may serve as technical liaisons between companies or departments, government, and labor unions.

Establishing and maintaining a firm's pay structure is the principal job of *compensation managers*. Assisted by compensation analysts or specialists, compensation managers devise ways to ensure fair and equitable pay rates. They may participate in or purchase salary surveys to see how their firm's pay compares with others, and they ensure that the firm's pay scale complies with changing laws and regulations. In addition, compensation managers often oversee the compensation side of their company's performance management system. They may design reward systems such as pay-for-performance plans, which might include setting merit pay guidelines and bonus or incentive pay criteria. Compensation managers also might administer executive compensation programs or determine commission rates and other incentives for corporate sales staffs.

Employee benefits managers and specialists administer a company's employee benefits program, most notably its health insurance and retirement plans. Expertise in designing, negotiating, and administering benefits programs continues to take on importance as employer-provided benefits account for a growing proportion of overall compensation costs and as benefit plans increase in number and complexity. For example, retirement benefits might include defined

benefit pension plans; defined contribution plans, such as 401(k) or thrift savings plans; and profit-sharing or stock ownership plans. Health benefits might include medical, dental, and vision insurance and protection against catastrophic illness. Familiarity with health benefits is a top priority for employee benefits managers and specialists because of the rising cost of providing health-care benefits to employees and retirees. In addition to health insurance and retirement coverage, many firms offer employees life and accidental death and dismemberment insurance; disability insurance; and benefits designed to meet the needs of a changing workforce, such as parental leave, long-term nursing or home care insurance, wellness programs, and flexible benefits plans. Working with employee assistance plan managers or work-life coordinators, many benefits managers work to integrate the growing number of programs that deal with mental and physical health, such as employee assistance, obesity, and smoking cessation, into their health benefits programs.

Employee assistance plan managers, also called *employee welfare managers* or *work-life managers*, are responsible for a wide array of programs to enhance employee safety and wellness and improve work-life balance. These may include occupational safety and health standards and practices; health promotion and physical fitness; medical examinations; and minor health treatment, such as first aid, flexible work schedules, food service and recreation activities, carpooling and transportation programs such as transit subsidies, employee suggestion systems, child care and elder care, and counseling services. Child care and elder care are increasingly significant because of growth in the number of dual-income households and the older population. Counseling may help employees deal with emotional disorders; alcoholism; or marital, family, consumer, legal, and financial problems. Some employers offer career counseling and outplacement services. In some companies, certain programs, such as those dealing with physical security or information technology, may be coordinated in separate departments by other managers.

> **CONSIDER THIS...**
> Benefits managers must keep abreast of changing federal and state regulations and legislation that may affect employee benefits.

Training and development managers and specialists create, procure, and conduct training and development programs for employees. Managers typically supervise specialists and make budget-impacting decisions in exchange for a reduced training portfolio. Increasingly, executives recognize that training offers a way of developing skills, enhancing productivity and quality of work, and building worker loyalty. Enhancing employee skills can increase individual and organizational performance and help to achieve business results. Increasingly, executives realize that developing the skills and knowledge of their workforce is a business imperative that can give them a competitive edge in recruiting and retaining high-quality employees and can lead to business growth.

Other factors involved in determining whether training is needed include the complexity of the work environment, the rapid pace of organizational and technological change, and the growing number of jobs in fields that constantly generate new knowledge and, thus, require new skills. In addition, advances in learning theory have provided insights into how people learn and how training can be organized most effectively.

Training managers oversee development of training programs, contracts, and budgets. They may perform needs assessments of the types of training needed, determine the best means of delivering training, and create the content. They may provide employee training in a classroom, computer laboratory, or onsite production facility or through a training film, Web video-on-demand, or self-paced or self-guided instructional guides. For live or in-person training, training managers ensure that teaching materials are prepared and the space appropriately set, training and instruction stimulate the class, and completion certificates are issued at the end of training. For computer-assisted or recorded training, trainers ensure that cameras, microphones, and other necessary technology platforms are functioning properly and that individual computers or other learning devices are configured for training purposes. They also have the responsibility for the entire learning process and its environment to ensure that the course meets its objectives and is measured and evaluated to understand how learning impacts performance.

Training specialists plan, organize, and direct a wide range of training activities. Trainers consult with training managers and employee supervisors to develop performance improvement measures, conduct orientation sessions, and arrange on-the-job training for new employees. They help employees maintain and improve their job skills and prepare for jobs requiring greater skill. They work with supervisors to improve their interpersonal skills and to deal effectively with employees. They may set up individualized training plans to strengthen employees' existing skills or teach new ones. Training specialists also may set up leadership or executive development programs for employees who aspire to move up in the organization. These programs are designed to develop or "groom" leaders to replace those leaving the organization and as part of a corporate succession plan. Trainers also lead programs to assist employees

with job transitions as a result of mergers or consolidation, as well as retraining programs to develop new skills that may result from technological changes in the workplace. In government-supported job-training programs, training specialists serve as case managers and provide basic job skills to prepare participants to function in the labor force. They assess the training needs of clients and guide them through the most appropriate training. After training, clients may either be referred to employer relations representatives or receive job placement assistance.

Planning and program development is an essential part of the training specialist's job. In order to identify and assess training needs, trainers may confer with managers and supervisors or conduct surveys. They also evaluate training effectiveness to ensure that employees actually learn and that the training they receive helps the organization meet its strategic goals and achieve results.

Depending on the size, goals, and nature of the organization, trainers may differ considerably in their responsibilities and in the methods they use. Training methods also vary by whether the training predominantly is knowledge-based or skill-based or is sometimes a combination of the two. For example, much knowledge-based training is conducted in a classroom setting. Most skill training provides some combination of hands-on instruction, demonstration, and practice at doing something and usually is conducted on a shop floor, in a studio, or in a laboratory where trainees gain experience and confidence. Some on-the-job training methods could apply equally to knowledge or skill training, and formal apprenticeship training programs combine classroom training and work experience. Increasingly, training programs involve interactive Internet-based training modules that can be downloaded for either individual or group instruction, for dissemination to a geographically dispersed class, or to be coordinated with other multimedia programs.

An organization's *director of industrial relations* forms labor policy, oversees industrial labor relations, negotiates collective bargaining agreements, and coordinates grievance procedures to handle complaints resulting from management disputes with employees. The director of industrial

CONSIDER THIS...

Trainers are using new technologies that allow employees to take advantage of distance learning alternatives and to attend conferences and seminars through satellite or Internet communications hookups. Other computer-aided instructional technologies have been developed for workers with hearing or sight impairment.

relations also advises and collaborates with the director of human resources, other managers, and members of their staffs because all aspects of human resources policy—such as wages, benefits, pensions, and work practices—may be involved in drawing up new or revised work rules that comply with a union contract.

Labor relations managers and their staffs implement industrial labor relations programs. Labor relations specialists prepare information for management to use during collective bargaining agreement negotiations, a process that requires the specialist to be familiar with economic and wage data and to have extensive knowledge of labor law and collective bargaining procedures. The labor relations staff interprets and administers the contract with respect to grievances, wages and salaries, employee welfare, health care, pensions, union and management practices, and other contractual stipulations. In the absence of a union, industrial relations personnel may work with employees individually or with employee association representatives.

Dispute resolution—attaining tacit or contractual agreements—has become increasingly significant as parties to a dispute attempt to avoid costly litigation, strikes, or other disruptions. Dispute resolution also has become more complex, involving employees, management, unions, other firms, and government agencies. Specialists involved in dispute resolution must be highly knowledgeable and experienced and often report to the director of industrial relations. *Mediators* advise and counsel labor and management to prevent and, when necessary, resolve disputes over labor agreements or other labor relations issues. *Arbitrators,* occasionally called umpires or referees, decide disputes that bind both labor and management to specific terms and conditions of labor contracts. Labor relations specialists who work for unions perform many of the same functions on behalf of the union and its members.

EEO officers, representatives, or *affirmative action coordinators* handle equal employment opportunity matters. They investigate and resolve EEO grievances, examine corporate practices for possible violations, and compile and submit EEO statistical reports.

Also Known As

Some emerging specialties in human resources include *international human resources managers*, who handle human resources issues related to a company's overseas operations; *human resources information system specialists*, who develop and apply computer programs to process human resources information, match jobseekers with job openings, and handle other human resources matters; and *total compensation* or *total rewards specialists*, who determine an appropriate mix of compensation, benefits, and incentives.

Dealing with people is an important part of the job of human resources specialists.

Job Fit

Personality Type
Enterprising-Social-Conventional

Career Cluster
04 Business, Management, and Administration

Skills
Social Skills
Management
Communications
Thought-Processing
Computer Programming
Mathematics

Work Styles
Leadership
Social Skills Orientation
Initiative
Analytical Thinking
Adaptability/Flexibility
Integrity
Achievement/Effort
Cooperation

Working Conditions

Human resources personnel usually work in clean, pleasant, and comfortable office settings. Although most human resources, training, and labor relations managers and specialists work in the office, some travel extensively. For example, recruiters regularly attend professional meetings, participate in job fairs, and visit college campuses to interview prospective employees. Arbitrators and mediators often must travel to the site chosen for negotiations; however, many of them work independently and may be based in home offices. Trainers and other specialists may travel to regional, satellite, or international offices of a company to meet with employees who work outside of the main corporate office.

Many human resources, training, and labor relations managers and specialists work a standard 40-hour week. However, longer hours might be necessary for some workers—for example, labor relations managers and specialists, arbitrators, and mediators—when contract agreements or dispute resolutions are being negotiated.

■ What's Required

The educational backgrounds of human resources, training, and labor relations managers and specialists vary considerably, reflecting the diversity of duties and levels of responsibility. In filling entry-level jobs, many employers seek college graduates who have majored in human resources, human resources administration, or industrial and labor relations. Other employers look for college graduates with a technical or business background or a well-rounded liberal arts education.

Education and Training

Although a bachelor's degree is a typical path of entry into these occupations, many colleges and universities do not offer degree programs in personnel administration, human resources, or labor relations until the graduate degree level. However, many offer individual courses in these subjects at the undergraduate level in addition to concentrations in human resources administration or human resources management, training and development, organizational development, and compensation and benefits.

Because an interdisciplinary background is appropriate in this field, a combination of courses in the social sciences, business administration, and behavioral sciences is useful. Some jobs may require more technical or specialized backgrounds in engineering, science, finance, or law. Most prospective human resources specialists should take courses in principles of management, organizational structure, and industrial psychology; however, courses in accounting or finance are becoming increasingly impor-

tant. Courses in labor law, collective bargaining, labor economics, and labor history also provide a valuable background for the prospective labor relations specialist. As in many other fields, knowledge of computers and information systems is useful.

An advanced degree is increasingly important for some jobs. A strong background in industrial relations and law is highly desirable for contract negotiators, mediators, and arbitrators; in fact, many people in these specialties have law degrees. A master's degree in human resources, labor relations, or in business administration with a concentration in human resources management is highly recommended for those seeking general and top management positions.

The duties given to entry-level workers vary, depending on whether the new workers have a degree in human resource management, have completed an intern-

> **CONSIDER THIS...**
> Many labor relations jobs require graduate study in industrial or labor relations.

ship, or have some other type of human resources-related experience. Entry-level employees commonly learn by performing administrative duties—helping to enter data into computer systems, compiling employee handbooks, researching information for a supervisor, or answering phone calls and handling routine questions. Entry-level workers often enter on-the-job training programs in which they learn how to classify jobs, interview applicants, or administer employee benefits; they then are assigned to specific areas in the human resources department to gain experience. Later, they may advance to supervisory positions, overseeing a major element of the human resources program—compensation or training, for example.

Postsecondary Programs to Consider

- Human resources development
- Human resources management/personnel administration, general
- Labor and industrial relations
- Organizational behavior studies

Additional Qualifications

Experience is an asset for many specialties in the human resources area and is essential for advancement to senior-level positions, including managers, arbitrators, and mediators. Employees in human resources administration and human resources development need the ability to work well with individuals and a commitment to organizational goals. This field demands skills that people may have developed elsewhere—teaching, supervising, and volunteering, among others. Human resources work also offers clerical workers opportunities to advance to more responsible or professional positions. Some positions occasionally are filled by experienced individuals from other backgrounds, including business, government, education, social services administration, and the military.

The human resources field demands a range of personal qualities and skills. Human resources, training, and labor relations managers and specialists must speak and write effectively. Ever-changing technologies and the growing complexities inherent in the many services human resources personnel provide require that they be knowledgeable about computer systems, storage and retrieval software, and how to use a wide array of digital communications devices.

The growing diversity of the workforce requires that human resources managers and specialists work with or supervise people of various ages, cultural backgrounds, levels of education, and experience. Ability to speak a foreign language is an asset, especially in an industry with a large immigrant workforce or for a company with many overseas operations. Human resources employees must be able to cope with conflicting points of view; function under pressure; and demonstrate discretion, integrity, fairmindedness, and a persuasive, genial personality. Because much of the information collected by these employees is confidential, they must also show the character and responsibility of dealing with sensitive employee information.

School Subjects to Study

- Algebra
- Computer science
- English
- Foreign language
- Geometry
- Public speaking
- Trigonometry

Moving Up

Most professional associations that specialize in human resources offer classes intended to enhance the skills of their members. Some organizations offer certification programs, which are signs of competence and credibility and can enhance advancement opportunities.

For example, the International Foundation of Employee Benefit Plans confers a designation in three distinct areas of specialization group benefit, retirement, and compensation—to persons who complete a series of college-level courses and pass exams. Candidates can earn a designation in each of the specialty tracks and, simultaneously, receive credit toward becoming a Certified Employee Benefits Specialist (CEBS).

The American Society for Training and Development (ASTD) Certification Institute offers professional certification in the learning and performance field. Addressing nine areas of expertise, certification requires passing a knowledge-based exam and successful work experience. In addition, ASTD offers 16 short-term certificate and workshop programs covering a broad range of professional training and development topics.

The Society for Human Resource Management offers two levels of certification, including the Professional in Human Resources (PHR) and the Senior Professional in Human Resources (SPHR). Additionally, the organization offers the Global Professional in Human Resources certification for those with international and cross-border responsibilities and the California Certification in Human Resources for those who plan to work in that state and become familiar with California's labor and human resources laws. All designations require experience and a passing score on a comprehensive exam.

The WorldatWork Society of Certified Professionals offers four distinct designations in the areas of compensation, benefits, work-life, and global remuneration that comprise the total rewards management practice. Candidates obtain the designations of Certified Compensation Professional (CCP), Certified Benefits Professional (CBP), Global Remuneration Professional (GRP), and Work-Life Certified Professional (WLCP). Certification is achieved after passing a series of knowledge-based exams within each designation. Additionally, WorldatWork offers online and classroom education covering a broad range of total rewards topics.

Exceptional human resources workers may be promoted to director of human resources or industrial relations, which can eventually lead to a top managerial or executive position. Others may join a consulting or outsourcing firm or open their own business. A Ph.D. is an asset for teaching, writing, or consulting work.

■ Employment

Human resources, training, and labor relations managers and specialists held about 904,900 jobs in 2008. Of these, 24 percent were training and development specialists; 23 percent were employment, recruitment, and placement specialists; 13 percent were compensation, benefits, and job analysis specialists; 4 percent were compensation and benefits managers; and 3 percent were training and development managers.

> ### CONSIDER THIS...
>
> Some companies prefer to outsource complex HR tasks, such as administering employee compensation packages or training workers; the firms providing these services may create many job openings for specialists.

Human resources, training, and labor relations managers and specialists were employed in virtually every industry. About 13 percent of human resources, training, and labor relations managers and specialists were employed in administrative and support services, 11 percent in professional, scientific, and technical services, 10 percent in health care and social assistance, and 9 percent in finance and insurance firms. About 12,900 managers and specialists were self-employed, working as consultants to public and private employers.

Job Prospects

Overall employment is projected to grow by 22 percent in the 10-year period ending in 2018, much faster than the average for all occupations. Legislation and court rulings revising standards in various areas—occupational safety and health, equal employment opportunity, wages, health care, retirement plans, and family leave, among others—will increase demand for human resources, training, and labor relations experts. Rising health-care costs and a growing number of health-care coverage options should continue to spur demand for specialists to develop creative compensation and benefits packages that companies can offer prospective employees.

Employment of labor relations staff, including arbitrators and mediators, should grow as companies attempt to resolve potentially costly labor-management disputes out of court. Additional job growth may stem from increasing demand for specialists in international human resources management and human resources information systems.

Job growth could be limited by the widespread use of computerized human resources information systems that make workers more productive. Like other workers, employment of human resources, training, and labor relations managers and specialists, particularly in larger companies, may be adversely affected by corporate downsizing, restructuring, and mergers; however, as companies once again expand operations, additional workers may be needed to manage company growth.

Demand may be particularly strong for certain specialists. For example, employers are expected to devote greater resources to job-specific training programs in response to the increasing complexity of many jobs and technological advances that can leave employees with obsolete skills. Additionally, as highly trained and skilled baby boomers retire, there should be strong demand for training and development specialists to impart needed skills to their replacements. In addition, increasing efforts throughout the industry to recruit and retain quality employees should create many jobs for employment, recruitment, and placement specialists.

Among industries, firms involved in management, consulting, and employment services should offer many job opportunities as businesses increasingly contract out human resources functions or hire human resources specialists on a temporary basis to deal with increasing costs and complexity of training and development programs.

College graduates and those who have earned certification should have the best job opportunities, particularly graduates with a bachelor's degree in human resources, human resources administration, or industrial and labor relations. Those with a technical or business background or a well-rounded liberal arts education also should find opportunities. Demand for human resources, training, and labor relations managers and specialists depends on general economic conditions and the business cycle as well as staffing needs of the companies in which they work. A rapidly expanding business is likely to hire additional human resources workers—either as permanent employees or consultants—while businesses that have consolidated operations or merged with another company may require fewer of these workers. Also, as human resources management becomes increasingly important to the success of an organization, some small and medium-size businesses that do not have separate human resources departments may assign various human resources responsibilities to some employees in addition to their usual responsibilities; others may contract with consulting firms to establish formal procedures and train current employees to administer programs on a long-term basis.

In addition to new human resources management and specialist jobs created over the 10-year projection period, many job openings will arise from the need to replace workers who transfer to other occupations, retire, or leave the labor force for other reasons.

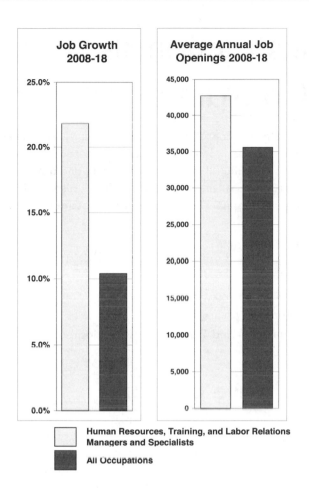

Job Growth 2008-18

Average Annual Job Openings 2008-18

Legend:
- Human Resources, Training, and Labor Relations Managers and Specialists
- All Occupations

Median annual wages of employment, recruitment, and placement specialists were $45,470 in May 2008. The middle 50 percent earned between $35,020 and $63,110. The lowest 10 percent earned less than $28,030, and the highest 10 percent earned more than $85,760.

Median annual wages of compensation, benefits, and job analysis specialists were $53,860 in May 2008. The middle 50 percent earned between $42,050 and $67,730. The lowest 10 percent earned less than $34,080, and the highest 10 percent earned more than $84,310.

Median annual wages of training and development specialists were $51,450 in May 2008. The middle 50 percent earned between $38,550 and $67,450. The lowest 10 percent earned less than $29,470, and the highest 10 percent earned more than $85,160.

According to a July 2009 salary survey conducted by the National Association of Colleges and Employers, bachelor's degree candidates majoring in human resources, including labor and industrial relations, received starting offers averaging $45,170 a year.

Income

Annual salary rates for human resources workers vary according to occupation, level of experience, training, location, and firm size.

Median annual wages of compensation and benefits managers were $86,500 in May 2008. The middle 50 percent earned between $64,930 and $113,480. The lowest 10 percent earned less than $49,350, and the highest 10 percent earned more than $147,050.

Median annual wages of training and development managers were $87,700 in May 2008. The middle 50 percent earned between $64,770 and $115,570. The lowest 10 percent earned less than $48,280, and the highest 10 percent earned more than $149,050.

Median annual wages of human resources managers, all other were $96,130 in May 2008. The middle 50 percent earned between $73,480 and $126,050. The lowest 10 percent earned less than $56,770, and the highest 10 percent earned more than $163,220.

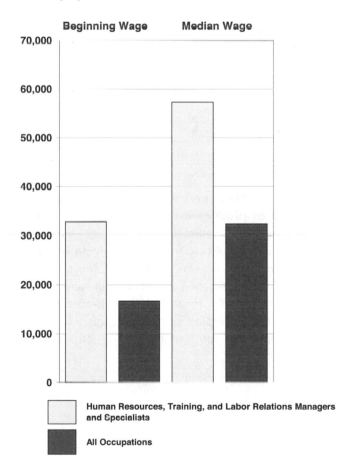

Beginning Wage   **Median Wage**

Legend:
- Human Resources, Training, and Labor Relations Managers and Specialists
- All Occupations

Related Jobs

- Counselors
- Education administrators
- Lawyers
- Psychologists
- Public relations specialists
- Social and human service assistants
- Social workers

▌ How to Learn More

For information about human resource management careers and certification, contact

- Society for Human Resource Management, 1800 Duke St., Alexandria, VA 22314. Internet: www.shrm.org

For information about careers in employee training and development and certification, contact

- American Society for Training and Development, 1640 King St., Box 1443, Alexandria, VA 22313-2043. Internet: www.astd.org

For information about careers and certification in employee compensation and benefits, contact

- International Foundation of Employee Benefit Plans, 18700 W. Bluemound Rd., Brookfield, WI 53045. Internet: www.ifebp.org
- WorldatWork, 14040 N. Northsight Blvd., Scottsdale, AZ 85260. Internet: www.worldatwork.org

Why It's Hot

Company managers know that their organization is only as productive as its workers. That's why they seek competent human resources managers and specialists to train and motivate workers and deal with workers' complaints. The demand for HR managers and specialists will increase as workers' benefits (especially health-care plans) grow more complex and as changing technologies require constant upgrading of workers' skills.

Instructional Coordinators

Instructional coordinators develop curricula, select textbooks and other materials, train teachers, and assess educational programs for quality and adherence to regulations and standards. They also assist in implementing new technology in the classroom.

Just the Facts

Earnings: $56,880

Job Growth: 23.2%

Annual Openings: 6,060

Education and Training: Master's degree

▌ While at Work

Instructional coordinators play a large role in improving the quality of education in the classroom. At the primary and secondary school level, they often specialize in specific subjects, such as reading, language arts, mathematics, or science. At the postsecondary level, they may work with employers to develop training programs that produce qualified workers.

Instructional coordinators evaluate how well a school or training program's curriculum, or plan of study, meets students' needs. Based on their research and observations of instructional practice, they recommend improvements. They research teaching methods and techniques and develop procedures to ensure that instructors are implementing the curriculum successfully and meeting program goals. To aid in their evaluation, they may meet with members of educational committees and advisory groups to learn about subjects—for example, English, history, or mathematics—and explore how curriculum materials meet students' needs and relate to occupations. Coordinators also may develop questionnaires and interview school staff about the curriculum.

CONSIDER THIS...

Instructional coordinators sometimes are involved in the hiring process for a new teacher. They may not actually screen resumes or interview job candidates, but they may help write the job description, basing it on instructional needs.

Some instructional coordinators also review textbooks, software, and other educational materials and make recommendations on purchases. They monitor the ways in which teachers use materials in the classroom, and they supervise workers who catalogue, distribute, and maintain a school's educational materials and equipment.

Some instructional coordinators find ways to use technology to enhance student learning. They monitor the introduction of new technology, including the Internet, into a school's curriculum. In addition, instructional coordinators might recommend installing educational software, such as interactive books and exercises designed to enhance student literacy and develop math skills. Instructional coordinators may invite experts—such as computer hardware, software, and library media specialists—to help integrate technological materials into the curriculum.

In addition to developing curriculum and instructional materials, many instructional coordinators also plan and provide onsite education for teachers and administrators. Instructional coordinators mentor new teachers and train experienced ones in the latest instructional methods. This role becomes especially important when a school district introduces new content, program innovations, or a different organizational structure.

Instructional coordinators research teaching methods and techniques and develop procedures to ensure that instructors implement curricula successfully.

Also Known As

Many instructional coordinators have titles such as *curriculum specialists, personnel development specialists, instructional coaches,* or *directors of instructional materials.*

Job Fit

Personality Type
Social-Investigative-Artistic

Career Cluster
05 Education and Training

Skills
Management
Social Skills
Thought-Processing
Communications
Equipment/Technology Analysis
Science
Mathematics
Computer Programming
Equipment Use/Maintenance

Work Styles
Leadership
Social Skills Orientation
Innovation
Concern for Others
Initiative
Achievement/Effort
Analytical Thinking
Persistence

Working Conditions

Many instructional coordinators work long hours. They often work year round. Some spend much of their time traveling between schools meeting with teachers and administrators. The opportunity to shape and improve instructional curricula and work in an academic environment can be satisfying. However, some instructional coordinators find the work stressful because they are continually accountable to school administrators.

■ What's Required

The minimum educational requirement for most instructional coordinator positions in public schools is a master's or higher degree—usually in education—plus a state teacher or administrator license. A master's degree also is preferred for positions in other settings.

Education and Training

Instructional coordinators should have training in curriculum development and instruction or in the specific field for which they are responsible, such as mathematics or history. Courses in research design teach how to create and implement research studies to determine the effectiveness of a given method of instruction or curriculum and how to measure and improve student performance.

> **CONSIDER THIS...**
> Instructional coordinators must be licensed to work in public schools. Check the licensing requirement for where you are planning to work; some states require a teaching license, whereas others require an education administrator license.

Instructional coordinators usually are also required to take continuing education courses to keep their skills current. Topics may include teacher evaluation techniques, curriculum training, new teacher induction, consulting and teacher support, and observation and analysis of teaching.

> **Postsecondary Programs to Consider**
> - Curriculum and instruction
> - Educational/instructional media design
> - International and comparative education

Additional Qualifications

Instructional coordinators must have a good understanding of how to teach specific groups of students and expertise in developing educational materials. As a result, many people become instructional coordinators after working for several years as teachers. Also beneficial is work experience in an education administrator position, such as a principal or assistant principal, or in another advisory role, such as a master teacher.

> **CONSIDER THIS...**
> Familiarity with computer technology also is important for instructional coordinators, who are increasingly involved in gathering technical information for students and teachers.

Instructional coordinators must be able to make sound decisions about curriculum options and to organize and coordinate work efficiently. They should have strong interpersonal and communication skills.

> **School Subjects to Study**
> - Algebra
> - Computer science
> - English
> - Geometry
> - Social studies
> - Trigonometry

Moving Up

Depending on experience and educational attainment, instructional coordinators may advance to higher administrative positions in a school system or to management or executive positions in private industry.

Employment

Instructional coordinators held about 133,900 jobs in 2008. About 70 percent worked in public or private educational institutions. Other employing industries included state and local government, individual and family services, and child day care services.

Job Prospects

The number of instructional coordinators is expected to grow by 23 percent over the 10-year period ending 2018, which is much faster than the average for all occupations. Although budget constraints may limit employment growth to some extent, a continuing emphasis on improving the quality of education should result in an increasing demand for these workers. The emphasis on accountability also should increase at all levels of government and cause more schools to focus on improving standards of educational quality and student performance. Growing numbers of coordinators will be needed to incorporate the new standards into existing curricula and ensure that teachers and administrators are informed of changes.

> **CONSIDER THIS...**
> Additional job growth for instructional coordinators will stem from an increasing emphasis on lifelong learning and on programs for students with special needs, including those for whom English is a second language. These students often require more educational resources and consolidated planning and management within the educational system.

Favorable job prospects are expected. Opportunities should be best for those who specialize in subjects targeted for improvement by the No Child Left Behind Act—reading, math, and science. There also will be a need for more instructional coordinators to show teachers how to use technology in the classroom.

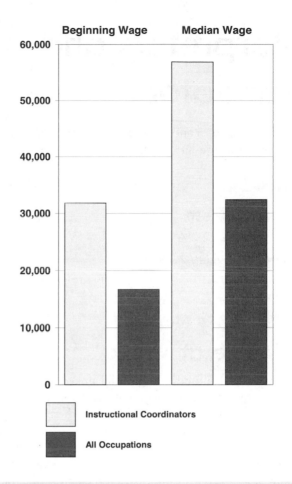

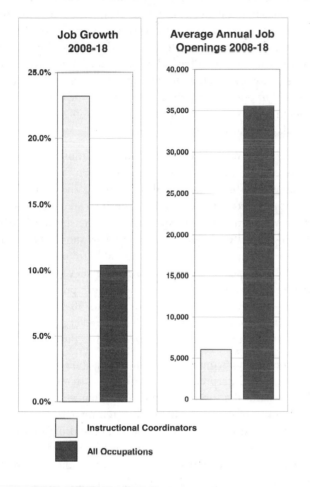

Income

Median annual earnings of instructional coordinators in May 2008 were $56,880. The middle 50 percent earned between $42,070 and $75,000. The lowest 10 percent earned less than $31,800, and the highest 10 percent earned more than $93,250.

Related Jobs

- Counselors
- Education administrators
- Elementary school teachers
- Human resources, training, and labor relations managers and specialists
- Kindergarten teachers
- Middle school teachers
- Postsecondary teachers
- Preschool teachers
- Secondary school teachers

How to Learn More

Information on requirements and job opportunities for instructional coordinators is available from local school systems and state departments of education.

Why It's Hot

Instructional coordinators will be in high demand because they will be instrumental in developing new curricula to meet the education needs of a changing society and in training teachers.

Interpreters and Translators

Interpreters and translators convert communications from one language into another.

Just the Facts

Earnings: $38,850

Job Growth: 22.2%

Annual Openings: 2,340

Education and Training: Long-term on-the-job training

■ While at Work

In today's multicultural and globally linked society, interpreters and translators play important roles, enabling cross-cultural communications. However, these language specialists do more than simply translate words—they relay concepts and ideas between languages. They must thoroughly understand the subject matter in which they work in order to convert information accurately from one language, known as the source language, into another, the target language. In addition, they must be sensitive to the cultures associated with their languages of expertise.

Interpreters and translators are often discussed together because they share some common traits. For example, both must be fluent in at least two languages—a native, or active, language and a secondary, or passive, language; a small number of interpreters and translators are fluent in two or more passive languages. Their active language is the one they know best and into which they interpret or translate, and their passive language is one for which they have nearly perfect knowledge.

Although some people do both, interpretation and translation are different professions. Interpreters deal with spoken words, translators with written words. Each task requires a distinct set of skills and aptitudes, and most people are better suited for one or the other. While interpreters often work into and from both languages, translators generally work only into their active language.

Interpreters convert one spoken language into another— or, in the case of sign-language interpreters, between spoken communication and sign language. This requires interpreters to pay attention carefully, understand what is communicated in both languages, and express thoughts and ideas clearly. Strong research and analytical skills, mental dexterity, and an exceptional memory also are important.

The first part of an interpreter's work begins before arriving at the job site. The interpreter must become familiar with the subject matter that the speakers will discuss, a task that may involve research to create a list of common words and phrases associated with the topic. Next, the interpreter usually travels to the location where his or her services are needed. Physical presence may not be required for some work, such as telephone interpretation. But it is usually important that the interpreter see the communicators in order to hear and observe the person speaking and to relay the message to the other party.

There are two types of interpretation: simultaneous and consecutive. Simultaneous interpretation requires interpreters to listen and speak (or sign) at the same time. In simultaneous interpretation, the interpreter begins to convey a sentence being spoken while the speaker is still talking. Ideally, *simultaneous interpreters* should be so familiar with a subject that they are able to anticipate the end of the speaker's sentence. Because they need a high degree of concentration, simultaneous interpreters work in pairs, with each interpreting for 20- to 30-minute periods. This type of interpretation is required at international conferences and is sometimes used in the courts.

In contrast to simultaneous interpretation's immediacy, consecutive interpretation begins only after the speaker has verbalized a group of words or sentences. *Consecutive interpreters* often take notes while listening to the speakers, so they must develop some type of note-taking or shorthand system. This form of interpretation is used most often for person-to-person communication, during which the interpreter is positioned near both parties.

Translators convert written materials from one language into another. They must have excellent writing and analytical ability. And because the documents that they translate must be as flawless as possible, they also need good editing skills.

Assignments may vary in length, writing style, and subject matter. When translators first receive text to convert into another language, they usually read it in its entirety to get an idea of the subject. Next, they identify and look up any unfamiliar words. Multiple additional readings are usually needed before translators begin to actually write and finalize the translation. Translators also might do additional research on the subject matter if they are unclear about anything in the text. They consult with the text's originator or issuing agency to clarify unclear or unfamiliar ideas, words, or acronyms.

Translating involves more than replacing a word with its equivalent in another language; sentences and ideas must be manipulated to flow with the same coherence as those in the source document so that the translation reads as though it originated in the target language. Translators also must bear in mind any cultural references that may need to be explained to the intended audience, such as colloquialisms, slang, and other expressions that do not translate literally. Some subjects may be more difficult than others to translate because words or passages may have multiple meanings that make several translations possible. Not surprisingly, translated work often goes through multiple revisions before final text is submitted.

The way in which translators do their jobs has changed with advances in technology. Today, nearly all translation work is done on a computer, and most assignments are received and submitted electronically. This enables translators to work from almost anywhere, and a large percentage of them work from home. The Internet provides advanced research capabilities and valuable language resources, such as specialized dictionaries and glossaries. In some cases, use of machine-assisted translation—including memory tools that provide comparisons of previous translations with current work—helps save time and reduce repetition.

The services of interpreters and translators are needed in a number of subject areas. While these workers may not completely specialize in a particular field or industry, many do focus on one area of expertise. Some of the most common areas are described here; however, interpreters and translators also may work in a variety of other areas, including business, social services, or entertainment.

Conference interpreters work at conferences that have non-English-speaking attendees. This work includes international business and diplomacy, although conference interpreters interpret for any organization that works with foreign language speakers. Employers prefer high-level interpreters who have the ability to translate from at least two passive languages into one active (native) language—for example, the ability to interpret from Spanish and French into English. For some positions, such as those with the United Nations, this qualification is mandatory.

Much of the interpreting performed at conferences is simultaneous; however, at some meetings with a small number of attendees, consecutive interpreting also may be used. Usually, interpreters sit in soundproof booths, listening to the speakers through headphones and interpreting into a microphone what is said. The interpreted speech is then relayed to the listener through headsets. When interpreting is needed for only one or two people, the interpreter generally sits behind or next to the attendee and whispers a translation of the proceedings.

Guide or escort interpreters accompany either U.S. visitors abroad or foreign visitors in the United States to ensure that they are able to communicate during their stay. These specialists interpret on a variety of subjects, both on an informal basis and on a professional level. Most of their interpretation is consecutive, and work is generally shared by two interpreters when the assignment requires more than an 8-hour day. Frequent travel, often for days or weeks at a time, is common, an aspect of the job that some find particularly appealing.

Judiciary interpreters and translators help people appearing in court who are unable or unwilling to communicate in English. These workers must remain detached from the content of their work and not alter or modify the meaning or tone of what is said. Legal translators must be thoroughly familiar with the language and functions of the U.S. judicial system, as well as other countries' legal systems. Court interpreters work in a variety of legal settings, such as attorney-client meetings, preliminary hearings, depositions, trials, and arraignments. Success as a court interpreter requires an understanding of both legal terminology and colloquial language. In addition to interpreting what is said, court interpreters also may be required to translate written documents and read them aloud, also known as sight translation.

Literary translators adapt written literature from one language into another. They may translate any number of documents, including journal articles, books, poetry, and short stories. Literary translation is related to creative writing; literary translators must create a new text in the target language that reproduces the content and style of the original. Whenever possible, literary translators work closely with authors to best capture their intended meanings and literary characteristics.

This type of work often is done as a sideline by university professors; however, opportunities exist for well-established literary translators. As with writers, finding a publisher and maintaining a network of contacts in the publishing industry is a critical part of the job. Most aspiring literary translators begin by submitting a short sample of their work, in the hope that it will be printed and give them recognition. For example, after receiving permission

CONSIDER THIS...

Self-employed and freelance interpreters and translators need general business skills to successfully manage their finances and careers. They must set prices for their work, bill customers, keep financial records, and market their services to attract new business and build their client base.

from the author, they might submit to a publishing house a previously unpublished short work, such as a poem or essay.

Medical interpreters and translators provide language services to health care patients with limited English proficiency. Medical interpreters help patients to communicate with doctors, nurses, and other medical staff. Translators working in this specialty primarily convert patient materials and informational brochures issued by hospitals and medical facilities into the desired language. Medical interpreters need a strong grasp of medical and colloquial terminology in both languages, along with cultural sensitivity regarding how the patient receives the information. They must remain detached but aware of the patient's feelings and pain.

Sign language interpreters facilitate communication between people who are deaf or hard of hearing and people who can hear. Sign language interpreters must be fluent in English and in American Sign Language (ASL), which combines signing, finger spelling, and specific body language. ASL has its own grammatical rules, sentence structure, idioms, historical contexts, and cultural nuances. Sign language interpreting, like foreign language interpreting, involves more than simply replacing a word of spoken English with a sign representing that word.

Most sign language interpreters either interpret, aiding communication between English and ASL, or transliterate, facilitating communication between English and contact signing—a form of signing that uses a more English language-based word order. Some interpreters specialize in oral interpreting for deaf or hard of hearing people who lip-read instead of sign. Other specialties include tactile signing, which is interpreting for people who are blind as well as deaf by making manual signs into a person's hands; cued speech; and signing exact English.

Also Known As

Localization translators constitute a relatively recent and rapidly expanding specialty. Localization involves the complete adaptation of a product for use in a different language and culture. At its earlier stages, this work dealt primarily with software localization, but the specialty has expanded to include the adaptation of Internet sites and products in manufacturing and other business sectors. The goal of these specialists is to make the product to appear as if it were originally manufactured in the country where it will be sold and supported.

Interpreters and translators must become familiar with the subject matter that will be discussed.

Job Fit

Personality Type
Artistic-Social

Career Clusters
05 Education and Training

10 Human Services

Skills
Communications

Thought-Processing

Social Skills

Computer Programming

Science

Work Styles
Social Skills Orientation

Independence

Dependability

Adaptability/Flexibility

Concern for Others

Self-Control

Integrity

Cooperation

Working Conditions

Interpreters work in a variety of settings, such as hospitals, courtrooms, and conference centers. They are required to travel to the site—whether it is in a neighboring town or on the other side of the world—where their services are needed. Interpreters who work over the telephone generally work in call centers in urban areas and keep to a standard 5-day, 40-hour work week. Interpreters for deaf students in schools usually work in a school setting for 9 months out of the year. Translators usually work alone and they must frequently perform under pressure of deadlines and tight schedules. Many translators choose to work at home; however, technology allows translators to work from almost anywhere.

CONSIDER THIS...
Some legal interpreters do much of their work in prisons, interviewing prisoners. This work setting is not dangerous but can feel harsh.

Because many interpreters and translators freelance, their schedules are often erratic, with extensive periods of no work interspersed with periods requiring long, irregular hours. For those who freelance, a significant amount of time must be dedicated to looking for jobs. In addition, freelancers must manage their own finances, and payment for their services may not always be prompt. Freelancing, however, offers variety, flexibility, and sometimes the chance to choose which jobs to accept or decline.

The work can be stressful and exhausting, and translation can be lonesome. However, interpreters and translators may use their irregular schedules to pursue other interests, such as traveling, dabbling in a hobby, or working a second job. Many interpreters and translators enjoy what they do and value the ability to control their schedules and workloads.

What's Required

Interpreters and translators must be fluent in at least two languages. Their educational backgrounds may vary widely, but most have a bachelor's degree. Many also complete job-specific training programs.

Education and Training

The educational backgrounds of interpreters and translators vary, but all know at least two languages. Although it is not necessary to have been raised bilingual to succeed, many interpreters and translators grew up speaking two languages.

Although a bachelor's degree is often required, the degree may be in something other than a language. An educational background in a particular field of study provides a natural area of subject matter expertise. However, specialized training in how to do the work is generally required. Formal programs in interpreting and translation are available at colleges nationwide and through nonuniversity training programs, conferences, and courses. Many people who work as conference interpreters or in more technical areas—such as localization, engineering, or finance—have master's degrees, while those working in the community as court or medical interpreters or translators are more likely to complete job-specific training programs.

CONSIDER THIS...
To prepare for this career, it helps to spend time abroad, engage in direct contact with foreign cultures, and read extensively on a variety of subjects in English and in at least one other language.

There is currently no universal form of certification required of interpreters and translators in the United States, but there are a variety of different tests that workers can take to demonstrate proficiency. The American Translators Association provides certification in more than 24 language combinations for its members; other options include a certification program offered by The Translators and Interpreters Guild. Many interpreters are not certified.

Federal courts have certification for Spanish, Navajo, and Haitian Creole interpreters, and many state and municipal courts offer their own forms of certification. The National Association of Judiciary Interpreters and Translators also offers certification for court interpreting.

The U.S. Department of State has a three-test series for interpreters, including simple consecutive interpreting (for escort work), simultaneous interpreting (for court or seminar work), and conference-level interpreting (for international conferences). These tests are not referred to directly as certification, but successful completion often indicates that a person has an adequate level of skill to work in the field.

The National Association of the Deaf and the Registry of Interpreters for the Deaf (RID) jointly offer certification for general sign interpreters. In addition, the registry offers specialty tests in legal interpreting, speech reading, and deaf-to-deaf interpreting—which includes interpreting between deaf speakers with different native languages and from ASL to tactile signing.

CONSIDER THIS...

Whatever path of entry they pursue, new interpreters and translators should establish mentoring relationships to build their skills, confidence, and a professional network. Mentoring may be formal, such as through a professional association, or informal with a co-worker or an acquaintance who has experience as an interpreter or translator. Both the American Translators Association and the Registry of Interpreters for the Deaf offer formal mentoring programs.

Once interpreters and translators have gained sufficient experience, they may then move up to more difficult or prestigious assignments, may seek certification, may be given editorial responsibility, or may eventually manage or start a translation agency.

A good way for translators to learn firsthand about the profession is to start out working in-house for a translation company; however, such jobs are not very numerous. People seeking to enter interpreter or translator jobs should begin by getting experience whatever way they can—even if it means doing informal or unpaid work.

Volunteer opportunities are available through community organizations, hospitals, and sporting events, such as marathons, that involve international competitors. The American Translators Association works with the Red Cross to provide volunteer interpreters in crisis situations. All translation can be used as examples for potential clients, even translation done as practice.

Paid or unpaid internships and apprenticeships are other ways for interpreters and translators to get started. Escort interpreting may offer an opportunity for inexperienced candidates to work alongside a more seasoned interpreter. Interpreters might also find it easier to break into areas with particularly high demand for language services, such as court or medical interpretation.

Postsecondary Programs to Consider

- American Sign Language (ASL)
- Education/teaching of individuals with hearing impairments
- Foreign language and literature
- Linguistics

Additional Qualifications

Translators working in localization need a solid grasp of the languages to be translated, a thorough understanding of technical concepts and vocabulary, and a high degree of knowledge about the intended target audience or users of the product. Because software often is involved, it is not uncommon for people who work in this area of translation to have a strong background in computer science or to have computer-related work experience.

School Subjects to Study

- Algebra
- Computer science
- English
- Foreign language
- Geometry
- Social studies

Moving Up

Many self-employed interpreters and translators start businesses by submitting resumes and samples to many different employment agencies and then wait to be contacted when an agency matches their skills with a job. After establishing a few regular clients, interpreters and translators may receive enough work from a few clients to stay busy, and they often hear of subsequent jobs by word of mouth or through referrals from existing clients.

Experience is an essential part of a successful career in either interpreting or translation. In fact, many agencies or companies use only the services of people who have worked in the field for 3 to 5 years or who have a degree in translation studies or both.

Employment

Interpreters and translators held about 50,900 jobs in 2008. However, the actual number of interpreters and translators is probably significantly higher because many work in the occupation only sporadically. Interpreters and translators are employed in a variety of industries, reflecting the diversity of employment options in the field. About 28 percent worked in public and private educational institutions, such as schools, colleges, and universities. About 13 percent worked in health care and social assistance, many of whom worked for hospitals. Another 9 percent worked in other areas of government, such as federal, state, and local courts. Other employers of interpreters and translators include interpreting and translation agencies, publishing companies, telephone companies, and airlines.

About 26 percent of interpreters and translators are self-employed. Many who freelance in the occupation work only part time, relying on other sources of income to supplement earnings from interpreting or translation.

Job Prospects

Employment of interpreters and translators is projected to increase 22 percent over the 10-year period ending 2018, which is much faster than the average for all occupations.

Demand will remain strong for translators of frequently translated languages, such as Portuguese, French, Italian, German, and Spanish. Demand should also be strong for translators of Arabic and other Middle Eastern languages and for the principal East Asian languages—Chinese, Japanese, and Korean. Demand for American Sign Language interpreters will grow rapidly, driven by the increasing use of video relay services, which allow individuals to conduct video calls using a sign language interpreter over an Internet connection.

Technology has made the work of interpreters and translators easier. However, technology is not likely to have a negative impact on employment of interpreters and translators because such innovations are incapable of producing work comparable with work produced by these professionals.

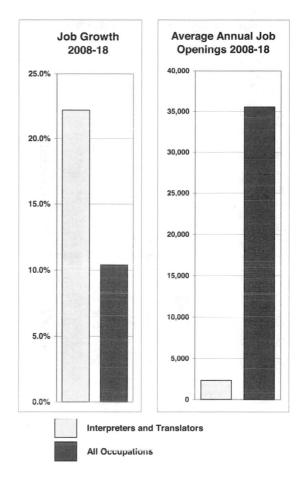

Job Growth 2008-18

Average Annual Job Openings 2008-18

☐ Interpreters and Translators

■ All Occupations

Job prospects for interpreters and translators vary by specialty and language. For example, interpreters and translators of Spanish should have good job opportunities because of expected increases in the Hispanic population in the United States. Demand is expected to be strong for interpreters and translators specializing in health care and law because it is critical that information be fully understood among all parties in these areas. Additionally, there should be demand for specialists in localization, driven by the globalization of business and the expansion of the Internet; however, demand may be dampened somewhat by outsourcing of localization work to other countries. Given the shortage of interpreters and translators meeting the desired skill level of employers, interpreters for the deaf will continue to have favorable employment prospects. On the other hand, competition can be expected for both conference interpreter and literary translator positions because of the small number of job opportunities in these specialties.

> ### CONSIDER THIS...
>
> Urban areas, especially Washington, D.C.; New York; and cities in California, provide the largest numbers of employment possibilities, especially for interpreters; however, as the immigrant population spreads into more rural areas, jobs in smaller communities will become more widely available.

Income

Wage-and-salary interpreters and translators had median annual wages of $38,850 in May 2008. The middle 50 percent earned between $28,940 and $52,240. The lowest 10 percent earned less than $22,170, and the highest 10 percent earned more than $69,190. Individuals classified as language specialists in the federal government earned an average of $79,865 annually in March 2009.

Earnings depend on language, subject matter, skill, experience, education, certification, and type of employer, and salaries of interpreters and translators can vary widely. Interpreters and translators who know languages for which there is a greater demand, or which relatively few people can translate, often have higher earnings, as do those who perform services requiring a high level of skill, such as conference interpreters.

For those who are not salaried, earnings typically fluctuate, depending on the availability of work. Freelance interpreters usually earn an hourly rate, whereas translators who freelance typically earn a rate per word or per hour.

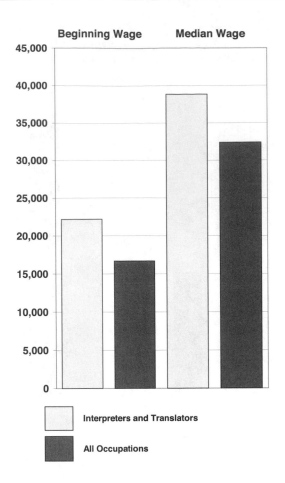

Beginning Wage   Median Wage

Legend:
- ☐ Interpreters and Translators
- ■ All Occupations

Related Jobs

- Court reporters
- Language teachers
- Medical transcriptionists
- Tour guides and escorts
- Writers and editors

How to Learn More

Organizations dedicated to these professions can provide valuable advice and guidance to people interested in learning more about interpretation and translation. The language services division of local hospitals or courthouses also may have information about available opportunities.

For general career information, contact

- American Translators Association, 225 Reinekers Ln., Suite 590, Alexandria, VA 22314. Internet: www.atanet.org

For more detailed information by specialty, contact the association affiliated with that subject area:

- American Literary Translators Association, The University of Texas at Dallas, Box 830688 Mail Station JO51, Richardson, TX 75083-0688. Internet: www.literarytranslators.org

- Localization Industry Standards Association, Domaine en Prael, CH-1323 Romainmôtier, Switzerland. Internet: www.lisa.org

- National Association of Judiciary Interpreters and Translators, 603 Stewart St., Suite 610, Seattle, WA 98101. Internet: www.najit.org

- National Council on Interpreting in Health Care, 270 West Lawrence St., Albany, NY 12208. Internet: www.ncihc.org

- Registry of Interpreters for the Deaf, 333 Commerce St., Alexandria, VA 22314. Internet: www.rid.org

For information about testing to become a contract interpreter or translator with the U.S. State Department, contact

- U.S. Department of State, Office of Language Services, 2401 E St. NW, SA-1, Room H1400, Washington, DC 20520-2204

Information on obtaining positions as interpreters and translators with the federal government is available at www.usajobs.opm.gov or through an interactive voice response telephone system at (703) 724-1850 or TDD (978) 461-8404. These numbers are not toll free, and charges may result.

Why It's Hot

Growth of this occupation will be driven partly by strong demand in health-care settings and work related to homeland security. Additionally, higher demand for interpreters and translators results directly from the broadening of international ties and the increase in the number of foreign language speakers in the United States. Both of these trends are expected to continue, contributing to relatively rapid growth in the number of jobs for interpreters and translators.

Licensed Practical and Licensed Vocational Nurses

Licensed practical and licensed vocational nurses care for people who are sick, injured, convalescent, or disabled.

While at Work

Licensed practical nurses (LPNs)—or *licensed vocational nurses (LVNs)* as they are known in Texas and California— care for people in hospitals, clinics, nursing care facilities, and doctor's offices under the direction of physicians and registered nurses. The nature of the direction and supervision required varies by state and job setting.

LPNs provide basic bedside care. They measure and record patients' vital signs such as height, weight, temperature, blood pressure, pulse, and respiration. They also prepare and give injections and enemas, monitor catheters, dress wounds, and give alcohol rubs and massages. To help keep patients comfortable, they assist with bathing, dressing, and personal hygiene, moving in bed, standing, and walking. They might also feed patients who need help eating. Experienced LPNs may supervise nursing assistants and aides.

As part of their work, LPNs collect samples for testing, perform routine laboratory tests, and record food and fluid intake and output. They clean and monitor medical equipment. Sometimes, they help physicians and registered nurses perform tests and procedures. Some LPNs help to deliver, care for, and feed infants. LPNs often teach family members how to care for a relative or teach patients about good health habits.

LPNs also monitor their patients and report reactions to medications or treatments. LPNs gather information from patients, including their health history and how they are currently feeling. They may use this information to complete insurance forms, pre-authorizations, and referrals, and they share information with registered nurses and doctors to help determine the best course of care for a patient.

Most LPNs are generalists and work in all areas of health care. However, some work in a specialized setting, such as a nursing home, a doctor's office, or in home health care. LPNs in nursing care facilities help to evaluate residents' needs, develop care plans, and supervise the care provided by nursing aides. In doctors' offices and clinics, they may be responsible for making appointments, keeping records, and performing other clerical duties. LPNs who work in home health care may prepare meals and teach family members simple nursing tasks.

Also Known As

Private-duty nurses provide in-home care to patients. They may work 8 to 12 hours per day caring for a single patient. In some cases, their duties involve cooking meals and caring for other members of the patient's family as well. At night, most return to their own homes and families, but some actually live with their patients' families while they provide care.

Job Fit

Personality Type
Social-Realistic

Career Cluster
08 Health Science

Skills
Social Skills
Communications
Thought-Processing
Computer Programming

Work Styles
Social Skills Orientation
Concern for Others
Self-Control
Leadership
Integrity
Stress Tolerance
Analytical Thinking
Initiative

Working Conditions

Most licensed practical nurses in hospitals and nursing care facilities work a 40-hour week, but because patients need round-the-clock care, some work nights, weekends, and holidays. They often stand for long periods and help patients move in bed, stand, or walk.

LPNs may face hazards from caustic chemicals, radiation, and infectious diseases. They are subject to back injuries

CONSIDER THIS...

In some states, LPNs are permitted to administer prescribed medicines, start intravenous fluids, and provide care to ventilator-dependent patients.

when moving patients. They often must deal with the stress of heavy workloads. In addition, the patients they care for may be confused, agitated, or uncooperative.

Licensed practical nurses measure and record patients' vital signs.

What's Required

Most training programs, lasting about 1 year, are offered by vocational or technical schools or community or junior colleges. LPNs must be licensed to practice. Successful completion of a practical nurse program and passing an examination are required to become licensed.

Education and Training

All states and the District of Columbia require LPNs to pass a licensing examination, known as the NCLEX-PN, after completing a state-approved practical nursing program. A high school diploma or its equivalent usually is required for entry, although some programs accept candidates without a diploma, and some programs are part of a high school curriculum.

CONSIDER THIS...

There are more than 1,500 state-approved training programs in practical nursing. Most training programs are available from technical and vocational schools or community and junior colleges. Other programs are available through high schools, hospitals, and colleges and universities.

Most year-long practical nursing programs include both classroom study and supervised clinical practice (patient care). Classroom study covers basic nursing concepts and subjects related to patient care, including anatomy, physiology, medical-surgical nursing, pediatrics, obstetrics, psychiatric nursing, the administration of drugs, nutrition,

and first aid. Clinical practice usually is in a hospital but sometimes includes other settings.

The NCLEX-PN licensing exam is required in order to obtain licensure as an LPN. The exam is developed and administered by the National Council of State Boards of Nursing. The NCLEX-PN is a computer-based exam and varies in length. The exam covers four major categories: safe and effective care environment, health promotion and maintenance, psychosocial integrity, and physiological integrity.

Postsecondary Program to Consider

- Licensed practical/vocational nurse training (LPN, LVN, Cert, Dipl, AAS)

Additional Qualifications

LPNs should have a caring, sympathetic nature. They should be emotionally stable because working with the sick and injured can be stressful. They also need to be observant, and to have good decision-making and communication skills. As part of a health-care team, they must be able to follow orders and work under close supervision.

School Subjects to Study

- Algebra
- Biology
- Chemistry
- English
- Geometry

Moving Up

In some employment settings, such as nursing homes, LPNs can advance to become charge nurses who oversee the work of other LPNs and of nursing aides. Some LPNs also choose to become registered nurses through numerous LPN-to-RN training programs.

Employment

Licensed practical and licensed vocational nurses held about 753,600 jobs in 2008. About 25 percent of LPNs worked in hospitals, 28 percent in nursing care facilities, and another 12 percent in offices of physicians. Others worked for home health-care services; employment services; residential care facilities; community care facilities for the elderly; outpatient care centers; and federal, state, and local government agencies.

Job Prospects

Employment of LPNs is expected to grow by 21 percent over the 10-year period ending 2018, much faster than the average for all occupations, in response to the long-term care needs of an increasing elderly population and the general increase in demand for health-care services.

Demand for LPNs will be driven by the increase in the share of the older population. Older persons have an increased incidence of injury and illness, which will increase their demand for health-care services. In addition, with better medical technology, people are living longer, increasing the demand for long-term health care. Job growth will occur over all health-care settings but especially those that service the geriatric population like nursing care facilities, community care facilities, and home health-care services.

In addition to projected job growth, job openings will result from replacement needs, as many workers leave the occupation permanently. Very good job opportunities are expected. Rapid employment growth is projected in most health-care industries, with the best job opportunities occurring in nursing care facilities and in home health-care services. There is a perceived inadequacy of available health care in many rural areas, so LPNs willing to locate in rural areas should have good job prospects.

Income

Median annual wages of licensed practical and licensed vocational nurses were $39,030 in May 2008. The middle 50 percent earned between $33,360 and $46,710. The lowest 10 percent earned less than $28,260, and the highest 10 percent earned more than $53,580.

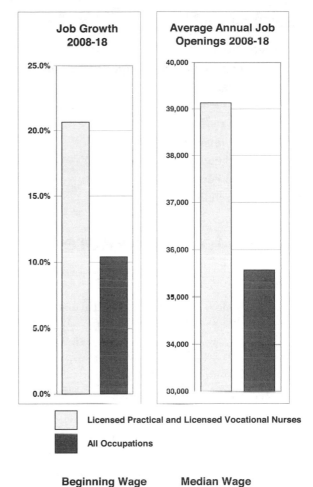

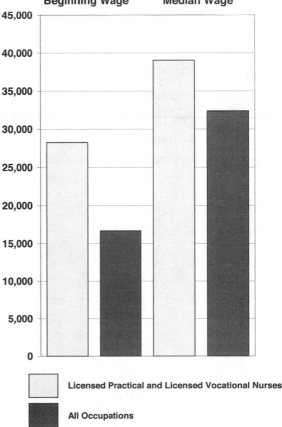

Related Jobs

- Athletic trainers
- Emergency medical technicians and paramedics
- Medical assistants
- Nursing, psychiatric, and home health aides
- Pharmacy aides
- Pharmacy technicians and aides
- Registered nurses
- Social and human service assistants
- Surgical technologists

How to Learn More

For information about practical nursing, contact the following organizations:

- National Association for Practical Nurse Education and Service, Inc., P.O. Box 25647, Alexandria, VA 22313. Internet: www.napnes.org

- National Federation of Licensed Practical Nurses, Inc., 605 Poole Dr., Garner, NC 27529. Internet: www.nflpn.org

- National League for Nursing, 61 Broadway, New York, NY 10006. Internet: www.nln.org

Information on the NCLEX-PN licensing exam is available from

- National Council of State Boards of Nursing, 111 East Wacker Dr., Suite 2900, Chicago, IL 60611. Internet: www.ncsbn.org

A list of state-approved LPN programs is available from individual state boards of nursing.

Why It's Hot

The American population is getting older and more in need of health care. Some of them will be cared for by LPNs in nursing homes. At the same time, in an attempt to cut costs, many doctors are shifting health-care procedures for people of all ages from hospitals to their own offices and to outpatient centers, where LPNs often play a large role.

Management Analysts

Management analysts analyze and propose ways to improve an organization's structure, efficiency, or profits.

Just the Facts

Earnings: $73,570

Job Growth: 23.9%

Annual Openings: 30,650

Education and Training: Bachelor's or higher degree, plus work experience

While at Work

As business becomes more complex, firms are continually faced with new challenges. They increasingly rely on management analysts to help them remain competitive amidst these changes. In private industry, management analysts are often called *consultants,* reflecting the fact that many are brought in on a temporary basis to solve a particular problem.

For example, a small but rapidly growing company might employ a consultant who is an expert in just-in-time inventory management to help improve its inventory-control system. In another case, a large company that has recently acquired a new division may hire management analysts to help reorganize the corporate structure and eliminate duplicate or nonessential jobs. In recent years, information technology and electronic commerce have provided new opportunities for management analysts. Companies hire consultants to develop strategies for entering and remaining competitive in the new electronic marketplace.

Management analysts might be single practitioners or part of large international organizations employing thousands of other consultants. Some analysts and consultants specialize in a specific industry, such as health care or telecommunications, while others specialize by type of business function, such as human resources, marketing, logistics, or information systems. In government, management analysts tend to specialize by type of agency. The work of management analysts and consultants varies with each client or employer and from project to project. Some projects require a team of consultants, each specializing in one area. In other projects, consultants work independently with the organization's managers. In all cases, ana-

CONSIDER THIS...

Management analysts often gain insight into business problems by building and solving mathematical models, such as one that shows how inventory levels affect costs and product delivery times. To use these models, they must have a strong foundation in mathematics, plus the experience to know which analytical approaches and tools are most appropriate for the given problem.

lysts and consultants collect, review, and analyze information in order to make recommendations to managers.

Both public and private organizations use consultants for a variety of reasons. Some lack the internal resources needed to handle a project, while others need a consultant's expertise to determine what resources will be required and what problems may be encountered if they pursue a particular opportunity. To retain a consultant, a company first solicits proposals from a number of consulting firms specializing in the area in which it needs assistance. These proposals include the estimated cost and scope of the project, staffing requirements, references from a number of previous clients, and a completion deadline. The company then selects the proposal that best suits its needs. Some firms, however, employ internal management consulting groups rather than hiring outside consultants.

After obtaining an assignment or contract, management analysts first define the nature and extent of the problem that they have been asked to solve. During this phase, they analyze relevant data—which may include annual revenues, employment, or expenditures—and interview managers and employees while observing their operations. The analysts or consultants then develop solutions to the problem. While preparing their recommendations, they take into account the nature of the organization, the relationship it has with others in the industry, and its internal organization and culture.

Once they have decided on a course of action, consultants report their findings and recommendations to the client. Their suggestions usually are submitted in writing, but oral presentations regarding findings also are common. For some projects, man-

agement analysts are retained to help implement the suggestions they have made.

Like their private-sector colleagues, management analysts in government agencies try to increase efficiency and worker productivity and to control costs. For example, if an agency is planning to purchase personal computers, it must first determine which type to buy, given its budget and data-processing needs. In this case, management analysts would assess the prices and characteristics of various machines and determine which ones best meet the agency's goals. Analysts may manage contracts for a wide range of goods and services to ensure quality performance and to prevent cost overruns.

Also Known As

Management analysts often have job titles that reflect a specialization in a certain kind of business problem; for example, some are called *clerical methods analysts, employment programs analysts, forms analysts, health program analysts, health systems analysts, purchase price analysts,* or *survey analysts.*

Job Fit

Personality Type
Investigative-Enterprising-Conventional

Career Cluster
04 Business, Management, and Administration

Skills
Equipment Use/Maintenance
Equipment/Technology Analysis
Management
Computer Programming
Social Skills
Science
Thought-Processing
Communications
Mathematics

Work Styles
Leadership
Adaptability/Flexibility
Concern for Others
Persistence
Analytical Thinking
Stress Tolerance
Social Skills Orientation
Innovation

CONSIDER THIS...

Management analysts often attempt to help a company adopt the "best practices" of its industry. To learn what these are, analysts may study a company with a track record of outstanding success with a particular business practice, a technique called *benchmarking.*

Management analysts propose ways to improve an organization's structure, efficiency, or profits.

Working Conditions

Management analysts usually divide their time between their offices and the client's site. In either situation, much of an analyst's time is spent indoors in clean, well-lit offices. Because they must spend a significant portion of their time with clients, analysts travel frequently.

Analysts and consultants generally work at least 40 hours a week. Uncompensated overtime is common, especially when project deadlines are approaching. Analysts may experience a great deal of stress when trying to meet a client's demands, often on a tight schedule.

Self-employed consultants can set their workload and hours and work at home. On the other hand, their livelihood depends on their ability to maintain and expand their client base. Salaried consultants also must impress potential clients to get and keep clients for their company.

CONSIDER THIS...

Analysts routinely attend conferences to keep abreast of current developments in their field. Every business specialization has at least one professional association, and most of them offer classes or workshops where members can learn the industry's newest tools and emerging challenges.

What's Required

Entry requirements for management analysts vary. For some entry-level positions, a bachelor's degree is sufficient. Other positions require a master's degree, specialized expertise, or both.

Education and Training

Educational requirements for entry-level jobs in this field vary between private industry and government. Many employers in private industry tend to seek individuals with a master's degree in business administration or a related discipline. Some employers also require additional years of experience in the field or industry in which the worker plans to consult. Other firms hire workers with a bachelor's degree as research analysts or associates and promote them to consultants after several years. Some government agencies require experience, graduate education, or both, but many also hire people with a bachelor's degree and little work experience for entry-level management analyst positions.

Few universities or colleges offer formal programs in management consulting; however, many fields of study provide a suitable educational background for this occupation, because of the wide range of areas addressed by management analysts. Most analysts also have years of experience in management, human resources, information technology, or other specialties.

Postsecondary Programs to Consider

- Accounting
- Business Administration and Management, General
- Computer and information science
- Economics
- Engineering
- Marketing
- Statistics

Additional Qualifications

Management analysts often work with minimal supervision, so they need to be self-motivated and disciplined. Analytical skills, the ability to get along with a wide range of people, strong oral and written communication skills, good judgment, time-management skills, and creativity are other desirable qualities. The ability to work in teams also is an important attribute as consulting teams become more common.

School Subjects to Study

- Algebra
- Computer science
- English
- Foreign language

- Geometry
- Pre-calculus and calculus
- Trigonometry

Moving Up

As consultants gain experience, they often become solely responsible for specific projects, taking on more responsibility and managing their own hours. At the senior level, consultants may supervise teams working on more complex projects and become more involved in seeking out new business. Those with exceptional skills may eventually become partners in the firm, focusing on attracting new clients and bringing in revenue. Senior consultants who leave their consulting firms often move to senior management positions at nonconsulting firms. Others with entrepreneurial ambition may open their own firms.

CONSIDER THIS...

A high percentage of management consultants are self-employed, partly because business startup and overhead costs are low. However, many small consulting firms fail each year because of lack of managerial expertise and clients. Therefore, persons interested in opening their own firm must have good organizational and marketing skills. Several years of consulting experience are also helpful.

The Institute of Management Consultants USA, Inc. offers the Certified Management Consultant (CMC) designation to those who meet minimum levels of education and experience, submit client reviews, and pass an interview and exam covering the IMC USA's Code of Ethics. Management consultants with a CMC designation must be recertified every 3 years. Certification is not mandatory for management consultants, but it may give a jobseeker a competitive advantage.

◾ Employment

Management analysts held about 746,900 jobs in 2008. About 26 percent of these workers, three times the average for all occupations, were self-employed. Management analysts are found throughout the country, but employment is concentrated in large metropolitan areas. Management analysts work in a range of industries, including management, scientific, and technical consulting firms; computer systems design and related services firms; and federal, state, and local governments.

Job Prospects

Employment of management analysts is expected to grow by 24 percent, much faster than the average, over the decade as industry and government increasingly rely on outside expertise to improve the performance of their organizations. Job growth is projected in very large consulting firms with international expertise and in smaller consulting firms that specialize in specific areas, such as biotechnology, health care, information technology, human resources, engineering, and marketing. Growth in the number of individual practitioners may be hindered by increasing use of consulting teams that are often more versatile.

As firms try to solve regulatory changes due to the current economic credit and housing crisis, consultants will be hired to render advice on the recovery process. Firms will also hire information technology consultants who specialize in "green" or environmentally safe use of technology management consulting to help lower energy consumption and implement "green" initiatives. Traditional companies hire analysts to help design intranets or company Web sites or to establish online businesses. New Internet startup companies hire analysts not only to design Web sites but also to advise them in traditional business practices, such as pricing strategies, marketing, and inventory and human resource management.

To offer clients better quality and a wider variety of services, consulting firms are partnering with traditional computer software and technology firms. Also, many computer firms are developing consulting practices of their own to take advantage of this expanding market. Although information technology consulting should remain one of the fastest-growing consulting areas, employment in the computer services industry can be volatile, and so the most successful management analysts may also consult in other business areas.

CONSIDER THIS...

The expanding role of management analysts in international business will create more opportunities for workers to travel or work abroad but also will require them to have a more comprehensive knowledge of international business and foreign cultures and languages.

The growth of international business will also contribute to an increase in demand for management analysts. As U.S. firms expand their business abroad, many will hire management analysts to help them form the right strategy for entering the market; to advise them on legal matters pertaining to specific countries; or to help them with organizational, administrative, and other issues, especially if the U.S. company is involved in a partnership or merger with a local firm. Just as globalization creates new opportunities for management analysts, it also allows U.S. firms to hire management analysts in other countries; however, because international work is expected to increase the total amount of work, this development is not expected to adversely affect employment in this occupation.

Furthermore, as international and domestic markets become more competitive, firms will need to use resources more efficiently. Management analysts will be increasingly sought to help reduce costs, streamline operations, and develop marketing strategies. As this process expands and as businesses downsize, even more opportunities will be created for analysts to perform duties that were previously handled internally. Finally, more management analysts will also be needed in the public sector as federal, state, and local government agencies seek to improve efficiency.

Despite rapid employment growth, keen competition is expected. The pool of applicants from which employers can draw is quite large, since analysts can have very diverse educational backgrounds and work experience. Furthermore, the independent and challenging nature of the work, combined with high earnings potential, makes this occupation attractive to many. Job opportunities are expected to be best for those with a graduate degree, specialized expertise, and a talent for salesmanship and public relations.

Economic downturns can also have adverse effects on employment for some management consultants. In these times, businesses look to cut costs, and consultants may be considered an excess expense. On the other hand, some consultants might experience an increase in work during recessions because they advise businesses on how to cut costs and remain profitable.

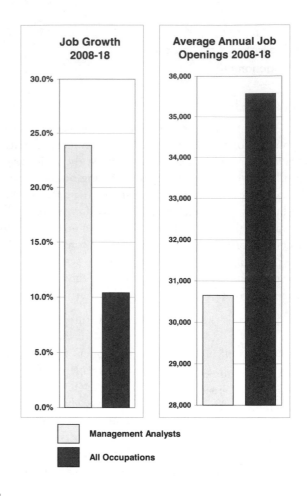

Income

Salaries for management analysts vary widely by years of experience and education, geographic location, specific expertise, and size of employer. Generally, management analysts employed in large firms or in metropolitan areas have the highest salaries. Median annual earnings of wage-and-salary management analysts in May 2008 were $73,570. The middle 50 percent earned between $54,890 and $99,700. The lowest 10 percent earned less than $41,910, and the highest 10 percent earned more than $133,850. Median annual May 2008 earnings in the industries employing the largest numbers of management analysts were $81,670 in management, scientific, and technical consulting services; $79,830 in federal executive branch; $55,590 in state government; $82,090 in computer systems design and related services; and $73,760 in management of companies and enterprises.

Salaried management analysts usually receive common benefits, such as health and life insurance, a retirement plan, vacation, and sick leave, as well as less common benefits, such as profit sharing and bonuses for outstanding work. In addition, all travel expenses usually are reimbursed by the employer. Self-employed consultants have to maintain their own office and provide their own benefits.

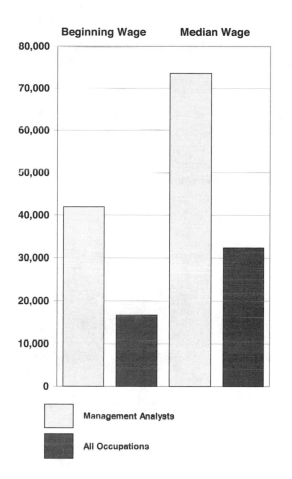

Beginning Wage   Median Wage

Management Analysts

All Occupations

How to Learn More

Information about career opportunities in management consulting is available from

- Association of Management Consulting Firms, 380 Lexington Ave., Suite 1700, New York, NY 10168. Internet: www.amcf. org

Information about the Certified Management Consultant designation can be obtained from

- Institute of Management Consultants USA, Inc., 2025 M St. NW, Suite 800, Washington, DC 20036. Internet: www. imcusa.org

Information on obtaining a management analyst position with the federal government is available at www.usajobs.opm.gov.

Why It's Hot

Job growth for management analysts has been driven by a number of changes in the business environment that have forced firms to take a closer look at their operations. These changes include regulatory changes, developments in information technology, and the growth of electronic commerce.

Market and Survey Researchers

Market and survey researchers gather information about people's preferences and opinions for companies, governments, and other organizations.

Just the Facts

Earnings: $58,982

Job Growth: 28.3%

Annual Openings: 15,070

Education and Training: Bachelor's degree

Related Jobs

- Accountants and auditors
- Administrative services managers
- Advertising, marketing, promotions, public relations, and sales managers
- Budget analysts
- Computer network, systems, and database administrators
- Computer systems analysts
- Cost estimators
- Economists
- Financial managers
- Human resources, training, and labor relations managers and specialists
- Industrial production managers
- Market and survey researchers
- Operations research analysts
- Personal financial advisors
- Top executives

While at Work

If you've ever been asked to rate a purchase or take a phone survey, you have been the target of market research. *Market research analysts* help companies understand what types of products people want and at what price. They also help companies market their products to the people most likely to buy them. Gathering statistical data on competitors and examining prices, sales, and methods of marketing and distribution, they analyze data on past sales to predict future sales.

Market research analysts devise methods and procedures for obtaining the data they need. Often, they design surveys to assess consumer preferences through Internet, telephone, or mail responses. They conduct some surveys as personal interviews, going door-to-door, leading focus group discussions, or setting up booths in public places such as shopping malls.

> **CONSIDER THIS...**
>
> Market research analysts often translate their research into sales. They might help develop advertising brochures and commercials, sales plans, and product promotions such as rebates and giveaways.

After compiling and evaluating the data, market research analysts make recommendations to their client or employer. They provide a company's management with information needed to make decisions on the promotion, distribution, design, and pricing of products or services. For example, the information may be used to determine the advisability of adding new lines of merchandise or opening branches of the company in a new location.

Survey researchers also gather information about people and their opinions, but these workers focus exclusively on designing and conducting surveys. They work for a variety of clients, such as corporations, government agencies, political candidates, and providers of various services. The surveys collect information that is used in performing research, making fiscal or policy decisions, measuring the effectiveness of those decisions, or improving customer satisfaction. Analysts may conduct opinion research to

> **CONSIDER THIS...**
>
> Survey researchers design surveys in many different formats, depending upon the scope of their research and the method of collection. Interview surveys, for example, are common because they can increase participation rates.

determine public attitudes on various issues; the research results may help political or business leaders to measure public support for their electoral prospects or social policies. Like market research analysts, survey researchers may use a variety of mediums to conduct surveys, such as the Internet, personal or telephone interviews, or questionnaires sent through the mail. They also may supervise interviewers who conduct surveys in person or over the telephone. Survey researchers may consult with economists, statisticians, market research analysts, or other data users in order to design surveys. They also may present survey results to clients.

Market and survey researchers may conduct opinion research to determine public attitudes on various issues.

Also Known As

One well-known form of survey research concerns people's opinions about political issues and candidates. *Pollsters* are professionals who conduct pre-election polls and then use that data to advise candidates on election strategy. Pollsters typically hold advanced degrees, such as master's degrees in political science or statistics.

Job Fit

Personality Type
Investigative-Enterprising-Conventional

Career Clusters
04 Business, Management, and Administration

14 Marketing, Sales, and Services

15 Science, Technology, Engineering, and Mathematics

Skills

Communications

Equipment/Technology Analysis

Management

Social Skills

Thought-Processing

Science

Mathematics

Computer Programming

Work Styles

Analytical Thinking

Achievement/Effort

Persistence

Innovation

Initiative

Integrity

Independence

Leadership

Working Conditions

Market and survey researchers generally have structured work schedules. They often work alone, writing reports, preparing statistical charts, and using computers, but they also may be an integral part of a research team. Market researchers who conduct personal interviews have frequent contact with the public. Most work under pressure of deadlines and tight schedules, which may require overtime. Travel may be necessary.

■ What's Required

A bachelor's degree is usually sufficient for entry-level market and survey research positions. Higher degrees may be required for some positions, however.

Education and Training

For many market and survey research jobs, a bachelor's degree is the minimum educational requirement. For more technical positions, however, a master's degree may be required.

In addition to completing courses in business, marketing, and consumer behavior, prospective market and survey researchers should take other liberal arts and social science courses, including economics, psychology, English, and sociology. Because of the importance of quantitative skills to market and survey researchers, courses in mathematics, statistics, sampling theory and survey design, and computer science are extremely helpful.

While in college, aspiring market and survey researchers should gain experience gathering and analyzing data, conducting interviews or surveys, and writing reports on their findings. This experience can prove invaluable later in obtaining a full-time position in the field. Some schools help graduate students find internships or part-time employment in government agencies, consulting firms, financial institutions, or marketing research firms prior to graduation.

CONSIDER THIS... Market and survey researchers often earn advanced degrees in business administration, marketing, statistics, communications, or other closely related disciplines.

Postsecondary Programs to Consider

- Applied economics
- Business/managerial economics
- Econometrics and quantitative economics
- Economics
- International economics
- Marketing research

Additional Qualifications

Market and survey researchers spend a lot of time performing precise data analysis, so those considering careers in the occupation should be able to pay attention to detail. Patience and persistence are also necessary qualities because these workers must spend long hours on independent study and problem solving.

Researchers must work well with others, however, as they often oversee the interviewing of a wide variety of individuals. Communication skills are important because researchers must be able to present their findings well both orally and in writing.

School Subjects to Study

- Algebra
- Computer science
- Economics
- English
- Pre-calculus
- Psychology
- Sociology
- Trigonometry

Moving Up

Researchers and analysts often begin by assisting others. With experience, market and survey analysts are eventually are assigned their own research projects. Continuing education and advanced degrees will be helpful to those looking to advance to more responsible positions in this occupation. It also is important to keep current with the latest methods of developing, conducting, and analyzing surveys and other data.

> **CONSIDER THIS...**
>
> Some people with expertise in marketing or survey research choose to teach others these skills. A master's degree usually is the minimum educational requirement for a job as a marketing or survey research instructor in junior and community colleges. In most colleges and universities, however, a Ph.D. is necessary for appointment as an instructor.

Advancement in this occupation may be helped by obtaining certification. The Marketing Research Association (MRA) offers a certification program for professional researchers who wish to demonstrate their expertise. The Professional Researcher Certification (PRC) is awarded for two levels of knowledge: practitioner and expert. Prior to gaining certification, each level of knowledge requires certain criteria to be met, consisting largely of education and experience, and also previous membership to at least one professional marketing research organization. Those who have been granted the PRC designation require continuing education within their particular discipline, and individuals must apply to renew their certification every 2 years.

Employment

Market and survey researchers held about 273,200 jobs in 2008, most of which—249,800—were held by market research analysts. Market research analysts are employed throughout the economy. The industries that employed the largest number of market research analysts in 2008 were management, scientific, and technical consulting services; management of companies and enterprises; computer systems design and related services; insurance carriers; and other professional, scientific, and technical services—which includes marketing research and public opinion polling.

Survey researchers held about 23,400 jobs in 2008. Most were employed primarily by firms in other professional, scientific, and technical services—which include market research and public opinion polling and scientific research and development services. About 9 percent of survey researchers worked in educational services.

Job Prospects

Overall employment of market and survey researchers is projected to grow 28 percent over the 10-year period ending 2018, much faster than the average for all occupations. Market research analysts, the larger specialty, will experience much faster than average job growth because competition between companies seeking to expand their market and sales of their products will generate a growing need for marketing professionals. Marketing research provides organizations valuable feedback from purchasers, allowing companies to evaluate consumer satisfaction and adjust their marketing strategies and plan more effectively for the future. In addition, globalization of the marketplace creates a need for more market researchers to analyze foreign markets and competition.

> **CONSIDER THIS...**
>
> Several market and survey researchers combine a full-time job in government, academia, or business with part-time consulting work in another setting. About 7 percent of market and survey researchers are self-employed.

Survey researchers, a much smaller specialty, will also increase much faster than average as public policy groups and all levels of governments increasingly use public opinion research to help determine a variety of issues, such as the best mass transit systems, social programs, and special services for school children and senior citizens that will be needed. Survey researchers will also be needed to meet the growing demand for market and opinion research as an increasingly competitive economy requires businesses and organizations to allocate advertising funds and other expenditures more effectively.

Despite the job growth, bachelor's degree holders may face competition for market research jobs, as many positions, especially technical ones, require a master's or doctoral degree. Among bachelor's degree holders, those with good quantitative skills, including a strong background in mathematics, statistics, survey design, and computer science, will have the best opportunities. Those with a background in consumer behavior or an undergraduate degree in a social science—psychology, sociology, or economics—may qualify for less technical positions, such as a public opinion researcher.

Overall, job opportunities should be best for jobseekers with a master's or Ph.D. degree in marketing or a related field and with strong quantitative skills. Market research analysts should have the best opportunities in consulting firms and marketing research firms as companies find it more profitable to contract for market research services rather than support their own marketing department. However, other organizations, including computer systems design companies, software publishers, financial services organizations, health-care institutions, advertising firms, and insurance companies, may also offer job opportunities for market research analysts.

than $112,410. Researchers in computer systems design or in company and enterprise management earned more than those in advertising, public relations, and technical consulting services.

Median annual wages of survey researchers in May 2008 were $36,220. The middle 50 percent earned between $22,290 and $54,480. The lowest 10 percent earned less than $17,650, and the highest 10 percent earned more than $75,940.

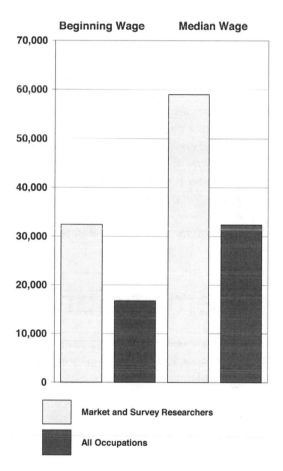

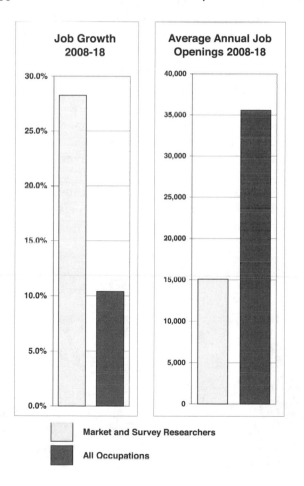

Related Jobs

- Actuaries
- Advertising, marketing, promotions, public relations, and sales managers
- Cost estimators
- Economists
- Management analysts
- Mathematicians
- Operations research analysts
- Psychologists
- Public relations specialists
- Sociologists and political scientists
- Statisticians
- Urban and regional planners

Income

Median annual wages of market research analysts in May 2008 were $61,070. The middle 50 percent earned between $43,990 and $85,510. The lowest 10 percent earned less than $33,770, and the highest 10 percent earned more

How to Learn More

For information about careers and certification in market research, contact

- Marketing Research Association, 110 National Dr., Glastonbury, CT 06033. Internet: www.mra-net.org

For information about careers in survey research, contact

- Council of American Survey Research Organizations, 170 North Country Rd., Suite 4, Port Jefferson, NY 11777. Internet: www.casro.org

Why It's Hot

Today's fast-paced business world is getting even more competitive in the expanding global marketplace. Businesses will need growing ranks of market and survey researchers to identify marketable products and services and to devise marketing campaigns that will open the wallets of buyers. Emerging media, such as smart phones, are opening new platforms for advertising, so businesses will need more guidance about how to invest their advertising dollars wisely.

Mathematicians

Mathematicians use mathematical theory and techniques to solve economic, scientific, engineering, physics, and business problems.

Just the Facts

Earnings: $95,150

Job Growth: 22.4%

Annual Openings: 150

Education and Training: Doctoral degree

While at Work

Mathematics is one of the oldest and most fundamental sciences. For millennia, mathematicians have been applying their theories and practices to a wide variety of scientific, social, and economic issues.

Theoretical mathematicians advance mathematical knowledge by developing new principles and recognizing previously unknown relationships between existing principles of mathematics. Although these workers seek to increase

basic knowledge without necessarily considering its practical use, such pure and abstract knowledge has been instrumental in producing or furthering many scientific and engineering achievements. Many theoretical mathematicians are employed as university faculty, dividing their time between teaching and conducting research.

Applied mathematicians, on the other hand, use theories and techniques, such as mathematical modeling and computational methods, to formulate and solve practical problems in business, government, engineering, and the physical, life, and social sciences. For example, they may analyze the most efficient way to schedule airline routes between cities, the effects and safety of new drugs, the aerodynamic characteristics of an experimental automobile, or the cost-effectiveness of alternative manufacturing processes.

Applied mathematicians working in industrial research and development may develop or enhance mathematical methods when solving a difficult problem. Some mathematicians, called *cryptanalysts,* analyze and decipher encryption systems—codes—designed to transmit military, political, financial, or law enforcement-related information. Applied mathematicians are frequently required to collaborate with other workers in their organizations to find common solutions to problems.

Consider This...

Applied mathematicians often use computers to analyze relationships among the variables and solve complex problems by developing models with alternative solutions.

Mathematicians may travel to seminars or conferences.

Also Known As

Individuals with titles other than mathematician do much of the work in applied mathematics. In fact, because mathematics is the foundation on which so many other academic disciplines are built, the number of workers using mathematical techniques is much greater than the number formally called mathematicians. For example, engineers, computer scientists, physicists, and economists are among those who use mathematics extensively. Some professionals, including statisticians, actuaries, and operations research analysts, are actually specialists in a particular branch of mathematics.

Job Fit

Personality Type

Investigative-Conventional-Artistic

Career Cluster

15 Science, Technology, Engineering, and Mathematics

Skills

Computer Programming

Science

Mathematics

Communications

Thought-Processing

Equipment/Technology Analysis

Social Skills

Management

Work Styles

Innovation

Analytical Thinking

Achievement/Effort

Persistence

Attention to Detail

Initiative

Independence

Working Conditions

Mathematicians usually work in comfortable offices. They often are part of interdisciplinary teams that may include economists, engineers, computer scientists, physicists, technicians, and others. Deadlines, overtime work, special requests for information or analysis, and prolonged travel to attend seminars or conferences may be part of their jobs.

Mathematicians who work in academia usually have a mix of teaching and research responsibilities. These mathematicians may conduct research alone or in close collabora-

tion with other mathematicians. Mathematicians in academia also may be aided by graduate students.

What's Required

A Ph.D. degree in mathematics usually is the minimum educational requirement for prospective mathematicians, except in the federal government.

Education and Training

In the federal government, entry level job candidates usually must have at least a bachelor's degree with a major in mathematics or 24 semester hours of mathematics courses. Most colleges and universities offer a bachelor's degree in mathematics. Courses usually required for this degree include calculus, differential equations, and linear and abstract algebra. Additional courses might include probability theory and statistics, mathematical analysis, numerical analysis, topology, discrete mathematics, and mathematical logic. High school students who are prospective college mathematics majors should take as many mathematics courses as possible while in high school.

Outside the federal government, bachelor's degree holders in mathematics usually are not qualified for most jobs, and many seek advanced degrees in mathematics or a related discipline. In private industry, candidates for mathematician jobs typically need a Ph.D., although there may be opportunities for those with a master's degree. Most of the positions designated for mathematicians are in research and development laboratories, as part of technical teams.

> **CONSIDER THIS...**
>
> Many colleges and universities advise or require students majoring in mathematics to take courses in a closely related field, such as computer science, engineering, life science, physical science, or economics. A double major in mathematics and another related discipline is particularly desirable to many employers.

Postsecondary Programs to Consider

- Algebra and number theory
- Analysis and functional analysis
- Applied mathematics
- Computational mathematics
- Geometry/geometric analysis
- Logic
- Mathematical statistics and probability
- Mathematics
- Topology and foundations

Additional Qualifications

For jobs in applied mathematics, training in the field in which mathematics will be used is very important. Mathematics is used extensively in physics, actuarial science, statistics, engineering, and operations research. Computer science, business and industrial management, economics, finance, chemistry, geology, life sciences, and behavioral sciences are likewise dependent on applied mathematics. Mathematicians also should have substantial knowledge of computer programming, because most complex mathematical computation and much mathematical modeling are done on a computer.

Mathematicians need to have good reasoning to identify, analyze, and apply basic principles to technical problems. Communication skills also are important, as mathematicians must be able to interact and discuss proposed solutions with people who may not have extensive knowledge of mathematics.

School Subjects to Study

- Algebra
- Chemistry
- Computer science
- English
- Geometry
- Physics
- Pre-calculus and calculus
- Trigonometry

Moving Up

Bachelor's degree holders who meet state certification requirements may become primary or secondary school mathematics teachers. The majority of those with a master's degree in mathematics who work in private industry do so not as mathematicians, however, but in related fields such as computer science, where they have titles such as computer programmer, systems analyst, or systems engineer.

◼ Employment

Mathematicians held about 2,900 jobs in 2008. Many people with mathematical backgrounds also worked in other occupations. For example, there were about 54,800 jobs for postsecondary mathematical science teachers in 2008.

Many mathematicians work for the federal government, primarily in the U.S. Department of Defense which ac-

counts for about 81 percent of the mathematicians employed by the federal government. Many of the other mathematicians employed by the federal government work for the National Institute of Standards and Technology (NIST) or the National Aeronautics and Space Administration (NASA).

In the private sector, major employers include scientific research and development services and management, scientific, and technical consulting services. Some mathematicians also work for insurance carriers.

Job Prospects

Employment of mathematicians is expected to increase by 22 percent during the 10-year period ending 2018, which is much faster than average for all occupations. Advancements in technology usually lead to expanding applications of mathematics, and more workers with knowledge of mathematics will be required in the future. However, jobs in industry and government often require advanced knowledge of related scientific disciplines in addition to mathematics. The most common fields in which mathematicians study and find work are computer science and software development, physics, engineering, and operations research. Many mathematicians also are involved in financial analysis and in life sciences research.

CONSIDER THIS...

Because the number of Ph.D. degrees awarded in mathematics continues to exceed the number of available university positions—especially tenure-track positions—many graduates will need to find employment in industry and government.

Job competition will remain keen, however, because few new jobs are expected compared to the number of college graduates with degrees in mathematics. Ph.D. holders with a strong background in mathematics and a related discipline, such as engineering or computer science, and who apply mathematical theory to real-world problems will have the best job prospects in related occupations. In addition, mathematicians with experience in computer programming will better their job prospects in many occupations.

Employment in theoretical mathematical research is sensitive to general economic fluctuations and to changes in government spending. Job prospects will be greatly influenced by changes in public and private funding for research and development.

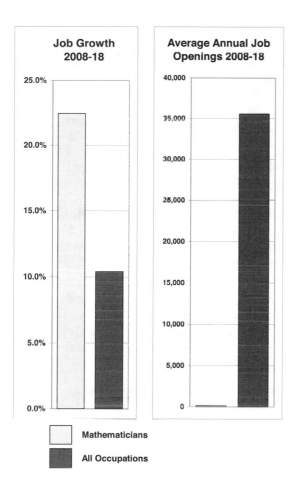

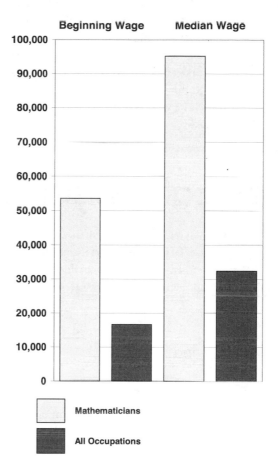

- Market and survey researchers
- Operations research analysts
- Personal financial advisors
- Physicists and astronomers
- Statisticians

Income

Median annual wages of mathematicians were $95,150 in May 2008. The middle 50 percent earned between $71,430 and $119,480. The lowest 10 percent had earnings of less than $53,570, while the highest 10 percent earned more than $140,500.

In March 2009, the average annual salary in the federal government was $107,051 for mathematicians; $107,015 for mathematical statisticians; and $101,645 for cryptanalysts.

Related Jobs

- Actuaries
- Computer network, systems, and database administrators
- Computer programmers
- Computer software engineers
- Computer systems analysts
- Economists
- Engineers

How to Learn More

For more information about careers and training in mathematics, especially for doctoral-level employment, contact

- American Mathematical Society, 201 Charles St., Providence, RI 02904-2294. Internet: www.ams.org

For specific information on careers in applied mathematics, contact

- Society for Industrial and Applied Mathematics, 3600 University City Science Center, Philadelphia, PA 19104-2688. Internet: www.siam.org

Information on obtaining positions as mathematicians with the federal government is available at www.usajobs.gov.

Why It's Hot

Computers are allowing more and more real-world problems to be reduced to mathematical models. Mathematicians with good computer skills will be needed to solve problems related to industrial production, national defense, environmental protection, and many other matters. Keep in mind that this occupation is small, with fewer than 3,000 workers, so its rapid growth will not result in a large number of job openings. Nevertheless, it is a field where workers will find many creative and useful projects to participate in.

Medical Assistants

Medical assistants perform administrative and clinical tasks to keep the offices of physicians, podiatrists, chiropractors, and other health practitioners running smoothly.

Just the Facts

Earnings: $28,300

Job Growth: 33.9%

Annual Openings: 21,780

Education and Training: Moderate-term on-the-job training

While at Work

The duties of medical assistants vary from office to office, depending on the location and size of the practice and the practitioner's specialty. In small practices, medical assistants usually do many different kinds of tasks, handling both administrative and clinical duties and reporting directly to an office manager, physician, or other health practitioner. Those in large practices tend to specialize in a particular area, under the supervision of department administrators.

Medical assistants who perform administrative tasks have many duties. They update and file patients' medical records, fill out insurance forms, and arrange for hospital admissions and laboratory services. They also perform tasks less specific to medical settings, such as answering telephones, greeting patients, handling correspondence, scheduling appointments, and handling billing and bookkeeping.

For clinical medical assistants, duties vary according to what is allowed by state law. Some common tasks include taking medical histories and recording vital signs, explaining treatment procedures to patients, preparing patients for examinations, and assisting physicians during examinations. Medical assistants collect and prepare laboratory specimens and sometimes perform basic laboratory tests on the premises, dispose of contaminated supplies, and sterilize medical instruments. They might instruct patients about medications and special diets, prepare and administer medications as directed by a physician, authorize drug refills as directed, telephone prescriptions to a pharmacy, draw blood, prepare patients for X-rays, take electrocardiograms, remove sutures, and change dressings.

Medical assistants also may arrange examining room instruments and equipment, purchase and maintain supplies and equipment, and keep waiting and examining rooms neat and clean.

CONSIDER THIS...

Medical assistants should not be confused with physician assistants, who examine, diagnose, and treat patients under the direct supervision of a physician.

Medical assistants perform clinical tasks to keep physicians' offices running smoothly.

Also Known As

Ophthalmic medical assistants, *optometric assistants*, and *podiatric medical assistants* are examples of specialized assistants who have additional duties. Ophthalmic medical assistants help ophthalmologists provide eye care. They conduct diagnostic tests, measure and record vision, and test eye muscle function. They also show patients how to insert, remove, and care for contact lenses, and they apply eye dressings. Under the direction of the physician, ophthalmic medical assistants may administer eye medications. They also maintain optical and surgical instruments and may assist the ophthalmologist in surgery. Optometric assistants also help provide eye care, working with optometrists. They provide chair-side assistance, instruct patients about contact lens use and care, conduct preliminary tests on patients, and otherwise provide assistance while working directly with an optometrist. Podiatric medical assistants make castings of feet, expose and develop X-rays, and assist podiatrists in surgery.

Job Fit

Personality Type
Conventional-Social-Realistic

Career Cluster
08 Health Science

Skills
Social Skills
Communications
Thought-Processing
Computer Programming

Work Styles
Concern for Others
Stress Tolerance
Social Skills Orientation
Self-Control
Adaptability/Flexibility
Cooperation
Integrity
Attention to Detail

Working Conditions

Medical assistants work in well-lighted, clean environments. They interact constantly with other people and may have to handle several responsibilities at once. Most full-time medical assistants work a regular 40-hour week. However, many medical assistants work part time, evenings, or weekends.

What's Required

Some medical assistants are trained on the job, but many complete 1-year or 2-year programs.

Education and Training

Postsecondary medical assisting programs are offered in vocational-technical high schools, postsecondary vocational schools, and community and junior colleges. Programs usually last either 1 year, resulting in a certificate or diploma, or 2 years, resulting in an associate degree. Courses cover anatomy, physiology, and medical terminology, as well as typing, transcription, recordkeeping, accounting, and insurance processing. Students learn laboratory techniques, clinical and diagnostic procedures, pharmaceutical principles, the administration of medications, and first aid. They study office practices, patient relations, medical law, and ethics. Various organizations accredit medical assisting programs. Accredited programs often include an internship that provides practical experience in physicians' offices, hospitals, or other health-care facilities.

CONSIDER THIS... Medical offices are governed by many laws and regulations, and part of medical assistant training is learning about these. For example, the Health Insurance Portability and Accountability Act of 1996 (HIPAA) puts limits on the use and sharing of information about patients. This applies not only to medical records, but also to conversations between doctors and other health providers.

Formal training in medical assisting, while generally preferred, is not always required. Some medical assistants are trained on the job, although this practice is less common than in the past. Applicants usually need a high school diploma or the equivalent. Volunteer experience in the health care field is helpful. Medical assistants who are trained on the job usually spend their first few months attending training sessions and working closely with more experienced workers.

Some states allow medical assistants to perform more advanced procedures, such as giving injections, after passing a test or taking a course.

- Allied health and medical assisting services, other
- Anesthesiologist assistant training
- Chiropractic assistant/technician training
- Medical administrative/executive assistant and medical secretary training
- Medical insurance coding specialist/coder training
- Medical office assistant/specialist training
- Medical office management/administration
- Medical reception/receptionist training
- Medical/clinical assistant training
- Ophthalmic technician/technologist training
- Optometric technician/assistant training
- Orthoptics/orthoptist training

Additional Qualifications

Medical assistants deal with the public; therefore, they must be neat and well groomed and have a courteous, pleasant manner, and they must be able to put patients at ease and explain physicians' instructions. They must respect the confidential nature of medical information. Clinical duties require a reasonable level of manual dexterity and visual acuity.

School Subjects to Study

- Algebra
- Bookkeeping
- Computer science
- English
- Typing

Moving Up

Medical assistants may advance to other occupations through experience or additional training. For example, some may go on to teach medical assisting, and others pursue additional education to become nurses or other health-care workers. Administrative medical assistants may advance to office manager or qualify for a variety of administrative support occupations.

Employment

Medical assistants held about 483,600 jobs in 2008. About 62 percent worked in offices of physicians; 13 percent worked in public and private hospitals, including inpatient and outpatient facilities; and 11 percent worked in offices of other health practitioners, such as chiropractors and optometrists. Most of the remainder worked in other health-care industries, such as outpatient care centers and nursing and residential care facilities.

Job Prospects

Employment of medical assistants is expected to grow 34 percent in the 10-year period ending in 2018, much faster than the average for all occupations. An aging population and the increasing prevalence of certain conditions, such as obesity and diabetes, will increase demand for health-care services and medical assistants. Increasing use of medical assistants to allow doctors to care for more patients will further stimulate job growth.

Helping to drive job growth is the increasing number of group practices, clinics, and other health-care facilities that need a high proportion of support personnel, particularly medical assistants who can handle both administrative and clinical duties. In addition, medical assistants work mostly in primary care, a consistently growing sector of the health-care industry.

CONSIDER THIS...

Employers prefer to hire experienced workers or those who are certified. Although not required, certification indicates that a medical assistant meets certain standards of competence. Various associations award certification credentials to medical assistants, and the certification process varies. It also is possible to become certified in a specialty, such as podiatry, optometry, or ophthalmology.

Jobseekers who want to work as a medical assistant should find excellent job prospects. Medical assistants are projected to account for a very large number of new jobs, and many other opportunities will come from the need to replace workers leaving the occupation. Medical assistants with formal training or experience—particularly those with certification—should have the best job opportunities, since employers generally prefer to hire these workers.

Income

The earnings of medical assistants vary, depending on their experience, skill level, and location. Median annual earnings of wage-and-salary medical assistants were $28,300 in May 2008. The middle 50 percent earned between $23,700 and $33,050. The lowest 10 percent earned less than $20,600, and the highest 10 percent earned more than $39,570. Median annual earnings in the industries employing the largest numbers of medical assistants in

May 2008 were $28,710 in offices of physicians; $29,720 in general medical and surgical hospitals; $24,730 in offices of chiropractors; $24,930 in offices of optometrists; and $26,560 in offices of all other health practitioners.

A 2009 survey of members of the American Association of Medical Assistants found that about 86 percent of full-time workers receive some form of benefits package from their employers.

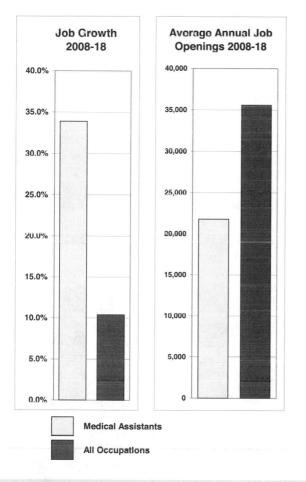

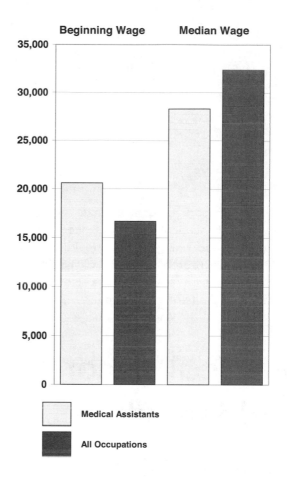

How to Learn More

Information about career opportunities and certification for medical assistants is available from

- American Association of Medical Assistants, 20 North Wacker Dr., Suite 1575, Chicago, IL 60606. Internet: www.aama-ntl.org

- American Medical Technologists, 10700 West Higgins Rd., Suite 150, Rosemont, IL 60018. Internet: www.amt1.com

- National Healthcareer Association, 7 Ridgedale Ave., Suite 203, Cedar Knolls, NJ 07927

Information about career opportunities, training programs, and certification for ophthalmic medical personnel is available from

- Joint Commission on Allied Health Personnel in Ophthalmology, 2025 Woodlane Dr., St. Paul, MN 55125. Internet: www.jcahpo.org/newsite/index.htm

Information about career opportunities, training programs and certification for optometric assistants is available from

- American Optometric Association, 243 N. Lindbergh Blvd., St. Louis, MO 63141. Internet: www.aoa.org

Information about certification for podiatric assistants is available from

- American Society of Podiatric Medical Assistants, 2124 South Austin Blvd., Cicero, IL 60804. Internet: www.aspma.org

Related Jobs

- Dental assistants
- Dental hygienists
- Licensed practical and licensed vocational nurses
- Medical records and health information technicians
- Medical secretaries
- Medical transcriptionists
- Nursing, psychiatric, and home health aides
- Occupational therapist assistants and aides
- Pharmacy aides
- Physical therapist assistants and aides
- Surgical technologists

For lists of accredited educational programs in medical assisting, contact

- Accrediting Bureau of Health Education Schools, 7777 Leesburg Pike, Suite 314 N, Falls Church, VA 22043. Internet: http://www.abhes.org

- Commission on Accreditation of Allied Health Education Programs, 1361 Park St., Clearwater, FL 33756. Internet: www.caahep.org

Why It's Hot

As the health-care industry expands rapidly because of technological advances in medicine and the growth and aging of the population, there will be an increased need for all health-care workers. Medical assistants are indispensible members of the health-care team.

Medical Records and Health Information Technicians

Medical records and health information technicians organize and evaluate medical records.

Just the Facts

Earnings: $30,610

Job Growth: 20.3%

Annual Openings: 7,030

Education and Training: Associate degree

While at Work

Every time a patient receives health care, it goes on his or her permanent record. *Medical* record, that is. Such records include information that the patient provides concerning his or her symptoms and medical history, the results of examinations, reports of X-rays and laboratory tests, diagnoses, treatment plans, and outcomes. Medical records and health information technicians evaluate these records for completeness and accuracy and keep them organized and secure.

Technicians assemble patients' health information, making sure that patients' initial medical charts are complete, that all forms are completed and properly identified and authenticated, and that all necessary information is in the computer. They regularly communicate with physicians and other health care professionals to clarify diagnoses or to obtain additional information.

Medical records and health information technicians' duties vary with the size of the facility where they work. In large facilities, technicians might specialize in one aspect of health information or might supervise health information clerks and transcriptionists while a medical records and health information administrator manages the department. In smaller facilities, a credentialed medical records and health information technician may have the opportunity to manage the department.

Medical records and health information technicians make sure that patients' medical charts are complete.

Some medical records and health information technicians specialize in coding patients' medical information for insurance purposes. Technicians who specialize in coding are called health information coders, medical record coders, or coding specialists. These technicians assign a code to each diagnosis and procedure, relying on their medical knowledge. Technicians then use classification systems software to assign the patient to one of several hundred "diagnosis-related groups," or DRGs. The DRG determines the amount for which the hospital will be reimbursed if the patient is covered by insurance.

Also Known As

Cancer registrars maintain facility, regional, and national databases of cancer patients. These specialized technicians review patient records and pathology reports, and assign codes for the diagnosis and treatment of different cancers and selected benign tumors. Registrars conduct annual follow-ups on all patients in the registry to track their treatment, survival, and recovery. Physicians and public health organizations then use this information to calculate success rates of various types of treatment and identify potential participants for clinical drug trials. Public health officials also use cancer registry data to target areas for the allocation of resources to provide intervention and screening.

Job Fit

Personality Type
Conventional-Enterprising

Career Cluster
08 Health Science

Skill
Computer Programming

Work Styles
Independence

Social Skills Orientation

Integrity

Attention to Detail

Adaptability/Flexibility

Concern for Others

Dependability

Cooperation

Working Conditions

Medical records and health information technicians work in pleasant and comfortable offices. Because accuracy is essential in their jobs, technicians must pay close attention to detail. Technicians who work at computer monitors for prolonged periods must guard against eyestrain and muscle pain.

Medical records and health information technicians usually work a 40-hour week. Some overtime may be required. In hospitals—where health information departments often are open 24 hours a day, 7 days a week—technicians may work day, evening, and night shifts.

What's Required

Medical records and health information technicians entering the field usually have an associate degree. Many employers favor technicians who have become Registered Health Information Technicians (RHIT).

Education and Training

Medical records and health information technicians generally obtain an associate degree from a community or junior college. Typically, community and junior colleges offer flexible course scheduling or online distance learning courses. In addition to general education, coursework includes medical terminology, anatomy and physiology, legal aspects of health information, health data standards, coding and abstraction of data, statistics, database management, quality improvement methods, and computer science.

> **CONSIDER THIS...**
>
> These workers are among the few who work in the health field but have little or no direct contact with patients.

Postsecondary Programs to Consider

- Health information/medical records technology/technician
- Medical insurance coding specialist/coder

Additional Qualifications

Most employers prefer to hire Registered Health Information Technicians (RHIT), who must pass a written examination offered by the American Health Information Management Association (AHIMA). To take the examination, a person must graduate from a 2-year associate degree program accredited by the Commission on Accreditation for Health Informatics and Information Management Education (CAHIIM). In 2009, there were more than 200 CAHIIM accredited programs in Health Informatics and Information Management Education.

The American Academy of Professional Coders (AAPC) offers coding credentials. The Board of Medical Specialty Coding (BMSC) and Professional Association of Healthcare Coding Specialists (PAHCS) both offer credentialing in specialty coding. The National Cancer Registrars Association (NCRA) offers a credential as a Certified Tumor Registrar (CTR). To learn more about the credentials available and their specific requirements, contact the credentialing organization.

Some employers prefer candidates with experience in a health care setting. Health information technicians should have good communication skills, as they often serve as a liaison between health care facilities, insurance companies, and other establishments. Accuracy is also essential because technicians must pay close attention to detail. Proficiency with computers is also useful, as most records exist in an electronic format.

School Subjects to Study

- Algebra
- Biology
- Chemistry
- Computer science
- English
- Geometry
- Pre-calculus
- Trigonometry

Moving Up

Experienced medical records and health information technicians usually advance in one of two ways—by specializing or by moving into a management position. Many senior technicians specialize in coding, in cancer registry, or in privacy and security. Most coding and registry skills are learned on the job. A number of schools offer certificate programs in coding or include coding as part of the associate degree program for health information technicians. For cancer registry, there are a few formal 2-year certificate programs approved by the National Cancer Registrars Association (NCRA). Some schools and employers offer intensive 1- to 2-week training programs in either coding or cancer registry.

In large medical records and health information departments, experienced technicians may advance to section supervisor, overseeing the work of the coding, correspondence, or discharge sections, for example. Senior technicians with RHIT credentials may become director or assistant director of a medical records and health information department in a small facility. However, in larger institutions, the director usually is an administrator with a bachelor's degree in medical records and health information administration.

◾ Employment

Medical records and health information technicians held about 172,500 jobs in 2008. About 2 out of 5 jobs were in hospitals. The rest were mostly in offices of physicians, nursing care facilities, outpatient care centers, and home

health care services. Insurance firms that deal in health matters employ a small number of health information technicians to tabulate and analyze health information. Public health departments also employ technicians to supervise data collection from health care institutions and to assist in research.

Job Prospects

Employment of medical records and health information technicians is expected to increase by 20 percent through 2018—faster than the average for all occupations—because of rapid growth in the number of medical tests, treatments, and procedures being used. Also, technicians will be needed to enter patient information into computer databases to comply with federal legislation mandating the use of electronic medical records.

New jobs are expected in offices of physicians as a result of increasing demand for detailed records, especially in large group practices. New jobs also are expected in home health care services, outpatient care centers, and nursing and residential care facilities.

Job prospects should be very good. In addition to job growth, openings will result from the need to replace technicians who retire or leave the occupation permanently.

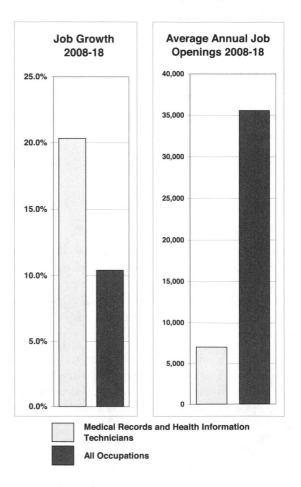

Income

The median annual wage of medical records and health information technicians was $30,610 in May 2008. The middle 50 percent earned between $24,290 and $39,490. The lowest 10 percent earned less than $20,440, and the highest 10 percent earned more than $50,060.

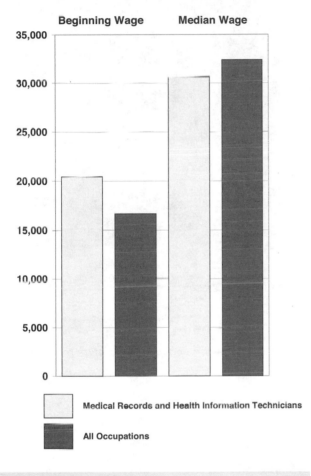

Beginning Wage Median Wage

☐ Medical Records and Health Information Technicians

■ All Occupations

Related Jobs

- Medical secretaries
- Medical transcriptionists

▣ How to Learn More

Information on careers in medical records and health information technology, and a list of accredited training programs is available from

- American Health Information Management Association, 233 N. Michigan Ave., Suite 2150, Chicago, IL 60601-5800. Internet: www.ahima.org

Information on training and certification for medical coders is available from

- American Academy of Professional Coders, 2480 South 3850 West, Suite B, Salt Lake City, UT 84120. Internet: www.aapc. com

Information on cancer registrars is available from

- National Cancer Registrars Association, 1340 Braddock Place Suite 203, Alexandria, VA 22314. Internet: www.ncra-usa.org

Why It's Hot

Changing government regulations and the growth of managed care have increased the amount of paperwork involved in filing insurance claims. Technicians with a strong background in medical coding will be in particularly high demand.

Medical Scientists

Medical scientists research human diseases to improve human health.

Just the Facts

Earnings: $72,590

Job Growth: 40.4%

Annual Openings: 6,620

Education and Training: Doctoral degree

▣ While at Work

If you've ever taken medication or been vaccinated for a disease, you no doubt have a medical scientist to thank for it. Most medical scientists conduct biomedical research and development to advance knowledge of life processes and living organisms, including viruses, bacteria, and other infectious agents. Their research results in advances in diagnosis, treatment, and prevention of many diseases. Basic medical research continues to build the foundation for new vaccines, drugs, and treatment procedures.

Medical scientists engage in laboratory research, clinical investigation, technical writing, drug application review, and related activities.

Medical scientists study biological systems to understand the causes of disease and other health problems. They develop treatments and design research tools and techniques that have medical applications. Medical scientists who are also physicians can administer these treatments to patients in clinical trials, monitor their reactions, and observe the results. They may draw blood, excise tissue, or perform other invasive procedures. Those who are not physicians normally collaborate with physicians who deal directly with patients. Medical scientists examine the results of clinical trials and adjust the dosage levels to reduce negative side effects or to induce better results.

Medical scientists who work in applied research or product development use knowledge discovered through basic research to develop new drugs and medical treatments. They usually have less autonomy than basic medical researchers do to choose the emphasis of their research. They spend more time working on marketable treatments to meet the business goals of their employers. Medical scientists doing applied research and product development in private industry may also be required to explain their research plans or results to nonscientists who are in a position to reject or approve their ideas.

> ### CONSIDER THIS...
> In addition to developing treatments for medical conditions, medical scientists attempt to discover ways to prevent health problems. For example, they may study the link between smoking and lung cancer or between alcoholism and liver disease.

Swift advances in basic medical knowledge related to genetics and organic molecules have spurred growth in the field of biotechnology. Discovery of important drugs, including human insulin and growth hormone, is the result of research using biotechnology techniques, such as recombining DNA. Many other substances not previously available in large quantities are now produced by biotechnological means; some may one day be useful in treating diseases such as Parkinson's or Alzheimer's.

> ### CONSIDER THIS...
> Scientists increasingly work as part of teams, interacting with engineers, scientists of other disciplines, business managers, and technicians.

Also Known As

Some medical scientists specialize in epidemiology. This branch of medical science investigates and describes the causes and spread of disease and develops the means for prevention or control. *Epidemiologists* may study many different illnesses, often focusing on major infectious diseases such as influenza or cholera. Epidemiologists can be separated into two groups—research and clinical. *Research epidemiologists* conduct research in an effort to eradicate or control infectious diseases. Research epidemiologists work at colleges and universities, schools of public health, medical schools, and independent research firms. *Clinical ep-*

idemiologists work primarily in consulting roles at hospitals, informing the medical staff of infectious outbreaks and providing containment solutions. These epidemiologists sometimes are referred to as infection control professionals, and some of them are also physicians.

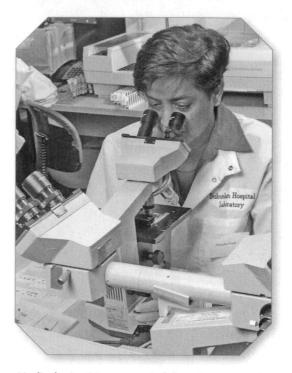

Medical scientists engage in laboratory research.

Job Fit

Personality Type
Investigative-Artistic-Realistic

Career Clusters
08 Health Science

15 Science, Technology, Engineering, and Mathematics

Skills
Science

Communications

Management

Thought-Processing

Mathematics

Computer Programming

Social Skills

Equipment/Technology Analysis

Equipment Use/Maintenance

Work Styles

Persistence

Analytical Thinking

Achievement/Effort

Innovation

Integrity

Initiative

Stress Tolerance

Leadership

Working Conditions

Many medical scientists work independently in private industry, university, or government laboratories, exploring new areas of research or expanding on specialized research that they began in graduate school. Medical scientists who rely on grant money may be under pressure to meet deadlines and to conform to rigid grant-writing specifications when preparing proposals to seek new or extended funding.

Medical scientists who conduct research usually work in laboratories and use a wide variety of equipment. Some may work directly with individual patients or larger groups as they administer drugs and monitor patients during clinical trials. Often, these medical scientists also spend time working in clinics and hospitals.

> **CONSIDER THIS...**
>
> Medical scientists usually are not exposed to unsafe or unhealthy conditions; however, those scientists who work with dangerous organisms or toxic substances must follow strict safety procedures to avoid contamination.

Medical scientists typically work regular hours in offices or laboratories, but longer hours are not uncommon. Researchers may be required to work odd hours in laboratories or other locations, depending on the nature of their research. On occasion, epidemiologists may be required to travel to meetings and hearings for medical investigations.

What's Required

A Ph.D. in a biological science is the minimum education required for most prospective medical scientists. However, some medical scientists also earn medical degrees in order to perform clinical work.

Education and Training

It is particularly helpful for medical scientists to earn both a Ph.D. and a medical degree. Students planning careers as medical scientists should start by pursuing a bachelor's degree in a biological science. In addition to required courses in chemistry and biology, undergraduates should study allied disciplines, such as mathematics, engineering, physics, and computer science. General humanities courses are also beneficial, as writing and communication skills are necessary for drafting grant proposals and publishing research results.

> **CONSIDER THIS...**
>
> In addition to formal education, medical scientists usually spend some time in a postdoctoral position before they apply for permanent jobs. Postdoctoral work provides valuable laboratory experience. In some institutions, the postdoctoral position can lead to a permanent job.

Once students have completed undergraduate studies, there are two main paths for prospective medical scientists. They can enroll in a university Ph.D. program in the biological sciences; these programs typically take about 6 years of study, and students specialize in one particular field, such as genetics, pathology, or bioinformatics. They can also enroll in a joint M.D.-Ph.D. program at a medical college; these programs typically take 7 to 8 years of study, where students learn both the clinical skills needed to be a physician and the research skills needed to be a scientist.

Medical scientists who administer drug or gene therapy to human patients, or who otherwise interact medically with patients—drawing blood, excising tissue, or performing other invasive procedures—must be licensed physicians. To be licensed, physicians must graduate from an accredited medical school, pass a licensing examination, and complete 1 to 7 years of graduate medical education.

Postsecondary Programs to Consider

- Anatomy
- Biochemistry
- Biomedical sciences
- Biophysics
- Biostatistics
- Cardiovascular science
- Cell/cellular biology and histology
- Endocrinology
- Environmental toxicology
- Epidemiology
- Exercise physiology
- Human/medical genetics
- Immunology
- Medical microbiology and bacteriology
- Medical science
- Molecular biology
- Molecular pharmacology
- Molecular toxicology
- Neuropharmacology
- Oncology and cancer biology
- Pathology/experimental pathology
- Pharmacology and toxicology
- Physiology
- Reproductive biology
- Toxicology
- Vision science/physiological optics

Additional Qualifications

Medical scientists should be able to work independently or as part of a team and be able to communicate clearly and concisely. Those in private industry, especially those who aspire to consulting and administrative positions, should possess strong communication skills so that they can provide instruction and advice to physicians and other healthcare professionals.

School Subjects to Study

- Algebra
- Biology
- Chemistry
- Computer science
- English
- Foreign language
- Geometry
- Physics
- Pre-calculus and calculus
- Public speaking
- Trigonometry

Moving Up

Medical scientists with more experience usually gain greater independence in their work, larger budgets, or tenure in university positions. Others choose to move into managerial positions and become natural science managers Those who pursue management careers spend more time preparing budgets and schedules.

Employment

Medical scientists held about 109,400 jobs in 2008. About 31 percent of medical scientists were employed in scientific research and development services firms. Another 27 percent were employed in educational services; 13 percent were employed in pharmaceutical and medicine manufacturing; and 10 percent were employed in hospitals.

Job Prospects

Employment of medical scientists is expected to increase 40 percent over the 10-year period ending 2018, much faster than the average for all occupations. In fact, medical scientists have enjoyed rapid gains in employment since the 1980s—reflecting, in part, the growth of biotechnology as an industry.

Much of the basic biological and medical research done in recent years has resulted in new knowledge. Medical scientists will be needed to take this knowledge to the next stage—for example, understanding how certain genes function within an entire organism—so that medical treatments can be developed for various diseases. Even pharmaceutical and other firms not solely engaged in biotechnology have adopted biotechnology techniques, thus creating employment for medical scientists. However, some companies may also conduct more of their research and development in lower-wage countries, limiting employment growth.

CONSIDER THIS... The federal government is a major source of funding for medical research. Going forward, the level of federal funding will continue to impact competition for winning and renewing research grants.

New jobs should also arise as a result of the expected expansion in research related to illnesses such as AIDS and cancer, along with growing treatment problems, such as antibiotic resistance. Moreover, environmental conditions such as overcrowding and the increasing frequency of international travel will tend to spread existing diseases and give rise to new ones. Medical scientists will continue to be needed because they greatly contribute to the development of treatments and medicines that improve human health.

Medical scientists with both doctoral and medical degrees are likely to experience the best opportunities. Workers with both a biological and professional medical background will have a distinct advantage in competing for research funding, as certain opportunities are only open to those with both qualifications.

Medical scientists are less likely to lose their jobs during recessions than workers in many other occupations because they are employed on long-term research projects. However, a recession could influence the amount of money allocated to new research and development, particularly in areas of risky or innovative medical research. A recession also could limit extensions or renewals of existing projects.

Income

Median annual wages of medical scientists, except epidemiologists, were $72,590 in May 2008. The middle 50 percent of these workers earned between $51,640 and $101,290. The lowest 10 percent earned less than $39,870, and the highest 10 percent earned more than $134,770. Those working in the private sector earn substantially more than those working in hospitals or at colleges and universities.

Earnings are lower and benefits limited for medical scientists in postdoctoral placements; workers in permanent positions typically receive higher wages and excellent benefits, in addition to job security.

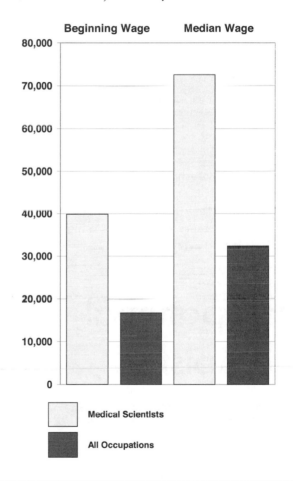

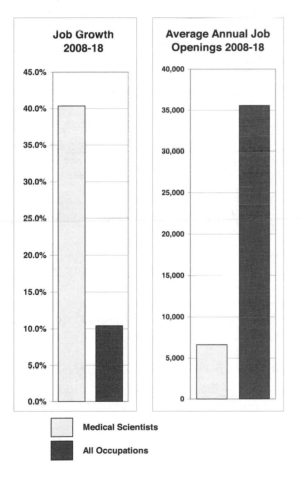

Related Jobs

- Agricultural and food scientists
- Biological scientists
- Epidemiologists
- Pharmacists
- Physicians and surgeons
- Teachers—Postsecondary
- Veterinarians

■ How to Learn More

For general information on medical scientists, contact

- Federation of American Societies for Experimental Biology, 9650 Rockville Pike, Bethesda, MD 20814. Internet: www.faseb.org

For information on and a listing of M.D.-Ph.D. programs, contact

- National Association of M.D.-Ph.D. Programs. Internet: www.aamc.org/students/considering/research/mdphd/

For information on pharmaceutical scientists, contact

- American Association of Pharmaceutical Scientists (AAPS), 2107 Wilson Blvd., Suite 700, Arlington, VA 22201. Internet: www.aapspharmaceutica.org

For information on careers in pharmacology, contact

- American Society for Pharmacology and Experimental Therapeutics, 9650 Rockville Pike, Bethesda, MD 20814. Internet: www.aspet.org

Information on obtaining a medical scientist position with the federal government is available at www.usajobs.opm.gov.

Why It's Hot

Advances in biotechnology have opened up research opportunities in almost all areas of medical science. Many projects will need qualified medical researchers, especially if a high level of federal funding continues.

Occupational Therapist Assistants and Aides

Occupational therapist assistants and aides work under the direction of occupational therapists to provide rehabilitative services to persons with mental, physical, emotional, or developmental impairments.

Just the Facts

Earnings: $43,457
Job Growth: 30.0%

Annual Openings: 1,530
Education and Training: Associate degree
Short-term on-the-job training

■ While at Work

The ultimate goal of occupational therapist assistants and aides is to help clients gain quality of life and ability to perform daily activities. For example, occupational therapist assistants help injured workers re-enter the labor force by teaching them how to compensate for lost motor skills or help individuals with learning disabilities increase their independence.

Occupational therapist assistants, commonly known as *occupational therapy assistants*, help clients with rehabilitative activities and exercises outlined in a treatment plan developed in collaboration with an occupational therapist. Activities range from teaching the proper method of moving from a bed into a wheelchair to the best way to stretch and limber the muscles of the hand. Assistants monitor an individual's activities to make sure that they are performed correctly and to provide encouragement. They also record their client's progress for the occupational therapist. If the treatment is not having the intended effect, or the client is not improving as expected, the therapist may alter the treatment program in hopes of obtaining better results. In addition, occupational therapist assistants document the billing of the client's health insurance provider.

> CONSIDER THIS...
>
> Occupational therapist aides are not licensed, so the law does not allow them to perform as wide a range of tasks as occupational therapist assistants.

Occupational therapist aides typically prepare materials and assemble equipment used during treatment. They are responsible for a range of clerical tasks, including scheduling appointments, answering the telephone, restocking or ordering depleted supplies, and filling out insurance forms or other paperwork.

Also Known As

Some common alternative titles for occupational therapist assistants and aides are *behavior specialists, independent living specialists,* or *rehabilitation assistants.*

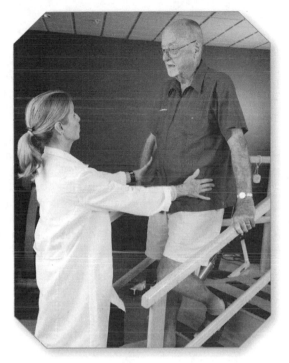

Occupational therapist assistants help clients gain the ability to perform daily activities.

Job Fit

Personality Type

Social-Realistic

Career Cluster

08 Health Science

Skills

Social Skills

Communications

Thought-Processing

Science

Equipment/Technology Analysis

Management

Equipment Use/Maintenance

Computer Programming

Work Styles

Social Skills Orientation

Concern for Others

Innovation

Cooperation

Adaptability/Flexibility

Stress Tolerance

Self-Control

Integrity

Working Conditions

Occupational therapist assistants and aides need to have a moderate degree of strength because of the physical exertion required to assist patients. For example, assistants and aides may need to lift patients. Constant kneeling, stooping, and standing for long periods also are part of the job.

The hours and days that occupational therapist assistants and aides work vary by facility and by work schedule (full-time or part time). For example, many outpatient therapy offices and clinics have evening and weekend hours to coincide with patients' schedules.

■ What's Required

An associate degree or a certificate from an accredited community college or technical school is generally required to qualify for occupational therapist assistant jobs. On the other hand, occupational therapist aides usually receive most of their training on the job.

Education and Training

Occupational therapist assistants must attend a school accredited by the Accreditation Council for Occupational Therapy Education (ACOTE) in order to sit for the national certifying exam for occupational therapist assistants. There were 135 ACOTE accredited occupational therapist assistant programs in 2009.

The first year of study typically involves an introduction to health care, basic medical terminology, anatomy, and physiology. In the second year, courses are more rigorous and usually include occupational therapist courses in areas such as mental health, adult physical disabilities, gerontology, and pediatrics. Students also must complete 16 weeks of supervised fieldwork in a clinic or community setting.

> ### CONSIDER THIS...
> Part of the training for occupational therapist assistants is learning the ethics expected of workers. Sometimes the issues can get complicated. For example, is it ever acceptable to cease providing treatment for a patient who needs it?

Applicants to occupational therapist assistant programs can improve their chances of admission by performing volunteer work in nursing care facilities, occupational or physical therapists' offices, or other health-care settings.

Occupational therapist aides usually learn their skills through on-the-job training. Qualified applicants must have a high school diploma, strong interpersonal skills, and a desire to help people in need. Applicants may increase their chances of getting a job by volunteering their services, thus displaying initiative and aptitude to the employer.

In most states, occupational therapist assistants are regulated and must pass a national certification examination after they graduate. Those who pass the test are awarded the title "Certified Occupational Therapy Assistant."

Postsecondary Program to Consider

- Occupational therapist assistant training

Additional Qualifications

Assistants and aides must be responsible, patient, and willing to take directions and work as part of a team. Furthermore, they should be caring and want to help people who are not able to help themselves.

School Subjects to Study

- Algebra
- Art
- Biology
- English
- Social studies

Moving Up

Occupational therapist assistants may advance into administration positions. They may organize all the assistants in a large occupational therapy department or act as the director for a specific department such as sports medicine. Some assistants go on to teach classes in accredited occupational therapist assistant academic programs or lead health risk reduction classes for the elderly.

◼ Employment

Occupational therapist assistants and aides held about 34,400 jobs in 2008, with assistants holding about 26,600 jobs and aides holding approximately 7,800 jobs. About 28 percent of jobs for assistants and aides were in offices of other health practitioners, 27 percent were in hospitals, and 20 percent were in nursing care facilities. The rest were primarily in community care facilities for the elderly, home health-care services, individual and family services, and government agencies.

Job Prospects

Employment of occupational therapist assistants and aides is expected to grow by 30 percent in the 10-year period ending in 2018, much faster than the average for all oc-

cupations. Demand for occupational therapist assistants and aides will continue to rise because of the aging population and the increasing number of individuals with disabilities or limited function.

Demand from adolescents will increase due to expansion of the school-age population and federal legislation mandating funding for education for the disabled.

CONSIDER THIS...

Occupational therapists are expected to increasingly utilize assistants and aides to reduce the cost of occupational therapy services. Once a patient is evaluated and a treatment plan is designed by the therapist, the occupational therapist assistant can provide many aspects of treatment as prescribed by the therapist.

Opportunities for occupational therapist assistants should be very good. However, individuals with only a high school diploma may face keen competition for occupational therapist aide jobs. Occupational therapist assistants and aides with prior experience working in an occupational therapy office or other health-care setting will have the best job opportunities. In addition to employment growth, job openings will result from the need to replace occupational therapist assistants and aides who leave the occupation permanently over the 10-year projection period ending in 2018.

Income

Median annual earnings of occupational therapist assistants were $48,230 in May 2008. The middle 50 percent earned between $39,240 and $57,810. The lowest 10 percent earned less than $31,150, and the highest 10 percent earned more than $65,160. Median annual earnings in the industries employing the largest numbers of occupational therapist assistants in May 2008 were $50,810 in offices of physical, occupational and speech therapists, and audiologists; $45,760 in general medical and surgical hospitals; and $50,790 in nursing care facilities.

Median annual earnings of occupational therapist aides were $26,960 in May 2008. The middle 50 percent earned between $21,930 and $33,340. The lowest 10 percent earned less than $17,850, and the highest 10 percent earned more than $46,910. Median annual earnings in the industries employing the largest numbers of occupational therapist aides in May 2008 were $26,850 in offices of physical, occupational and speech therapists, and audiologists; $27,750 in general medical and surgical hospitals; and $25,790 in nursing care facilities.

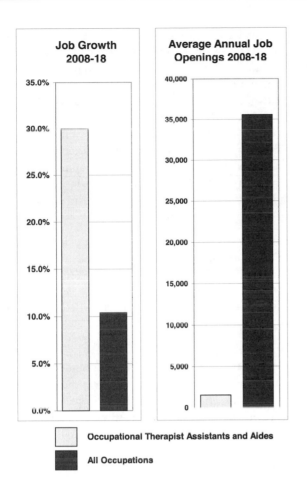

Job Growth 2008-18

Average Annual Job Openings 2008-18

☐ Occupational Therapist Assistants and Aides

■ All Occupations

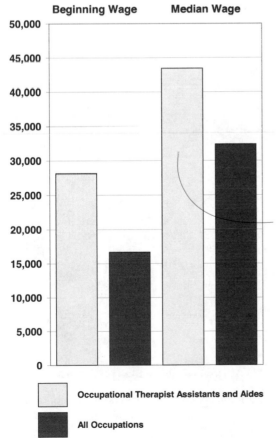

Beginning Wage   Median Wage

☐ Occupational Therapist Assistants and Aides

■ All Occupations

Related Jobs

- Dental assistants
- Medical assistants
- Nursing, psychiatric, and home health aides
- Personal and home care aides
- Pharmacy aides
- Pharmacy technicians and aides
- Physical therapist assistants and aides

How to Learn More

For information on a career as an occupational therapist assistant or aide, together with a list of accredited programs, contact

- American Occupational Therapy Association, 4720 Montgomery Lane, Bethesda, MD 20824-1220. Internet: www.aota.org

Why It's Hot

The growing elderly population is particularly vulnerable to chronic and debilitating conditions that require therapeutic services. These patients often need additional assistance in their treatment, making the roles of assistants and aides vital. Also, the large baby-boom generation is entering the prime age for heart attacks and strokes, further increasing the demand for cardiac and physical rehabilitation. In addition, future medical developments should permit an increased percentage of trauma victims to survive, creating added demand for therapy services. An increase of sensory disorders in children will also spur demand for occupational therapy services.

Occupational Therapists

Occupational therapists help patients improve their ability to perform tasks in living and working environments.

Just the Facts

Earnings: $66,780

Job Growth: 25.6%

Annual Openings: 4,580

Education and Training: Master's degree

◾ While at Work

Occupational therapists work with individuals who suffer from a mentally, physically, developmentally, or emotionally disabling condition. Therapists use treatments to develop, recover, or maintain the daily living and work skills of their patients. They help clients not only to improve their basic motor functions and reasoning abilities, but also to compensate for permanent loss of function. The goal is to help clients have independent, productive, and satisfying lives.

Occupational therapists help clients to perform all types of activities, from using a computer to caring for daily needs such as dressing, cooking, and eating. Physical exercises may be used to increase strength and dexterity, while other activities may be chosen to improve visual acuity or the ability to discern patterns. For example, a client with short-term memory loss might be encouraged to make lists to aid recall, and a person with coordination problems might be assigned exercises to improve hand-eye coordination. Occupational therapists also use computer programs to help clients improve decision-making, abstract-reasoning, problem-solving, and perceptual skills, as well as memory, sequencing, and coordination—all of which are important for independent living.

Patients with permanent disabilities, such as spinal cord injuries, cerebral palsy, or muscular dystrophy, often need special instruction to master certain daily tasks. For these individuals, therapists demonstrate the use of adaptive equipment, including wheelchairs, orthoses, eating aids, and dressing aids. They also design or build special equipment needed at home or at work, including computer-aided adaptive equipment. They teach clients how to use the equipment to improve communication and control various situations in their environment.

Some occupational therapists treat individuals whose ability to function in a work environment has been impaired. These practitioners might arrange employment, evaluate the work space, plan work activities, and assess the client's progress. Therapists also may collaborate with the client and the employer to modify the work environment so that the client can successfully complete the work.

Occupational therapists may work exclusively with individuals in a particular age group or with a particular disability. In schools, for example, they evaluate children's capabilities, recommend and provide therapy, modify classroom equipment, and help children participate in school activities. A therapist may work with children individually, lead small groups in the classroom, consult with a teacher, or serve on an administrative committee. Some therapists provide early intervention therapy to infants and toddlers who have, or are at risk of having, developmental delays. Therapies may include facilitating the use of the hands and promoting skills for listening, following directions, social play, dressing, or grooming.

Other occupational therapists work with elderly patients. These therapists help the elderly lead more productive, active, and independent lives through a variety of methods. They may work with clients to assess their homes for hazards and to identify environmental factors that contribute to falls.

Occupational therapists in mental health settings treat individuals who are mentally ill, developmentally challenged, or emotionally disturbed. To treat these problems, therapists choose activities that help people learn to engage in and cope with daily life. Activities might include time management skills, budgeting, shopping, homemaking, and the use of public transportation. Occupational therapists also work with individuals who are dealing with alcoholism, drug abuse, depression, eating disorders, or stress-related disorders.

CONSIDER THIS...

Occupational therapists take care to assess and record a client's activities and progress in detail. Accurate records are essential for evaluating clients, for billing, and for reporting to physicians and other health-care providers.

Occupational therapists help patients to perform all types of activities.

Also Known As

Driver rehabilitation therapists assess an individual's ability to drive, using both clinical and on-the-road tests. The evaluations allow the therapist to make recommendations for adaptive equipment, training to prolong driving independence, and alternative transportation options.

Job Fit

Personality Type
Social-Investigative

Career Cluster
08 Health Science

Skills
Social Skills
Communications
Management
Thought-Processing
Computer Programming

Work Styles
Social Skills Orientation
Concern for Others
Adaptability/Flexibility
Self-Control
Integrity
Analytical Thinking
Innovation
Cooperation

Working Conditions

In large rehabilitation centers, therapists may work in spacious rooms equipped with machines, tools, and other noisy devices. The work can be tiring because therapists are on their feet much of the time. Those providing home health-care services may spend time driving from appointment to appointment. Therapists also face hazards such as back strain from lifting and moving clients and equipment.

Occupational therapists in hospitals and other health-care and community settings usually work a 40-hour week. Those in schools may participate in meetings and other activities during and after the school day. In 2008, more than a quarter of occupational therapists worked part time.

What's Required

Occupational therapists must be licensed, requiring a master's degree in occupational therapy, 6 months of supervised fieldwork, and passing scores on national and state examinations.

Education and Training

A master's degree or higher in occupational therapy is the typical minimum requirement for entry into the field. In addition, occupational therapists must attend an academic program accredited by the Accreditation Council for Occupational Therapy Education (ACOTE) in order to sit for the national certifying exam. In 2009, 150 master's degree programs or combined bachelor's and master's degree programs were accredited, and four doctoral degree programs were accredited. Most schools have full-time programs, although a growing number are offering weekend or part-time programs as well. Coursework in occupational therapy programs include the physical, biological, and behavioral sciences as well as the application of occupational therapy theory and skills. All accredited programs require at least 24 weeks of supervised fieldwork as part of the academic curriculum.

> **CONSIDER THIS...**
> Occupational therapists are expected to continue their professional development by participating in continuing education courses and workshops. In fact, a number of states require continuing education as a condition of maintaining licensure. Some therapists take courses online; others attend workshops at professional meetings.

People considering this profession should get paid or volunteer experience in the health-care field. Relevant undergraduate majors include biology, psychology, sociology, anthropology, liberal arts, and anatomy.

All states, Puerto Rico, Guam, and the District of Columbia regulate the practice of occupational therapy. To obtain a license, applicants must graduate from an accredited educational program and pass a national certification examination. Those who pass the exam are awarded the title "Occupational Therapist Registered (OTR)." Some states have additional requirements for therapists who work in schools or early intervention programs. These requirements may include education-related classes, an education practice certificate, or early intervention certification.

- Occupational therapy/therapist training

Additional Qualifications

Occupational therapists need patience and strong interpersonal skills to inspire trust and respect in their clients. Patience is necessary, because many clients may not show rapid improvement. Ingenuity and imagination in adapting activities to individual needs are assets. Those working in home health-care services also must be able to adapt to a variety of settings.

School Subjects to Study

- Algebra
- Art
- Biology
- Chemistry
- English
- Geometry
- Social science

Moving Up

Therapists are increasingly taking on supervisory roles. Because of rising health-care costs, third-party payers are beginning to encourage occupational therapist assistants and aides to take more hands-on responsibility for clients. Occupational therapists can choose to advance their careers by taking on administrative duties and supervising assistants and aides.

Occupational therapists also can advance by specializing in a clinical area and gaining expertise in treating a certain type of patient or ailment. Therapists have specialized in gerontology, mental health, pediatrics, and physical rehabilitation. In addition, some occupational therapists choose to teach classes in accredited occupational therapy educational programs.

Employment

Occupational therapists held about 104,500 jobs in 2008. The largest number of occupational therapist jobs was in ambulatory health-care services, which employed about 29 percent of occupational therapists. Other major employers were hospitals, offices of other health practitioners (including offices of occupational therapists), public and private educational services, and nursing care facilities. Some occupational therapists were employed by home health-care services, outpatient care centers, offices of physicians, individual and family services, community care facilities for the elderly, and government agencies.

A small number of occupational therapists were self-employed in private practice. These practitioners treated clients referred by other health professionals. They also provided contract or consulting services to nursing care facilities, schools, adult day care programs, and home health-care agencies.

Job Prospects

Employment of occupational therapists is expected to increase by 26 percent in the 10-year period ending 2018, much faster than the average for all occupations. The increasing elderly population will drive growth in the demand for occupational therapy services. The demand for occupational therapists should continue to rise as a result of the increasing number of individuals with disabilities or limited function who require therapy services.

CONSIDER THIS...
Occupational therapists with specialized knowledge in a treatment area will have increased job prospects. Driver rehabilitation and fall-prevention training for the elderly are emerging practice areas for occupational therapy.

Hospitals will continue to employ a large number of occupational therapists to provide therapy services to acutely ill inpatients. Hospitals also will need occupational therapists to staff their outpatient rehabilitation programs.

Employment growth in schools will result from the expansion of the school-age population and the federally funded extension of services for disabled students. Therapists will be needed to help children with disabilities prepare to enter special education programs.

Job opportunities should be good for licensed occupational therapists in all settings, particularly in acute hospital, rehabilitation, and orthopedic settings, because the elderly receive most of their treatment in these settings.

Income

Median annual earnings of occupational therapists were $66,780 in May 2008. The middle 50 percent earned between $55,090 and $81,290. The lowest 10 percent earned less than $42,820, and the highest 10 percent earned more than $98,310. Median annual earnings in the industries employing the largest numbers of occupational therapists in May 2008 were $68,100 in general medical and surgical hospitals; $69,360 offices of physical, occupational and speech therapists, and audiologists; $60,020 elementary and secondary schools; $72,790 in nursing care facilities; and $74,510 in home health care services.

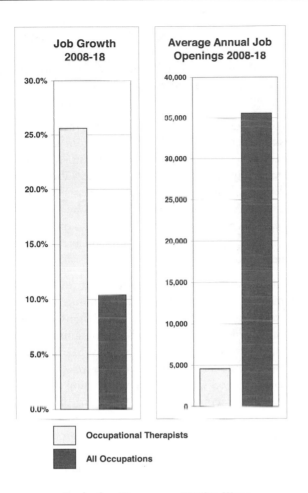

Job Growth 2008-18 / Average Annual Job Openings 2008-18

- Occupational Therapists
- All Occupations

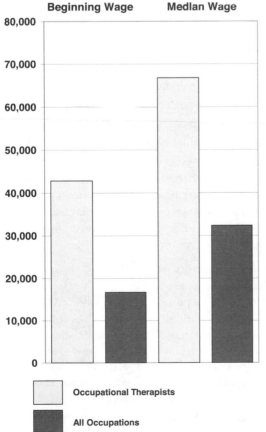

Beginning Wage / Median Wage

- Occupational Therapists
- All Occupations

Related Jobs

- Athletic trainers
- Audiologists
- Chiropractors
- Physical therapists
- Recreational therapists
- Rehabilitation counselors
- Respiratory therapists
- Speech-language pathologists

How to Learn More

For more information on occupational therapy as a career, contact

- American Occupational Therapy Association, 4720 Montgomery Lane, Bethesda, MD 20824-1220. Internet: www. aota.org

For information regarding the requirements to practice as an occupational therapist in schools, contact the appropriate occupational therapy regulatory agency for your state.

Why It's Hot

The baby-boom generation's movement into middle age, a period when the incidence of heart attack and stroke increases, will spur demand for therapeutic services. Growth in the population 75 years and older—an age group that suffers from high incidences of disabling conditions—also will increase demand for therapeutic services. In addition, medical advances now enable more patients with critical problems to survive—patients who ultimately may need extensive occupational therapy.

Operations Research Analysts

Operations research analysts assist managers with decision making, policy formulation, or other managerial functions by creating and applying mathematical models and other optimizing methods.

Just the Facts

Earnings: $69,000

Job Growth: 22.0%

Annual Openings: 3,220

Education and Training: Master's degree

While at Work

Managers need to base their decisions on more than just hunches. Operations research analysts formulate and apply mathematical models that help managers make better decisions and solve problems. Operations research is used in planning business ventures and analyzing options by using statistical analysis, data mining, simulation, computer modeling, linear programming, and other mathematical techniques.

Operations research analysts today are employed in almost every industry, as companies and organizations must effectively manage money, materials, equipment, people, and time. Operations research analysts reduce the complexity of these elements by applying analytical methods from mathematics, science, and engineering to help companies make better decisions and improve efficiency. Using sophisticated software tools, operations research analysts are largely responsible for solving complex problems, such as setting up schedules for sports leagues or determining how to organize products in supermarkets. Presenting the pros and cons of each possible scenario, analysts present solutions to managers, who use the information to make decisions.

CONSIDER THIS...

The procedures of operations research were first formalized by the military. They have been used in wartime to effectively deploy radar, search for enemy submarines, and get supplies to where they are most needed.

Analysts are often involved in top-level strategizing, planning, and forecasting. They help to allocate resources, measure performance, schedule, design production facilities and systems, manage the supply chain, set prices, coordinate transportation and distribution, or analyze large databases.

The duties of operations research analysts vary according to the structure and management of the organizations they are assisting. Some firms centralize operations research in one department; others use operations research in each division. Many analysts work with management consulting companies that perform contract work for other firms. Analysts working in these positions often have areas of specialization, such as transportation or finance.

Teams of analysts usually start projects by listening to managers describe problems. Analysts ask questions and search for data that may help to formally define a problem. For example, an operations research team for an auto manufacturer may be asked to determine the best inventory level for each of the parts needed on a production line and to determine the optimal number of windshields to be kept in stock. Too many windshields would be wasteful and expensive, whereas too few could halt production.

Analysts study the problem, breaking it into its components. Then they gather information from a variety of sources. To determine the optimal inventory, operations research analysts might talk with engineers about production levels, discuss purchasing arrangements with buyers, and examine storage-cost data provided by the accounting department. They might also find data on past inventory levels or other statistics that may help them to project their needs.

With relevant information in hand, the team determines the most appropriate analytical technique. Techniques used may include Monte Carlo simulations, linear and nonlinear programming, dynamic programming, queuing and other stochastic-process models, Markov decision processes, econometric methods, data envelopment analysis, neural networks, expert systems, decision analysis, and the analytic hierarchy process. Nearly all of these techniques involve the construction of mathematical models that attempt to describe the system. The problem of the windshields, for example, would be described as a set of equations that represent real-world conditions.

Using these models, the team can explicitly describe the different components and clarify the relationships among them. The model's inputs can then be altered to examine what might happen to the system under different circumstances. In most cases, a computer program is used to numerically evaluate the model.

A team will often run the model with a variety of different inputs to determine the results of each change. A model for airline flight scheduling, for example, might stipulate such things as connecting cities, the amount of fuel required to fly the routes, projected levels of passenger demand, varying ticket and fuel prices, pilot scheduling, and maintenance costs. Analysts may also use optimization techniques to determine the most cost-effective or profit-maximizing solution for the airline.

Based on the results of the analysis, the operations research team presents recommendations to managers. Managers may ask analysts to modify and rerun the model with different inputs or change some aspect of the model before

CONSIDER THIS...

Because problems the workers deal with are very complex and often require expertise from many disciplines, most analysts work in teams.

making their decisions. Once a manager reaches a final decision, the team usually works with others in the organization to ensure the plan's successful implementation.

Operations research analysts are often involved in strategizing, planning, and forecasting.

Also Known As

Many job titles for operations research analysts reflect specializations, such as *file system installers, material requirements workers,* and *supply chain analysts.*

Job Fit

Personality Type
Investigative-Conventional-Enterprising

Career Clusters
04 Business, Management, and Administration
15 Science, Technology, Engineering, and Mathematics

Skills
Computer Programming
Mathematics
Science
Equipment/Technology Analysis
Communications
Thought-Processing
Management
Social Skills
Equipment Use/Maintenance

Work Styles
Analytical Thinking
Innovation

Achievement/Effort
Persistence
Initiative
Independence
Integrity

Working Conditions

Operations research analysts generally work 40 hours a week; some, however, work longer. While most of their work is done in an office environment, they may spend time in the field, analyzing processes through direct observation. Because they work on projects that are of immediate interest to top managers, operations research analysts often are under pressure to meet deadlines.

■ What's Required

Some entry-level positions are available to those with a bachelor's degree in operations research, management science, or a related field, but higher degrees are required for many positions. Strong quantitative and computer skills are essential. Employers prefer workers who have completed advanced math courses.

Education and Training

A bachelor's degree coupled with extensive coursework in mathematics and other quantitative subjects usually is the minimum education requirement. Many employers, however, prefer applicants with a master's degree in operations research, management science, or a closely related field—such as computer science, engineering, business, applied mathematics, or information systems. Dual graduate degrees in operations research and computer science are especially attractive to employers. There are numerous degree programs in operations research and closely related fields in colleges and universities across the United States.

> #### CONSIDER THIS...
> Because operations research is a multi-disciplinary field, a background in political science, economics, statistics, engineering, accounting, and management can also be useful.

Continuing education is important for operations research analysts. Keeping up to date with technological advances, software tools, and improvements in analytical methods is vital for maintaining problem-solving skills.

- Management science
- Management sciences and quantitative methods, other
- Operations research

Additional Qualifications

Those considering careers as operations research analysts should be able to pay attention to detail because much time is spent on data analysis. Candidates should also have strong computer and quantitative skills and be able to perform complex research. Employers prefer analysts who understand how to use advanced operations research software and statistical packages. Although not always required, having programming skills can be very helpful.

Operations research analysts must be able to think logically, work well with people, and write and speak well.

School Subjects to Study

- Algebra
- Chemistry
- Computer science
- English
- Geometry
- Physics
- Pre-calculus and calculus
- Trigonometry

Moving Up

Beginning analysts usually perform routine computational work under the supervision of more experienced analysts. As novices gain knowledge and experience, they are assigned more complex tasks and are given greater autonomy to design models and solve problems.

Operations research analysts can advance by becoming technical specialists or project team leaders. Analysts also gain valuable insights into the industry where they work and may assume higher-level managerial or administrative positions. Operations research analysts with significant experience or expertise may become independent consultants. Others may move into corporate management, where they eventually may become chief operating officers.

Employment

Operations research analysts held about 63,000 jobs in 2008. Major employers include computer systems design firms; insurance carriers and other financial institutions; management; telecommunications companies; and scientific, and technical consulting services firms. Most operations research analysts in the federal government work for the Department of Defense.

Job Prospects

Employment of operations research analysts is expected to grow 22 percent in the 10-year period ending 2018, much faster than the average for all occupations. As technology advances and companies further emphasize efficiency, demand for operations research analysis should continue to grow. Technological advancements have extended the availability of data access and storage, making information more readily available. Advancements in computing capabilities and analytical software have made it cheaper and faster for analysts to solve problems. As problem solving becomes cheaper and faster with technological advances, more firms will have the ability to employ or consult with analysts.

CONSIDER THIS...
Operations research is not a particularly well-known field, which means there are fewer applicants competing for each job.

Additionally, organizations increasingly will be faced with the pressure of growing domestic and international competition and must work to maximize organizational efficiency. As a result, businesses increasingly will rely on operations research analysts to optimize profits by improving productivity and reducing costs. As new technologies are introduced into the marketplace, operations research analysts will be needed to determine how to best use those new technologies.

Jobs for operations research analysts exist in almost every industry because of the diversity of applications for their work. As businesses and government agencies continue to contract out jobs to cut costs, opportunities for operations research analysts will be best in management, scientific, and technical consulting firms. The relatively small pool of qualified candidates will result in excellent opportunities for those with a master's or Ph.D. degree in operations research or management science.

In addition to job growth, some openings will result from the need to replace analysts retiring or leaving the occupation for other reasons.

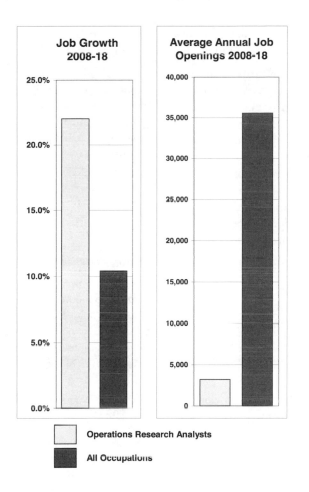

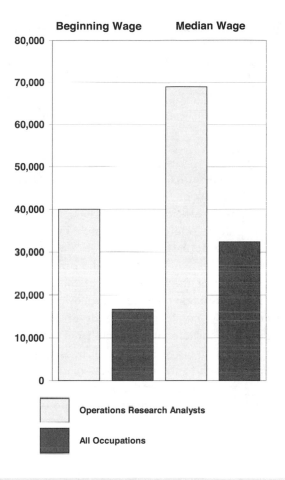

Income

Median annual wages of operations research analysts were $69,000 in May 2008. The middle 50 percent earned between $51,780 and $92,920. The lowest 10 percent had wages of less than $40,000, while the highest 10 percent earned more than $118,130. Median annual wages of operations research analysts working in management, scientific, and technical consulting services were $80,290 in May 2008. The average annual salary for operations research analysts in the federal government was $107,198 in March 2009.

Operations research analysts generally are paid fixed annual salaries with the possibility of bonuses. They also receive benefits typical of professional employees, such as medical and life insurance and 401(k) programs. Many employers offer training programs, including tuition reimbursement programs that allow analysts to attend advanced university classes.

Related Jobs

- Computer programmers
- Computer software engineers
- Computer systems analysts
- Economists
- Engineers
- Management analysts
- Market and survey researchers
- Mathematicians
- Statisticians

How to Learn More

For information on career opportunities and a list of degree programs for operations research analysts, contact

- Institute for Operations Research and the Management Sciences, 7240 Parkway Dr., Suite 300, Hanover, MD 21076. Internet: www.informs.org

For information on operations research careers and degree programs in the Armed Forces, contact

- Military Operations Research Society, 1703 N. Beauregard St., Suite 450, Alexandria, VA 22311. Internet: www.mors.org

Information on obtaining positions as operations research analysts with the federal government is available at www.usajobs.opm.gov.

Why It's Hot

Operations research will grow rapidly because global competition is compelling companies to improve their efficiency. Meanwhile, new technology allows operations research analysts to create more sophisticated models and simulations than were ever possible in the past. For example, think of the complexity of the purchasing and distribution network that allows Walmart to keep its prices low. Thousands of ships and trucks move millions of products from manufacturers to consumers, whose preferences may shift from one week to the next. Fine-tuning this intricate system requires mathematical models that can try out various scenarios to anticipate problems and suggest solutions.

Optometrists

Optometrists diagnose, manage, and treat conditions and diseases of the human eye and visual system.

Just the Facts

Earnings: $96,320

Job Growth: 24.4%

Annual Openings: 2,010

Education and Training: First professional degree

While at Work

Optometrists, also known as *doctors of optometry*, or *ODs*, are the main providers of vision care. They examine people's eyes to diagnose vision problems, such as nearsightedness and farsightedness, and they test patients' depth and color perception and ability to focus and coordinate the eyes. Optometrists may prescribe eyeglasses or contact lenses, or they may provide other treatments, such as vision therapy or low-vision rehabilitation.

Optometrists also test for glaucoma and other eye diseases and diagnose conditions caused by systemic diseases such as diabetes and high blood pressure, referring patients to other health practitioners as needed. They prescribe medication to treat vision problems or eye diseases, and some provide preoperative and postoperative care to cataract patients, as well as to patients who have had corrective laser surgery.

Although most work in a general practice as a primary care optometrist, some optometrists prefer to specialize in a particular field, such as contact lenses, geriatrics, pediatrics, or vision therapy. As a result, an increasing number of optometrists are forming group practices in which each group member specializes in a specific area while still remaining a full scope practitioner. For example, an expert in low-vision rehabilitation may help legally blind patients by custom fitting them with a magnifying device that will enable them to read. Some may specialize in occupational vision, developing ways to protect workers' eyes from on-the-job strain or injury. Others may focus on sports vision, head trauma, or ocular disease and special testing. A few optometrists teach optometry, perform research, or consult.

Also Known As

Optometrists should not be confused with ophthalmologists or dispensing opticians. Ophthalmologists are physicians who perform eye surgery, as well as diagnose and treat eye diseases and injuries. Like optometrists, they also examine eyes and prescribe eyeglasses and contact lenses. Dispensing opticians fit and adjust eyeglasses and, in some states, may fit contact lenses according to prescriptions written by ophthalmologists or optometrists.

> **CONSIDER THIS...**
> Like other physicians, optometrists encourage preventative measures by promoting nutrition and hygiene education to their patients to minimize the risk of eye disease.

> **CONSIDER THIS...**
> Most optometrists are private practitioners who also handle the business aspects of running an office, such as developing a patient base, hiring employees, keeping paper and electronic records, and ordering equipment and supplies. Optometrists who operate franchise optical stores also may have some of these duties.

Optometrists examine people's eyes to diagnose vision problems.

Job Fit

Personality Type

Investigative-Social-Realistic

Career Cluster

08 Health Science

Skills

Computer Programming

Communications

Management

Thought-Processing

Social Skills

Mathematics

Science

Work Styles

Concern for Others

Analytical Thinking

Integrity

Leadership

Social Skills Orientation

Attention to Detail

Cooperation

Dependability

Working Conditions

Optometrists usually work in their own offices that are clean, well lighted, and comfortable. Although most full-time optometrists work standard business hours, some work weekends and evenings to suit the needs of patients. Emergency calls, once uncommon, have increased with the passage of therapeutic-drug laws expanding optometrists' ability to prescribe medications.

◼ What's Required

The Doctor of Optometry degree requires the completion of a 4-year program at an accredited school of optometry, preceded by at least 3 years of preoptometric study at an accredited college or university. All states require optometrists to be licensed.

Education and Training

Optometrists need a Doctor of Optometry degree, which requires the completion of a 4-year program at an accredited school of optometry. In 2009, there were 19 colleges of optometry in the U.S. and one in Puerto Rico that offered programs accredited by the Accreditation Council on Optometric Education of the American Optometric Association. Requirements for admission to optometry schools include college courses in English, mathematics, physics, chemistry, and biology.

> ### CONSIDER THIS...
>
> Because a strong background in science is important, many applicants to optometry school major in a science, such as biology or chemistry, as undergraduates. Other applicants major in another subject and take many science courses offering laboratory experience.

Admission to optometry school is competitive; about one in three applicants was accepted in 2007. All applicants must take the Optometry Admissions Test (OAT), a standardized exam that measures academic ability and scientific comprehension. The OAT consists of four tests: survey of the natural sciences, such as biology, general chemistry, and organic chemistry; reading comprehension; physics; and quantitative reasoning. As a result, most applicants take the test after their sophomore or junior year in college, allowing them an opportunity to take the test again and raise their score. A few applicants are accepted to optometry school after 3 years of college and complete their bachelor's degree while attending optometry school. However, most students accepted by a school or college of optometry have completed an undergraduate degree.

Optometry programs include classroom and laboratory study of health and visual sciences and clinical training in the diagnosis and treatment of eye disorders. Courses in pharmacology, optics, vision science, biochemistry, and systemic diseases are included.

One-year postgraduate clinical residency programs are available for optometrists who wish to obtain advanced clinical competence within a particular area of optometry. Specialty areas for residency programs include family practice optometry, pediatric optometry, geriatric optometry, vision therapy and rehabilitation, low-vision rehabilitation, cornea and contact lenses, refractive and ocular surgery, primary eye care optometry, and ocular disease.

All states and the District of Columbia require that optometrists be licensed. Applicants for a license must have a Doctor of Optometry degree from an accredited optometry school and must pass both a written National Board examination and a national, regional, or state clinical examination. The written and clinical examinations of the National Board of Examiners in Optometry usually are taken during the student's academic career. Many states also require applicants to pass an examination on relevant state laws. Licenses must be renewed every 1 to 3 years and, in all states, continuing education credits are needed for renewal.

Postsecondary Program to Consider

- Optometry (OD)

Additional Qualifications

Business acumen, self-discipline, and the ability to deal tactfully with patients are important for success. The work of optometrists also requires attention to detail and manual dexterity.

School Subjects to Study

- Algebra
- Biology
- Chemistry
- Computer science
- English
- Geometry
- Physics
- Pre-calculus and calculus
- Trigonometry

Moving Up

Optometrists who wish to teach or conduct research may study for a master's degree or Ph.D. in visual science, physiological optics, neurophysiology, public health, health administration, health information and communication, or health education.

Employment

Optometrists held about 34,800 jobs in 2008. Salaried jobs for optometrists were primarily in offices of optometrists; offices of physicians, including ophthalmologists; and health and personal care stores, including optical goods stores. A few salaried jobs for optometrists were in hospitals, the federal government, or outpatient care centers, including health maintenance organizations. About 25 percent of optometrists are self-employed. According to a 2008 survey by the American Optometric Association, most self-employed optometrists worked in private practice or in partnership with other health-care professionals. A small number worked for optical chains or franchises or as independent contractors.

Job Prospects

Employment of optometrists is projected to grow 24 percent in the 10-year period ending in 2018. A growing population that recognizes the importance of good eye care will increase demand for optometrists. Also, an increasing number of health insurance plans that include vision care should generate more job growth.

As the population ages, there will likely be more visits to optometrists and ophthalmologists because of the onset of vision problems that occur at older ages, such as cataracts, glaucoma, and macular degeneration. In addition, increased incidences of diabetes and hypertension in the general population as well as in the elderly will generate greater demand for optometric services as these diseases often affect eyesight.

Employment of optometrists would grow more rapidly if not for productivity gains expected to allow each optometrist to see more patients. These expected gains stem from greater use of optometric assistants and other support personnel, who can reduce the amount of time optometrists need with each patient.

Excellent job opportunities are expected over the next decade because there are only 19 schools of optometry in the United States, resulting in a limited number of graduates—about 1,200—each year. This number is not expected to keep pace with demand. However, admission to optometry school is competitive.

In addition to job growth, the need to replace optometrists who retire will also create many employment opportunities.

Income

Median annual wages of salaried optometrists were $96,320 in May 2008. The middle 50 percent earned between $70,140 and $125,460. Median annual wages of salaried optometrists in offices of optometrists were $92,670. Salaried optometrists tend to earn more initially than do optometrists who set up their own practices. In the long run, however, those in private practice usually earn more.

According to the American Optometric Association, average annual income for self-employed optometrists was $175,329 in 2007.

Self-employed optometrists, including those in individual, partnerships, and group practice, continue to earn higher income than those in other settings. Earnings also vary by group size. For example, practitioners in large groups—six or more—earn $159,300; practitioners in mid-sized groups—three to five people—earn $179,205; those in small practices—two people—earn $176,944; and individual practitioners earn an average of $134,094. Self-employed optometrists must also provide their own benefits. Practitioners associated with optical chains earn $100,704 on average. However, they typically enjoy paid vacation, sick leave, and pension contributions.

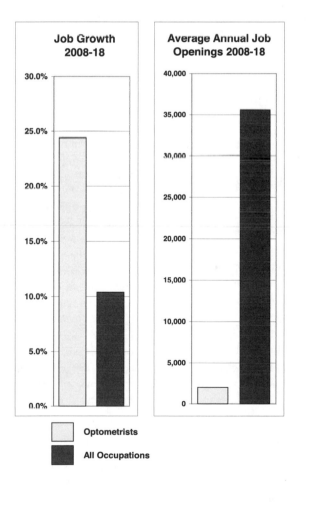

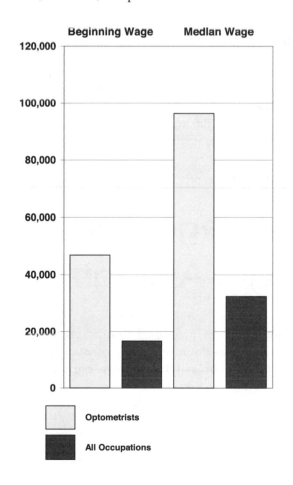

Related Jobs

- Chiropractors
- Dentists
- Physicians and surgeons
- Podiatrists
- Psychologists
- Veterinarians

How to Learn More

For information on optometry as a career and a list of accredited optometric institutions of education, contact

- Association of Schools and Colleges of Optometry, 6110 Executive Blvd., Suite 420, Rockville, MD 20852. Internet: www.opted.org

Additional career information is available from

- American Optometric Association, Educational Services, 243 N. Lindbergh Blvd., St. Louis, MO 63141. Internet: www.aoa.org

The board of optometry in each state can supply information on licensing requirements. For information on specific admission requirements and sources of financial aid, contact the admissions officers of individual optometry schools.

Why It's Hot

Americans are needing more vision care. This results partly from aging and partly from chronic diseases that can affect sight. Fortunately, more of us have health insurance plans that cover eye care, so optometrists will find plenty of work in the coming years.

Paralegals and Legal Assistants

Paralegals and legal assistants assist lawyers by researching legal precedent, investigating facts, or preparing legal documents. They conduct research to support a legal proceeding, to formulate a defense, or to initiate legal action.

Just the Facts

Earnings: $46,120
Job Growth: 28.1%
Annual Openings: 10,400
Education and Training: Associate degree

While at Work

While lawyers assume ultimate responsibility for legal work, they often delegate many of their tasks to *paralegals*. In fact, paralegals—also called *legal assistants*—are continuing to assume a growing range of tasks in legal offices and perform many of the same tasks as lawyers. Nevertheless, they are explicitly prohibited from carrying out duties considered to be the practice of law, such as setting legal fees, giving legal advice, and presenting cases in court.

One of a paralegal's most important tasks is helping lawyers prepare for closings, hearings, trials, and corporate meetings. Paralegals may investigate the facts of cases and ensure that all relevant information is considered. They also identify appropriate laws, judicial decisions, legal articles, and other materials that are relevant to assigned cases. After they analyze and organize the information, paralegals may prepare written reports that attorneys use in determining how cases should be handled. If attorneys decide to file lawsuits on behalf of clients, paralegals may help prepare the legal arguments, draft pleadings and motions to be filed with the court, obtain affidavits, and assist attorneys during trials. Paralegals also organize and track files of all important case documents and make them available and easily accessible to attorneys.

CONSIDER THIS...

Paralegals need to be skilled with computer software packages and the Internet. They use these resources to search legal literature stored in computer databases and on CD-ROM. In litigation involving many supporting documents, paralegals usually use computer databases to retrieve, organize, and index various materials. Imaging software allows paralegals to scan documents directly into a database, while billing programs help them to track hours billed to clients. Computer software packages also are used to perform tax computations and explore the consequences of various tax strategies for clients.

In addition to this preparatory work, paralegals perform a number of other functions. For example, they help draft contracts, mortgages, and separation agreements. They also may assist in preparing tax returns, establishing trust funds, and planning estates. Some paralegals coordinate the activities of other law office employees and maintain financial office records.

Paralegals are found in all types of organizations, but most are employed by law firms, corporate legal departments, and various government offices. In these organizations, they can work in many different areas of the law, including litigation, personal injury, corporate law, criminal law, employee benefits, intellectual property, labor law, bankruptcy, immigration, family law, and real estate.

Paralegals help lawyers prepare for closings, hearings, trials, and corporate meetings.

The tasks of paralegals differ widely according to the type of organization for which they work. A corporate paralegal often assists attorneys with employee contracts, shareholder agreements, stock-option plans, and employee benefit plans. They also may help prepare and file annual financial reports, maintain corporate minutes, and prepare forms to secure loans for the corporation. Corporate paralegals often monitor and review government regulations to ensure that the corporation is aware of new requirements and is operating within the law. Increasingly, experienced corporate paralegals or paralegal managers are assuming additional supervisory responsibilities, such as overseeing team projects.

The duties of paralegals who work in the public sector usually vary by agency. In general, litigation paralegals analyze legal material for internal use, maintain reference files, conduct research for attorneys, and collect and analyze evidence for agency hearings. They may prepare informative or explanatory material on laws, agency regulations, and agency policy for general use by the agency and the public. Paralegals employed in community legal-service projects help the poor, the aged, and others who are in need of legal assistance. They file forms, conduct research, prepare documents, and, when authorized by law, may represent clients at administrative hearings.

> ### CONSIDER THIS...
>
> As the law becomes more complex, paralegals become more specialized. Within specialties, functions are often broken down further. For example, paralegals specializing in labor law may concentrate exclusively on employee benefits. In small and medium-size law firms, duties are often more general.

Also Known As

Many paralegals have job titles that reflect a specialization, such as *bankruptcy assistants, closing agents, contract preparers, eviction specialists, immigration specialists, litigation paralegals, probate paralegals, real estate closers,* or *title curators.*

Job Fit

Personality Type
Conventional-Investigative-Enterprising

Career Cluster
12 Law, Public Safety, Corrections, and Security

Skills
Communications
Computer Programming
Mathematics
Management
Thought-Processing
Social Skills
Equipment/Technology Analysis

Work Styles
Attention to Detail
Social Skills Orientation
Persistence
Initiative
Dependability
Cooperation
Stress Tolerance
Achievement/Effort

Working Conditions

Paralegals do most of their work in offices and law libraries. Occasionally, they travel to gather information and perform other duties.

Paralegals employed by corporations and government usually work a standard 40-hour week. Although most paralegals work year round, some are temporarily employed during busy times of the year and then released. Paralegals who work for law firms sometimes work very long hours when under pressure to meet deadlines.

■ What's Required

Most entrants have an associate degree in paralegal studies; some have a bachelor's degree coupled with a certificate in paralegal studies. Some employers train paralegals on the job.

Education and Training

There are several ways to become a paralegal. The most common is through a community college paralegal program that leads to an associate degree. Another common method of entry, mainly for those who already have a college degree, is earning a certificate in paralegal studies. A small number of schools offer a bachelor's and master's degree in paralegal studies. Finally, some employers provide on-the-job training.

Associate and bachelor's degree programs usually combine paralegal training with courses in other academic subjects. Certificate programs vary significantly, with some only taking a few months to complete. Most certificate programs provide intensive paralegal training for individuals who already hold college degrees.

About 1,000 colleges and universities, law schools, and proprietary schools offer formal paralegal training programs. Approximately 260 paralegal programs are approved by the American Bar Association (ABA). Although many employers do not require such approval, graduation from an ABA-approved program can enhance employment opportunities. Admission requirements vary. Some require certain college courses or a bachelor's degree, while others accept high school graduates or those with legal experience. A few schools require standardized tests and personal interviews.

Any training program usually includes courses in legal research and the legal applications of computers. Many paralegal training programs also offer an internship, in which students gain practical experience by working for several months in a private law firm, the office of a public defender or attorney general, a corporate legal department, a legal aid organization, a bank, or a government agency. Internship experience is an asset when one is seeking a job after graduation.

Some employers train paralegals on the job, hiring college graduates with no legal experience or promoting experienced legal secretaries. Other entrants have experience in a technical field that is useful to law firms, such as a background in tax preparation or criminal justice. Nursing or health administration experience is valuable in personal-injury law practices.

Although most employers do not require certification, earning a voluntary certification from a professional society may offer advantages in the labor market. The National Association of Legal Assistants (NALA), for example, has established standards for certification requiring various combinations of education and experience. Paralegals who meet these standards are eligible to take a 2-day examination. Those who pass the exam may use the Certified Legal Assistant (CLA) or Certified Paralegal (CP) credential. The NALA also offers the Advanced Paralegal Certification for experienced paralegals who want to specialize. The Advanced Paralegal Certification program is a curriculum-based program offered on the Internet.

The American Alliance of Paralegals, Inc., offers the American Alliance Certified Paralegal (AACP) credential, a voluntary certification program. Paralegals seeking the AACP certification must possess at least 5 years of paralegal experience and meet one of the three educational criteria. Certification must be renewed every 2 years, including the completion of 18 hours of continuing education.

In addition, the National Federation of Paralegal Association offers the Registered Paralegal (RP) designation to paralegals with a bachelor's degree and at least 2 years of experience who pass an exam. To maintain the credential, workers must complete 12 hours of continuing education every 2 years. The National Association for Legal Professionals offers the Professional Paralegal (PP) certification to those who pass a four-part exam. Recertification requires 75 hours of continuing education.

> **CONSIDER THIS...**
>
> The quality of paralegal training programs varies; some programs may include job placement services. If possible, prospective students should examine the experiences of recent graduates before enrolling in a paralegal program.

- Legal assistant/paralegal training

Additional Qualifications

Paralegals must be able to document and present their findings and opinions to their supervising attorney. They need to understand legal terminology and have good research and investigative skills. Familiarity with the operation and applications of computers in legal research and litigation support also is important. Paralegals should stay informed of new developments in the laws that affect their area of practice. Participation in continuing legal education seminars allows paralegals to maintain and expand their knowledge of the law. In fact, all paralegals in California must complete 4 hours of mandatory continuing education in either general law or in a specialized area of law.

Because paralegals frequently deal with the public, they should be courteous and uphold the ethical standards of the legal profession. The National Association of Legal Assistants, the National Federation of Paralegal Associations, and a few states have established ethical guidelines for paralegals to follow.

School Subjects to Study

- Algebra
- Computer science
- English
- Geometry
- Office skills
- Social studies

Moving Up

Paralegals handle many routine assignments, particularly when they are inexperienced. As they gain experience, paralegals usually assume more varied tasks, with additional responsibility and less supervision. Experienced paralegals who work in large law firms, corporate legal departments, or government agencies may supervise and delegate assignments to other paralegals and clerical staff. Advancement opportunities also include promotion to managerial and other law-related positions

CONSIDER THIS...

A small number of paralegals own their own businesses and work as freelance legal assistants, contracting their services to attorneys or corporate legal departments.

within the firm or corporate legal department. However, some paralegals find it easier to move to another law firm when seeking increased responsibility or advancement.

Employment

Paralegals and legal assistants held about 263,800 jobs in 2008. Private law firms employed 71 percent; most of the remainder worked for corporate legal departments and various levels of government. Within the federal government, the U.S. Department of Justice is the largest employer, followed by the Social Security Administration and the U.S. Department of the Treasury.

Job Prospects

Employment of paralegals and legal assistants is projected to grow 28 percent in the 10-year period ending in 2018, much faster than the average for all occupations.

Private law firms will continue to be the largest employers of paralegals, but a growing array of other organizations, such as corporate legal departments, insurance companies, real-estate and title insurance firms, and banks also hire paralegals. Corporations in particular are expected to increase their in-house legal departments to cut costs. The wide range of tasks paralegals can perform has helped to increase their employment in small and medium-size establishments of all types.

In addition to new jobs created by employment growth, more job openings will arise as people leave the occupation. There will be demand for paralegals who specialize in areas such as real estate, bankruptcy, medical malpractice, and product liability. Community legal service programs, which provide assistance to the poor, elderly, minorities, and middle-income families, will employ additional paralegals to minimize expenses and serve the most people. Job opportunities also are expected in federal, state, and local government agencies, consumer organizations, and the courts. However, this occupation attracts many applicants, creating competition for jobs. Experienced, formally trained paralegals should have the best job prospects.

To a limited extent, paralegal jobs are affected by the business cycle. During recessions, demand declines for some discretionary legal services, such as planning estates, drafting wills, and handling real estate transactions. Corporations are less inclined to initiate certain types of litigation when falling sales and profits lead to fiscal belt tightening. As a result, full-time paralegals employed in offices adversely affected by a recession may be laid off or have their work hours reduced. However, during recessions, corporations and individuals are more likely to face problems that require legal assistance, such as bankruptcies, foreclosures, and divorces. Paralegals, who provide many of the same legal services as lawyers at a lower cost, tend to fare relatively better in difficult economic conditions.

ing to work long hours. Paralegals also receive vacation, paid sick leave, a 401(k) savings plan, life insurance, personal paid time off, dental insurance, and reimbursement for continuing legal education.

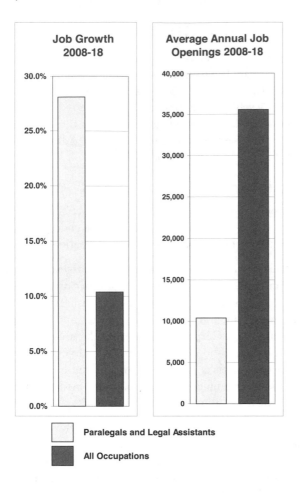

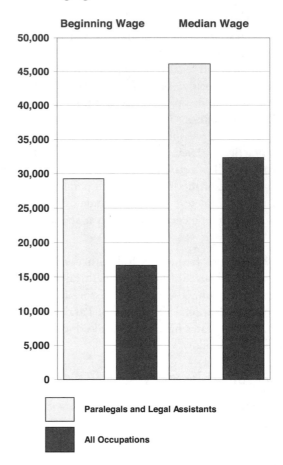

Income

Earnings of paralegals and legal assistants vary greatly. Salaries depend on education, training, experience, the type and size of employer, and the geographic location of the job. In general, paralegals who work for large law firms or in large metropolitan areas earn more than those who work for smaller firms or in less populated regions. In May 2008, full-time wage-and-salary paralegals and legal assistants had median annual earnings, including bonuses, of $46,120. The middle 50 percent earned between $36,080 and $59,310. The top 10 percent earned more than $73,450, and the bottom 10 percent earned less than $29,260. In 2008, median annual earnings in the industries employing the largest numbers of paralegals were $44,480 in legal services; $58,540 in federal government; $55,910 in management of companies and enterprises; $52,200 in insurance carriers; and $50,050 in employment services.

In addition to earning a salary, many paralegals receive bonuses, in part, to compensate them for sometimes hav-

Related Jobs

- Claims adjusters, appraisers, examiners, and investigators
- Law clerks
- Occupational health and safety specialists and technicians
- Title examiners, abstractors, and searchers

How to Learn More

General information on a career as a paralegal can be obtained from

- Standing Committee on Paralegals, American Bar Association, 321 North Clark St., Chicago, IL 60610. Internet: www. abanet.org/legalservices/paralegals

For information on the Certified Legal Assistant exam, schools that offer training programs in a specific state, and standards and guidelines for paralegals, contact

- National Association of Legal Assistants, Inc., 1516 South Boston St., Suite 200, Tulsa, OK 74119. Internet: www.nala.org

Information on the Paralegal Advanced Competency Exam, paralegal careers, paralegal training programs, job postings, and local associations is available from

- National Federation of Paralegal Associations, PO Box 2016, Edmonds, WA 98020. Internet: www.paralegals.org

Information on paralegal training programs, including the pamphlet *How to Choose a Paralegal Education Program,* may be obtained from

- American Association for Paralegal Education, 19 Mantua Rd., Mt. Royal, NJ 08061. Internet: www.aafpe.org

Information on paralegal careers, certification, and job postings is available from

- American Alliance of Paralegals, Inc., 16815 East Shea Boulevard, Suite 110, No. 101, Fountain Hills, Arizona, 85268. Internet: www.aapipara.org

For information on the Professional Paralegal exam, schools that offer training programs in a specific state, and standards and guidelines for paralegals, contact

- NALS, 314 E. 3rd St., Suite 210, Tulsa, OK 74120. Internet: www.nals.org

Information on obtaining positions as a paralegal or legal assistant with the federal government is available at www.usajobs.opm.gov.

Why It's Hot

Employers are trying to reduce costs and increase the availability and efficiency of legal services by hiring paralegals to perform tasks once done by lawyers. Paralegals are performing a wider variety of duties, making them more useful to businesses. Demand for paralegals also is expected to grow as an expanding population increasingly requires legal services, especially in areas such as intellectual property, health care, international law, elder issues, criminal law, and environmental law. The growth of prepaid legal plans also should contribute to the demand for legal services.

Personal Financial Advisors

Personal financial advisors assess the financial needs of individuals and assist them with investments, tax laws, and insurance decisions.

Just the Facts

Earnings: $69,050
Job Growth: 30.1%
Annual Openings: 8,530
Education and Training: Bachelor's degree

While at Work

Personal financial advisors help their clients identify and plan for short-term and long-term goals. Advisors help clients plan for retirement, education expenses, and general investment choices. Many also provide tax advice or sell insurance. Although most planners offer advice on a wide range of topics, some specialize in areas such as retirement and estate planning or risk management.

> **CONSIDER THIS...**
> Finding clients and building a customer base are some of the most important aspects of becoming a successful financial advisor.

Personal financial advisors usually work with many clients and often must find their own customers. Many personal financial advisors spend a great deal of their time marketing their services. Many advisors meet potential clients by giving seminars or through business and social networking.

Financial advisors begin work with a client by setting up a consultation. This is usually an in-person meeting where the advisor obtains as much information as possible about the client's finances and goals. The advisor creates a comprehensive financial plan that identifies problem areas; makes recommendations for improvement; and selects appropriate investments compatible with the client's goals, attitude toward risk, and expectation or need for investment returns. Advisors sometimes seek advice from financial analysts, accountants, or lawyers.

> **CONSIDER THIS...**
> Financial planners must educate their clients about risks and possible scenarios so that the clients don't harbor unrealistic expectations about investments.

Financial advisors usually meet with established clients at least once a year to update them on potential investments and adjust their financial plan to any life changes, such as marriage, disability, or retirement. Financial advisors also answer clients' questions regarding changes in benefit plans or the consequences of changing their job.

Many personal financial advisors are licensed to directly buy and sell financial products, such as stocks, bonds, derivatives, annuities, and insurance products. Depending upon the agreement they have with their clients, personal financial advisors may have their clients' permission to make decisions regarding the buying and selling of stocks and bonds.

Personal financial advisors usually meet with established clients at least once a year to update them on potential investments and adjust their financial plan.

Also Known As

Private bankers or *wealth managers* are personal financial advisors who work for people who have a lot of money to invest. Because they have so much capital, these clients resemble institutional investors and approach investing differently from the general public. Private bankers manage portfolios for these individuals using the resources of the bank, including teams of financial analysts, accountants, lawyers, and other professionals. Private bankers sell these services to wealthy individuals, generally spending most of their time working with a small number of clients. Private bankers normally directly manage their customers' finances.

Job Fit

Personality Type
Enterprising-Conventional-Social

Career Cluster
06 Finance

Skills
Mathematics

Communications
Thought-Processing
Management
Social Skills
Computer Programming
Equipment/Technology Analysis

Work Styles
Persistence
Integrity
Independence
Analytical Thinking
Initiative
Achievement/Effort
Attention to Detail
Concern for Others

Working Conditions

Personal financial advisors usually work in offices or their own homes. Personal financial advisors usually work standard business hours, but they also schedule meetings with clients in the evenings or on weekends. Many also teach evening classes or hold seminars to bring in more clients. Some personal financial advisors spend a fair amount of their time traveling to attend conferences or training sessions or to visit clients.

Private bankers also generally work during standard business hours, but because they work so closely with their clients, they may have to be available outside normal hours upon request.

■ What's Required

Personal financial advisors must have a bachelor's degree. Many also earn a master's degree in finance or business administration or get professional designations. Math, analytical, and interpersonal skills are important.

Education and Training

A bachelor's or graduate degree is strongly preferred for personal financial advisors. Employers usually do not require a specific field of study for personal financial advisors. Courses in investments, taxes, estate planning, and risk management are helpful if they are not a required part of the major.

Personal financial advisors who directly buy or sell stocks, bonds, insurance policies, or specific investment advice need a combination of licenses that varies based upon the products they sell. In addition to those licenses, smaller firms that manage clients' investments must be registered with state regulators, and larger firms must be registered with the Securities and Exchange Commission. Personal financial advisors who choose to sell insurance need licenses issued by state boards. State licensing board information and requirements for registered investment advisors are available from the North American Securities Administrator Association.

Although not always required, certifications enhance professional standing and are recommended by employers. Personal financial advisors may obtain the Certified Financial Planner (CFP) credential. This certification, issued by the Certified Financial Planner Board of Standards, requires 3 years of relevant experience; the completion of education requirements, including a bachelor's degree; passing a comprehensive examination, and adherence to a code of ethics. The exam tests the candidate's knowledge of the financial planning process, insurance and risk management, employee benefits planning, taxes and retirement planning, and investment and estate planning. Candidates are also required to have a working knowledge of debt management, planning liability, emergency fund reserves, and statistical modeling.

Postsecondary Programs to Consider

- Accounting
- Economics
- Finance, general
- Financial planning and services
- Law
- Mathematics

Additional Qualifications

Personal financial advisors need strong math, analytical, and interpersonal skills. They need strong sales ability, including the ability to make a wide range of customers feel comfortable. Personal financial advisor training emphasizes the different types of investors and how to tailor advice to the investor's personality. They need the ability to present financial concepts to clients in easy-to-understand language. Some advisors have experience in a related occupation, such as accountant, auditor, insurance sales agent, or broker.

Private bankers may have previously worked as a financial analyst and need to understand and explain highly technical investment strategies and products.

School Subjects to Study

- Algebra
- Computer science
- English
- Geometry
- Pre-calculus and calculus
- Trigonometry

Moving Up

Personal financial advisors have several different paths to advancement. Those who work in firms may move into managerial positions. Others may choose to open their own branch offices for securities firms and serve as independent registered representatives of those firms.

Employment

Personal financial advisors held 208,400 jobs in May 2008. Jobs were spread throughout the country, although a significant number are located in New York, California, and Florida. About 63 percent worked in finance and insurance industries, including securities and commodity brokers, banks, insurance carriers, and financial investment firms. About 29 percent of personal financial advisors were self-employed, operating small investment advisory firms.

Job Prospects

Personal financial advisors are projected to grow by 30 percent in the 10-year period ending in 2018, which is much faster than the average for all occupations. Growing numbers of advisors will be needed to assist the millions of workers expected to retire in the next 10 years. As more members of the large baby boom generation reach their peak years of retirement savings, personal investments are expected to increase and more people will seek the help of experts. Many companies also have replaced traditional pension plans with retirement savings programs, so more individuals are managing their own retirements than in the past, creating jobs for advisors. In addition, as people are living longer, they should plan to finance longer retirements.

The growing number and assets of very wealthy individuals will help drive growth of private bankers and wealth managers. The need for private bankers to explain and manage the increasing complexity of financial and investment products will continue to drive growth.

Personal financial advisors will face keen competition, as relatively low barriers to entry and high wages attract many new entrants. Many individuals enter the field by working for a bank or full-service brokerage. A college degree and certification can lend credibility.

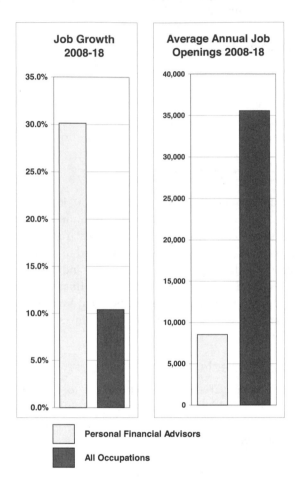

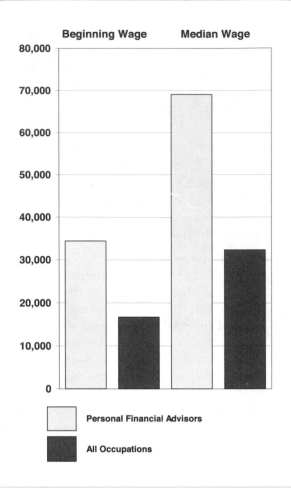

Income

Median annual wages of wage-and-salary personal financial advisors were $69,050 in May 2008. The middle 50 percent earned between $46,390 and $119,290. Personal financial advisors who work for financial services firms are often paid a salary plus bonus. Bonuses are not included in the wage data listed here. Advisors who work for financial investment or planning firms or who are self-employed typically earn their money by charging a percentage of the clients' assets under management. They may also earn money by charging hourly fees for their services or through fees on stock and insurance purchases. Advisors generally receive commissions for financial products they sell in addition to charging a fee. Wages of self-employed workers are not included in the earnings given here.

Related Jobs

- Accountants and auditors
- Actuaries
- Budget analysts
- Financial analysts
- Financial managers
- Insurance sales agents
- Insurance underwriters
- Real estate brokers and sales agents
- Securities, commodities, and financial services sales agents

■ How to Learn More

For general information on securities industry employment, contact

- Financial Industry Regulatory Authority (FINRA), 1735 K St. NW, Washington, DC 20006. Internet: www.finra.org
- Securities Industry and Financial Markets Association, 120 Broadway, 35th Floor, New York, NY 10271. Internet: www.sifma.org

For information on state and federal investment advisor registration, contact

- North American Securities Administrator Association, 750 First St. NE, Suite 1140, Washington, DC 20002. Internet: www.nasaa.org

- Securities and Exchange Commission (SEC), 100 F St. NE, Washington, DC 20549. Internet: www.sec.gov

For information on personal financial advisor careers, contact

- Certified Financial Planner Board of Standards, Inc., 1425 K St. NW, Suite 500, Washington, DC 20005. Internet: www.cfp.net
- Financial Planning Association, 4100 E. Mississippi Ave., Suite 400, Denver, CO 80246-3053. Internet: www.fpanet.org

For additional career information, see the Occupational Outlook Quarterly article "Financial analysts and personal financial advisors" online at www.bls.gov/opub/ooq/2000/summer/art03.pdf and in print at many libraries and career centers.

Why It's Hot

Each year, more and more baby boomers retire or start making serious plans for retirement. Financial planning is one of their most important considerations, so they need advisors to help them with decisions about their assets. The financial near-meltdown of 2008 raised the stakes even higher, making the public aware that investing is a very complex undertaking.

Pharmacy Technicians and Aides

Pharmacy technicians and aides help licensed pharmacists prepare prescription medications, provide customer service, and perform administrative duties within a pharmacy setting.

Just the Facts

Earnings: $26,637
Job Growth: 25.3%
Annual Openings: 18,810
Education and Training: Short-term on-the-job training
Moderate-term on-the-job training

While at Work

Pharmacy technicians generally are responsible for receiving prescription requests, counting tablets, and labeling bottles, while *pharmacy aides* perform administrative functions such as answering phones, stocking shelves, and operating cash registers. In organizations that do not have aides, however, pharmacy technicians may be responsible for these clerical duties.

Pharmacy technicians who work in retail or mail-order pharmacies have various responsibilities, depending on state rules and regulations. Technicians receive written prescription requests from patients. They also may receive prescriptions sent electronically from doctors' offices, and in some states they are permitted to process requests by phone. They must verify that the information on the prescription is complete and accurate. To prepare the prescription, technicians retrieve, count, pour, weigh, measure, and sometimes mix the medication. Then they prepare the prescription labels, select the type of container, and affix the prescription and auxiliary labels to the container. Once the prescription is filled, technicians price and file the prescription, which must be checked by a pharmacist before it is given to the patient. Technicians may establish and maintain patient profiles, as well as prepare insurance claim forms. Technicians always refer any questions regarding prescriptions, drug information, or health matters to a pharmacist.

In hospitals, nursing homes, and assisted-living facilities, technicians have added responsibilities, including preparing sterile solutions and delivering medications to nurses or physicians. Technicians may also record the information about the prescribed medication onto the patient's profile.

CONSIDER THIS...

Although pharmacy technicians and aides perform many of the same tasks as pharmacists, they are not allowed to counsel patients about specific medicines or take new prescriptions that are called in via the telephone.

Pharmacy technicians often have varying schedules that include nights, weekends, and holidays.

Pharmacy aides work closely with pharmacy technicians. They primarily perform administrative duties such as answering telephones, stocking shelves, and operating cash registers. They also may prepare insurance forms and maintain patient profiles. Unlike pharmacy technicians, pharmacy aides do not prepare prescriptions or mix medications.

Also Known As

Pharmacy technicians sometimes are called *drug coordinators, pharmaceutical care associates,* or *pharmacy technologists.* Pharmacy aides sometimes are called *dispensary attendants, pharmacy clerks,* or *prescription clerks.*

Job Fit

Personality Type

Conventional-Realistic

Career Cluster

08 Health Science

Skills

Mathematics

Communications

Science

Thought-Processing

Social Skills

Equipment Use/Maintenance

Work Styles

Concern for Others

Social Skills Orientation

Self-Control

Cooperation

Integrity

Stress Tolerance

Adaptability/Flexibility

Attention to Detail

Working Conditions

Pharmacy technicians and aides work in clean, organized, well-lighted, and well-ventilated areas. Most of their workday is spent on their feet. They may be required to lift heavy boxes or to use stepladders to retrieve supplies from high shelves.

Technicians and aides often have varying schedules that include nights, weekends, and holidays. In facilities that are open 24 hours a day, such as hospital pharmacies, technicians and aides may be required to work nights. Many technicians and aides work part time.

What's Required

There is no national training standard for pharmacy technicians, but employers favor applicants who have formal training, certification, or previous experience. There also are no formal training requirements for pharmacy aides, but a high school diploma may increase an applicant's prospects for employment.

Education and Training

Some states require pharmacy technicians to have a high school diploma or its equivalent. Although most pharmacy technicians receive informal on-the-job training, employers favor those who have completed formal training and certification. On-the-job training generally ranges between 3 and 12 months.

Formal technician education programs are available through a variety of organizations, including community colleges, vocational schools, hospitals, and the military. These programs range from 6 months to 2 years and include classroom and laboratory work. They cover a variety of subject areas, such as medical and pharmaceutical terminology, pharmaceutical calculations, pharmacy recordkeeping, pharmaceutical techniques, and pharmacy law and ethics. Technicians also are required to learn the names, actions, uses, and doses of the medications they work with. After completing training, students receive a diploma, a certificate, or an associate degree, depending on the program.

For jobs as pharmacy aides, employers may favor applicants with a high school diploma or its equivalent. Experience operating a cash register, interacting with customers, managing inventory, and using computers may be helpful. Pharmacy aides also receive informal on-the-job training that generally lasts less than 3 months.

In most states, pharmacy technicians must be registered with the state board of pharmacy. Eligibility requirements vary, but in some states applicants must possess a high school diploma or its equivalent and pay an application fee.

Most states do not require technicians to be certified, but voluntary certification is available through several private organizations. The Pharmacy Technician Certification Board (PTCB) and the Institute for the Certification of Pharmacy Technicians (ICPT) administer national certification examinations. Certification through such programs may enhance an applicant's prospects for employment and is required by some states and employers. Many employers will reimburse the cost of the certifying exams.

Under the certification programs, technicians must be recertified every 2 years. Recertification requires 20 hours of continuing education within the 2-year certification period. Continuing education hours can be earned from several different sources, including colleges, pharmacy associations, and pharmacy technician training programs. Up to 10 hours of continuing education also can be earned on the job under the direct supervision and instruction of a pharmacist.

Postsecondary Program to Consider

- Pharmacy technician/assistant training

Additional Qualifications

Good customer service and communication skills are needed because pharmacy technicians and aides interact with patients, coworkers, and health-care professionals. Basic mathematics, spelling, and reading skills also are important, as technicians must interpret prescription orders and verify drug doses. Technicians also must be precise: details are sometimes a matter of life and death.

School Subjects to Study

- Algebra
- Biology
- Chemistry
- Computer science
- English

Moving Up

Advancement opportunities generally are limited, but in large pharmacies and health systems pharmacy technicians and aides with significant training or experience can be promoted to supervisory positions. Some may advance into specialty positions such as chemotherapy technician or nuclear pharmacy technician. Others may move into sales. With a substantial amount of formal training, some technicians and aides go on to become pharmacists.

Employment

Pharmacy technicians and aides held about 381,200 jobs in 2008. Of these, about 326,300 were pharmacy technicians and about 54,900 were pharmacy aides. About 75 percent of jobs were in a retail setting, and about 16 percent were in hospitals.

Job Prospects

Employment of pharmacy technicians and aides is expected to increase by 25 percent in the 10-year period ending 2018, which is much faster than the average for all occupations. An aging population will contribute to this growth.

Employment of pharmacy technicians is expected to increase by 31 percent. As cost-conscious insurers begin to use pharmacies as patient-care centers and pharmacists become more involved in patient care, pharmacy technicians will continue to see an expansion of their role in the pharmacy. In addition, they will increasingly adopt some of the administrative duties that were previously performed by pharmacy aides, such as answering phones and stocking shelves. As a result of this development, demand for pharmacy aides should decrease, and employment is expected to decline moderately, decreasing by 6 percent over the projection period.

> **CONSIDER THIS...**
>
> Almost all states have legislated the maximum number of technicians who can safely work under a pharmacist at one time. Changes in these laws could directly affect employment.

Job opportunities for pharmacy technicians are expected to be good, especially for those with previous experience, formal training, or certification. Job openings will result from employment growth, as well as the need to replace workers who transfer to other occupations or leave the labor force.

Despite declining employment, job prospects for pharmacy aides also are expected to be good. As people leave this occupation, new applicants will be needed to fill the positions that remain.

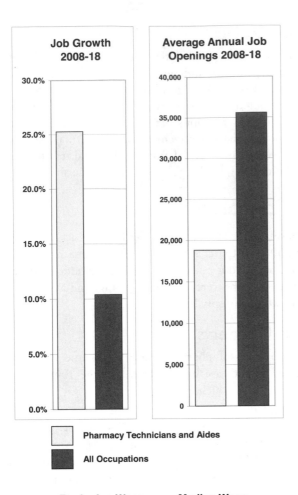

Job Growth 2008-18

Average Annual Job Openings 2008-18

□ Pharmacy Technicians and Aides

■ All Occupations

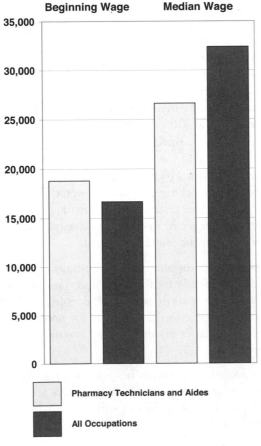

Beginning Wage   **Median Wage**

□ Pharmacy Technicians and Aides

■ All Occupations

Income

Median hourly wages of wage-and-salary pharmacy technicians in May 2008 were $13.32. The middle 50 percent earned between $10.95 and $15.88. The lowest 10 percent earned less than $9.27, and the highest 10 percent earned more than $18.98.

Median hourly wages of wage-and-salary pharmacy aides were $9.66 in May 2008. The middle 50 percent earned between $8.47 and $11.62. The lowest 10 percent earned less than $7.69, and the highest 10 percent earned more than $14.26.

Certified technicians may earn more than non-certified technicians. Some technicians and aides belong to unions representing hospital or grocery store workers.

Related Jobs

- Dental assistants
- Medical assistants
- Medical records and health information technicians
- Medical transcriptionists
- Pharmacists

How to Learn More

For information on pharmacy technician certification programs, contact

- Pharmacy Technician Certification Board, 2215 Constitution Ave. NW, Washington DC 20037-2985. Internet: www.ptcb. org

- Institute for the Certification of Pharmacy Technicians, 2536 S. Old Hwy 94, Suite 214, St. Charles, MO 63303. Internet: www.nationaltechexam.org

For a list of accredited pharmacy technician training programs, contact

- American Society of Health-System Pharmacists, 7272 Wisconsin Ave., Bethesda, MD 20814. Internet: www.ashp.org

For pharmacy technician career information, contact

- National Pharmacy Technician Association, P.O. Box 683148, Houston, TX 77268. Internet: www.pharmacytechnician.org

Why It's Hot

The increased number of middle-aged and elderly people—who use more prescription drugs than younger people—will spur demand for technicians over the next decade. In addition, as scientific advances bring treatments for an increasing number of conditions, more pharmacy technicians will be needed to fill a growing number of prescriptions. Even though the number of pharmacy aides will decrease, the occupation has a high turnover rate, making room for many new hires.

Physical Therapist Assistants and Aides

Physical therapist assistants and aides help physical therapists to provide treatment that improves patient mobility, relieves pain, and prevents or lessens physical disabilities of patients.

Just the Facts

Earnings: $36,784
Job Growth: 34.5%
Annual Openings: 5,390
Education and Training: Associate degree
Short-term on-the-job training

■ While at Work

Physical therapy helps patients suffering from injuries or disease to regain functions, improve their mobility, and experience less pain. As part of a program of physical therapy, a therapist might ask an assistant to help a patient exercise or learn to use crutches, for example, or might ask an aide to gather and prepare therapy equipment. Patients include accident victims and individuals with disabling conditions such as lower-back pain, arthritis, heart disease, fractures, head injuries, and cerebral palsy.

Physical therapist assistants perform a variety of tasks to help with

CONSIDER THIS...

The duties of aides include some clerical tasks, such as ordering depleted supplies, answering the phone, and filling out insurance forms and other paperwork. The extent to which an aide or an assistant performs clerical tasks depends on the size and location of the facility.

treatment under the direction and supervision of physical therapists. This might involve exercises, massages, electrical stimulation, paraffin baths, hot and cold packs, traction, or ultrasound. Physical therapist assistants record the patient's responses to treatment and report the outcome of each treatment to the physical therapist.

Physical therapist aides help make therapy sessions productive, under the direct supervision of a physical therapist or physical therapist assistant. They usually are responsible for keeping the treatment area clean and organized and for preparing for each patient's therapy. When patients need assistance moving to or from a treatment area, aides push them in a wheelchair or provide them with a shoulder to lean on. Because they are not licensed, aides do not perform the clinical tasks of a physical therapist assistant in states where licensure is required.

Also Known As

In states where licensure is required, workers may use the job title *licensed physical therapist assistants*. Other titles that are sometimes used are *rehabilitation assistants, rehabilitation aides*, and *restorative care technicians*.

Job Fit

Personality Type
Social-Realistic

Career Cluster
08 Health Science

Skills
Computer Programming
Social Skills
Communications

Work Styles
Concern for Others
Social Skills Orientation
Cooperation
Self-Control
Adaptability/Flexibility
Integrity
Dependability
Attention to Detail

Working Conditions

Physical therapist assistants and aides need a moderate degree of strength because of the physical exertion required in assisting patients with their treatment. In some cases, assistants and aides need to lift patients. Frequent kneeling, stooping, and standing for long periods also are part of the job.

Physical therapist assistants demonstrate exercises to patients.

■ What's Required

Most physical therapist aides are trained on the job, but most physical therapist assistants earn an associate degree from an accredited physical therapist assistant program. Some states require licensing for physical therapist assistants.

Education and Training

Employers typically require physical therapist aides to have a high school diploma. They are trained on the job, and most employers provide clinical on-the-job training.

> **CONSIDER THIS...**
>
> The hours and days that physical therapist assistants and aides work vary with the facility. About one-quarter of all physical therapist assistants and aides work part time. Many outpatient physical therapy offices and clinics have evening and weekend hours to coincide with patients' personal schedules.

In many states, physical therapist assistants are required by law to hold at least an associate degree. According to the American Physical Therapy Association, there were 232 accredited physical therapist assistant programs in the United States as of 2009. Accredited programs usually last 2 years, or 4 semesters, and culminate in an associate degree.

Programs are divided into academic study and hands-on clinical experience. Academic course work includes algebra, anatomy and physiology, biology, chemistry, and psychology. Clinical work includes certifications in cardiopulmonary resuscitation (CPR) and other first aid and field experience in treatment centers. Both educators and prospective employers view clinical experience as essential to ensuring that students understand the responsibilities of a physical therapist assistant.

Postsecondary Program to Consider

- Physical therapist assistant training

Additional Qualifications

Physical therapist assistants and aides should be well-organized, detail oriented, and caring. They usually have strong interpersonal skills and a desire to help people in need.

School Subjects to Study

- Algebra
- Biology
- Chemistry
- English
- Geometry
- Physics

Moving Up

Some physical therapist aides advance to become therapist assistants after gaining experience and, often, additional education. Sometimes, this education is required by law.

Some physical therapist assistants advance by specializing in a clinical area. They gain expertise in treating a certain type of patient, such as geriatric or pediatric, or a type of ailment, such as sports injuries. Many physical therapist assistants advance to administration positions. These positions might include organizing all the assistants in a large physical therapy organization or acting as the director for a specific department such as sports medicine. Other assistants go on to teach in

> **CONSIDER THIS...**
>
> Licensing is not required to practice as a physical therapist aide, but some states require licensure or registration for physical therapist assistants. States that require licensure stipulate specific educational and examination criteria. Additional requirements may include certification in CPR and other first aid and a minimum number of hours of clinical experience. Complete information on regulations can be obtained from state licensing boards.

an accredited physical therapist assistant academic program, lead health risk reduction classes for the elderly, or organize community activities related to fitness and risk reduction.

Employment

Physical therapist assistants and aides held about 109,900 jobs in 2008. Physical therapist assistants held about 63,800 jobs; physical therapist aides held 46,100. Both work with physical therapists in a variety of settings. About 72 percent of jobs were in offices of other health practitioners and in hospitals. Others worked primarily in nursing care facilities, home health-care services, and outpatient care centers.

Job Prospects

Employment of physical therapist assistants and aides is expected to grow by 35 percent in the 10-year period ending 2018, much faster than the average for all occupations.

The elderly population is vulnerable to conditions that require therapeutic services and often need additional assistance in their treatment. In addition, the baby-boom generation is entering the prime age for heart attacks and strokes, further increasing the demand for cardiac and physical rehabilitation. Medical developments should permit more trauma victims to survive, creating demand for therapy services.

> ### CONSIDER THIS...
> Some physical therapy assistants get the additional education they need to become physical therapists, but others choose not to do so because they are not interested in evaluating and diagnosing patients, supervising assistants and aides, or dealing with the paperwork required by that occupation.

> ### CONSIDER THIS...
> Physical therapist assistants and aides with prior experience working in a physical therapy office or other health-care setting will have the best job opportunities.

Physical therapists are expected to increasingly use assistants to reduce the cost of physical therapy services. Once a patient is evaluated and a treatment plan is designed by the physical therapist, the physical therapist assistant can provide many parts of the treatment, as approved by the therapist.

Opportunities for individuals interested in becoming physical ther-

apist assistants are expected to be very good. Physical therapist aides may face keen competition from the large pool of qualified individuals. In addition to employment growth, job openings will result from the need to replace workers who leave the occupation permanently.

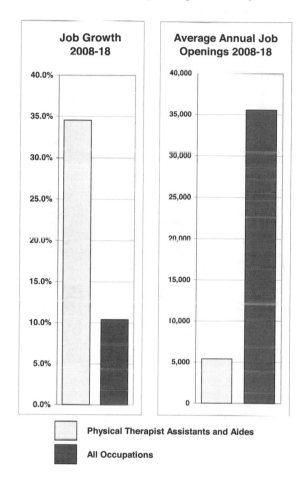

Physical Therapist Assistants and Aides

All Occupations

Income

Median annual earnings of physical therapist assistants were $46,140 in May 2008. The middle 50 percent earned between $37,170 and $54,900. The lowest 10 percent earned less than $28,580, and the highest 10 percent earned more than $63,830. Median May 2008 annual earnings in the industries employing the largest numbers of physical therapist assistants were $51,950 in home health care services, $51,090 in nursing care facilities, $45,510 in general medical and surgical hospitals, $44,580 in offices of other health practitioners, and $43,390 in offices of physicians.

Median annual earnings of physical therapist aides were $23,760 in May 2008. The middle 50 percent earned between $19,910 and $28,670. The lowest 10 percent earned less than $17,270, and the highest 10 percent earned more than $33,540. Median May 2008 annual earnings in the industries employing the largest numbers of physical therapist aides were $26,530 in nursing care facilities, $24,780 in general medical and surgical hospitals, $24,590 in specialty hospitals, $23,730 in offices of physicians, and $22,550 in offices of other health practitioners.

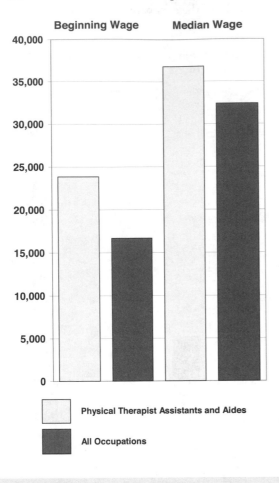

Beginning Wage   **Median Wage**

- ☐ Physical Therapist Assistants and Aides
- ■ All Occupations

Related Jobs

- Dental assistants
- Medical assistants
- Nursing, psychiatric, and home health aides
- Occupational therapist assistants and aides
- Personal and home care aides
- Pharmacy aides
- Pharmacy technicians and aides
- Social and human service assistants

▢ How to Learn More

Career information on physical therapist assistants and a list of schools offering accredited programs can be obtained from

- The American Physical Therapy Association, 1111 North Fairfax St., Alexandria, VA 22314-1488. Internet: www.apta.org

Why It's Hot

Changes to restrictions on reimbursement for physical therapy services by third-party payers will increase patient access to services and thus increase demand. Therapists are assigning more and more tasks to assistants in order to bring down costs. Aides should experience keen competition for jobs because the entry requirements for the occupation are low.

Physical Therapists

Physical therapists assess, plan, organize, and participate in rehabilitative programs that improve mobility, relieve pain, increase strength, and decrease or prevent deformity of patients suffering from disease or injury.

Just the Facts

Earnings: $72,790
Job Growth: 30.3%
Annual Openings: 7,860
Education and Training: Master's degree

▢ While at Work

Physical therapists provide services that help restore function, improve mobility, relieve pain, and prevent or limit permanent physical disabilities of patients suffering from injuries or disease. They restore, maintain, and promote overall fitness and health. Their patients include accident victims and individuals with disabling conditions, such as low-back pain, arthritis, heart disease, fractures, head injuries, and cerebral palsy.

Therapists examine patients' medical histories and then test and measure the patients' strength, range of motion, balance and coordination, posture, muscle performance, respiration, and motor function. Next, physical therapists develop plans describing a treatment strategy and its anticipated outcome.

Treatment often includes exercise, especially for patients who have been immobilized or who lack flexibility, strength, or endurance. Physical therapists encourage patients to use their muscles to increase their flexibility and range of motion. More advanced exercises focus on

CONSIDER THIS...

Physical therapists often consult and practice with a variety of other professionals, such as physicians, dentists, nurses, educators, social workers, occupational therapists, speech-language pathologists, and audiologists.

improving strength, balance, coordination, and endurance. The goal is to improve how an individual functions at work and at home.

Physical therapists also use electrical stimulation, hot packs or cold compresses, and ultrasound to relieve pain and reduce swelling. They may use traction or deep-tissue massage to relieve pain and improve circulation and flexibility. Therapists also teach patients to use assistive and adaptive devices, such as crutches, prostheses, and wheelchairs. They also may show patients how to do exercises at home to expedite their recovery.

As treatment continues, physical therapists document the patient's progress, conduct periodic examinations, and modify treatments when necessary.

Some physical therapists treat a wide range of ailments; others specialize in areas such as pediatrics, geriatrics, orthopedics, sports medicine, neurology, and cardiopulmonary physical therapy.

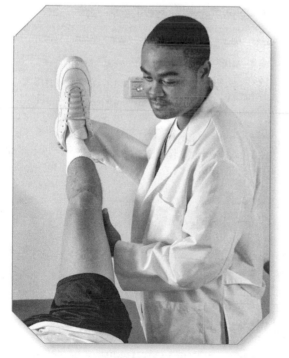

Physical therapists test and measure patients' strength and range of motion.

Also Known As

Many job titles of physical therapists are based on specializations—for example, *kinesiotherapists, pediatric physical therapists, pulmonary physical therapists,* or *sports physical therapists.*

Job Fit

Personality Type
Social-Investigative-Realistic

Career Cluster
08 Health Science

Skills
Communications
Social Skills
Management
Thought-Processing
Computer Programming

Work Styles
Concern for Others
Social Skills Orientation
Innovation
Analytical Thinking
Cooperation
Integrity
Self-Control
Independence

Working Conditions

Physical therapists practice in hospitals, clinics, and private offices that have specially equipped facilities. They also treat patients in hospital rooms, homes, or schools. These jobs can be physically demanding because therapists often have to stoop, kneel, crouch, lift, and stand for long periods. In addition, physical therapists move heavy equipment and lift patients or help them turn, stand, or walk.

In 2008, most full-time physical therapists worked a 40-hour week; some worked evenings and weekends to fit their patients' schedules. About one in five physical therapists worked part time.

What's Required

Physical therapists need a master's degree from an accredited physical therapy program and a state license, which requires passing scores on national and state examinations.

Education and Training

According to the American Physical Therapy Association, there were approximately 200 accredited physical therapist education programs in 2009. Of these, about 40 offer master's degrees and typically last 2 years; about 165 offer doctoral degrees and typically last 3 years. These are the only degrees for which the Commission on Accreditation in Physical Therapy Education accredits educational programs. In the future, the doctoral degree may be the required entry-level degree.

Physical therapist education programs start with basic science courses such as biology, chemistry, and physics; then they introduce specialized courses, including biomechanics, neuroanatomy, human growth and development, manifestations of disease, examination techniques, and therapeutic procedures. Besides getting classroom and laboratory instruction, students receive supervised clinical experience.

> ### CONSIDER THIS...
> Physical therapists are expected to continue their professional development by participating in continuing education courses and workshops. In fact, a number of states require continuing education as a condition of maintaining licensure.

Among the undergraduate courses that are useful when one applies to a physical therapist education program are anatomy, biology, chemistry, social science, mathematics, and physics. Before granting admission, many programs require volunteer experience in the physical therapy department of a hospital or clinic. For high school students, volunteering with the school athletic trainer is a good way to gain experience.

All states require physical therapists to pass national and state licensure exams before they can practice. Therapists must also graduate from an accredited physical therapist education program.

Postsecondary Programs to Consider

- Kinesiotherapy/kinesiotherapist training
- Physical therapy/therapist training

Additional Qualifications

Physical therapists should have strong interpersonal skills so that they can educate patients about their physical therapy treatments and communicate with patients' families. Physical therapists also should be compassionate and possess a desire to help patients.

School Subjects to Study

- Algebra
- Biology
- Chemistry
- English
- Geometry
- Physics
- Social studies
- Trigonometry

Moving Up

Therapists may advance to a managerial position with a title such as rehabilitation services director. They also may start their own physical therapy practice.

Employment

Physical therapists held about 185,500 jobs in 2008. The number of physical therapist jobs is probably greater than the number of practicing physical therapists, because some physical therapists work part time, holding two or more jobs. For example, some may work in a private practice, but also work part time in another health-care facility.

About 60 percent of physical therapists worked in hospitals or in offices of other health practitioners. Other jobs were in the home health-care services industry, nursing care facilities, outpatient care centers, and offices of physicians. Some physical therapists were self-employed in private practices, seeing individual patients and contracting to provide services in hospitals, rehabilitation centers, nursing care facilities, home health-care agencies, adult day care programs, and schools. Physical therapists also teach in academic institutions and conduct research.

> ### CONSIDER THIS...
> Improved health care in the United States is unlikely to decrease the number of people who need physical therapy. In fact, a recent study found that people currently in their 60s have *more* disabilities than previous generations did at that age.

Job Prospects

Employment of physical therapists is expected to grow by 30 percent in the 10-year period ending 2018, much faster than the average for all occupations.

The increasing elderly population will drive growth in the demand for physical therapy services. The elderly population is particularly vulnerable to chronic and debilitating conditions that require therapeutic services. Medical and technological developments will permit a greater percentage of trauma victims and newborns with birth defects to survive, creating additional demand for rehabilitative care. In addition, growth may result from advances in medical technology and the use of evidence-based practices, which could permit the treatment of an increasing number of disabling conditions that were untreatable in the past.

In addition, the federally mandated Individuals with Disabilities Education Act guarantees that students have access to services from physical therapists and other therapeutic and rehabilitative services. Demand for physical therapists will continue in schools.

Job opportunities will be good for licensed physical therapists in all settings. Job opportunities should be particularly good in acute hospital, skilled nursing, and orthopedic settings, where the elderly are most often treated. Job prospects should be especially favorable in rural areas as many physical therapists tend to cluster in highly populated urban and suburban areas.

Income

Median annual earnings of physical therapists were $72,790 in May 2008. The middle 50 percent earned between $60,300 and $85,540. The lowest 10 percent earned less than $50,350, and the highest 10 percent earned more than $104,350. Median annual earnings in the industries employing the largest numbers of physical therapists in May 2008 were $71,400 in offices of health practitioners (other than physicians); $73,270 in general medical and surgical hospitals, $77,630 in home health-care services; $76,680 in nursing care facilities; and $72,790 in offices of physicians.

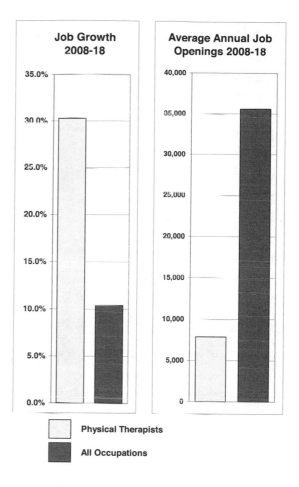

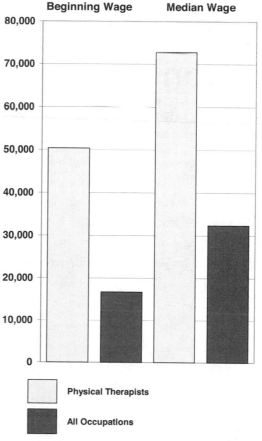

Related Jobs

- Audiologists
- Chiropractors
- Occupational therapists
- Recreational therapists
- Rehabilitation counselors
- Respiratory therapists
- Speech-language pathologists

How to Learn More

Additional career information and a list of accredited educational programs in physical therapy are available from

- American Physical Therapy Association, 1111 North Fairfax St, Alexandria, VA 22314-1488. Internet: www.apta.org

Why It's Hot

The long-run demand for physical therapists should continue to rise as new treatments and techniques expand the scope of physical therapy practices. Moreover, demand will be spurred by the increasing numbers of individuals with disabilities or limited function.

Physician Assistants

Physician assistants (PAs) practice medicine under the supervision of physicians and surgeons.

Just the Facts

Earnings: $81,230

Job Growth: 39.0%

Annual Openings: 4,280

Education and Training: Master's degree

■ While at Work

Physician assistants are formally trained to provide diagnostic, therapeutic, and preventive health-care services, as delegated by a physician. Working as members of the health-care team, they take medical histories, examine and treat patients, order and interpret laboratory tests and X-rays, and make diagnoses. They also treat minor injuries by suturing, splinting, and casting. PAs record progress notes, instruct and counsel patients, and order or carry out therapy. In all 50 states and the District of Columbia, physician assistants may prescribe some medications. In some establishments, a PA is responsible for managerial duties, such as ordering medical supplies or equipment and supervising technicians and assistants.

The duties of physician assistants are determined by the supervising physician and by state law. Aspiring PAs should investigate the laws and regulations in the states in which they wish to practice.

> **CONSIDER THIS...**
>
> Although supervised by physicians, PAs sometimes work with a lot of independence. For example, PAs may be the principal care providers in rural or inner-city clinics where a physician is present for only 1 or 2 days each week. In such cases, the PA confers with the supervising physician and other medical professionals as needed and as required by law. PAs also may make house calls or go to hospitals and nursing care facilities to check on patients, after which they report back to the physician.

Many PAs work in primary care specialties, such as general internal medicine, pediatrics, and family medicine. Other specialty areas include general and thoracic surgery, emergency medicine, orthopedics, and geriatrics. PAs specializing in surgery provide preoperative and postoperative care and may work as first or second assistants during major surgery.

Also Known As

Physician assistants often have job titles that indicate a branch of medicine in which they specialize—for example, *anesthesiologist assistants, cardiothoracic surgery physician assistants, emergency room physician assistants, gynecological assistants,* or *pediatric physician assistants.*

Physician assistants take medical histories and examine and treat patients.

Job Fit

Personality Type
Social-Investigative-Realistic

Career Cluster
08 Health Science

Skills
Social Skills
Communications
Thought-Processing
Mathematics
Computer Programming
Science
Management

Work Styles
Concern for Others
Social Skills Orientation
Analytical Thinking
Integrity
Stress Tolerance
Initiative
Dependability
Achievement/Effort

Working Conditions

Although PAs usually work in a comfortable, well-lighted environment, those in surgery often stand for long periods. At times, the job requires a considerable amount of walking. Schedules vary according to the practice setting and often depend on the hours of the supervising physician. The work week of hospital-based PAs may include weekends, nights, or early morning hospital rounds to visit patients. These workers also may be on call. PAs in clinics usually work a 40-hour week.

What's Required

Physician assistant programs usually last at least 2 years. Admission requirements vary by program, but many require at least 2 years of college and some health-care experience. All states require that PAs complete an accredited, formal education program and pass a national exam to obtain a license.

Education and Training

Physician assistant education programs usually are full time and take at least 2 years to complete. Most programs are in schools of allied health, academic health centers, medical schools, or 4-year colleges; a few are in community colleges, the military, or hospitals. Many accredited PA programs have clinical teaching affiliations with medical schools.

In 2009, more than 140 education programs for physician assistants were accredited or provisionally accredited by the American Academy of Physician Assistants. More than 90 of these programs offered the option of a master's degree, and the rest offered either a bachelor's degree or an associate degree. Most applicants to PA educational programs already have a bachelor's degree.

> **CONSIDER THIS...**
>
> The profession hasn't yet agreed on what title to use for a physician assistant who earns a Ph.D. degree. Although people with doctoral degrees in other fields commonly use the title "Doctor," it could cause confusion in a medical setting.

Admission requirements vary, but many programs require 2 years of college and some work experience in the health care field. Students should take college courses in biology, English, chemistry, mathematics, psychology, and the social sciences. Many PAs have prior experience as registered nurses, and others come from varied backgrounds, including military corpsmen or medics and allied health occupations such as respiratory therapists, physical therapists, and emergency medical technicians and paramedics.

PA education includes classroom instruction in biochemistry, pathology, human anatomy, physiology, microbiology, clinical pharmacology, clinical medicine, geriatric and home health care, disease prevention, and medical ethics. Students obtain supervised clinical training in several areas, including family medicine, internal medicine, surgery, prenatal care and gynecology, geriatrics, emergency medicine, psychiatry, and pediatrics.

All states and the District of Columbia have legislation governing the qualifications or practice of physician assistants. All jurisdictions require physician assistants to pass the Physician Assistant National Certifying Examination, administered by the National Commission on Certification of Physician Assistants (NCCPA) and open only to graduates of accredited PA education programs. Only those successfully completing the examination may use the credential "Physician Assistant-Certified." To remain certified, PAs must complete 100 hours of continuing medical education every 2 years. Every 6 years, they must pass a recertification examination or complete an alternative program combining learning experiences and a take-home examination.

Postsecondary Program to Consider

- Physician assistant training

Additional Qualifications

Physician assistants must have a desire to serve patients and be self-motivated. PAs also must have a good bedside manner, emotional stability, and the ability to make decisions in emergencies. Physician assistants must be willing to study throughout their career to keep up with medical advances.

School Subjects to Study

- Algebra
- Biology
- Chemistry
- English
- Geometry
- Trigonometry

Moving Up

Some PAs pursue additional education in a specialty such as surgery, neonatology, or emergency medicine. PA post-graduate educational programs are available in areas such as internal medicine, rural primary care, emergency medicine, surgery, pediatrics, neonatology, and occupational medicine. Candidates must be graduates of an accredited program and be certified by the NCCPA.

As they attain greater clinical knowledge and experience, PAs can advance to added responsibilities and higher earnings. However, by the very nature of the profession, clinically practicing PAs always are supervised by physicians.

Employment

Physician assistants held about 74,800 jobs in 2008. The number of jobs is greater than the number of practicing PAs because some hold two or more jobs. For example, some PAs work with a supervising physician but also work in another health-care facility. According to the American Academy of Physician Assistants, about 15 percent of actively practicing PAs worked in more than one clinical job concurrently in 2008.

More than 53 percent of jobs for PAs were in the offices of physicians. About 24 percent were in general medical and surgical hospitals, public or private. The rest were mostly in outpatient care centers, including health maintenance organizations; the federal government; and public or private colleges, universities, and professional schools. Very few were self-employed.

Job Prospects

Employment of physician assistants is expected to grow by 39 percent in the 10-year period ending 2018, much faster than the average for all occupations.

Physicians and institutions are expected to employ more PAs to provide primary care and to assist with medical and surgical procedures because PAs are cost-effective and productive members of the health-care team. Physician assistants can relieve physicians of routine duties and procedures.

Health-care providers will use more physician assistants as states continue to expand PAs' scope of practice by allowing them to perform more procedures.

Besides working in traditional office-based settings, PAs should find a growing number of jobs in institutional settings such as hospitals, academic medical centers, public clinics, and prisons.

Job openings will result both from employment growth and from the need to replace physician assistants who retire or leave the occupation permanently. Opportunities will be best in states that allow PAs a wider scope of practice.

first-year graduates was $74,470. Income varies by specialty, practice setting, geographical location, and years of experience. Employers often pay for their employees' liability insurance, registration fees with the Drug Enforcement Administration, state licensing fees, and credentialing fees.

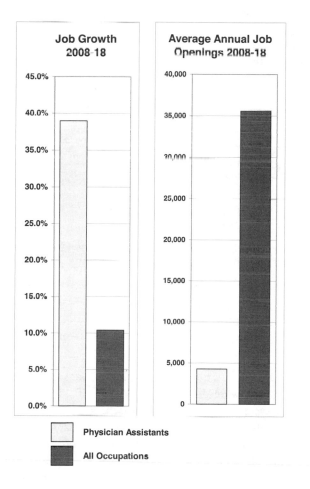

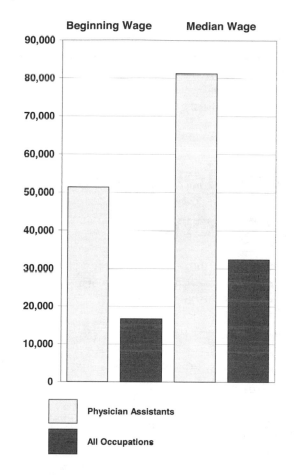

Income

Median annual earnings of wage-and-salary physician assistants were $81,230 in May 2008. The middle 50 percent earned between $68,210 and $97,070. The lowest 10 percent earned less than $51,360, and the highest 10 percent earned more than $110,240. Median annual earnings in the industries employing the largest numbers of physician assistants in May 2008 were $80,440 in offices of physicians; $84,550 in general medical and surgical hospitals; $84,390 in outpatient care centers; $78,200 in federal government; and $74,200 in colleges, universities, and professional schools.

According to the American Academy of Physician Assistants, median income for physician assistants in full-time clinical practice was $87,710 in 2008; median income for

Related Jobs

- Audiologists
- Occupational therapists
- Physical therapists
- Registered nurses
- Speech-language pathologists

How to Learn More

For information on a career as a physician assistant, including a list of accredited programs, contact

- American Academy of Physician Assistants Information Center, 950 North Washington St., Alexandria, VA 22314. Internet: www.aapa.org

For eligibility requirements and a description of the Physician Assistant National Certifying Examination, contact

- National Commission on Certification of Physician Assistants, Inc., 12000 Findley Rd., Suite 200, Duluth, GA 30097. Internet: http://www.nccpa.net

Why It's Hot

The rapid job growth expected for physician assistants reflects the expansion of the health-care industry and an emphasis on cost containment, which results in increasing use of PAs by health-care establishments.

Physicians and Surgeons

Physicians and surgeons diagnose illnesses and prescribe and administer treatment for people suffering from injury or disease.

Just the Facts

Earnings: $163,170

Job Growth: 21.8%

Annual Openings: 26,050

Education and Training: First professional degree

■ While at Work

Physicians examine patients, obtain medical histories, and order, perform, and interpret diagnostic tests. They counsel patients on diet, hygiene, and preventive health care.

There are two types of physicians: *M.D.* (*Medical Doctor*) and *D.O.* (*Doctor of Osteopathic Medicine*). M.D.s also are known as *allopathic physicians*. While both M.D.s and D.O.s may use all accepted methods of treatment, including drugs and surgery, D.O.s place special emphasis on the body's musculoskeletal system, preventive medicine, and holistic patient care. D.O.s are most likely to be primary care specialists although they can be found in all specialties. About half of D.O.s practice general or family medicine, general internal medicine, or general pediatrics.

Physicians work in one or more of several specialties, including, but not limited to, anesthesiology, family and general medicine, general internal medicine, general pediatrics, obstetrics and gynecology, psychiatry, and surgery.

Anesthesiologists focus on the care of surgical patients and pain relief. Like other physicians, they evaluate and treat patients and direct the efforts of their staffs. Through continual monitoring and assessment, these critical care specialists are responsible for maintenance of the patient's vital life functions—heart rate, body temperature, blood pressure, breathing—during surgery. They also work outside of the operating room, providing pain relief in the intensive care unit, during labor and delivery, and for those who suffer from chronic pain. Anesthesiologists confer with other physicians and surgeons about appropriate treatments and procedures before, during, and after operations.

> ## CONSIDER THIS...
> Family and general physician typically have a base of regular, long-term patients. These doctors refer patients with more serious conditions to specialists or other health-care facilities for more intensive care.

Family and general physicians often provide the first point of contact for people seeking health care, by acting as the traditional family physician. They assess and treat a wide range of conditions, from sinus and respiratory infections to broken bones.

General internists diagnose and provide nonsurgical treatment for a wide range of problems that affect internal organ systems, such as the stomach, kidneys, liver, and digestive tract. Internists use a variety of diagnostic techniques to treat patients through medication or hospitalization. Like general practitioners, general internists commonly act as primary care specialists. They treat patients referred from other specialists and, in turn, they refer patients to other specialists when more complex care is required.

General pediatricians care for the health of infants, children, teenagers, and young adults. They specialize in the diagnosis and treatment of a variety of ailments specific to young people and track patients' growth to adulthood. Like most physicians, pediatricians work with different health-care workers, such as nurses and other physicians, to assess and treat children with various ailments. Most of the work of pediatricians involves treating day-to-day illnesses—minor injuries, infectious diseases, and immunizations—that are common to children, much as a general practitioner treats adults. Some pediatricians specialize in pediatric surgery or serious medical conditions, such as autoimmune disorders or serious chronic ailments.

Obstetricians and gynecologists (OB/GYNs) specialize in women's health. They are responsible for women's general medical care, and they also provide care related to pregnancy and the reproductive system. Like general practitioners, OB/GYNs attempt to prevent, diagnose, and treat general health problems, but they focus on ailments specific to the female anatomy, such as cancers of the breast or cervix, urinary tract and pelvic disorders, and hormonal disorders. OB/GYNs also specialize in childbirth, which includes treating and counseling women throughout their pregnancy, from giving prenatal diagnoses to assisting with delivery and providing postpartum care.

Psychiatrists are the primary mental health-care-givers. They assess and treat mental illnesses through a combination of psychotherapy, psychoanalysis, hospitalization, and medication. Psychotherapy involves regular discussions with patients about their problems; the psychiatrist helps them find solutions through changes in their behavioral patterns, the exploration of their past experiences, or group and family therapy sessions.

Surgeons specialize in the treatment of injury, disease, and deformity through operations. Using a variety of instruments, and with patients under anesthesia, a surgeon corrects physical deformities, repairs bone and tissue after injuries, or performs preventive surgeries on patients with debilitating diseases or disorders. Although a large number perform general surgery, many surgeons choose to specialize in a specific area. One of the most prevalent specialties is orthopedic surgery: the treatment of the musculoskeletal system. Others include neurological surgery (treatment of the brain and nervous system), cardiovascular surgery, otolaryngology (treatment of the ear, nose, and throat), and plastic or reconstructive surgery. Like other physicians, surgeons also examine patients, perform and interpret diagnostic tests, and counsel patients on preventive health care.

Also Known As

Physicians and surgeons who work in a number of other medical and surgical specializations include *allergists, cardiologists, dermatologists, emergency physicians, gastroenterologists, ophthalmologists, pathologists,* and *radiologists.*

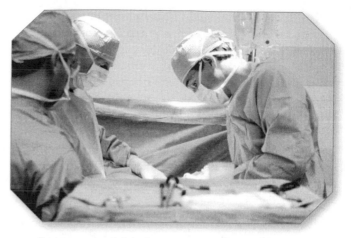

Surgeons repair injuries or remove diseased tissue.

Job Fit

Personality Type
Investigative-Social-Realistic

Career Cluster
08 Health Science

Skills
Science
Social Skills
Thought-Processing
Communications
Management
Mathematics
Equipment/Technology Analysis
Equipment Use/Maintenance
Computer Programming

Work Styles
Concern for Others
Analytical Thinking
Social Skills Orientation
Achievement/Effort
Persistence
Stress Tolerance
Leadership
Self-Control

Working Conditions

Many physicians—primarily general and family practitioners, general internists, pediatricians, OB/GYNs, and psychiatrists—work in small private offices or clinics, often assisted by a small staff of nurses and other administrative personnel. Increasingly, physicians are practicing in groups or health-care organizations that provide backup coverage and allow for more time off. Physicians in a group practice or health-care organization often work as part of a team that coordinates care for a number of patients; they are less independent than the solo practitioners of the past. Surgeons and anesthesiologists usually work in well-lighted, sterile environments while performing surgery and often stand for long periods. Most work in hospitals or in surgical outpatient centers.

Many physicians and surgeons work long, irregular hours. In 2008, 43 percent of all physicians and surgeons worked 50 or more hours a week. Nine percent of all physicians and surgeons worked part-time. Physicians and surgeons travel between office and hospital to care for their patients. While on call, a physician will deal with many patients' concerns over the phone and make emergency visits to hospitals or nursing homes.

What's Required

The common path to practicing as a physician requires 8 years of education beyond high school and 3 to 8 additional years of internship and residency. All states, the District of Columbia, and U.S. territories license physicians.

Education and Training

Formal education and training requirements for physicians are among the most demanding of any occupation—4 years of undergraduate school, 4 years of medical school, and 3 to 8 years of internship and residency, depending on the specialty selected. A few medical schools offer combined undergraduate and medical school programs that last 6 or 7 years rather than the customary 8 years.

Premedical students must complete undergraduate work in physics, biology, mathematics, English, and inorganic and organic chemistry. Students also take courses in the humanities and the social sciences. Some students volunteer at local hospitals or clinics to gain practical experience in the health professions.

The minimum educational requirement for entry into medical school is 3 years of college; most applicants, however, have at least a bachelor's degree, and many have advanced degrees. In 2008, there were 129 medical schools accredited by the Liaison Committee on Medical Education (LCME). The LCME is the national accrediting body for M.D. medical education programs. The American Osteopathic Association accredits schools that award a D.O. degree; there were 25 schools accredited in 31 locations in 2008.

Acceptance to medical school is highly competitive. Most applicants must submit transcripts, scores from the Medical College Admission Test, and letters of recommendation. Schools also consider an applicant's character, personality, leadership qualities, and participation in extracurricular activities. Most schools require an interview with members of the admissions committee.

Students spend most of the first 2 years of medical school in laboratories and classrooms, taking courses such as anatomy, biochemistry, physiology, pharmacology, psychology, microbiology, pathology, medical ethics, and laws governing medicine. They also learn to take medical histories, examine patients, and diagnose illnesses. During their last 2 years, students work with patients under the supervision of experienced physicians in hospitals and clinics, learning acute, chronic, preventive, and rehabilitative care. Through rotations in internal medicine, family practice, obstetrics and gynecology, pediatrics, psychiatry, and surgery, they gain experience in the diagnosis and treatment of illness.

Following medical school, almost all M.D.s enter a residency—graduate medical education in a specialty that takes the form of paid on-the-job training, usually in a hospital. Most D.O.s serve a 12-month rotating internship after graduation and before entering a residency, which may last 2 to 6 years.

All physicians and surgeons practicing in the United States must pass the United States Medical Licensing Examination (USMLE). To be eligible to take the USMLE in its entirety, physicians must graduate from an accredited medical school. Although physicians licensed in one state usually can get a license to practice in another without further examination, some states limit reciprocity. Graduates of foreign medical schools generally can qualify for licensure after passing an examination and completing a

CONSIDER THIS...

Although a large percentage of applicants to medical school are rejected, those who do get in usually go on to become physicians.

CONSIDER THIS...

A physician's training is costly. According to the Association of American Medical Colleges, in 2007 85 percent of public medical school graduates and 86 percent of private medical school graduates were in debt for educational expenses.

U.S. residency. For specific information on licensing in a given state, contact that state's medical board.

M.D.s and D.O.s seeking board certification in a specialty may spend up to 7 years in residency training, depending on the specialty. A final examination immediately after residency or after 1 or 2 years of practice is also necessary for certification by a member board of the American Board of Medical Specialists (ABMS) or the American Osteopathic Association (AOA). The ABMS represents 24 boards related to medical specialties ranging from allergy and immunology to urology. The AOA has approved 18 specialty boards, ranging from anesthesiology to surgery. For certification in a subspecialty, physicians usually need another 1 to 2 years of residency.

Postsecondary Programs to Consider

- Allergy and immunology residency program
- Dermatology residency program
- Diagnostic radiology residency program
- Medicine (MD)
- Neurology residency program
- Nuclear medicine residency program
- Ophthalmology residency program
- Orthopedic sports medicine residency program
- Osteopathic medicine/osteopathy (DO)
- Pathology residency program
- Physical medicine and rehabilitation residency program
- Radiologic physics residency program
- Urology residency program

Additional Qualifications

People who wish to become physicians must have a desire to serve patients, be self-motivated, and be able to survive the pressures and long hours of medical education and practice. Physicians also must have a good bedside manner, emotional stability, and the ability to make decisions in emergencies. Prospective physicians must be willing to study throughout their career to keep up with medical advances.

School Subjects to Study

- Algebra
- Biology
- Chemistry
- English
- Geometry
- Pre-calculus and calculus
- Trigonometry

Moving Up

Some physicians and surgeons advance by gaining expertise in specialties and subspecialties and by developing a reputation for excellence among their peers and patients. Physicians and surgeons may also start their own practice or join a group practice. Others teach residents and other new doctors, and some advance to supervisory and managerial roles in hospitals, clinics, and other settings.

■ Employment

Physicians and surgeons held about 661,400 jobs in 2008; approximately 12 percent were self-employed. About 53 percent of wage-and-salary physicians and surgeons worked in offices of physicians, and 19 percent were employed by hospitals. Others practiced in federal, state, and local governments, educational services, and outpatient care centers.

According to 2007 data from the American Medical Association (AMA), 32 percent of physicians in patient care were in primary care, but not in a subspecialty of primary care.

> **CONSIDER THIS...**
>
> A growing number of physicians are partners or wage-and-salary employees of group practices. Organized as clinics or as associations of physicians, medical groups can more easily afford expensive medical equipment, share support staff, and benefit from other business advantages.

According to the AMA, the New England and Middle Atlantic states have the highest ratios of physicians to population; the South Central and Mountain states have the lowest. Physicians tend to locate in urban areas, close to hospitals and education centers. AMA data showed that in 2007, about 75 percent of physicians in patient care were located in metropolitan areas while the remaining 25 percent were located in rural areas.

Job Prospects

Employment of physicians and surgeons is projected to grow 22 percent in the 10-year period ending 2018, much faster than the average for all occupations. Job growth will occur because of continued expansion of health-care-related industries. The growing and aging population will drive growth in the demand for physician services, as consumers continue to demand high levels of care using the latest technologies, diagnostic tests, and therapies. Many medical schools are increasing their enrollments based on perceived new demand for physicians.

Despite growing demand for physicians and surgeons, some factors will temper growth. For example, new technologies allow physicians to be more productive. This means physicians can diagnose and treat more patients in the same amount of time. The rising cost of health care can dramatically affect demand for physicians' services. Physician assistants and nurse practitioners, who can perform many of the routine duties of physicians at a fraction of the cost, may be increasingly used. Furthermore, demand for physicians' services is highly sensitive to changes in health-care reimbursement policies. If changes to health coverage result in higher out-of-pocket costs for consumers, they may demand fewer physician services.

Opportunities for individuals interested in becoming physicians and surgeons are expected to be very good. In addition to job openings from employment growth, openings will result from the need to replace the relatively high number of physicians and surgeons expected to retire over the projection decade ending in 2018.

Income

Earnings of physicians and surgeons are among the highest of any occupation. According to the Medical Group Management Association's Physician Compensation and Production Survey, median total compensation for physicians varied by their type of practice. In 2008, physicians practicing primary care had total median annual compensation of $186,044, and physicians practicing in medical specialties earned total median annual compensation of $339,738.

Self-employed physicians—those who own or are part owners of their medical practice—generally have higher median incomes than salaried physicians. Earnings vary according to number of years in practice, geographic region, hours worked, skill, personality, and professional reputation. Self-employed physicians and surgeons must provide for their own health insurance and retirement.

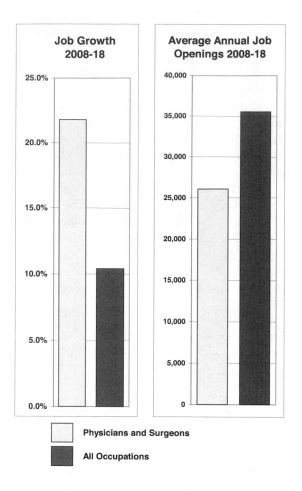

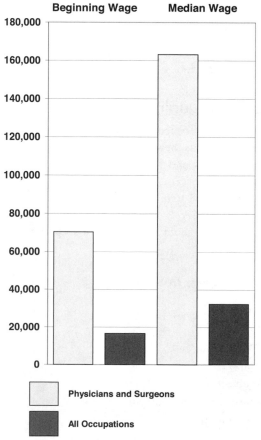

Related Jobs

- Chiropractors
- Dentists
- Optometrists
- Physician assistants
- Podiatrists
- Registered nurses
- Veterinarians

How to Learn More

For a list of medical schools and residency programs, as well as general information on premedical education, financial aid, and medicine as a career contact

- Association of American Medical Colleges, Section for Student Services, 2450 N St. NW, Washington, DC 20037. Internet: www.aamc.org/students

For information on licensing, contact

- Federation of State Medical Boards, P.O. Box 619850 Dallas, TX 75261-9850. Internet: www.fsmb.org

For general information on physicians, contact

- American Medical Association, 515 N. State St., Chicago, IL 60654. Internet: www.ama-assn.org/go/becominganmd

- American Osteopathic Association, Department of Communications, 142 E. Ontario St., Chicago, IL 60611. Internet: www.osteopathic.org

For information about various medical specialties, contact

- American Academy of Family Physicians, Resident Student Activities Department, P.O. Box 11210, Shawnee Mission, KS 66207-1210. Internet: http://fmignet.aafp.org

- American Board of Medical Specialties, 222 N. LaSalle St., Suite 1500, Chicago, IL 60601. Internet: www.abms.org

- American College of Obstetricians and Gynecologists, P.O. Box 96920, Washington, DC 20090. Internet: www.acog.org

- American College of Surgeons, Division of Education, 633 N. Saint Clair St., Chicago, IL 60611. Internet: www.facs.org

- American Psychiatric Association, 1000 Wilson Blvd., Suite 1825, Arlington, VA 22209. Internet: www.psych.org

- American Society of Anesthesiologists, 520 N. Northwest Hwy., Park Ridge, IL 60068. Internet: www.asahq.org/career/homepage.htm

Information on federal scholarships and loans is available from the directors of student financial aid at schools of medicine. Information on licensing is available from state boards of examiners.

Why It's Hot

As America's population ages, growing more frail and suffering the effects of chronic diseases, more physicians will be needed to treat them. Although some health-care tasks are being shifted to lower-paid nurses and technicians, physicians will continue to be needed as the gatekeepers for medical care.

Private Detectives and Investigators

Private detectives and investigators assist individuals, businesses, and attorneys by finding and analyzing information.

Just the Facts

Earnings: $41,760

Job Growth: 22.0%

Annual Openings: 1,930

Education and Training: Work experience in a related occupation

While at Work

Private detectives and investigators connect clues to uncover facts about legal, financial, or personal matters. Private detectives and investigators offer many services, including executive, corporate, and celebrity protection; pre-employment verification; and individual background profiles. Some investigate computer crimes, such as identity theft, harassing e-mails, and illegal downloading of copyrighted material. They also provide assistance in criminal and civil liability cases, insurance claims and fraud cases, child custody and protection cases, missing-persons cases, and premarital screening. They are sometimes hired to investigate individuals to prove or disprove infidelity.

Private detectives and investigators may use many methods to determine the facts in a case. Much of their work is done with a computer. For example, they often recover deleted e-mails and documents. They also may perform computer database searches or work with someone who does.

Detectives and investigators also perform various other types of surveillance or searches. To verify facts, such as an individual's income or place of employment, they may make phone calls or visit a subject's workplace. In other cases, especially those involving missing persons and background checks, investigators interview people to gather as much information as possible about an individual. Sometimes investigators go undercover, pretending to be someone else in order to get information or to observe a subject inconspicuously. They even arrange to be hired in businesses to observe workers for wrongdoing.

Most detectives and investigators are trained to perform physical surveillance, which may be high tech or low tech. They may observe a site, such as the home of a subject, from an inconspicuous location or a vehicle. Using photographic and video cameras, binoculars, cell phones, and GPS systems, detectives gather information on an individual. Surveillance can be time consuming.

The duties of private detectives and investigators depend on the needs of their clients. In cases that involve fraudulent workers' compensation claims, for example, investigators may carry out long-term covert observation of a person suspected of fraud. If an investigator observes the person performing an activity that contradicts injuries stated in a worker's compensation claim, the investigator would take video or still photographs to document the activity and report it to the client.

Detectives and investigators must be mindful of the law in conducting investigations. They keep up with federal, state, and local legislation, such as privacy laws and other legal issues affecting their work. They must also know how to collect evidence properly so that they do not compromise its admissibility in court.

Private detectives and investigators often specialize. Those who focus on intellectual property theft, for example, investigate and document acts of piracy, help clients stop illegal activity, and provide intelligence for prosecution and civil action. Other investigators specialize in developing financial profiles and carrying out asset searches. Their reports reflect information gathered through interviews, investigation and surveillance, and research, including reviews of public documents.

Computer forensic investigators specialize in recovering, analyzing, and presenting data from computers for use in investigations or as evidence. They determine the details of intrusions into computer systems, recover data from encrypted or erased files, and recover e-mails and deleted passwords.

Legal investigators assist in preparing criminal defenses, locating witnesses, serving legal documents, interviewing police and prospective witnesses, and gathering and reviewing evidence. Legal investigators also may collect information on the parties to a litigation, take photographs, testify in court, and assemble evidence and reports for trials. They often work for law firms or lawyers.

Corporate investigators conduct internal and external investigations for corporations. In internal investigations, they may investigate drug use in the workplace, ensure that expense accounts are not abused, or determine whether employees are stealing assets, merchandise, or information. External investigations attempt to thwart criminal schemes from outside the corporation, such as fraudulent billing by a supplier. Investigators may spend months posing as employees of the company in order to find misconduct.

Financial investigators may be hired to develop confidential financial profiles of individuals or companies that are prospective parties to large financial transactions. These investigators often are certified public accountants (CPAs) who work closely with investment bankers and other accountants. They also might search for assets in order to recover damages awarded by a court in fraud or theft cases.

Detectives who work for retail stores or hotels are responsible for controlling losses and protecting assets. *Store detectives*, also known as *loss prevention agents*, safeguard the assets of retail stores by apprehending anyone attempting to steal merchandise or destroy store property. They prevent theft by shoplifters, vendor representatives, delivery personnel, and store employees. Store detectives also conduct periodic inspections of stock areas, dressing rooms, and rest rooms, and sometimes assist in opening and closing the store. They may prepare loss prevention and security reports for management and testify in court against people they apprehend. *Hotel detectives* protect guests of the establishment from theft of their belongings and preserve order in hotel restaurants and bars. They also may keep undesirable individuals, such as known thieves, off the premises.

Private investigators may need to blend in to conduct surveillance.

Also Known As

Some private investigators have job titles that reflect a specialization, such as *background investigators, cash shortage investigators, missing persons investigators,* and *skip tracers.*

Job Fit

Personality Type
Enterprising-Conventional

Career Cluster
12 Law, Public Safety, Corrections, and Security

Skills
Communications
Thought-Processing
Equipment/Technology Analysis
Social Skills
Management
Computer Programming
Science
Mathematics

Work Styles
Self-Control
Analytical Thinking
Innovation
Independence
Dependability
Attention to Detail
Persistence

Working Conditions

Many detectives and investigators spend time away from their offices conducting interviews or doing surveillance, but some work in the office most of the day conducting computer searches and making phone calls. When an investigator is working on a case, the environment might range from plush boardrooms to seedy bars. Store and hotel detectives work in the businesses that they protect.

Investigators generally work alone, but they sometimes work with others, especially during surveillance or when they follow a subject. Some of the work involves confrontation, so the job can be stressful and dangerous. Some situations, such as certain bodyguard assignments for corporate or celebrity clients, call for the investigator to be armed. In most cases, however, a weapon is not necessary, because the purpose of the work is gathering information and not law enforcement or criminal apprehension. Owners of investigative agencies have the added stress of having to deal with demanding and sometimes distraught clients.

> **CONSIDER THIS...**
> Although considered a dangerous occupation, private detectives and investigators have a relatively low incidence of nonfatal work-related injuries.

Private detectives and investigators often work irregular hours because of the need to conduct surveillance and contact people who are not available during normal working hours. Early morning, evening, weekend, and holiday work is common.

■ What's Required

Most private detectives and investigators have some college education and previous experience in investigative work. In the majority of states, they are required to be licensed.

Education and Training

There are no formal education requirements for most private detective and investigator jobs, although many have postsecondary degrees. Courses in criminal justice and police science are helpful to aspiring private detectives and investigators. Although related experience is usually required, some people enter the occupation directly after graduation from college, generally with an associate or bachelor's degree in criminal justice or police science. Experience in police investigation is viewed favorably.

Most corporate investigators must have a bachelor's degree, preferably in a business-related field. Some corporate investigators have a master's degree in business administration or a law degree; others are CPAs.

For computer forensics work, a computer science or accounting degree is more helpful than a criminal justice degree. An accounting degree provides good background knowledge for investigating computer fraud. Either of these two degrees provides a good starting point, after which investigative techniques can be learned on the job. Alternatively, many colleges and universities now offer certificate programs, requiring from 15 to 21 credits, in computer forensics. These programs are most beneficial to law enforcement officers, paralegals, or others who already are involved in investigative work. A few colleges and universities now offer bachelor's or master's degrees in computer forensics, and others are planning to begin offering such degrees. Most computer forensic investigators learn their trade while working for a law enforcement agency, either as a sworn officer or a civilian computer forensic analyst. They are trained at their agency's computer forensics training program.

Most of the work of private detectives and investigators is learned on the job. New investigators will usually start by learning how to use databases to gather information. The training they receive depends on the type of firm. At an insurance company, a new investigator will learn to recognize insurance fraud. At a firm that specializes in domestic cases, a new worker might observe a senior investigator performing surveillance. Learning by doing, in which new investigators are put on cases and gain skills as they go, is a common approach. Corporate investigators hired by large companies, however, may receive formal training in business

> **CONSIDER THIS...**
> Many people enter law enforcement specifically to get training in computer forensic investigation and establish a reputation before moving to the private sector.

practices, management structure, and various finance-related topics.

Most states and the District of Columbia require private detectives and investigators to be licensed. Licensing requirements vary, however. Seven states—Alabama, Alaska, Colorado, Idaho, Mississippi, South Dakota, and Wyoming—have no statewide licensing requirements. Some states have few requirements, and many others have stringent regulations. For example, the Bureau of Security and Investigative Services of the California Department of Consumer Affairs requires private investigators to be 18 years of age or older; have a combination of education in police science, criminal law, or justice and experience equaling 3 years (6,000 hours); pass a criminal history background check by the California Department of Justice and the FBI (in most states, convicted felons cannot be issued a license); and receive a qualifying score on a 2-hour written examination covering laws and regulations. In all states, detectives and investigators who carry handguns must meet additional requirements. Because laws change, it is important to verify the licensing laws related to private investigators in the state and locality where work will be performed.

> **CONSIDER THIS...**
> Because they work with changing technologies, computer forensic investigators never stop training. They learn the latest methods of fraud detection and new software programs and operating systems by attending conferences and courses offered by software vendors and professional associations.

There are no licenses specifically for computer forensic investigators, but some states require them to be licensed private investigators. Even where licensure is not required, a private investigator license is useful to some because it allows them to perform follow-up or related tasks.

Postsecondary Program to Consider

• Criminal justice/police science

Additional Qualifications

Private detectives and investigators typically have previous experience in other occupations. Some have worked in other occupations for insurance or collections companies, in the private security industry, or as paralegals. Many investigators enter the field after serving in law enforcement, the military, government auditing and investigative positions, or federal intelligence jobs. Former law enforcement officers, military investigators, and government agents, who frequently are able to retire after 25 years of service, often become private detectives or investigators in a second career. Others enter from jobs in finance, accounting, commercial credit, investigative reporting, insurance, and law. These individuals often can apply their previous work experience in a related investigative specialty.

For private detective and investigator jobs, most employers look for individuals with ingenuity, persistence, and assertiveness. A candidate must not be afraid of confrontation, should communicate well, and should be able to think on his or her feet. Good interviewing and interrogation skills also are important and usually are acquired in earlier careers in law enforcement or other fields. Because the courts often are the judge of a properly conducted investigation, the investigator must be able to present the facts in a manner that a jury will believe.

Some investigators receive certification from a professional organization to demonstrate competency in a field. For example, the National Association of Legal Investigators confers the Certified Legal Investigator designation upon licensed investigators who devote a majority of their practice to negligence or criminal defense investigations. To receive the designation, applicants must have 5 years of investigations experience. They also must satisfy educational requirements and continuing-training requirements and must pass written and oral exams.

> ### CONSIDER THIS...
>
> Employers don't want investigators to use the information they obtain for illegal purposes (for example, blackmail). Therefore, the screening process for potential employees typically includes a background check for a criminal history.

ASIS International, a trade organization for the security industry, offers the Professional Certified Investigator certification. To qualify, applicants must have a high school diploma or the equivalent; must have 5 years of investigations experience, including 2 years managing investigations; and must pass an exam.

School Subjects to Study

- Algebra
- Biology
- Computer science
- English
- Geometry
- Public speaking

Moving Up

Most private detective agencies are small, with little room for advancement. Usually, there are no defined ranks or steps, so advancement takes the form of increases in salary and assignment status. Many detectives and investigators start their own firms after gaining a few years of experience. Corporate and legal investigators may rise to supervisor or manager of the security or investigations department.

Employment

Private detectives and investigators held about 45,500 jobs in 2008. About 21 percent were self-employed, including many for whom investigative work was a second job. Around 41 percent of detective and investigator jobs were in investigation and security services, including private detective agencies. The rest worked mostly in state and local government, legal services firms, department or other general merchandise stores, employment services companies, insurance agencies, and credit mediation establishments, including banks and other depository institutions.

Job Prospects

Employment of private detectives and investigators is expected to grow 22 percent over the 10-year period ending 2018, much faster than the average for all occupations. Increased demand for private detectives and investigators will result from heightened security concerns, increased litigation, and the need to protect confidential information and property of all kinds. The proliferation of criminal activity on the Internet, such as identity theft, spamming, e-mail harassment, and illegal downloading of copyrighted materials, also will increase the demand for private investigators. Employee background checks, conducted by private investigators, have become standard for an increasing number of jobs. Growing financial activity worldwide will increase the demand for investigators to control internal and external financial losses, to monitor competitors, and to prevent industrial spying. More individuals are investigating care facilities, such as childcare providers, hospices, and hospitals.

Keen competition is expected for most jobs because private detective and investigator careers attract many qualified people, including relatively young retirees from law enforcement and military careers. The best opportunities for new jobseekers will be in entry-level jobs in detective agencies. Opportunities are expected to be favorable for qualified computer forensic investigators.

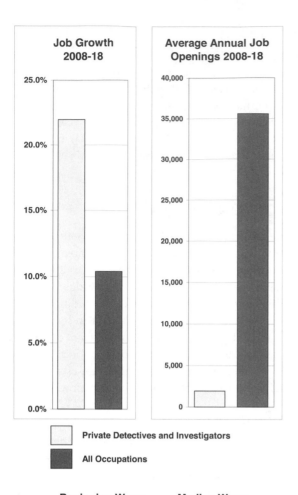

Job Growth 2008-18

Average Annual Job Openings 2008-18

☐ Private Detectives and Investigators

■ All Occupations

Income

Median annual wages of salaried private detectives and investigators were $41,760 in May 2008. The middle 50 percent earned between $30,870 and $59,060. The lowest 10 percent earned less than $23,500, and the highest 10 percent earned more than $76,640. Wages of private detectives and investigators vary greatly by employer, specialty, and geographic area.

Related Jobs

- Accountants and auditors
- Bill and account collectors
- Claims adjusters, appraisers, examiners, and investigators
- Financial analysts
- Personal financial advisors
- Police and detectives
- Security guards and gaming surveillance officers

■ How to Learn More

For information on local licensing requirements, contact your State Department of Public Safety, State Division of Licensing, or local or state police headquarters.

For information on a career as a legal investigator and about the Certified Legal Investigator credential, contact

- National Association of Legal Investigators, NALI World Headquarters, 235 N. Pine St., Lansing, MI. 48933. Internet: www.nalionline.org

For more information about investigative and other security careers, about the Professional Certified Investigator credential, and for a list of colleges and universities offering security-related courses and majors, contact

- ASIS International, 1625 Prince St., Alexandria, VA 22314-2818. Internet: www.asisonline.org

Why It's Hot

The computer-based economy we now live in permits many new kinds of crimes, including identity theft and computer vandalism. It has also made industrial espionage and intellectual property theft easier. But it also has created many new tools for investigation. For example, it's much cheaper nowadays for businesses to order background checks of potential employees. Companies wanting to stay competitive in the global market are cutting their losses to theft and fraud and monitoring the activities of their competitors by hiring private investigators.

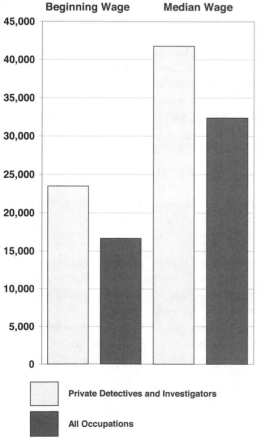

Beginning Wage

Median Wage

☐ Private Detectives and Investigators

■ All Occupations

Public Relations Specialists

Public relations specialists engage in promoting or creating good will for individuals, groups, or organizations by writing or selecting favorable publicity material and releasing it through various communications media.

Just the Facts

Earnings: $51,280

Job Growth: 24.0%

Annual Openings: 13,130

Education and Training: Bachelor's degree

While at Work

An organization's reputation, profitability, and its continued existence can depend on the degree to which its targeted public supports its goals and policies. Public relations specialists—also referred to as *communications specialists* and *media specialists*, among other titles—serve as advocates for clients seeking to build and maintain positive relationships with the public. Their clients include businesses, nonprofit associations, universities, hospitals, and other organizations that want to build and maintain positive relationships with the public. As managers recognize the link between good public relations and the success of their organizations, they increasingly rely on public relations specialists for advice on the strategy and policy of their communications.

Public relations specialists handle organizational functions, such as media, community, consumer, industry, and governmental relations; political campaigns; interest-group representation; conflict mediation; and employee and investor relations.

Public relations specialists draft press releases and contact people in the media who might print or broadcast their material. Sometimes, the subject of a press release is an organization and its policies toward employees or its role in the community. For example, a press release might describe a public issue, such as health, energy, or the environment, and what an organization does to advance that issue.

Public relations specialists also arrange and conduct programs to maintain contact between organization representatives and the public. For example, public relations specialists set up speaking engagements and prepare speeches for officials. These media specialists represent employers at community projects; make film, slide, and other visual presentations for meetings and school assemblies; and plan conventions.

In large organizations, the key public relations executive, who often is a vice president, may develop overall plans and policies with other executives. In addition, public relations departments employ public relations specialists to write, research, prepare materials, maintain contacts, and respond to inquiries.

People who handle publicity for an individual or who direct public relations for a small organization may deal with all aspects of the job. These public relations specialists contact people, plan and research, and prepare materials for distribution. They also may handle advertising or sales promotion work to support marketing efforts.

Public relations specialists draft press releases and contact people in the media who might print or broadcast their material.

Also Known As

In government, public relations specialists may be called *press secretaries.* They keep the public informed about the activities of agencies and officials. For example, *public affairs specialists* in the U.S. Department of State alert the public of travel advisories and of U.S. positions on foreign issues. A press secretary for a member of Congress informs constituents of the representative's accomplishments.

Job Fit

Personality Type

Enterprising-Artistic-Social

Career Clusters

03 Arts, Audio/Video Technology, and Communications

04 Business, Management, and Administration

Skills

Social Skills

Thought-Processing

Communications

Management

Equipment/Technology Analysis

Work Styles

Adaptability/Flexibility

Innovation

Independence

Social Skills Orientation

Integrity

Initiative

Achievement/Effort

Leadership

Working Conditions

Public relations specialists work in busy offices. The pressures of deadlines and tight work schedules can be stressful.

Some public relations specialists work a standard 35- to 40-hour week, but overtime is common, and work schedules can be irregular and are frequently interrupted. Occasionally, they must be at the job or on call around the clock, especially if there is an emergency or crisis. Schedules often have to be rearranged so workers can meet deadlines, deliver speeches, attend meetings and community activities, and travel.

What's Required

A bachelor's degree in a communications-related field combined with public relations experience is excellent preparation for a person interested in public relations work.

Education and Training

Many entry-level public relations specialists have a college degree in public relations, journalism, marketing, or communications. Some firms seek college graduates who have worked in electronic or print journalism. Other employers seek applicants with demonstrated communication skills and training or experience in a field related to the firm's business—information technology, health care, science, engineering, sales, or finance, for example.

Many colleges and universities offer bachelor's and post-secondary programs leading to a degree in public relations. In addition, many other colleges offer courses in this field. Courses in advertising, business administration, finance, political science, psychology, sociology, and creative writing also are helpful. Specialties may be offered in public relations for business, government, and nonprofit organizations.

Internships in public relations provide students with valuable experience and training and are the best route to finding entry-level employment. Membership in local chapters of the Public Relations Student Society of America (affiliated with the Public Relations Society of America) or in student chapters of the International Association of Business Communicators provides an opportunity for students to exchange views with public relations specialists and to make professional contacts that may help them to find a full-time job after graduation.

> **CONSIDER THIS...**
> Colleges usually offer the public relations major within the journalism or communications department.

Some organizations, particularly those with large public relations staffs, have formal training programs for new employees. In smaller organizations, new employees work under the guidance of experienced staff members. Entry-level workers often maintain files of material about company activities, skim newspapers and magazines for appropriate articles to clip, and assemble information for speeches and pamphlets. New workers also may answer calls from the press and the public, prepare invitation lists and details for press conferences, or escort visitors and clients. After gaining experience, they write news releases, speeches, and articles for publication or plan and carry out public relations programs. Public relations specialists in smaller firms usually get well-rounded experience, whereas those in larger firms become more specialized.

The Universal Accreditation Board accredits public relations specialists who are members of the Public Relations Society of America and who participate in the Examination for Accreditation in Public Relations process. This process includes both a readiness review and an examination, which are designed for candidates who have at least 5 years of full-time work or teaching experience in public relations and who have earned a bachelor's degree in a communications related field. The readiness review includes a written submission by each candidate, a portfolio review, and dialogue between the candidate and a three-member panel. Candidates who successfully advance through readiness review and pass the computer-based examination earn the Accredited in Public Relations (APR) designation.

The International Association of Business Communicators (IABC) also has an accreditation program for professionals in the communications field, including public relations specialists. Those who meet all the requirements of the program earn the Accredited Business Communicator (ABC) designation. Candidates must have at least 5 years of experience and a bachelor's degree in a communications field and must pass written and oral examinations. They also must submit a portfolio of work samples that demonstrate involvement in a range of communications projects and a thorough understanding of communications planning.

Postsecondary Programs to Consider

- Family and consumer sciences/human sciences communication
- Health communication
- Political communication
- Public relations/image management
- Speech communication and rhetoric

Additional Qualifications

In addition to the ability to communicate thoughts clearly and simply, public relations specialists must show cre-

ativity, initiative, and good judgment. Decision-making, problem-solving, and research skills also are important. People who choose public relations as a career should have an outgoing personality, self-confidence, an understanding of human psychology, and an enthusiasm for motivating people. They should be assertive but able to participate as part of a team and be open to new ideas.

School Subjects to Study

- Algebra
- English
- Foreign language
- Geometry
- Public speaking
- Trigonometry

Moving Up

Public relations specialists who show that they can handle more demanding assignments are more likely to be promoted to supervisory jobs than those who are unable to do so. In public relations firms, an entry-level worker might be hired as a junior account executive and be promoted over the course of a career to account executive, senior account executive, account manager, and, eventually, vice president. Specialists in corporate public relations follow a similar career path, although the job titles may differ.

Some experienced public relations specialists start their own consulting firms.

Employment

Public relations specialists held about 275,200 jobs in 2008. They are concentrated in service-providing industries, such as advertising and related services; health care and social assistance; educational services; and government. Others work for communications firms, financial institutions, and government agencies.

Public relations specialists are concentrated in large cities, where press services and other communications facilities are readily available and where many businesses and trade associations have their headquarters. Many public relations consulting firms, for example, are in New York, Los Angeles, San Francisco, Chicago, and Washington, D.C. There is a trend, however, toward public relations jobs to be dispersed throughout the nation, closer to clients.

Job Prospects

Employment of public relations specialists is expected to grow 24 percent in the 10-year period ending 2018, much faster than the average for all occupations. The need for good public relations in an increasingly competitive and global business environment should spur demand for these workers, especially those with specialized knowledge or international experience. Employees who possess additional language capabilities also are in great demand.

Employment in public relations firms is expected to grow as firms hire contractors to provide public relations services, rather than support more full-time staff when additional work is needed.

Among detailed industries, the largest job growth will continue to be in advertising and related services.

Keen competition likely will continue for entry-level public relations jobs, as the number of qualified applicants is expected to exceed the number of job openings. Many people are attracted to this profession because of the high-profile nature of the work. Opportunities should be best for college graduates who combine a degree in journalism, public relations, or another communications-related field with a public relations internship or other related work experience. Applicants who do not have the appropriate educational background or work experience will face the toughest obstacles.

Additional job opportunities should result from the need to replace public relations specialists who retire or leave the occupation for other reasons.

Income

Median annual wages for salaried public relations specialists were $51,280 in May 2008. The middle 50 percent earned between $38,400 and $71,670; the lowest 10 percent earned less than $30,140, and the top 10 percent earned more than $97,910.

Related Jobs

- Advertising, marketing, promotions, public relations, and sales managers
- Demonstrators and product promoters
- Lawyers
- Market and survey researchers
- News analysts, reporters, and correspondents
- Sales representatives, wholesale and manufacturing

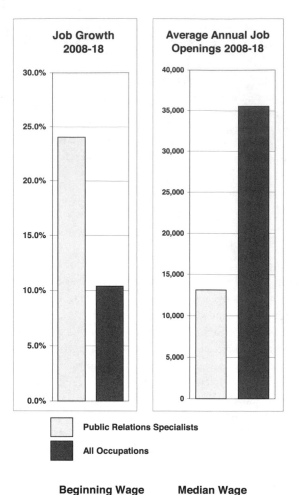

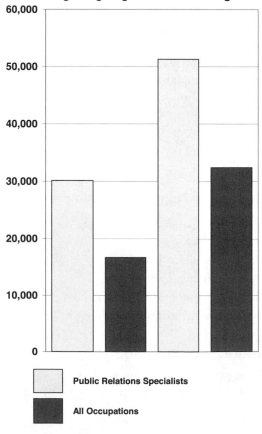

How to Learn More

A comprehensive directory of schools offering degree programs, a sequence of study in public relations, a brochure on careers in public relations, and an online brochure entitled *Where Shall I Go to Study Advertising and Public Relations?* are available from

- Public Relations Society of America, Inc., 33 Maiden Lane, New York, NY 10038-5150. Internet: www.prsa.org

For information on accreditation for public relations professionals and the IABC Student Web site, contact

- International Association of Business Communicators, 601 Montgomery St. Suite 1900, San Francisco, CA 94111.

Why It's Hot

In the highly competitive global marketplace, and in an era when the Internet can spread bad news in a heartbeat, good publicity is essential to a company's survival. Public relations professionals, especially those who can communicate effectively across borders, will be in great demand, although competition will be keen.

Radiation Therapists

Radiation therapists provide radiation therapy to patients as prescribed by a radiologist, according to established practices and standards.

Just the Facts

Earnings: $72,910

Job Growth: 27.1%

Annual Openings: 690

Education and Training: Associate degree

While at Work

Radiation therapy is an important medical technique for treating cancer in the human body. As part of a medical radiation oncology team, radiation therapists use machines called linear accelerators to administer radiation treatment to patients. In the procedure called external beam therapy, the linear accelerator projects high-energy X-rays at targeted cancer cells. As the X-rays collide with human tissue, they produce highly energized ions that can shrink and eliminate cancerous tumors. Radiation therapy is sometimes used as the sole treatment for cancer, but it is usually used in conjunction with chemotherapy or surgery.

The radiation therapy process consists of several steps. In the first step, simulation, the radiation therapist uses an X-ray imaging machine or computer tomography (CT) scan to pinpoint the location of the tumor. The radiation therapist then develops a treatment plan in conjunction with a radiation oncologist (a physician who specializes in therapeutic radiology) and a dosimetrist (a technician who calculates the dose of radiation that will be used for treatment). The therapist then explains the treatment plan to the patient and answers any questions that the patient may have.

The next step in the process is treatment. To begin, the radiation therapist positions the patient so that radiation exposure is concentrated on the tumor cells and adjusts the linear accelerator according to the guidelines established in simulation. Then, from a separate room that is protected from the X-ray radiation, the therapist operates the linear accelerator and monitors the patient's condition through a TV monitor and an intercom system. Treatment can take anywhere from 10 to 30 minutes and is usually administered once a day, 5 days a week, for 2 to 9 weeks.

During the treatment phase, the radiation therapist monitors the patient's physical condition to determine whether any adverse side effects are taking place.

CONSIDER THIS...

To hold the patient's body still during treatment, radiation therapists sometimes make body molds from foam, plastic, or plaster. They may also make shields that block radiation from body parts near the treatment site.

CONSIDER THIS...

The therapist needs to stay aware of the patient's emotional well-being during the period of treatment. Because many patients are under stress and are emotionally fragile, it is important for the therapist to maintain a positive attitude and provide emotional support. The therapist may refer to the patient to an appropriate counselor or social worker.

Radiation therapists keep detailed records of their patients' treatments. These records include information such as the dose of radiation used for each treatment, the total amount of radiation used to date, the area treated, and the patient's reactions. Radiation oncologists and dosimetrists review these records to ensure that the treatment plan is working, to monitor the amount of radiation exposure that the patient has received, and to keep side effects to a minimum.

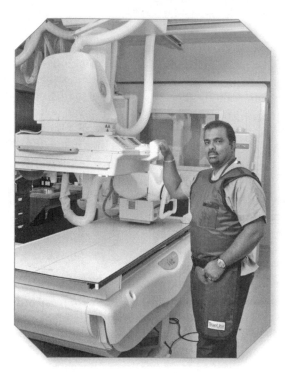

Radiation therapists use machines to administer radiation to patients.

Also Known As

Radiation therapists should not be confused with some other technicians who work with them, although their duties sometimes partially overlap. *Medical radiation physicists* monitor and adjust the linear accelerator. Because radiation therapists often work alone during the treatment phase, they sometimes check the linear accelerator for problems and make adjustments that are needed. *Dosimetrists* specialize in calculating the dose of radiation that will be used in a treatment plan, but therapists sometimes assist dosimetrists with routine aspects of dosimetry.

Job Fit

Personality Type
Social Realistic-Conventional

Career Cluster
08 Health Science

Skills
Computer Programming
Equipment Use/Maintenance
Communications
Social Skills
Mathematics
Thought-Processing
Science
Management

Work Styles
Concern for Others
Social Skills Orientation
Integrity
Stress Tolerance
Self-Control
Adaptability/Flexibility
Attention to Detail
Cooperation

Working Conditions

Radiation therapists work in hospitals or in cancer treatment centers. These places are clean, well lighted, and well ventilated. Therapists do a considerable amount of lifting and must be able to help disabled patients get on and off treatment tables. They spend most of their time on their feet.

Radiation therapists generally work 40 hours a week, and unlike those in other health care occupations, they normally work only during the day. However, because radiation therapy emergencies do occur, some therapists are required to be on call and may have to work outside of their normal hours.

> **CONSIDER THIS...**
> Because they work around radioactive materials, radiation therapists take great care to ensure that they are not exposed to dangerous levels of radiation. Following standard safety procedures can prevent overexposure.

Working with cancer patients can be stressful, but many radiation therapists also find it rewarding.

■ What's Required

A bachelor's degree, associate degree, or certificate in radiation therapy generally is required. Many states also require radiation therapists to be licensed. With experience, therapists can advance to managerial positions.

Education and Training

Employers usually require applicants to complete an associate or a bachelor's degree program in radiation therapy. Radiation therapy programs include core courses on radiation therapy procedures and the scientific theories behind them. In addition, such programs often include courses on human anatomy and physiology, physics, algebra, pre-calculus, writing, public speaking, computer science, and research methodology. In 2009 there were 123 radiation therapy programs accredited by the American Registry of Radiologic Technologists (ARRT).

In 2009, 35 states required radiation therapists to be licensed by a state accrediting board. Licensing requirements vary by state, but many states require applicants to pass the ARRT certification examination. Further information is available from individual state licensing offices.

Even in states where licensing is not linked to ARRT certification, many employers require this credential. To become ARRT-certified, an applicant must complete an accredited radiation therapy program, adhere to ARRT ethical standards, and pass the ARRT certification examination. The examination and accredited academic programs cover radiation protection and quality assurance, clinical concepts in radiation oncology, treatment planning, treatment delivery, and patient care and education. Candidates also must demonstrate competency in several clinical practices, including patient care activities; simulation procedures; dosimetry calculations; fabrication of beam modification devices; low-volume, high-risk procedures; and the application of radiation.

ARRT certification is valid for 1 year, after which therapists renew certification through a procedure that the ARRT calls registration. Requirements include abiding by the ARRT ethical standards, paying annual dues, and satisfying continuing education requirements. Continuing education requirements must be met every 2 years and include either the completion of 24 credits of radiation therapy-related courses or the attainment of ARRT certification in a discipline other than radiation therapy. Reg-

CONSIDER THIS...

Some therapists become qualified by completing an associate or bachelor's degree program in radiography, which is the study of radiological imaging, and then completing a 12-month certificate program in radiation therapy.

istration, however, may not be required by all states or employers that require initial certification.

Postsecondary Program to Consider

• Medical radiologic technology/science—radiation therapist training

Additional Qualifications

All radiation therapists need good communication skills because their work involves a great deal of patient interaction. Individuals interested in becoming radiation therapists should be psychologically capable of working with cancer patients. They should be caring and empathetic because they work with patients who are ill and under stress. They should be able to keep accurate, detailed records. They also should be physically fit because they work on their feet for long periods and lift and move disabled patients.

School Subjects to Study

• Algebra
• Biology
• English
• Geometry
• Physics
• Pre-calculus and calculus
• Trigonometry

Moving Up

Experienced radiation therapists may advance to manage radiation therapy programs in treatment centers or other health-care facilities. Managers generally continue to treat patients while taking on management responsibilities. Other advancement opportunities include teaching, technical sales, and research. With additional training and certification, therapists also can become dosimetrists, who use complex mathematical formulas to calculate proper radiation doses.

Employment

Radiation therapists held about 15,200 jobs in 2008. About 70 percent worked in hospitals, and about 18 percent worked in the offices of physicians. A small proportion worked in outpatient care centers and medical and diagnostic laboratories.

Job Prospects

Employment of radiation therapists is projected to grow by 27 percent in the 10-year period ending 2018, which is much faster than the average for all occupations. The growing elderly population is expected to cause an increase in the number of people needing treatment. In addition, as radiation technology becomes safer and more effective, it will be prescribed more often, leading to an increased demand for radiation therapists. Growth is likely to be rapid across all practice settings, including hospitals, physicians' offices, and outpatient centers.

Job prospects are expected to be good. Job openings will result from employment growth and from the need to replace workers who retire or leave the occupation for other reasons. Applicants with a bachelor's degree and related work experience may have the best opportunities.

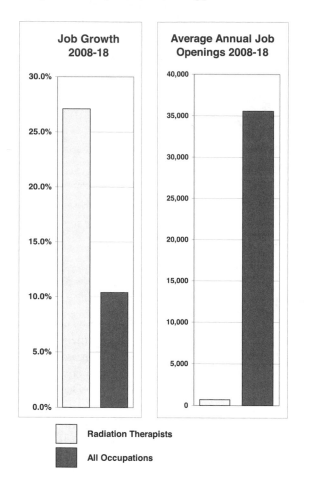

Income

Median annual earnings of wage-and-salary radiation therapists were $72,910 in May 2008. The middle 50 percent earned between $59,050 and $87,910. The lowest 10 percent earned less than $47,910, and the highest 10 percent earned more than $104,350. Median annual earnings in the industries that employed the largest numbers of radiation therapists in May 2008 are as follows: $71,310 in general medical and surgical hospitals; $74,720 in offices

of physicians; $81,280 in specialty hospitals; $79,660 in employment services; and $80,540 in colleges, universities, and professional schools.

Some employers also reimburse their employees for the cost of continuing education.

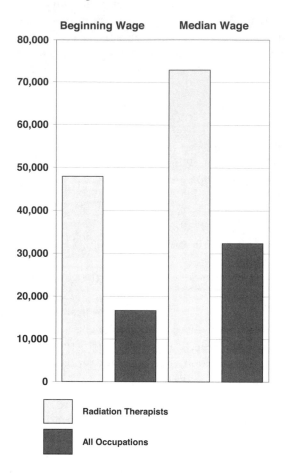

Related Jobs

- Cardiovascular technologists and technicians
- Counselors
- Dental hygienists
- Diagnostic medical sonographers
- Nuclear medicine technologists
- Nursing, psychiatric, and home health aides
- Physical therapist assistants and aides
- Physicians and surgeons
- Psychologists
- Radiologic technologists and technicians
- Registered nurses
- Respiratory therapists
- Social and human service assistants
- Social workers

How to Learn More

Information on certification by the American Registry of Radiologic Technologists and on accredited radiation therapy programs may be obtained from

- American Registry of Radiologic Technologists, 1255 Northland Dr., St. Paul, MN 55120. Internet: www.arrt.org

Information on careers in radiation therapy may be obtained from

- American Society of Radiologic Technologists, 15000 Central Ave., SE, Albuquerque, NM 87123. Internet: www.asrt.org

Why It's Hot

As the U.S. population grows and an increasing share of it is in the older age groups, the number of people requiring treatment will spur demand for radiation therapists. In addition, as radiation technology advances and is able to treat more types of cancer, radiation therapy will be prescribed more often.

Registered Nurses

Registered nurses administer nursing care to ill, injured, convalescent, or disabled patients.

Just the Facts

Earnings: $62,450

Job Growth: 22.2%

Annual Openings: 103,900

Education and Training: Associate degree

Bachelor's degree

While at Work

Registered nurses (RNs) work in various specializations and settings, but all of them treat patients, educate patients and the public about various medical conditions, and provide advice and emotional support to patients' family members. RNs record patients' medical histories and symptoms, help perform diagnostic tests and analyze results, operate medical machinery, administer treatment and medications, and help with patient follow-up and rehabilitation.

RNs teach patients and their families how to manage their illness or injury, explaining post-treatment home care needs; diet, nutrition, and exercise programs; and self-administration of medication and physical therapy. Some RNs work to promote general health by educating the public on warning signs and symptoms of disease. RNs also may run general health screening or immunization clinics, blood drives, and public seminars on various conditions.

When caring for patients, RNs establish a plan of care or contribute to an existing plan. Plans may include numerous activities, such as administering medication, including careful checking of dosages and avoiding interactions; starting, maintaining, and discontinuing intravenous (IV) lines for fluid, medication, blood, and blood products; administering therapies and treatments; observing the patient and recording those observations; and consulting with physicians and other health-care clinicians. Some RNs provide direction to licensed practical nurses and nursing aids regarding patient care. RNs with advanced educational preparation and training may perform diagnostic and therapeutic procedures and may have prescriptive authority.

RNs can specialize in one or more areas of patient care. There generally are four ways to specialize. RNs can choose a particular work setting or type of treatment, such as *perioperative nurses,* who work in operating rooms and assist surgeons. RNs also may choose to specialize in specific health conditions, as do *diabetes management nurses,* who assist patients to manage diabetes. Other RNs specialize in working with one or more organs or body system types, such as *dermatology nurses,* who work with patients who have skin disorders. RNs also can choose to work with a well-defined population, such as *geriatric nurses,* who work with the elderly. Some RNs may combine specialties. For example, *pediatric oncology nurses* deal with children and adolescents who have cancer.

There are many options for RNs who specialize in a work setting or type of treatment. *Ambulatory care nurses* provide preventive care and treat patients with a variety of illnesses and injuries in physicians' offices or in clinics. Some ambulatory care nurses are involved in telehealth, providing care and advice through electronic communications media such as videoconferencing, the Internet, or by telephone. *Critical care nurses* provide care to patients with serious, complex, and acute illnesses or injuries that require very close monitoring and extensive medication protocols and therapies. Critical care nurses often work in critical or intensive care hospital units. *Emergency,* or *trauma, nurses* work in hospital or stand-alone emergency departments, providing initial assessments and care for patients with life-threatening conditions. Some emergency nurses may become qualified to serve as *transport nurses,* who provide medical care to patients who are transported by helicopter or airplane to the nearest medical facility. *Holistic nurses* provide care such as acupuncture, massage and aroma therapy, and biofeedback, which are meant to treat patients' mental and spiritual health in addition to their physical health. *Home health-care nurses* provide at-home nursing care for patients, often as follow-up care after discharge from a hospital or from a rehabilitation, long-term care, or skilled nursing facility. *Hospice and palliative care nurses* provide care, most often in home or hospice settings, focused on maintaining quality of life for terminally ill patients. *Infusion nurses* administer medications, fluids, and blood to patients through injections into patients' veins. *Long-term care nurses* provide health-care services on a recurring basis to patients with chronic physical or mental disorders, often in long-term care or skilled nursing facilities.

Medical-surgical nurses provide health promotion and basic medical care to patients with various medical and surgical diagnoses. *Occupational health nurses* seek to prevent job-related injuries and illnesses, provide monitoring and emergency care services, and help employers implement health and safety standards. *Perianesthesia nurses* provide preoperative and postoperative care to patients undergoing anesthesia during surgery or other procedure. *Perioperative nurses* assist surgeons by selecting and handling instruments, controlling bleeding, and suturing incisions. Some of these nurses also can specialize in plastic and reconstructive surgery. *Psychiatric-mental health nurses* treat patients with personality and mood disorders. *Radiology nurses* provide care to patients undergoing diagnostic radiation procedures such as ultrasounds, magnetic resonance imaging, and radiation therapy for oncology diagnoses. *Rehabilitation nurses* care for patients with temporary and permanent disabilities. *Transplant nurses* care for both transplant recipients and living donors and monitor signs of organ rejection.

RNs specializing in a particular disease, ailment, or health care condition are employed in virtually all work settings, including physicians' offices, outpatient treatment facilities, home health-care agencies, and hospitals. *Addictions nurses* care for patients seeking help with alcohol, drug, tobacco, and other addictions. *Intellectual and developmen-*

CONSIDER THIS...

Some RNs provide basic health care to patients outside of traditional health-care settings in such venues as correctional facilities, schools, summer camps, and the military. Other RNs travel around the United States and abroad providing care to patients in areas with shortages of health-care workers.

tal disabilities nurses provide care for patients with physical, mental, or behavioral disabilities; care may include help with feeding, controlling bodily functions, sitting or standing independently, and speaking or other communication. *Diabetes management nurses* help diabetics to manage their disease by teaching them proper nutrition and showing them how to test blood sugar levels and administer insulin injections. *Genetics nurses* provide early detection screenings, counseling, and treatment of patients with genetic disorders, including cystic fibrosis and Huntington's disease. *HIV/AIDS nurses* care for patients diagnosed with HIV and AIDS. *Oncology nurses* care for patients with various types of cancer and may assist in the administration of radiation and chemotherapies and follow-up monitoring. *Wound, ostomy, and continence nurses* treat patients with wounds caused by traumatic injury, ulcers, or arterial disease; provide postoperative care for patients with openings that allow for alternative methods of bodily waste elimination; and treat patients with urinary and fecal incontinence.

RNs specializing in treatment of a particular organ or body system usually are employed in hospital specialty or critical care units, specialty clinics, and outpatient care facilities. *Cardiovascular nurses* treat patients with coronary heart disease and those who have had heart surgery, providing services such as postoperative rehabilitation. *Dermatology nurses* treat patients with disorders of the skin, such as skin cancer and psoriasis. *Gastroenterology nurses* treat patients with digestive and intestinal disorders, including ulcers, acid reflux disease, and abdominal bleeding. Some nurses in this field also assist in specialized procedures such as endoscopies, which look inside the gastrointestinal tract using a tube equipped with a light and a camera that can capture images of diseased tissue. *Gynecology nurses* provide care to women with disorders of the reproductive system, including endometriosis, cancer, and sexually transmitted diseases. *Nephrology nurses* care for patients with kidney disease caused by diabetes, hypertension, or substance abuse. *Neuroscience nurses* care for patients with dysfunctions of the nervous system, including brain and spinal cord injuries and seizures. *Ophthalmic nurses* provide care to patients with disorders of the eyes, including blindness and glaucoma, and to patients undergoing eye surgery. *Orthopedic nurses* care for patients with muscular and skeletal problems, including arthritis, bone fractures, and muscular dystrophy. *Otorhinolaryngology nurses* care for patients with ear, nose, and throat disorders, such as cleft palates, allergies, and sinus disorders. *Respiratory nurses* provide care to patients with respiratory disorders such as asthma, tuberculosis, and cystic fibrosis. *Urology nurses* care for patients with disorders of the kidneys, urinary tract, and male reproductive organs, including infections, kidney and bladder stones, and cancers.

RNs who specialize by population provide preventive and acute care in all health-care settings to the segment of the population in which they specialize, including newborns (neonatology), children and adolescents (pediatrics), adults, and the elderly (gerontology or geriatrics).

Most RNs work as staff nurses: members of a team providing critical health care. However, some RNs choose to become advanced practice nurses, who work independently or in collaboration with physicians and may focus on the provision of primary care services. *Clinical nurse specialists* provide direct patient care and expert consultations in one of many nursing specialties, such as mental health. *Nurse anesthetists* provide anesthesia and related care before and after surgical, therapeutic, diagnostic and obstetrical procedures. They also provide pain management and emergency services, such as airway management. *Nurse-midwives* provide primary care to women, including gynecological exams, family planning advice, prenatal care, assistance in labor and delivery, and neonatal care. *Nurse practitioners* serve as primary and specialty care providers, providing a blend of nursing and health-care services to patients and families. The most common specialty areas for nurse practitioners are family practice, adult practice, women's health, pediatrics, acute care, and geriatrics. However, there are a variety of other specialties that nurse practitioners can choose, including neonatology and mental health. Advanced practice nurses can prescribe medications in all states and in the District of Columbia.

Also Known As

Some nurses have jobs that require little or no direct patient care, but still require an active RN license. *Case managers* ensure that all of the medical needs of patients with severe injuries and severe or chronic illnesses are met. *Forensics nurses* participate in the scientific investigation and treatment of abuse victims, violence, criminal activity, and traumatic accident. *Infection control nurses* identify, track, and control infectious outbreaks in health-care facilities and develop programs for outbreak prevention and response to biological terrorism. *Legal nurse consultants* assist lawyers in medical cases by interviewing patients and witnesses, organizing medical records, determining damages and costs, locating evidence, and educating lawyers about medical issues. *Nurse administrators* supervise nursing staff, establish work schedules and budgets, maintain medical supply inventories, and manage resources to ensure high-quality care. *Nurse educators* plan, develop, implement, and evaluate educational programs and curricula for the professional development of student nurses and RNs. *Nurse informaticists* manage and communicate nursing data and information to improve decision making by consumers, patients, nurses, and other health-care

providers. RNs also may work as health-care consultants, public policy advisors, pharmaceutical and medical supply researchers and salespersons, and medical writers and editors.

Job Fit

Personality Type
Social-Investigative

Career Cluster
08 Health Science

Skills
Social Skills
Management
Computer Programming
Thought-Processing
Communications
Mathematics
Science

Work Styles
Concern for Others
Social Skills Orientation
Stress Tolerance
Self-Control
Integrity
Adaptability/Flexibility
Achievement/Effort
Analytical Thinking

Working Conditions

Most RNs work in well-lighted, comfortable health-care facilities. Home health and public health nurses travel to patients' homes, schools, community centers, and other sites. RNs may spend considerable time walking, bending, stretching, and standing. Patients in hospitals and nursing care facilities require 24-hour care; consequently, nurses in these institutions may work nights, weekends, and holidays. RNs also may be on call—available to work on short notice.

> **CONSIDER THIS...**
> Nurses who work in offices, schools, and other settings that do not provide 24-hour care are more likely to work regular business hours.

Most registered nurses work as part of a team providing critical health care.

Nursing has its hazards, especially in hospitals, nursing care facilities, and clinics, where nurses may be in close contact with individuals who have infectious diseases and with toxic, harmful, or potentially hazardous compounds, solutions, and medications. RNs must observe rigid, standardized guidelines to guard against disease and other dangers, such as those posed by radiation, accidental needle sticks, chemicals used to sterilize instruments, and anesthetics. In addition, they are vulnerable to back injury when moving patients, shocks from electrical equipment, and hazards posed by compressed gases. RNs also may suffer emotional strain from caring for patients suffering unrelieved intense pain, close personal contact with patients' families, the need to make critical decisions, and ethical dilemmas and concerns.

What's Required

The three major educational paths to registered nursing are a bachelor's degree (BSN), an associate degree (ADN), and a diploma from an approved nursing program. Nurses most commonly enter the occupation by completing an associate degree or bachelor's degree program. Individuals then must complete a national licensing examination in order to obtain a nursing license. Further training or education can qualify nurses to work in specialty areas and may help improve advancement opportunities.

Education and Training

BSN programs, offered by more than 700 colleges and universities, take about 4 years to complete. ADN programs, offered by about 850 community and junior colleges, take about 2 to 3 years to complete. Diploma programs, administered in hospitals, last about 3 years. Only about 70 programs offer diplomas. Generally, licensed graduates of any of the three types of educational programs qualify for entry-level positions.

Many RNs with an ADN or diploma later enter bachelor's programs to prepare for a broader scope of nursing practice. Often, they can find an entry-level position and then take advantage of tuition reimbursement benefits to work toward a BSN by completing an RN-to-BSN program. There are more than 600 RN-to-BSN programs in the United States. Accelerated master's degree in nursing (MSN) programs also are available by combining 1 year of an accelerated BSN program with 2 years of graduate study. There are about 150 RN-to-MSN programs.

> **CONSIDER THIS...**
> Some RN-to-BSN and RN-to-MSN programs include coursework that can be taken online, which is a convenient way for some people to complete the classroom requirements for the degree. However, all such programs also include a clinical learning component, which you usually can complete at a health-care agency in your community.

About 200 accelerated BSN programs also are available for individuals who have a bachelor's or higher degree in another field and who are interested in moving into nursing. Accelerated BSN programs last 12 to 18 months and provide the fastest route to a BSN for individuals who already hold a degree. MSN programs also are available for individuals who hold a bachelor's or higher degree in another field.

Individuals considering nursing should carefully weigh the advantages and disadvantages of enrolling in a BSN or MSN program because, if they do, their advancement opportunities usually are broader. In fact, some career paths are open only to nurses with a bachelor's or master's degree. A bachelor's degree often is necessary for administrative positions and is a prerequisite for admission to graduate nursing programs in research, consulting, teaching, and all four advanced practice nursing specialties—clinical nurse specialists, nurse anesthetists, nurse-midwives, and nurse practitioners. Individuals who complete a bachelor's receive more training in areas such as communication, leadership, and critical thinking, all of which are becoming more important as nursing care becomes more complex. Additionally, bachelor's degree programs offer more clinical experience in non-hospital settings.

CONSIDER THIS...

Do you want a credential that's accepted everywhere? Go into advanced practice or a specialization. Most advanced practice nurses become nationally certified in their area of specialization after completing their educational programs. Certification also is available in specialty areas for all nurses. In some states, certification in a specialty is required in order to practice that specialty.

Education beyond a bachelor's degree can also help students looking to enter certain fields or increase advancement opportunities. About 450 nursing schools offer master's degrees, about 100 offer doctoral degrees, and about 50 offer accelerated BSN-to-doctoral programs.

All four advanced practice nursing specialties require at least a master's degree. Most programs require a BSN degree for entry; some programs require at least 1 to 2 years of clinical experience as an RN for admission. There are about 350 master's and post-master's programs offered for nurse practitioners, about 200 master's and post-master's programs for clinical nurse specialists, about 100 programs for nurse anesthetists, and about 40 programs for nurse-midwives.

All nursing education programs include classroom instruction and supervised clinical experience in hospitals and other health-care facilities. Students take courses in anatomy, physiology, microbiology, chemistry, nutrition, psychology and other behavioral sciences, and nursing. Coursework also includes the liberal arts for ADN and BSN students.

Supervised clinical experience is provided in hospital departments such as pediatrics, psychiatry, maternity, and surgery. A growing number of programs include clinical experience in nursing care facilities, public health departments, home health agencies, and ambulatory clinics.

In all states, the District of Columbia, and U.S. territories, students must graduate from an approved nursing program and pass a national licensing examination, known as the NCLEX-RN, in order to obtain a nursing license. Nurses may be licensed in more than one state, either by examination or by the endorsement of a license issued by another state. The Nurse Licensure Compact Agreement allows a nurse who is licensed and permanently resides in one of the member states to practice in the other member states without obtaining additional licensure. In 2009, 23 states were members of the Compact, while one more was pending membership. All states require periodic renewal of licenses, which may require continuing education.

Foreign-educated and foreign-born nurses wishing to work in the United States must obtain a work visa. To obtain the visa, nurses must undergo a federal screening program to ensure that their education and licensure are comparable to that of a U.S. educated nurse, that they have proficiency in written and spoken English, and that they have passed either the Commission on Graduates of Foreign Nursing Schools (CGFNS) Qualifying Examination or the NCLEX-RN. CGFNS administers the VisaScreen Program. (The Commission is an immigration-neutral, nonprofit organization that is recognized internationally as an authority on credentials evaluation in the health-care field.) Nurses educated in Australia, Canada (except Quebec), Ireland, New Zealand, and the United Kingdom, or foreign-born nurses who were educated in the United States, are exempt from the language proficiency testing. In addition to these national requirements, foreign-born nurses must obtain state licensure to practice in the United States. Each state has its own requirements for licensure.

Postsecondary Programs to Consider

- Adult health nurse training/nursing
- Clinical nurse specialist training
- Critical care nursing
- Maternal/child health and neonatal nursing
- Nurse anesthetist training
- Nurse practitioner training
- Nursing midwifery
- Nursing science (M.S., Ph.D.)
- Nursing/registered nurse training (RN, ASN, BSN, MSN)
- Occupational and environmental health nursing
- Pediatric nursing
- Perioperative/operating room and surgical nurse training/nursing
- Psychiatric/mental health nurse training/nursing
- Public health/community nurse training/nursing

Additional Qualifications

Nurses should be caring, sympathetic, responsible, and detail-oriented. They must be able to direct or supervise others, correctly assess patients' conditions, and determine when consultation is required. They need emotional stability to cope with human suffering, emergencies, and other stresses.

- Algebra
- Biology
- Chemistry
- English
- Geometry
- Trigonometry

Moving Up

Some RNs start their careers as licensed practical nurses or nursing aides, and then go back to school to receive their RN degree. Most RNs begin as staff nurses in hospitals and, with experience and good performance, often move to other settings or are promoted to more responsible positions. In management, nurses can advance from assistant unit manager or head nurse to more senior-level administrative roles of assistant director, director, vice president, or chief nurse. Increasingly, management-level nursing positions require a graduate or an advanced degree in nursing or health services administration. Administrative positions require leadership, communication and negotiation skills, and good judgment.

Some nurses move into the business side of health care. Their nursing expertise and experience on a health-care team equip them to manage ambulatory, acute, home-based, and chronic care. Employers—including hospitals, insurance companies, pharmaceutical manufacturers, and managed care organizations, among others—need RNs for health planning and development, marketing, consulting, policy development, and quality assurance. Other nurses work as college and university faculty or conduct research.

Employment

As the largest health-care occupation, registered nurses held about 2.6 million jobs in 2008. Hospitals employed the majority of RNs, with 60 percent of such jobs. About 8 percent of jobs were in offices of physicians, 5 percent in home health-care services, 5 percent in nursing care facilities, and 3 percent in employment services. The remainder worked mostly in government agencies, social assistance agencies, and educational services.

Job Prospects

Employment of registered nurses is expected to grow by 22 percent in the 10-year period ending 2018, much faster than the average for all occupations.

However, employment of RNs will not grow at the same rate in every industry. The projected growth rates for RNs in the industries with the highest employment of these workers are offices of physicians (48%); home health care services (33%); nursing care facilities (25%); employment services (24%); and hospitals, public and private (17%).

Employment is expected to grow more slowly in hospitals—health care's largest industry—than in most other health-care industries. While the intensity of nursing care is likely to increase, requiring more nurses per patient, the number of inpatients (those who remain in the hospital for more than 24 hours) is not likely to grow by much. Patients are being discharged earlier, and more procedures are being done on an outpatient basis, both inside and outside hospitals. Rapid growth is expected in hospital outpatient facilities, such as those providing same-day surgery, rehabilitation, and chemotherapy.

More and more sophisticated procedures, once performed only in hospitals, are being performed in physicians' offices and in outpatient care centers, such as freestanding ambulatory surgical and emergency centers. Accordingly, employment of nurses is expected to grow very fast in these places as health care in general expands.

Employment in nursing care facilities is expected to grow because of increases in the number of elderly, many of whom require long-term care. However, this growth will be relatively slower than in other health-care industries because of the desire of patients to be treated at home or in residential care facilities, and the increasing availability of that type of care. The financial pressure on hospitals to discharge patients as soon as possible should produce more admissions to nursing and residential care facilities and to home health care. Job growth also is expected in units that provide specialized long-term rehabilitation for stroke and head injury patients, as well as units that treat Alzheimer's victims.

> **CONSIDER THIS...**
> Generally, RNs with at least a bachelor's degree will have better job prospects than those with less than a bachelor's. In addition, all four advanced practice specialties—clinical nurse specialists, nurse practitioners, nurse midwives, and nurse anesthetists—will be in high demand, particularly in medically underserved areas such as inner cities and rural areas. Relative to physicians, these RNs increasingly serve as lower-cost primary care providers.

Employment in home health care is expected to increase rapidly in response to the growing number of older persons with functional disabilities, consumer preference for care in the home, and technological advances that make it possible to bring increasingly complex treatments into the home. The type of care demanded will require nurses who are able to perform complex procedures.

Rapid employment growth in the employment services industry is expected as hospitals, physician's offices, and other health-care establishments utilize temporary workers to fill short-term staffing needs. And as the demand for nurses grows, temporary nurses will be needed more often, further contributing to employment growth in this industry.

Overall, job opportunities are expected to be excellent for registered nurses. Employers in some parts of the country and in certain employment settings report difficulty in attracting and retaining an adequate number of RNs, primarily because of an aging RN workforce and a lack of younger workers to fill positions. Enrollments in nursing programs at all levels have increased more rapidly in the past few years as students seek jobs with stable employment. However, many qualified applicants are being turned away because of a shortage of nursing faculty. The need for nursing faculty will only increase as many instructors near retirement. Many employers also are relying on foreign-educated nurses to fill vacant positions.

Even though overall employment opportunities for all nursing specialties are expected to be excellent, they can vary by employment setting. Despite the slower employment growth in hospitals, job opportunities should still be excellent because of the relatively high turnover of hospital nurses. RNs working in hospitals frequently work overtime and night and weekend shifts and also treat seriously ill and injured patients, all of which can contribute to stress and burnout. Hospital departments in which these working conditions occur most frequently—critical care units, emergency departments, and operating rooms—generally will have more job openings than other departments. To attract and retain qualified nurses, hospitals may offer signing bonuses, family-friendly work schedules, or subsidized training. A growing number of hospitals also are experimenting with online bidding to fill open shifts, in which nurses can volunteer to fill open shifts at premium wages. This can decrease the amount of mandatory overtime that nurses are required to work.

Although faster employment growth is projected in physicians' offices and outpatient care centers, RNs may face greater competition for these positions because they generally offer regular working hours and more comfortable working environments. There also may be some competition for jobs in employment services, despite a high rate of employment growth, because a large number of workers are attracted by the industry's relatively high wages and the flexibility of the work in this industry.

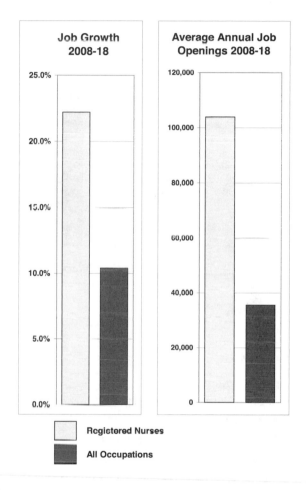

Income

Median annual earnings of registered nurses were $62,450 in May 2008. The middle 50 percent earned between $51,640 and $76,570. The lowest 10 percent earned less than $43,410, and the highest 10 percent earned more than $92,240. Median annual earnings in the industries employing the largest numbers of registered nurses in May 2008 were $63,880 in general medical and surgical hospitals; $59,210 in offices of physicians; $58,740 in home health care services; $57,060 in nursing care facilities; and $68,160 in employment services.

Many employers offer flexible work schedules, child care, educational benefits, and bonuses.

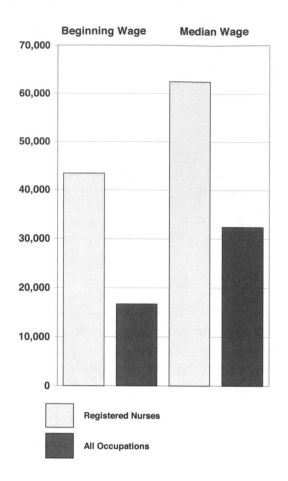

Beginning Wage   Median Wage

Registered Nurses

All Occupations

Related Jobs

- Athletic trainers
- Cardiovascular technologists and technicians
- Dental hygienists
- Diagnostic medical sonographers
- Dietitians and nutritionists
- Emergency medical technicians and paramedics
- Licensed practical and licensed vocational nurses
- Massage therapists
- Medical and health services managers
- Nursing, psychiatric, and home health aides
- Occupational therapists
- Physical therapists
- Physician assistants
- Physicians and surgeons
- Radiation therapists
- Radiologic technologists and technicians
- Respiratory therapists
- Surgical technologists

How to Learn More

For information on a career as a registered nurse and nursing education, contact

- National League for Nursing, 61 Broadway, New York, NY 10006. Internet: www.nln.org

For information on baccalaureate and graduate nursing education, nursing career options, and financial aid, contact

- American Association of Colleges of Nursing, 1 Dupont Circle NW, Suite 530, Washington, DC 20036. Internet: www. aacn.nche.edu

For additional information on registered nurses, including credentialing, contact

- American Nurses Association, 8515 Georgia Ave., Suite 400, Silver Spring, MD 20910. Internet: http://nursingworld.org

For information on the NCLEX-RN exam and a list of individual state boards of nursing, contact

- National Council of State Boards of Nursing, 111 E. Wacker Dr., Suite 2900, Chicago, IL 60611. Internet: www.ncsbn.org

For information on the nursing population, including facts about workforce shortages, contact

- Bureau of Health Professions, 5600 Fishers Lane, Room 8-05, Rockville, MD 20857. Internet: http://bhpr.hrsa.gov

For information on obtaining U.S. certification and work visas for foreign-educated nurses, contact

- Commission on Graduates of Foreign Nursing Schools, 3600 Market St., Suite 400, Philadelphia, PA 19104. Internet: www.cgfns.org

For a list of accredited clinical nurse specialist programs, contact

- National Association of Clinical Nurse Specialists, 2090 Linglestown Rd., Suite 107, Harrisburg, PA 17110. Internet: www.nacns.org

For information on nurse anesthetists, including a list of accredited programs, contact

- American Association of Nurse Anesthetists, 222 Prospect Ave., Park Ridge, IL 60068.

For information on nurse-midwives, including a list of accredited programs, contact

- American College of Nurse-Midwives, 8403 Colesville Rd., Suite 1550, Silver Spring, MD 20910. Internet: www. midwife.org

For information on nurse practitioners, including a list of accredited programs, contact

- American Academy of Nurse Practitioners, P.O. Box 12846, Austin, TX 78711. Internet: www.aanp.org

For information on education for nurse practitioners, contact

- National Organization of Nurse Practitioner Faculties, 1522 K St. NW, Suite 702, Washington, DC 20005. Internet: www. nonpf.org

For information on critical care nurses, contact

- American Association of Critical-Care Nurses, 101 Columbia, Aliso Viejo, CA 92656. Internet: www.aacn.org

For additional information on registered nurses in all fields and specialties, contact

- American Society of Registered Nurses, 1001 Bridgeway, Suite 411, Sausalito, CA 94965. Internet: www.asrn.org

Why It's Hot

Job growth for nurses will be driven by technological advances in patient care, which permit a greater number of health problems to be treated, and by an increasing emphasis on preventive care. In addition, the number of older people, who are much more likely than younger people to need nursing care, is projected to grow rapidly.

Respiratory Therapists

Respiratory therapists evaluate, treat, and care for patients with breathing or other cardiopulmonary disorders.

Just the Facts

Earnings: $52,200
Job Growth: 20.9%
Annual Openings: 4,140
Education and Training: Associate degree

While at Work

Respiratory therapists—also known as *respiratory care practitioners*—practice under the direction of a physician and assume primary responsibility for all respiratory care therapeutic treatments and diagnostic procedures, including the supervision of respiratory therapy technicians. They consult with physicians and other health-care staff to help develop and modify patient care plans. Therapists also provide complex therapy requiring considerable independent judgment, such as caring for patients on life support in intensive-care units of hospitals.

Respiratory therapists evaluate and treat all types of patients, ranging from premature infants whose lungs are not fully developed to elderly people whose lungs are diseased. They provide temporary relief to patients with chronic asthma or emphysema and give emergency care to patients who are victims of a heart attack, stroke, drowning, or shock.

Respiratory therapists interview patients, perform limited physical examinations, and conduct diagnostic tests. For example, respiratory therapists test a patient's breathing capacity and determine the concentration of oxygen and other gases in a patient's blood. They also measure a patient's pH, which indicates the acidity or alkalinity of the blood. To evaluate a patient's lung capacity, respiratory therapists have the patient breathe into an instrument that measures the volume and flow of oxygen during inhalation and exhalation. By comparing the reading with the norm for the patient's age, height, weight, and sex, respiratory therapists can provide information that helps determine whether the patient has any lung deficiencies. To analyze oxygen, carbon dioxide, and blood pH levels, therapists draw an arterial blood sample, place it in a blood gas analyzer, and relay the results to a physician, who then makes treatment decisions.

To treat patients, respiratory therapists use oxygen or oxygen mixtures, chest physiotherapy, and aerosol medications—liquid medications suspended in a gas that forms a mist that is inhaled. They teach patients how to inhale the aerosol properly to ensure its effectiveness. When a patient has difficulty getting enough oxygen into his or her blood, therapists increase the patient's concentration of oxygen by placing an oxygen mask or nasal cannula on the patient and setting the oxygen flow at the level prescribed by a physician. Therapists also connect patients who cannot breathe on their own to ventilators that deliver pressurized oxygen into the lungs. The therapists insert a tube into the patient's trachea, or windpipe; connect the tube to the ventilator; and set the rate, volume, and oxygen concentration of the oxygen mixture entering the patient's lungs.

CONSIDER THIS...

Some therapists provide services for pulmonary rehabilitation, smoking-cessation counseling, disease prevention, case management, or polysomnography—the diagnosis of breathing disorders during sleep, such as apnea. Respiratory therapists also increasingly treat critical-care patients, either as part of surface and air transport teams or as part of rapid-response teams in hospitals.

Therapists perform regular assessments of patients and equipment. If a patient appears to be having difficulty breathing or if the oxygen, carbon dioxide, or pH level of the blood is abnormal, therapists change the ventilator setting according to the doctor's orders or check the equipment for mechanical problems.

Respiratory therapists perform chest physiotherapy on patients to remove mucus from their lungs and make it easier for them to breathe. Therapists place patients in positions that help drain mucus, and then vibrate the patients' rib cages, often by tapping on the chest, and tell the patients to cough. Chest physiotherapy may be needed after surgery, for example, because anesthesia depresses respiration. As a result, physiotherapy may be prescribed to help get the patient's lungs back to normal and to prevent congestion. Chest physiotherapy also helps patients suffering from lung diseases, such as cystic fibrosis, that cause mucus to collect in the lungs.

Therapists who work in home care teach patients and their families to use ventilators and other life-support systems. In addition, these therapists visit patients in their homes to inspect and clean equipment, evaluate the home environment, and ensure that patients have sufficient knowledge of their diseases and the proper use of their medications and equipment.

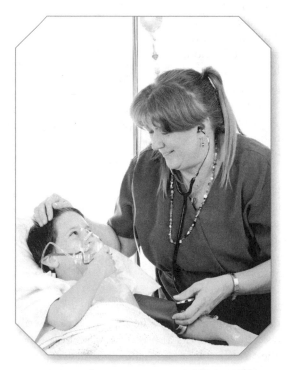

Respiratory therapists test a patient's breathing capacity and determine the concentration of oxygen and other gases in the blood.

Also Known As

Some respiratory therapists have job titles that reflect a specialization, such as *oxygen therapists* or *sleep lab technicians*. The title *inhalation therapist* is sometimes used in the United States but is more common abroad.

Job Fit

Personality Type
Social-Investigative-Realistic

Career Cluster
08 Health Science

Skills
Science
Mathematics
Communications
Thought-Processing
Equipment Use/Maintenance
Social Skills
Equipment/Technology Analysis
Computer Programming
Management

Work Styles
Concern for Others
Social Skills Orientation
Independence
Stress Tolerance
Cooperation
Integrity
Leadership
Initiative

Working Conditions

Respiratory therapists generally work between 35 and 40 hours a week. Because hospitals operate around the clock, therapists can work evenings, nights, or weekends. They spend long periods standing and walking between patients' rooms. In an emergency, therapists work under the stress of the situation.

Respiratory therapists are trained to work with

CONSIDER THIS...
Respiratory therapists employed in home health care must travel frequently to patients' homes. They may need to make emergency visits if equipment problems arise.

gases stored under pressure. Adherence to safety precautions and regular maintenance and testing of equipment minimize the risk of injury. As in many other health occupations, respiratory therapists are exposed to infectious diseases, but by carefully following proper procedures, they can minimize these risks.

What's Required

An associate degree is the minimum educational requirement, but a bachelor's or master's degree may be important for advancement. All states, except Alaska and Hawaii, require respiratory therapists to be licensed.

Education and Training

An associate degree is required to become a respiratory therapist. Training is offered at the postsecondary level by colleges and universities, medical schools, vocational-technical institutes, and the Armed Forces. Most programs award associate or bachelor's degree and prepare graduates for jobs as advanced respiratory therapists. A limited number of associate degree programs lead to jobs as entry-level respiratory therapists. According to the Commission on Accreditation of Allied Health Education Programs (CAAHEP), 31 entry-level and 346 advanced respiratory therapy programs were accredited in the United States in 2008.

> **CONSIDER THIS...**
>
> Knowledge of math and science is important. Respiratory care involves basic mathematical problem solving and an understanding of chemical and physical principles. For example, respiratory care workers must be able to compute dosages of medication and calculate gas concentrations.

Among the areas of study in respiratory therapy programs are human anatomy and physiology, pathophysiology, chemistry, physics, microbiology, pharmacology, and mathematics. Other courses deal with therapeutic and diagnostic procedures and tests, equipment, patient assessment, cardiopulmonary resuscitation, the application of clinical practice guidelines, patient care outside of hospitals, cardiac and pulmonary rehabilitation, respiratory health promotion and disease prevention, and medical recordkeeping and reimbursement.

A license is required to practice as a respiratory therapist, except in Alaska and Hawaii. Also, most employers require respiratory therapists to maintain a cardiopulmonary resuscitation (CPR) certification.

Licensure is usually based, in large part, on meeting the requirements for certification from the National Board for Respiratory Care (NBRC). The board offers the Certified Respiratory Therapist (CRT) credential to those who graduate from entry-level or advanced programs accredited by CAAHEP or the Committee on Accreditation for Respiratory Care (CoARC) and who also pass an exam.

The board also awards the Registered Respiratory Therapist (RRT) to CRTs who have graduated from advanced programs and pass two separate examinations. Supervisory positions and intensive-care specialties usually require the RRT.

Postsecondary Program to Consider

- Respiratory care therapy/therapist

Additional Qualifications

Therapists should be sensitive to a patient's physical and psychological needs. Respiratory care practitioners must pay attention to detail, follow instructions, and work as part of a team. In addition, operating advanced equipment requires proficiency with computers.

School Subjects to Study

- Algebra
- Biology
- Computer science
- Chemistry
- English
- Geometry
- Physics
- Trigonometry

Moving Up

Respiratory therapists advance in clinical practice by moving from general care to the care of critically ill patients who have significant problems in other organ systems, such as the heart or kidneys. Respiratory therapists, especially those with a bachelor's or master's degree, also may advance to supervisory or managerial positions in a respiratory therapy department. Respiratory therapists in home health care and equipment rental firms may become branch managers. Some respiratory therapists advance by moving into teaching positions. Some others use the knowledge gained as a respiratory therapist to work in another industry, such as developing, marketing, or selling pharmaceuticals and medical devices.

Employment

Respiratory therapists held about 105,900 jobs in 2008. About 81 percent of jobs were in hospitals, mainly in departments of respiratory care, anesthesiology, or pulmonary medicine. Most of the remaining jobs were in offices of physicians or other health practitioners, consumer-goods rental firms that supply respiratory equipment for home use, nursing care facilities, employment services, and home health-care services.

Job Prospects

Employment of respiratory therapists is expected to grow by 21 percent in the 10-year period ending 2018, much faster than the average for all occupations. The increasing demand will come from substantial growth in the middle-aged and elderly population—a development that will heighten the incidence of cardiopulmonary disease. Growth in demand also will result from the expanding role of respiratory therapists in case management, disease prevention, emergency care, and the early detection of pulmonary disorders.

> **CONSIDER THIS...**
>
> Some patients are the opposite of elderly: premature infants whose lungs aren't yet working well and who therefore depend on a ventilator. As medicine improves the outlook for these infants, respiratory therapists will be needed to help them survive.

Older Americans suffer most from respiratory ailments and cardiopulmonary diseases, such as pneumonia, chronic bronchitis, emphysema, and heart disease. As the number of older persons increases, the need for respiratory therapists is expected to increase as well.

Job opportunities are expected to be very good, especially for those with a bachelor's degree and certification, and those with cardiopulmonary care skills or experience working with infants. The vast majority of job openings will continue to be in hospitals. However, a growing number of openings are expected to be outside of hospitals, especially in home health-care services, offices of physicians or other health practitioners, consumer-goods rental firms, or in the employment services industry as a temporary worker in various settings.

Income

Median annual wages of wage-and-salary respiratory therapists were $52,200 in May 2008. The middle 50 percent earned between $44,490 and $61,720. The lowest 10 percent earned less than $37,920 and the highest 10 percent earned more than $69,800.

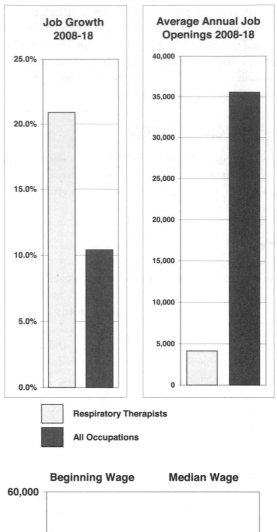

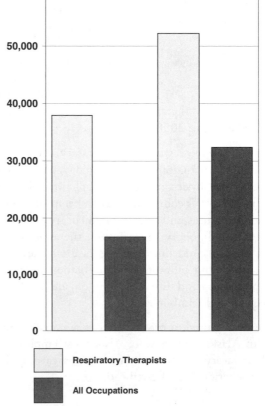

Related Jobs

- Athletic trainers
- Cardiovascular technologists and technicians
- Diagnostic medical sonographers
- Nuclear medicine technologists
- Occupational therapists
- Physical therapists
- Radiation therapists
- Radiologic technologists and technicians
- Registered nurses

How to Learn More

Information concerning a career in respiratory care is available from

- American Association for Respiratory Care, 9425 N. MacArthur Blvd., Suite 100, Irving, TX 75063. Internet: www.aarc.org

For a list of accredited educational programs for respiratory care practitioners, contact either of the following organizations:

- Commission on Accreditation for Allied Health Education Programs, 1361 Park St., Clearwater, FL 33756. Internet: www.caahep.org

- Committee on Accreditation for Respiratory Care, 1248 Harwood Rd., Bedford, TX 76021.

Information on gaining credentials in respiratory care and a list of state licensing agencies can be obtained from

- National Board for Respiratory Care, Inc., 18000 W. 105th St., Olathe, KS 66061. Internet: www.nbrc.org

Why It's Hot

Lung function often deteriorates as people age, so the aging American population will create a demand for respiratory therapists. In addition, advances in inhalable medications and in the treatment of lung transplant patients, heart attack patients, accident victims, and premature infants will increase the demand for the services of respiratory care practitioners. The best opportunities will be in hospitals and for workers with a bachelor's degree.

Social and Human Service Assistants

Social and human service assistants help professionals from a wide variety of fields, such as psychology, rehabilitation, or social work, to provide client services, as well as support for families.

Just the Facts

Earnings: $27,280

Job Growth: 22.6%

Annual Openings: 15,390

Education and Training: Moderate-term on-the-job training

While at Work

Social and human service assistants help social workers, health-care workers, and other professionals to provide services to people. They usually work under the direction of workers from a variety of fields, such as nursing, psychiatry, psychology, rehabilitative or physical therapy, or social work. The amount of responsibility and supervision they are given varies a great deal. Some have little direct supervision—they may run a group home, for example. Others work under close direction.

Social and human service assistants provide services to clients to help them improve their quality of life. They assess clients' needs, investigate their eligibility for benefits and services such as food stamps, Medicaid, or welfare, and help to obtain them. They also arrange for transportation and escorts, if necessary, and provide emotional support. Social and human service assistants monitor and keep case records on clients and report progress to supervisors and case managers.

Social and human service assistants play a variety of roles in a community. They may organize and lead group activities, assist clients in need of counseling or crisis intervention, or administer food banks or emergency fuel programs, for example. In halfway houses, group homes, and government-supported housing programs, they assist adults who need supervision with personal hygiene and daily living skills. They review clients' records, ensure that they take their medication, talk with family members, and confer with medical personnel and other caregivers to provide insight into clients' needs. Social and human service assistants also give emotional support and help clients become involved in community recreation programs and other activities.

In psychiatric hospitals, rehabilitation programs, and outpatient clinics, social and human service assistants work with psychiatrists, psychologists, social workers, and others to help clients master everyday living skills, communicate more effectively, and live well with others. They support the client's participation in a treatment plan, such as individual or group counseling or occupational therapy.

Social and human service assistants help clients with community services and benefits.

Also Known As

Because this is a very diverse group of occupations, workers have a wide variety of job titles, such as *case aides, child care workers, community development workers, correctional case managers, domestic violence advocates, housing assistants, independent living specialists, job opportunity specialists, mental health technicians, peer counselors, shelter advocates,* or *welfare service aides.*

Job Fit

Personality Type
Conventional-Social-Enterprising

Career Cluster
10 Human Services

Skills
Social Skills
Communications
Computer Programming
Thought-Processing
Management
Work Styles
Social Skills Orientation
Concern for Others
Self-Control
Cooperation
Stress Tolerance
Dependability
Persistence
Integrity

Working Conditions

Working conditions of social and human service assistants vary. Some work in offices, clinics, and hospitals, while others work in group homes, shelters, sheltered workshops, and day programs. Traveling to see clients is also required for some jobs. Sometimes working with clients can be dangerous, even though most agencies do everything they can to ensure their workers' safety. Most assistants work 40 hours a week; some work in the evening and on weekends.

▮ What's Required

A bachelor's degree is not required for most jobs in this occupation, but employers increasingly seek individuals with relevant work experience or education beyond high school.

Education and Training

Certificates or associate degrees in appropriate subjects meet many employers' requirements, but some jobs may require a bachelor's or master's degree.

Human services degree programs have a core curriculum that trains students to observe patients and record information, conduct patient interviews, implement treatment plans, employ problem-solving techniques, handle crisis intervention matters, and use proper case management and referral procedures. Many programs utilize field work to give students hands-on experience. General education courses in liberal arts, sciences, and the humanities also are part of most curriculums. Most programs also offer specialized courses related to addictions, gerontology, child protection, and other areas. Many degree programs require completion of a supervised internship.

Regardless of the academic or work background of employees, most employers provide some form of in-service training to their employees, such as seminars and workshops.

Postsecondary Programs to Consider

- Counseling
- Gerontology
- Human services
- Mental and social health services and allied professions, other
- Psychology
- Rehabilitation
- Social work
- Sociology

Additional Qualifications

These workers should have a strong desire to help others, effective communication skills, a sense of responsibility, and the ability to manage time effectively. Many human services jobs involve direct contact with people who are vulnerable to exploitation or mistreatment, so patience and understanding are also highly valued characteristics.

It is becoming more common for employers to require a criminal background check, and in some settings, workers may be required to have a valid driver's license.

School Subjects to Study

- Algebra
- English
- Geometry
- Public speaking
- Social studies

Moving Up

Social and human service assistants with proven leadership ability, especially from paid or volunteer experience in social services, often gain greater autonomy in their work.

Formal education is almost always necessary for advancement. In general, advancement to case management, rehabilitation, or social work jobs requires a bachelor's or master's degree in human services, counseling, rehabilitation, social work, or a related field.

Employment

Social and human service assistants held about 352,000 jobs in 2008. More than 65 percent were employed in the health-care and social assistance industries and almost 24 percent were employed by state and local governments.

Job Prospects

The number of social and human service assistants is expected to grow by nearly 23 percent in the 10-year period ending 2018, which is much faster than the average for all occupations. This is due in large part to the aging population and increased demand for mental health and substance abuse treatment.

Demand for social services will expand with the growing elderly population, who are more likely to need adult day care, meal delivery programs, support during medical crises, and other services. In addition, more social and human service assistants will be needed to provide services to pregnant teenagers, people who are homeless, people who are mentally disabled or developmentally challenged, and people who are substance abusers.

Job training programs are also expected to require additional social and human service assistants. As social welfare policies shift focus from benefit-based programs to work-based initiatives, there will be more demand for people to teach job skills to the people who are new to, or returning to, the workforce.

Residential care establishments should face increased pressures to respond to the needs of the mentally and physically disabled. The number of people who are disabled is increasing, and many need help to care for themselves. More community-based programs and supportive

CONSIDER THIS...

The level of education workers have often influences the kind of work they are assigned and the degree of responsibility that is given to them. For example, workers with no more than a high school education are likely to receive extensive on-the-job training to work in direct-care services—helping clients to fill out paperwork, for example. Workers with a college degree, however, might do supportive counseling, coordinate program activities, or manage a group home.

independent-living sites are expected to be established to house and assist the homeless and the mentally and physically disabled. Furthermore, as substance abusers are increasingly being sent to treatment programs instead of prison, employment of social and human service assistants in substance abuse treatment programs also will grow.

> **CONSIDER THIS...**
>
> There will be more competition for jobs in urban areas than in rural ones, but qualified applicants should have little difficulty finding employment.

Opportunities are expected to be good in private social service agencies. Employment in private agencies will grow as state and local governments continue to contract out services to the private sector in an effort to cut costs. Also, some private agencies have been employing more social and human service assistants in place of social workers, who are more educated and more highly paid.

The number of jobs for social and human service assistants in local governments will grow, but not as fast as employment for social and human service assistants in other industries. Employment in the public sector may fluctuate with the level of funding provided by state and local governments and with the number of services contracted out to private organizations.

Job prospects for social and human service assistants are expected to be excellent, particularly for individuals with appropriate education after high school. Job openings will come from job growth, but also from the need to replace workers who advance into new positions, retire, or leave the workforce for other reasons.

Income

Median annual earnings of social and human service assistants were $27,280 in May 2008. The middle 50 percent earned between $21,860 and $34,590. The top 10 percent earned more than $43,510, while the lowest 10 percent earned less than $17,900.

Median annual earnings in the industries employing the largest numbers of social and human service assistants in May 2008 were $26,250 in individual and family services; $32,560 in local government; $23,580 in residential mental retardation, mental health and substance abuse facilities; $35,510 in state government; and $23,910 in vocational rehabilitation services.

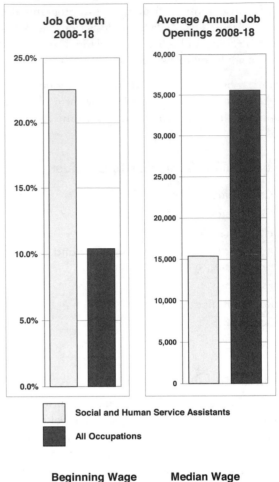

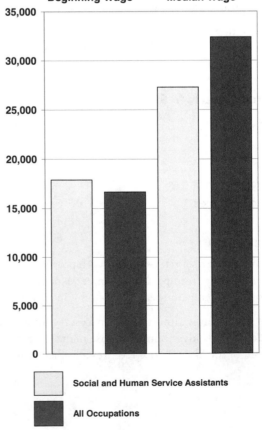

Related Jobs

- Child care workers
- Clergy
- Counselors
- Nursing, psychiatric, and home health aides
- Occupational therapist assistants and aides
- Physical therapist assistants and aides
- Social workers

How to Learn More

For information on programs and careers in human services, contact

- Council for Standards in Human Services Education, PMB 703, 1050 Larrabee Avenue, Suite 104, Bellingham, WA 98225-7367. Internet: www.cshse.org

- National Organization for Human Services, 90 Madison Street, Suite 206, Denver, CO 80206. Internet: www. nationalhumanservices.org

Information on job openings may be available from state employment service offices or directly from city, county, or state departments of health, mental health and mental retardation, and human resources.

Why It's Hot

As the population ages, the rapidly changing economy throws people out of work, and substance abuse grows, a wide variety of social and human services are needed. Many employers are responding to these needs by relying on social and human service assistants.

Social Scientists, Other

Social scientists research, analyze, and report on all aspects of human society.

Just the Facts

Earnings: $55,552
Job Growth: 21.7%
Annual Openings: 800
Education and Training: Master's degree

While at Work

Social scientists study all aspects of society—from past events and achievements to human behavior and relationships among groups. Their research provides insights into the different ways individuals, groups, and institutions make decisions, exercise power, and respond to change. They look at data in detail, such as studying the data they've collected, reanalyzing already existing data, analyzing historical records and documents, and interpreting the effect of location on culture and other aspects of society. Through their studies and analyses, social scientists offer insight into the physical, social, and cultural development of humans, as well as the links between human activity and the environment.

Following are brief discussions of several major types of social scientists. Specialists in one field may find that their research overlaps work being conducted in another discipline.

Anthropologists study the origin, development, and behavior of humans. They examine the ways of life, languages, archaeological remains, and physical characteristics of people in various parts of the world. They also examine the customs, values, and social patterns of different cultures. Some anthropologists study current human concerns, such as overpopulation, warfare, and poverty, while others study the prehistory of *Homo sapiens*, including the evolution of the human brain. *Sociocultural anthropologists* study the customs, cultures, and social lives of groups in settings that range from unindustrialized societies to modern urban centers. They often do this through observation or face-to-face interviews with a particular group, comparing findings of one particular group with that of another. *Linguistic anthropologists* investigate the history of, role of, and changes to language over time in various cultures. *Biological anthropologists* research the evolution of the human body, look for the earliest evidences of human life, and analyze how culture and biology influence one another. *Physical anthropologists* examine human remains found at archaeological sites in order to understand population demographics and factors, such as nutrition and disease, that affected these populations.

Archaeologists examine and recover material evidence, including tools, pottery, cave paintings, the ruins of buildings, and other objects remaining from past human cultures in order to learn about the history, customs, and living habits of earlier civilizations. Most archaeologists work at consulting and research firms—specifically, at cultural resource management (CRM) firms, whose services often are contracted by developers, construction companies, and, sometimes, the federal government. CRM workers are responsible mainly for identifying, assessing, and preserving archaeological and historical sites on private and public land, such as national parks, to ensure that the builder is complying with legislation pertaining to preservation. Archaeologists in museums and historic sites often handle the locale's artifacts collection, educate the public through interactive programs and presentations, or become administrators who supervise programs related to research, collections, and exhibitions. Many archaeologists in the federal government conduct research for the U.S. Department of Interior's National Park Service.

CONSIDER THIS...

With continued technological advances making it increasingly possible to detect the presence of underground anomalies without digging, archaeologists can now target excavation sites better than they previously could.

Geographers study the earth and its land, features, inhabitants, and phenomena. *Physical geographers* examine the physical aspects of a region, including its land forms, climates, soils, vegetation, water, plants, and animals. *Cultural geographers* analyze the spatial implications of human activities within a given area, including its economic activities, social characteristics, and political organization. For example, they might study the distribution of resources and economic activities or investigate health-care delivery systems and the effect of the environment on health.

Geographers incorporate many different technologies into their work, such as geographic information systems (GISs), global positioning systems (GPSs), and remote sensing. For example, a geographer may use GIS and GPS to track information on population growth, traffic patterns, environmental hazards, natural resources, and weather patterns, all in digital format. By overlaying remotely sensed aerial or satellite images with GIS data, such as population density, they create computerized maps that can advise governments, businesses, and the general public on a variety of issues, including the impact of natural disasters and the development of houses, roads, and landfills. As more of these systems are created and

CONSIDER THIS...

Most historians conduct some form of research and analysis for state and local government. Others help study and preserve archival materials and artifacts in museums, visitor centers, and historic buildings and sites.

refined, a good number of mapping specialists are being called *geographic information specialists.*

Historians research, analyze, and interpret the past. They use many sources of information in their research, including government and institutional records, newspapers and other periodicals, photographs, interviews, films, and unpublished manuscripts such as personal diaries and letters. Historians usually specialize in a country or region, a particular period, or a particular field, such as social, intellectual, cultural, political, or diplomatic history. Many communicate their research and findings through books, articles, or essays.

Social scientists study all aspects of society—from past events and achievements to human behavior and relationships.

Also Known As

Many of the people who study geography and work with GIS technology are classified into other occupations, such as *surveyors, cartographers, photogrammetrists, and survey and mapping technicians* (who develop maps and other location-based information), *urban and regional planners* (who help to decide on and evaluate the locations of building and roads and other aspects of physical society), and *geoscientists* (who study earthquakes and other physical aspects of the Earth).

Job Fit

Personality Type
Investigative-Artistic

Career Clusters
03 Arts, Audio/Video Technology, and Communications

05 Education and Training

15 Science, Technology, Engineering, and Mathematics

Skills

Science

Communications

Management

Thought-Processing

Computer Programming

Social Skills

Mathematics

Equipment/Technology Analysis

Work Styles

Analytical Thinking

Persistence

Integrity

Innovation

Achievement/Effort

Initiative

Adaptability/Flexibility

Social Orientation

Working Conditions

Most social scientists have regular hours. Although they often work as part of a research team, they sometimes work alone, writing reports of their findings. Travel may be necessary to collect information or attend meetings, and those on foreign assignment must adjust to unfamiliar cultures, climates, and languages.

Some social scientists do fieldwork. For example, anthropologists, archaeologists, and geographers may travel to remote areas, live among the people they study, learn their languages, and stay for long periods at the site of their investigations. They may work under rugged conditions, and their work may involve strenuous physical exertion.

Social scientists employed by colleges and universities usually have flexible work schedules, often dividing their time among teaching, research, writing, consulting, and administrative responsibilities.

■ What's Required

Most positions require a master's or Ph.D. degree. Some entry-level positions are available to those with a bachelor's degree. All social scientists need good analytical skills.

Education and Training

Graduates with master's degrees in applied specialties usually are qualified for positions outside of colleges and universities, although requirements vary by field. A Ph.D.

may be required for higher level teaching positions. Bachelor's degree holders have limited opportunities; however, a bachelor's degree does provide a suitable background for many different kinds of entry-level jobs in related occupations, such as research assistant, writer, management trainee, and market analyst. In addition, bachelor's degree holders in history often qualify for elementary, middle, and high school teaching positions.

> **CONSIDER THIS...**
>
> Training in statistics and mathematics is essential for many social scientists, most of whom increasingly are using mathematical and quantitative research methods. The ability to use computers for research purposes is mandatory in most disciplines.

Many social science students also benefit from internships or field experience. Numerous local museums, historical societies, government agencies, and nonprofit and other organizations offer internships or volunteer research opportunities. Archaeological field schools instruct future anthropologists, archaeologists, and historians in how to excavate, record, and interpret historical sites.

Postsecondary Programs to Consider

- American history (United States)
- Ancient studies/civilization
- Anthropology
- Archeology
- Asian history
- Canadian history
- Classical, ancient Mediterranean, and near eastern studies and archaeology
- Classics and classical languages, literatures, and linguistics
- Cultural resource management and policy analysis
- European history
- Geography
- Historic preservation and conservation
- History and philosophy of science and technology
- History
- Holocaust and related studies
- Medieval and renaissance studies
- Physical and biological anthropology

Additional Qualifications

Social scientists need excellent written and oral communication skills to report research findings and to collaborate on research. The ability to think logically and methodically also is essential. Objectivity, an open mind, and systematic work habits are important in all kinds of social science research. Patience and persistence are required, for example, when an anthropologist spends years studying artifacts from an ancient civilization before making a final analysis and interpretation.

School Subjects to Study

- Algebra
- Computer science
- English
- Foreign language
- Geography
- Geometry
- History
- Public speaking
- Trigonometry

Moving Up

Some social scientists advance to top-level research and administrative positions. Advancement often depends on the number and quality of reports that social scientists publish or their ability to design studies.

Certification can increase one's prospects for advancement. The GIS Certification Institute (GISCI) has voluntary certification programs for geography professionals in GIS. To qualify for professional distinction, individuals must meet education and experience requirements and pass a written examination. The professional recognition these certifications bestow can often help geographers find employment—especially those who do not have a master's or Ph.D. degree. Workers in these jobs, however, may not be called "geographers," but instead may be referred to by a different title, such as "GIS analyst" or "GIS specialist."

■ Employment

Anthropologists and archaeologists, geographers, and historians held about 11,100 jobs in 2008. Professional, scientific, and technical services employed 37 percent of all workers. About 2 percent were self-employed.

Job Prospects

Overall employment of anthropologists and archaeologists, geographers, and historians is expected to grow by 22 percent in the 10-year period 2018, which is much faster than the average for all occupations. Anthropologists and archaeologists, the largest specialty, is expected to grow by 28 percent, driven by growth in the management, scientific, and technical consulting services industry. Anthropologists who work as consultants will be needed to apply their analytical skills and knowledge to problems ranging from economic development to forensics.

Employment growth of archaeologists will be driven by higher levels of overall construction, including large-scale transportation projects and upgrades to the nation's infrastructure. As construction projects increase, more archaeologists will be needed to ensure that federal laws related to the preservation of archaeological and historical sites and artifacts are met.

> ### CONSIDER THIS...
>
> A growing number of anthropologists will be needed in specific segments of the federal government, such as the U.S. Department of Defense, to assess the regional customs and values—or "cultural terrain"—of a particular society in specific parts of the world.

Employment of geographers is expected to increase by 26 percent because the federal government—the largest employer—is projected to grow faster than in the past. Outside of the federal government, geographers will be needed to advise businesses, local municipalities, real estate developers, utilities, and telecommunications firms regarding where to build new roads, buildings, powerplants, and cable lines. Geographers also will be needed to advise about environmental matters, such as where to build a landfill and where to preserve wetland habitats.

Employment of historians is expected to grow by 11 percent, about as fast as the average for all occupations, reflecting the relatively few jobs outside of federal, state, and local government. Nonetheless, historians possess broad training and education in writing, analytical research, and coherent thinking, so their skills can be applied to many different occupations. As a result, many workers with a history background will find work in niche areas with specialized titles, such as researcher, writer, or policy analyst.

> ### CONSIDER THIS...
>
> Many workers with a history background also choose to teach in elementary, middle, and secondary schools.

In addition to opportunities arising from employment growth, some job openings for social scientists will come from the need to replace those who retire or who leave the

occupation for other reasons. Some social scientists leave the occupation to become professors, but competition for tenured teaching positions will be keen.

Overall, people seeking social science positions are likely to face competition for jobs. Candidates who have a master's or Ph.D. degree in a social science, who are skilled in quantitative research methods, and who also have good written and communications skills are likely to have the best job opportunities. In addition, many jobs in policy, research, or marketing, for which social scientists qualify, are not advertised exclusively as social scientist positions.

Anthropologists and archaeologists will experience the best job prospects at management, scientific, and technical consulting firms. Those with a bachelor's degree in archaeology usually qualify to be a field technician.

Geographers with a background in GIS will find numerous job opportunities applying GIS technology in nontraditional areas, such as emergency assistance, where GISs can track the locations of ambulances, police, and fire rescue units and their proximity to the emergency.

Historians will find jobs mainly in policy or research. Historians may find opportunities with historic preservation societies or by working as a consultant as public interest in preserving and restoring historical sites increases.

Income

Wages of anthropologists and archaeologists, geographers, and historians vary. Median annual wages for anthropologists and archaeologists were $53,910 in May 2008. The middle 50 percent earned between $39,200 and $70,980. The lowest 10 percent earned less than $32,150, and the highest 10 percent earned more than $89,490.

Median annual wages of geographers were $66,600 in May 2008. The middle 50 percent earned between $51,390 and $82,590. The lowest 10 percent earned less than $38,780, and the highest 10 percent earned more than $97,540.

For historians, median annual wages were $54,530 in May 2008. The middle 50 percent earned between $33,570 and $77,290. The lowest 10 percent earned less than $25,670, and the highest 10 percent earned more than $96,530.

In March 2009, the federal government's average annual salary for anthropologists was $88,302; for archaeologists, $70,606; for geographers, $79,223; and for historians, $87,730. Beginning salaries were higher in selected areas of the country where the prevailing local pay level was higher.

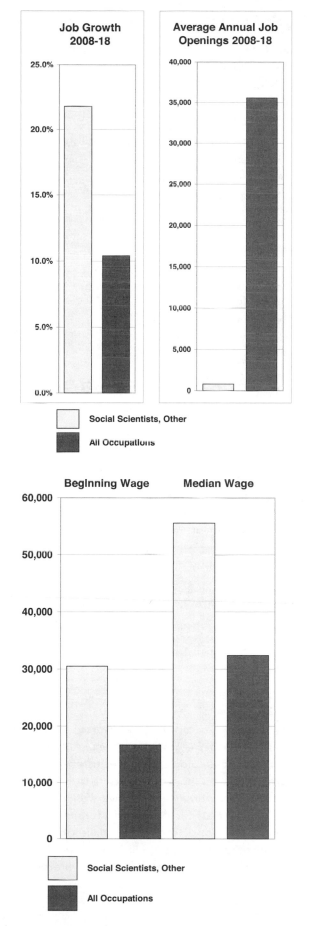

Related Jobs

- Archivists, curators, and museum technicians
- Atmospheric scientists
- Conservation scientists and foresters
- Counselors
- Economists
- Environmental scientists and specialists
- Geoscientists and hydrologists
- Market and survey researchers
- Psychologists
- Social workers
- Statisticians
- Surveyors, cartographers, photogrammetrists, and surveying and mapping technicians
- Teachers—kindergarten, elementary, middle, and secondary
- Teachers—postsecondary
- Urban and regional planners

How to Learn More

For information about careers in anthropology, contact

- American Anthropological Association, 2200 Wilson Blvd., Suite 600, Arlington, VA 22201. Internet: www.aaanet.org

For information about careers in archaeology, contact

- Archaeological Institute of America, 656 Beacon St., 6th Floor, Boston, MA 02215. Internet: www.archaeological.org
- Society for American Archaeology, 900 2nd St. NE, Suite 12, Washington, DC 20002. Internet: www.saa.org

For information about careers in geography, contact

- Association of American Geographers, 1710 16th St. NW, Washington, DC 20009. Internet: www.aag.org

Information on careers for historians is available from

- American Historical Association, 400 A St. SE, Washington, DC 20003. Internet: www.historians.org

Why It's Hot

This family of occupations is diverse, with some growing much faster than others. Anthropologists and archaeologists are the fastest-growing, partly because they are needed to help businesses and government agencies work with subcultures in the United States and foreign cultures around the world. Those with skills at analyzing bones and artifacts will be needed for forensic work and for interpreting sites threatened by construction projects. Geographers, especially those with good GIS skills, will be in demand because they can advise businesses and government agencies about where infrastructure projects are needed and how to minimize the environmental impact of construction.

Sociologists and Political Scientists

Sociologists and political scientists study all aspects of human society and political systems—from social behavior and the origin of social groups to the origin, development, and operation of political systems.

Just the Facts

Earnings: $84,419

Job Growth: 20.8%

Annual Openings: 480

Education and Training: Master's degree

While at Work

Sociologists and political scientists do research that provides insights into different ways individuals, groups, and governments make decisions, exercise power, and respond to change. Through their studies and analyses, sociologists and political scientists suggest solutions to social, business, personal, and governmental problems.

Sociologists study society and social behavior by examining the groups, cultures, organizations, and social institutions people form. They also study the activities in which people participate, including activities conducted in social, religious, political, economic, and business organizations. They study the behavior of, and interaction among, groups, organizations, institutions, and nations, and how they react to phenomena such as the spread of technology, crime, social movements, and epidemics of illness. They also trace the origin and growth of these groups and interactions. Sociologists analyze how social influences affect different individuals and groups, and the ways organizations and institutions affect the daily lives of those same people.

To analyze these social patterns, sociologists usually begin by designing research projects that incorporate a variety of methods, including historical analysis, comparative analysis, and quantitative and qualitative techniques. Through this process of applied research, they construct theories and produce information that attempts to explain certain social trends or that will enable people to make better decisions or manage their affairs more effectively. Most sociologists work in one or more specialties, such as social organization, stratification, and mobility; racial and ethnic relations; education; the family; social psychology; urban, rural, political, and comparative sociology; gender relations; demography; gerontology; criminology; and sociological practice.

Political scientists conduct research on a wide range of subjects, such as relations between the United States and other countries, the institutions and political life of nations, the politics of small towns or major metropolises, and the decisions of the U.S. Supreme Court. Studying and evaluating topics such as public opinion, political decision making, ideology, and public policy, they analyze the structure and operation of governments, as well as various other entities. Depending on the topic, a political scientist might analyze a public-opinion survey, study election results or public documents, or interview public officials. Occasionally, they may collaborate with government economists to assess the effects of specific changes in legislation or public policy, such as the effects of the deregulation of industries or of changes in Social Security. Through academic publications, written reports, or public presentations, political scientists present their research reports and often identify new issues for research and analysis.

Most political scientists—about 63 percent—work for the federal government. Some find work in research and development firms performing work for the federal government on a contract basis. The relatively few who work in the Foreign Service may help formulate and implement foreign policy.

Political scientists conduct research on a wide range of subjects.

Also Known As

Political scientists who are *policy analysts* work for government or in labor, political, or professional organizations, some of which are nonprofit. These workers gather and analyze information to assist in the planning, development, review, and interpretation of government or industrial policies. They use the results of their research to raise public awareness of social issues, such as crime prevention, access to health care, and protection of the environment, hoping to influence government action.

Job Fit

Personality Type
Investigative-Artistic-Social

Career Cluster
07 Government and Public Administration

Skills
Science
Communications
Computer Programming
Thought-Processing
Mathematics
Management
Social Skills

Work Styles
Analytical Thinking
Achievement/Effort
Innovation
Independence
Persistence
Initiative
Integrity

Working Conditions

Most sociologists and political scientists have regular hours. Generally working behind a desk, either alone or in collaboration with other social scientists, they read and write research articles or reports. Many experience the pressures of writing and publishing, as well as those associated with deadlines and tight schedules. Some sociologists may be required to attend meetings. Political scientists on foreign assignment must adjust to unfamiliar cultures, climates, and languages.

Sociologists and political scientists employed by colleges and universities usually have flexible work schedules, often dividing their time among teaching, research, writing, consulting, and administrative responsibilities. Those who teach in these settings are classified as postsecondary teachers.

■ What's Required

Some entry-level positions for sociologists and political scientists are available to those with a bachelor's degree, but higher degrees are required for the majority of positions. Prospects need good quantitative and qualitative skills.

Education and Training

Whether working in government, industry, research organizations, or consulting firms, sociologists and political scientists with a bachelor's degree usually qualify for entry-level positions as a market analyst, research assistant, writer, or policy analyst. Graduates with master's degrees in applied specialties usually qualify for most administrative and research positions, while a Ph.D. degree is typically required for college and university teaching positions.

> ### CONSIDER THIS...
>
> Training in statistics and mathematics is essential for many political scientists, who increasingly are using mathematical and quantitative research methods. The ability to use computers for research purposes is mandatory in most disciplines.

Many sociology and political science students can benefit greatly from internships. Numerous government agencies, as well as nonprofit and other organizations, offer internships or volunteer research opportunities. Also, the vast majority of colleges and universities have student organizations devoted to specific public policy issues, and many provide opportunities for debates, often hosted by the political science department.

- American government and politics
- Criminology
- Demography and population studies
- International relations and affairs
- International/global studies
- Political science and government, general
- Sociology
- Urban studies/affairs

Additional Qualifications

Sociologists and political scientists need excellent written and oral communication skills to report research findings and to collaborate on research. Successful workers also need intellectual curiosity and creativity because they constantly are seeking new information about people, things, and ideas. The ability to think logically and methodically also is essential in analyzing complicated issues, such as the relative merits of various forms of government.

School Subjects to Study

- Algebra
- Computer science
- English
- Geometry
- History
- Public speaking
- Trigonometry

Moving Up

Many sociologists and political scientists choose to teach in their field, often while pursuing their own research. These workers are usually classified as postsecondary teachers. The minimum requirement for most positions in colleges and universities is a Ph.D. degree. Graduates with a master's degree in sociology or political science may qualify for teaching positions in community colleges.

■ Employment

Sociologists and political scientists held about 9,000 jobs in 2008, of which 4,900 were held by sociologists. Most sociologists worked as researchers, administrators, and counselors for a wide range of employers. The industries that employed the largest number of sociologists in 2008 were scientific research and development services, social advocacy organizations, and state and local government, excluding education and hospitals.

Many sociologists—about 37 percent—teach in colleges and universities and in secondary and elementary schools.

Political scientists held about 4,100 jobs in 2008. About 63 percent worked for the federal government. Most of the remainder worked in scientific research and development services and religious, grantmaking, civic, professional, and similar organizations.

Job Prospects

Overall employment of sociologists and political scientists is expected to grow 21 percent in the 10-year period ending 2018, much faster than the average for all occupations. Sociologists will experience much faster than average job growth because the incorporation of sociology into research in other fields continues to increase. Sociologists possess broad training and education in analytical, methodological, conceptual, and quantitative and qualitative analysis and research, so their skills can be applied to many different occupations. As a result, many workers with sociology backgrounds will find work in niche areas with specialized titles, such as market analyst, research assistant, writer, and policy analyst. Some sociologists may find work conducting policy research for consulting firms, and their knowledge of society and social behavior may be used as well by a variety of companies in product development, marketing, and advertising. Demand for sociologists also will stem from growth in the number of social, political, and business associations and organizations, including many nonprofit organizations, to conduct various evaluations and statistical work.

Employment of political scientists is projected to grow faster than average, reflecting the growing importance of public policy and research. Demand for political science research is growing because of increasing interest in politics, foreign affairs, and public policy, including social and environmental policy issues, health care, and immigration. Political scientists will use their knowledge of political institutions to further the interests of nonprofit, political lobbying, and social and civic organizations. Job growth also may be driven by the budget constraints of public resources. As a growing population exerts excess demand on certain public services, political scientists will be needed to analyze the effects and efficiencies of those services, as well as to offer solutions.

In addition to opportunities arising from employment growth, a growing number of job openings will come from the need to replace those who retire, enter teaching or other occupations, or leave their social science occupation for other reasons.

People seeking sociologist and political scientist positions may face competition for jobs, and those with higher educational attainment will have the best prospects. Many jobs in policy, research, or marketing, for which bachelor's degree holders qualify, are not advertised exclusively as sociologist or political scientist positions.

Some people with a Ph.D. degree in sociology will find opportunities as university faculty rather than as applied sociologists. Although there will be competition for tenured positions, the number of faculty expected to retire over the decade and the increasing number of part-time or short-term faculty positions will lead to better opportunities in colleges and universities than in the past. The growing importance and popularity of social science subjects in secondary schools also is strengthening the demand for social science teachers at that level.

People who have a master's or Ph.D. degree in political science, who are skilled in quantitative and qualitative techniques, and who also have specialized skills should have the best opportunities. Some will find jobs in the federal government as the expected number of retirements increases.

> **CONSIDER THIS...**
>
> While in college, aspiring sociologists and political scientists should gain experience gathering and analyzing data, conducting interviews or surveys, and writing reports on their findings. This experience can prove invaluable later in obtaining a full-time position in the field because much of the work, especially in the beginning, may center on these duties.

> **CONSIDER THIS...**
>
> Because of the wide range of skills and knowledge possessed by these workers, many compete for jobs with other workers, such as anthropologists and archaeologists, geographers, historians, market and survey researchers, psychologists, engineers, and statisticians.

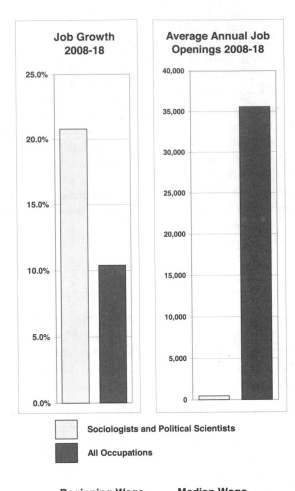

Job Growth 2008-18

Average Annual Job Openings 2008-18

☐ Sociologists and Political Scientists

■ All Occupations

Income

Median annual wages of sociologists in May 2008 were $68,570. The middle 50 percent earned between $51,110 and $92,220. The lowest 10 percent earned less than $40,720, and the highest 10 percent earned more than $122,130. Median annual wages of sociologists in scientific research and development services were $72,170.

Median annual wages of political scientists in May 2008 were $104,130. The middle 50 percent earned between $74,040 and $124,490. The lowest 10 percent earned less than $47,220, and the highest 10 percent earned more than $146,880.

In March 2009, the federal government's average salary was $100,824 for sociologists. Beginning salaries were higher in selected areas of the country where the prevailing local pay level was higher.

Related Jobs

- Archivists, curators, and museum technicians
- Counselors
- Economists
- Market and survey researchers
- Psychologists
- Social workers
- Social scientists, other
- Statisticians
- Teachers—kindergarten, elementary, middle, and secondary
- Teachers—postsecondary
- Urban and regional planners

How to Learn More

Information about careers in sociology is available from

- American Sociological Association, 1430 K St. NW, Suite 600, Washington, DC 20005. Internet: www.asanet.org

For information about careers in political science, contact

- American Political Science Association, 1527 New Hampshire Ave. NW, Washington, DC 20036. Internet: www.apsanet.org

For information about careers in public policy, contact

- National Association of Schools of Public Affairs and Administration, 1029 Vermont Ave. NW, Suite 1100, Washington, DC 20005. Internet: www.naspaa.org

For information about careers in policy analysis, an important task for some social scientists, see "Policy analysts: Shaping society through research and problem-solving," online at www.bls.gov/opub/ooq/2007/spring/art03.pdf and in the spring 2007 issue of the *Occupational Outlook Quarterly*.

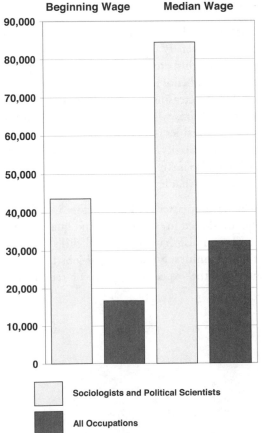

Beginning Wage

Median Wage

☐ Sociologists and Political Scientists

■ All Occupations

Surgical Technologists

Surgical technologists assist in operations, under the supervision of surgeons, registered nurses, or other surgical personnel.

Just the Facts

Earnings: $38,740

Job Growth: 25.3%

Annual Openings: 4,630

Education and Training: Postsecondary vocational training

While at Work

Surgical technologists, also called *scrubs* and *surgical or operating room technicians,* assist in surgical operations. Surgical technologists are supervised by other members of the operating room team, which most commonly includes surgeons, anesthesiologists, and circulating nurses.

Before an operation, surgical technologists help prepare the operating room by setting up surgical instruments and equipment, sterile drapes, and sterile solutions. They assemble both sterile and nonsterile equipment, checking and adjusting it to ensure it is working properly. Technologists also get patients ready for surgery by washing, shaving, and disinfecting incision sites. They transport patients to the operating room, help position them on the operating table, and cover them with sterile surgical drapes. Technologists also observe patients' vital signs, check charts, and help the surgical team put on sterile gowns and gloves.

During surgery, technologists pass instruments and other sterile supplies to surgeons and surgeon assistants. They may hold retractors, cut sutures, and help count sponges, needles, supplies, and instruments. Surgical technologists help prepare, care for, and dispose of specimens taken for laboratory analysis and help apply dressings. Some operate sterilizers, lights, or suction machines and help operate diagnostic equipment.

After an operation, surgical technologists may help transfer patients to the recovery room and clean and restock the operating room.

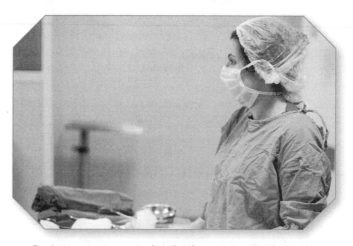

During surgery, surgical technologists pass instruments and other sterile supplies to surgeons.

Also Known As

Certified surgical technologists with additional specialized education or training also may act in the role of the *surgical first assistant* or *circulating technologist*. The surgical first assistant, as defined by the American College of Surgeons (ACS), provides aid in exposure, hemostasis (controlling blood flow and stopping or preventing hemorrhage), and other technical functions under the surgeon's direction that help the surgeon carry out a safe operation. A circulating technologist is the "unsterile" member of the surgical team who interviews the patient before surgery; prepares the patient; helps with anesthesia; obtains and opens packages from which the "sterile" people remove the sterile contents during the procedure; keeps a written account of the surgical procedure; and answers the surgeon's questions about the patient during the surgery.

Job Fit

Personality Type

Realistic-Social-Conventional

Career Cluster

08 Health Science

Skills

Equipment Use/Maintenance

Management

Social Skills

Communications

Work Styles

Social Skills Orientation

Achievement/Effort

Stress Tolerance

Self-Control

Adaptability/Flexibility

Concern for Others

Initiative

Persistence

Working Conditions

Surgical technologists work in clean, well-lighted, cool environments. They must stand for long periods and remain alert during operations. At times, they may be exposed to communicable diseases and unpleasant sights, odors, and materials.

Most surgical technologists work a regular 40-hour week, although they may be on call or work nights, weekends, and holidays on a rotating basis.

■ What's Required

Training programs last 9 to 24 months and lead to a certificate, diploma, or associate degree. Professional certification can help in getting jobs and promotions.

Education and Training

Surgical technologists receive their training in formal programs offered by community and junior colleges, vocational schools, universities, hospitals, and the military. In 2009, the Commission on Accreditation of Allied Health Education Programs (CAAHEP) recognized more than 450 accredited training programs. Programs last from 9 to 24 months and lead to a certificate, diploma, or associate degree. High school graduation normally is required for admission.

Programs provide classroom education and supervised clinical experience. Students take courses in anatomy, physiology, microbiology, pharmacology, professional ethics, and medical terminology. Other topics covered include the care and safety of patients during surgery, sterile techniques, and surgical procedures. Students also learn to sterilize instruments; prevent and control infection; and handle special drugs, solutions, supplies, and equipment.

> **CONSIDER THIS...**
>
> About 10 CAAHEP-accredited programs offer online learning. To cover the skills that cannot be learned from a computer screen, all such programs require students to get a certain amount of supervised clinical training at a local health-care facility.

> **CONSIDER THIS...**
>
> The "technologist" part of this occupation name is not just a synonym for "assistant" or "aide." Work in the operating room involves many technologies, which are always advancing. This is why continuing education is a necessary requirement for staying in this career.

Most employers prefer to hire certified technologists. Technologists may obtain voluntary professional certification from the Liaison Council on Certification for the Surgical Technologist by graduating from a CAAHEP-accredited program and passing a national certification examination. They may then use the Certified Surgical Technologist (CST) designation. Continuing education or reexamination is required to maintain certification, which must be renewed every 4 years.

Certification also may be obtained from the National Center for Competency Testing (NCCT). To qualify to take the exam, candidates follow one of three paths: complete an accredited training program; undergo a 2-year hospital on-the-job training program; or acquire 7 years of experience working in the field. After passing the exam, individuals may use the designation Tech in Surgery-Certified, TS-C (NCCT). This certification must be renewed every 5 years through either continuing education or reexamination.

Postsecondary Programs to Consider

- Pathology/pathologist assistant training
- Surgical technology/technologist training

Additional Qualifications

Surgical technologists need manual dexterity to handle instruments quickly. They also must be conscientious, orderly, and emotionally stable to handle the demands of the operating room environment. Technologists must respond quickly and must be familiar with operating procedures in order to have instruments ready for surgeons without having to be told. They are expected to keep abreast of new developments in the field.

School Subjects to Study

- Algebra
- Biology
- Chemistry
- English
- Geometry
- Trigonometry

Moving Up

Technologists advance by specializing in a particular area of surgery, such as neurosurgery or open heart surgery. They also may work as circulating technologists. With additional training, some technologists advance to first assistant. Some surgical technologists manage central supply departments in hospitals or take positions with insurance companies, sterile supply services, and operating equipment firms.

■ Employment

Surgical technologists held about 91,500 jobs in 2008. About 71 percent of jobs for surgical technologists were in hospitals, mainly in operating and delivery rooms. Other jobs were in offices of physicians or dentists who perform outpatient surgery and in outpatient care centers, including ambulatory surgical centers. A few technologists, known as private scrubs, are employed directly by surgeons who have special surgical teams, such as those for liver transplants.

Job Prospects

Employment of surgical technologists is expected to grow 25 percent in the 10-year period ending 2018, much faster than the average for all occupations, as the volume of surgeries increases.

Hospitals will continue to be the primary employer of surgical technologists, although much faster employment growth is expected in offices of physicians and in outpatient care centers, including ambulatory surgical centers.

Job opportunities will be best for technologists who are certified.

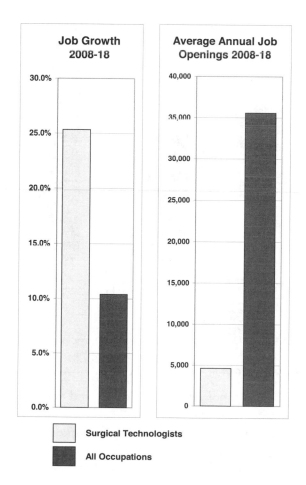

Income

Median annual earnings of wage-and-salary surgical technologists were $38,740 in May 2008. The middle 50 percent earned between $32,490 and $46,910. The lowest 10 percent earned less than $27,510, and the highest 10 percent earned more than $54,300. Median annual earnings in the industries employing the largest numbers of surgical technologists were $38,640 in general medical and surgical hospitals; $38,520 in offices of physicians; $39,660 in outpatient care centers; $36,380 in offices of dentists; and $40,880 in specialty hospitals.

Benefits provided by most employers include paid vacation and sick leave, health, medical, vision, dental insurance and life insurance, and a retirement program. A few employers also provide tuition reimbursement and child care benefits.

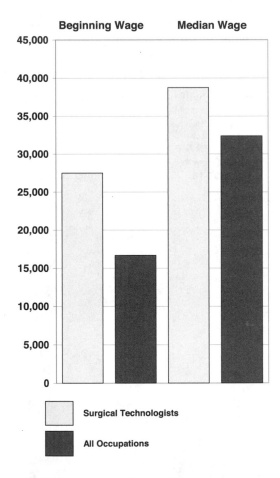

Beginning Wage   **Median Wage**

- Surgical Technologists
- All Occupations

Related Jobs

- Clinical laboratory technologists and technicians
- Dental assistants
- Licensed practical and licensed vocational nurses
- Medical assistants

How to Learn More

For additional information on a career as a surgical technologist and a list of CAAHEP-accredited programs, contact

- Association of Surgical Technologists, 6 West Dry Creek Circle, Suite 200, Littleton, CO 80120. Internet: www.ast.org

For information on becoming a Certified Surgical Technologist, contact

- Liaison Council on Certification for the Surgical Technologist, 6 West Dry Creek Circle, Suite 100, Littleton, CO 80120. Internet: www.lcc-st.org

For information on becoming a Tech in Surgery-Certified, contact

- National Center for Competency Testing, 7007 College Blvd., Suite 705, Overland Park, KS 66211.

Why It's Hot

The number of surgical procedures is expected to rise as the population grows and ages. Older people, including the baby-boom generation, who generally require more surgical procedures, will account for a larger portion of the general population. In addition, technological advances, such as fiber optics and laser technology, will permit an increasing number of new surgical procedures to be performed and also will allow surgical technologists to assist with a greater number of procedures.

Teachers— Self-Enrichment Education

Self-enrichment teachers provide instruction in a wide variety of subjects that students take for fun or self-improvement.

Just the Facts

Earnings: $35,720

Job Growth: 32.0%

Annual Openings: 12,030

Education and Training: Work experience in a related occupation

While at Work

Some self-enrichment teachers teach a series of classes that provide students with useful life skills, such as cooking, personal finance, and time management. Others provide group instruction intended solely for recreation, such as photography, pottery, and painting. Many others provide one-on-one instruction in a variety of subjects, including dance, singing, or playing a musical instrument. Some teachers conduct courses on academic subjects, such as literature, foreign language, and history, in a nonacademic setting. The classes self-enrichment teachers give seldom lead to a degree and attendance is voluntary, but dedicated, talented students sometimes go on to careers in the arts.

Self-enrichment teachers may have styles and methods of instruction that differ greatly. Most self-enrichment classes are relatively informal. Some classes, such as pottery or sewing, may be largely hands-on, with the instructor demonstrating methods or techniques for the class, observing students as they attempt to do it themselves, and pointing out mistakes to students and offering suggestions to improve techniques. Other classes, such as those involving financial planning or religion and spirituality, may center on lectures or might rely more heavily on group discussions. Self-enrichment teachers may also teach classes offered through religious institutions, such as marriage preparation or classes in religion for children.

Many of the classes that self-enrichment educators teach are shorter in duration than classes taken for academic credit; some finish in 1 or 2 days or several weeks. These brief classes tend to be introductory in nature and generally focus on only one topic—for example, a cooking class that teaches students how to make bread. Some self-enrichment classes introduce children and youth to activities such as piano or drama and may be designed to last anywhere from 1 week to several months.

Many self-enrichment teachers provide one-on-one lessons to students. The instructor may work with the student for only an hour or two a week, telling the student what to practice in the interim until the next lesson. Many instructors work with the same students on a weekly basis for years and derive satisfaction from observing them mature and gain expertise. The most talented students may go on to paid careers as craft artists, painters, sculptors, dancers, singers, or musicians.

All self-enrichment teachers must prepare lessons beforehand and stay current in their fields. Although not a requirement for most types of classes, teachers may use computers and other modern technologies in their instruction or to maintain business records.

Also Known As

Most self-enrichment teachers have job titles that refer to the subject being taught, such as *acting teachers, art instructors, ceramics instructors, drama coaches, ESL teachers, guitar teachers, martial arts instructors, speed reading teachers,* or *water safety teachers.*

Job Fit

Personality Type
Social-Artistic-Enterprising

Career Cluster
05 Education and Training

Skills
Social Skills

Thought-Processing

Communications

Management

Science

Work Styles
Leadership

Self-Control

Social Skills Orientation

Concern for Others

Innovation

Independence

Integrity

Dependability

Working Conditions

Few self-enrichment education teachers are full-time, salaried workers. Most either work part time or are self-employed. Some have several part-time teaching assignments, but it is most common for teachers to have a full-time job in another occupation, often related to the subject that they teach, in addition to their part-time teaching job. Although jobs in this occupation are primarily part time and pay is low, most teachers enjoy their work because it gives them the opportunity to share a subject they enjoy with others.

Many classes for adults are held in the evenings and on weekends to accommodate students who have a job or family responsibilities. Similarly, self-enrichment classes for children are usually held after school, on weekends, or during school vacations.

Self-enrichment teachers teach classes that provide students with useful life skills.

■ What's Required

The main qualification for self-enrichment teachers is expertise in their subject area, but requirements vary greatly with the type of class taught and the place of employment.

Education and Training

In general, there are few educational or training requirements for a job as a self-enrichment teacher beyond being an expert in the subject taught. To demonstrate expertise, however, self-enrichment teachers may be required to have formal training in disciplines, such as art or music, where specific teacher training programs are available. Prospective dance teachers, for example, may complete programs that prepare them to teach many types of dance, from ballroom to ballet. Other employers may require a portfolio of a teacher's work. For example, to secure a job teaching a photography course, an applicant often needs

to show examples of previous work. Some self-enrichment teachers are trained educators or other professionals who teach enrichment classes in their spare time. In many self-enrichment fields, however, instructors are simply experienced in the field, and want to share that experience with others.

Postsecondary Programs to Consider

- Adult and continuing education and teaching
- Any program that contributes to expertise in a subject that people would study for self-enrichment

Additional Qualifications

In addition to knowledge of their subject, self-enrichment teachers should have good speaking skills and a talent for making the subject interesting. Patience and the ability to explain and instruct students at a basic level are important as well, particularly for teachers who work with children.

School Subjects to Study

- Any subject that contributes to expertise in a subject that people would study for self-enrichment

Moving Up

Opportunities for advancement in this occupation are limited. Some part-time teachers are able to move into full-time teaching positions or program administrator positions, such as coordinator or director. Experienced teachers may mentor new instructors.

■ Employment

Teachers of self-enrichment education held about 253,600 jobs in 2008. The largest numbers of teachers were employed by public and private educational institutions and providers of social assistance.

Job Prospects

Employment of self-enrichment education teachers is expected to increase in the 10-year period ending 2018 by 32 percent, which is much faster than the average for all occu-

Consider This...

Opportunities should be best for teachers of subjects that are not easily researched on the Internet and those that benefit from hands-on experiences, such as cooking, crafts, and the arts. Classes on self-improvement, personal finance, and computer and Internet-related subjects are also expected to be popular.

pations. The need for self-enrichment teachers is expected to grow as more people embrace lifelong learning and course offerings expand. Demand for self-enrichment education will also increase, as more people seek to gain or improve skills that will make them more attractive to prospective employers. Some self-enrichment teachers offer instruction in foreign languages, computer programming or applications, public speaking, and many other subjects that help students gain marketable skills. People increasingly take courses to improve their job skills, which creates more demand for self-enrichment teachers.

10 percent earned less than $9.15, and the highest 10 percent earned more than $32.68. Self-enrichment teachers are generally paid by the hour or for each class that they teach. Earnings may also be tied to the number of students enrolled in the class.

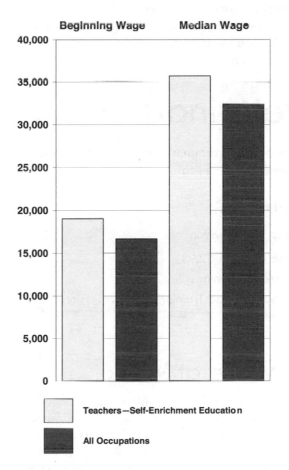

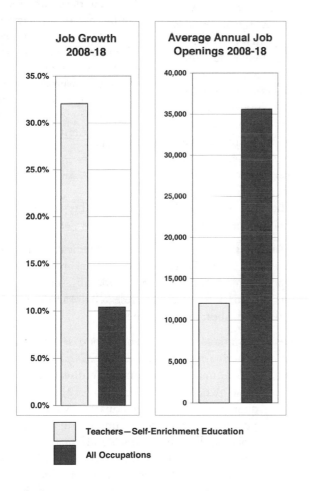

Related Jobs

- Artists and related workers
- Athletes, coaches, umpires, and related workers
- Dancers and choreographers
- Elementary school teachers
- Kindergarten teachers
- Middle school teachers
- Musicians, singers, and related workers
- Preschool teachers
- Recreation workers
- Secondary school teachers

Income

Median hourly earnings of wage-and-salary self-enrichment teachers were $17.17 in May 2008. The middle 50 percent earned between $12.50 and $24.98. The lowest

How to Learn More

For information on employment of self-enrichment teachers, contact local schools, colleges, or companies that offer self-enrichment programs.

Veterinarians

Veterinarians diagnose and treat diseases and dysfunctions of animals.

Just the Facts

Earnings: $79,050

Job Growth: 32.9%

Annual Openings: 3,020

Education and Training: First professional degree

While at Work

Veterinarians care for the health of pets, livestock, and animals in zoos, racetracks, and laboratories. Some veterinarians use their skills to protect humans against diseases carried by animals and conduct clinical research on human and animal health problems. Others work in basic research, broadening our knowledge of animals and medical science, and in applied research, developing new ways to use knowledge about animals.

Most veterinarians diagnose animal health problems; vaccinate against diseases, such as distemper and rabies; medicate animals suffering from infections or illnesses; treat and dress wounds; set fractures; perform surgery; and advise owners about animal feeding, behavior, and breeding.

According to the American Medical Veterinary Association, more than 70 percent of veterinarians who work in private medical practices predominately, or exclusively, treat small animals. *Small-animal practitioners* usually care for companion animals, such as dogs and cats, but also treat birds, reptiles, rabbits, ferrets, and other animals that can be kept as pets. About one-fourth of all veterinarians work in mixed animal practices, where they see pigs, goats, cattle, sheep, and some wild animals in addition to companion animals.

A small number of *private-practice veterinarians* work exclusively with large animals, mostly horses or cattle; some also care for various kinds of food animals. These veterinarians usually drive to farms or ranches to provide veterinary services for herds or individual animals. Much of this work involves preventive care to maintain the health of the animals. These veterinarians test for and vaccinate against diseases and consult with farm or ranch owners and managers regarding animal production, feeding, and housing issues. They also treat and dress wounds, set fractures, and perform surgery, including cesarean sections on birthing animals. Other veterinarians care for zoo, aquarium, or laboratory animals. Veterinarians of all types euthanize animals when necessary.

Veterinarians who treat animals use medical equipment such as stethoscopes, surgical instruments, and diagnostic equipment, including radiographic and ultrasound equipment. Veterinarians working in research use a full range of sophisticated laboratory equipment.

Some veterinarians are involved in food safety and inspection. Veterinarians who are *livestock inspectors,* for example, check animals for transmissible diseases, such as E. coli, advise owners on the treatment of their animals, and may quarantine animals. Veterinarians who are *meat, poultry, or egg product inspectors* examine slaughtering and processing plants, check live animals and carcasses for disease, and enforce government regulations regarding food purity and sanitation. More veterinarians are finding opportunities in food security as they ensure that the nation has abundant and safe food supplies. Veterinarians involved in food security often work along the nation's borders as *animal and plant health inspectors,* where they examine imports and exports of animal products to prevent disease here and in foreign countries. Many of these workers are employed by the Department of Homeland Security or the Department of Agriculture's Animal and Plant Health Inspection Service division.

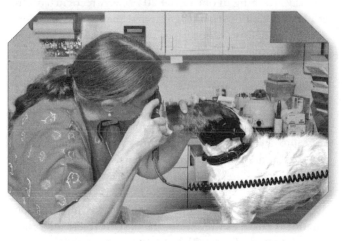

Veterinarians who treat animals use medical equipment such as stethoscopes, surgical instruments, and diagnostic equipment.

Also Known As

Some veterinarians have job titles that reflect the kinds of animals they work with—for example, *large animal veterinarians, poultry veterinarians, small animal veterinarians,* or *wildlife veterinarians.* Others have job titles that indicate specializations in certain animal health issues, such as *animal anatomists, animal chiropractors, veterinarian epidemiologists, veterinary dentists,* or *veterinary parasitologists.* Still others have job titles that indicate some other work role, such as *treatment coordinators* or *veterinary inspectors.*

Job Fit

Personality Type
Investigative-Realistic

Career Clusters
01 Agriculture, Food, and Natural Resources

08 Health Science

Skills
Science

Management

Thought-Processing

Mathematics

Communications

Social Skills

Equipment/Technology Analysis

Equipment Use/Maintenance

Computer Programming

Work Styles
Social Skills Orientation

Concern for Others

Persistence

Analytical Thinking

Leadership

Integrity

Stress Tolerance

Achievement/Effort

Working Conditions

Veterinarians in private or clinical practice often work long hours in a noisy indoor environment. Sometimes they have to deal with emotional or demanding pet owners. When working with animals that are frightened or in pain, veterinarians risk being bitten, kicked, or scratched.

Veterinarians in large-animal practice spend time driving between their office and farms or ranches. They work outdoors in all kinds of weather and may have to perform surgery or other treatments under unsanitary conditions.

Veterinarians working in nonclinical areas, such as public health and research, have working conditions similar to those of other professionals in those lines of work. These veterinarians enjoy clean, well-lit offices or laboratories and spend much of their time dealing with people rather than animals.

Veterinarians often work long hours. Those in group practices may take turns being on call for evening, night, or weekend work; solo practitioners may work extended and weekend hours, responding to emergencies or squeezing in unexpected appointments.

■ What's Required

Veterinarians must obtain a Doctor of Veterinary Medicine degree and a state license. There is keen competition for admission to veterinary school.

Education and Training

Prospective veterinarians must graduate with a Doctor of Veterinary Medicine (D.V.M. or V.M.D.) degree from a 4-year program at an accredited college of veterinary medicine. There are 28 colleges in 26 states that meet accreditation standards set by the Council on Education of the American Veterinary Medical Association (AVMA).

The prerequisites for admission to veterinary programs vary. Many programs do not require a bachelor's degree for entrance, but all require a significant number of credit hours—ranging from 45 to 90 semester hours—at the undergraduate level. However, most of the students admitted have completed an undergraduate program and earned a bachelor's degree. Applicants without a degree face a difficult task gaining admittance.

Preveterinary courses should emphasize the sciences. Veterinary medical colleges typically require applicants to have taken classes in organic and inorganic chemistry, physics, biochemistry, general biology, animal biology, animal nutrition, genetics, vertebrate embryology, cellular biology, microbiology, zoology, and systemic physiology. Some programs require calculus; some require only statistics, college algebra and trigonometry, or pre-calculus. Most veterinary medical colleges also require some courses in English or literature, other humanities, and the social sciences. Increasingly, courses in general business management and career development have become a standard part of the preveterinary curriculum to teach new graduates how to run a practice effectively.

In addition to satisfying preveterinary course requirements, applicants must submit test scores from the Graduate Record Examination (GRE), the Veterinary College Admission Test (VCAT), or the Medical College Admission Test (MCAT), depending on the preference of the college to which they are applying. Currently, 22 schools require the GRE, four require the VCAT, and two accept the MCAT.

New graduates with a Doctor of Veterinary Medicine degree may begin to practice veterinary medicine once they receive their license, but many new graduates choose to enter a 1-year internship. Interns receive a small salary but often find that their internship experience leads to better paying opportunities later, relative to those of other veterinarians. Veterinarians who then seek board certification also must complete a 3- to 4-year residency program that provides intensive training in one of the 20 AVMA-recognized veterinary specialties including internal medicine, oncology, pathology, dentistry, nutrition, radiology, surgery, dermatology, anesthesiology, neurology, cardiology, ophthalmology, preventive medicine, and exotic small-animal medicine.

All states and the District of Columbia require that veterinarians be licensed before they can practice. The only exemptions are for veterinarians working for some federal agencies and some state governments. Licensing is controlled by the states and is not strictly uniform, although all states require the successful completion of the D.V.M. degree—or equivalent education—and a passing grade on a national board examination, the North American Veterinary Licensing Exam. This 8-hour examination consists of 360 multiple-choice questions covering all aspects of veterinary medicine as well as visual materials designed to test diagnostic skills.

The Educational Commission for Foreign Veterinary Graduates grants certification to individuals trained outside the United States who demonstrate that they meet specified requirements for English language and clinical proficiency. This certification fulfills the educational requirement for licensure in all states.

Most states also require candidates to pass a state jurisprudence examination covering state laws and regulations. Some states do additional testing on clinical competency as well. There are few reciprocal agreements between states, so veterinarians who wish to practice in a different state usually must first pass that state's examinations.

Postsecondary Programs to Consider

- Laboratory animal medicine
- Veterinary anatomy (Cert., M.S., Ph.D.)
- Veterinary anesthesiology
- Veterinary dentistry
- Veterinary emergency and critical care medicine
- Veterinary internal medicine
- Veterinary medicine (DVM)
- Veterinary nutrition
- Veterinary pathology
- Veterinary radiology
- Veterinary surgery
- Veterinary toxicology
- Zoological medicine

Additional Qualifications

When deciding whom to admit, some veterinary medical colleges place heavy consideration on a candidate's veterinary and animal experience. Formal experience, such as work with veterinarians or scientists in clinics, agribusiness, research, or some area of health science, is particularly advantageous. Less formal experience, such as working with animals on a farm or ranch or at a stable or animal shelter, also can be helpful. Students must demonstrate ambition and an eagerness to work with animals.

Prospective veterinarians must have good manual dexterity. They should have an affinity for animals and the ability to get along with their owners, especially pet owners, who usually have strong bonds with their pets. Veterinarians who intend to go into private practice should possess excellent communication and business skills, because they will need to manage their practice and employees successfully and to promote, market, and sell their services.

School Subjects to Study

- Algebra
- Biology
- Computer science
- English
- Geometry
- Pre-calculus
- Trigonometry

Moving Up

Most veterinarians begin as employees in established group practices. Despite the substantial financial investment in equipment, office space, and staff, many veterinarians with experience eventually set up their own practice or purchase an established one.

Newly trained veterinarians can become U.S. Government meat and poultry inspectors, disease-control workers, animal welfare and safety workers, epidemiologists, research assistants, or commissioned officers in the U.S. Public Health Service or various branches of the U.S. Armed Forces. A state license may be required.

Nearly all states have continuing education requirements for licensed veterinarians. Requirements differ by state and may involve attending a class or otherwise demonstrating knowledge of recent medical and veterinary advances.

▮ Employment

Veterinarians held about 59,700 jobs in 2008. According to the American Veterinary Medical Association, 80 percent of veterinarians were employed in a solo or group practice. Most others were salaried employees of colleges or universities; medical schools; private industry, such as research laboratories and pharmaceutical companies; and federal, state, or local government. Data from the U.S. Bureau of Labor Statistics show that the federal government employed about 1,300 civilian veterinarians, chiefly in the U.S. Department of Agriculture and the U.S. Food and Drug Administration's Center for Veterinary Medicine. A few veterinarians work for zoos, but most veterinarians caring for zoo animals are private practitioners who contract with the zoos to provide services, usually on a part-time basis.

In addition, many veterinarians hold veterinary faculty positions in colleges and universities and are classified as teachers.

Job Prospects

Employment of veterinarians is expected to increase 33 percent over the 10-year period ending 2018, much faster than the average for all occupations. Veterinarians usually practice in animal hospitals or clinics and care primarily for small pets. Recent trends indicate particularly strong interest in cats as pets. Faster growth of the cat population is expected to increase the demand for feline medicine and veterinary services, while demand for veterinary care for dogs should continue to grow at a more modest pace.

Many pet owners consider their pets as members of the family, which serves as evidence that people are placing a higher value on their pets and is an example of the human-animal bond. These pet owners are becoming more aware of the availability of advanced care and are more willing to pay for intensive veterinary care than owners in the past. Furthermore, the number of pet owners purchasing pet insurance is rising, increasing the likelihood that considerable money will be spent on veterinary care.

More pet owners also will take advantage of nontraditional veterinary services, such as cancer treatment and preventive dental care. Modern veterinary services have caught up to human medicine; certain procedures, such as hip replacement, kidney transplants, and blood transfusions, which were once only available for humans, are now available for animals.

Continued support for public health and food and animal safety, national disease control programs, and biomedical research on human health problems will contribute to the demand for veterinarians, although the number of positions in these areas is smaller than the number in private practice. Homeland security also may provide opportunities for veterinarians involved in efforts to maintain abundant food supplies and minimize animal diseases in the United States and in foreign countries.

Beginning veterinarians may take positions requiring evening or weekend work to accommodate the extended hours of operation that many practices are offering. Some veterinarians take salaried positions in retail stores offering veterinary services. Self-employed veterinarians usually have to work hard and long to build a sufficient client base.

The number of jobs for farm-animal veterinarians is likely to grow more slowly than the number of jobs for companion-animal veterinarians. Nevertheless, job prospects should be excellent for farm-animal veterinarians because of their lower earnings and because many veterinarians do not want to work outside or in rural or isolated areas.

Veterinarians with training in food safety and security, animal health and welfare, and public health and epidemiology should have the best opportunities for a career in the federal government.

Income

Median annual earnings of veterinarians were $79,050 in May 2008. The middle 50 percent earned between $61,370 and $104,110. The lowest 10 percent earned less than $46,610, and the highest 10 percent earned more than $143,660.

The average annual salary for veterinarians in the federal government was $78,140 in May 2008.

According to a survey by the American Veterinary Medical Association, average starting salaries of veterinary medical college graduates in 2009 were $64,826. In the private sector, average starting salaries were $72,318 for those working exclusively with food animals, $69,154 for those working with companion animals, and $37,854 for those working with horses.

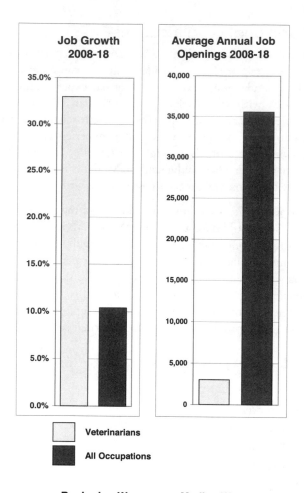

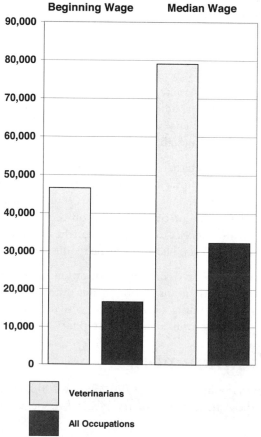

Veterinary Technologists and Technicians

Related Jobs

- Animal care and service workers
- Biological scientists
- Chiropractors
- Dentists
- Medical scientists
- Optometrists
- Physicians and surgeons
- Podiatrists
- Veterinary technologists and technicians

How to Learn More

For additional information on careers in veterinary medicine, a list of U.S. schools and colleges of veterinary medicine, and accreditation policies, send a letter-size, self-addressed, stamped envelope to

- American Veterinary Medical Association, 1931 N. Meacham Rd., Suite 100, Schaumburg, IL 60173. Internet: www.avma. org

For information on veterinary education, contact

- Association of American Veterinary Medical Colleges, 1101 Vermont Ave. NW, Suite 301, Washington, DC 20005. www. aavmc.org

For information on scholarships, grants, and loans, contact the financial aid officer at the veterinary schools to which you wish to apply.

For information on veterinarians working in zoos, see the *Occupational Outlook Quarterly* article "Wild Jobs with Wildlife," online at www.bls.gov/opub/ooq/2001/spring/art01.pdf.

Information on obtaining a veterinary position with the federal government is available at www.usajobs.opm.gov.

Why It's Hot

Excellent job opportunities are expected because there are only 28 accredited schools of veterinary medicine in the United States, resulting in a limited number of graduates—about 2,700—each year. However, applicants face keen competition for admission to veterinary school.

Veterinary technologists and technicians perform medical tests in a laboratory environment for use in the treatment and diagnosis of diseases in animals.

Just the Facts

Earnings: $28,900

Job Growth: 35.8%

Annual Openings: 4,850

Education and Training: Associate degree

While at Work

Owners of pets and other animals today expect state-of-the-art veterinary care. To provide this service, veterinarians use the skills of veterinary technologists and technicians, who perform many of the same duties for a veterinarian that a nurse would for a physician, including routine laboratory and clinical procedures. Although specific job duties vary by employer, there often is little difference between the tasks carried out by technicians and by technologists, despite some differences in formal education and training. As a result, most workers in this occupation are called technicians.

Veterinary technologists and technicians typically conduct clinical work in a private practice under the supervision of a licensed veterinarian. They often perform various medical tests and treat and diagnose medical conditions and diseases in animals. For example, they may perform laboratory tests such as urinalysis and blood counts, assist with dental prophylaxis, prepare tissue samples, take blood samples, or assist veterinarians in a variety of tests and analyses in which they often use various items of medical equipment, such as test tubes and diagnostic equipment. While most of these duties are performed in a laboratory setting, many are not. For example, some veterinary technicians obtain and record patients' case histories, expose and develop X-rays and radiographs, and provide specialized nursing care. In addition, experienced veterinary technicians may discuss a pet's condition with its owners and train new clinic personnel. Veterinary technologists and technicians assisting small-animal practitioners usu-

CONSIDER THIS...

While the goal of most veterinary technologists and technicians is to promote animal health, some contribute to human health as well. Veterinary technologists occasionally assist veterinarians in implementing research projects as they work with other scientists in medical-related fields such as gene therapy and cloning. Some find opportunities in biomedical research, wildlife medicine, the military, livestock management, or pharmaceutical sales.

CONSIDER THIS...

Veterinary technologists and technicians who witness abused animals or who euthanize unwanted, aged, or hopelessly injured animals may experience emotional stress. Those working for humane societies and animal shelters often deal with the public, some of whom might react with hostility to any implication that the owners are neglecting or abusing their pets. Such workers must maintain a calm and professional demeanor while they enforce the laws regarding animal care.

ally care for companion animals, such as cats and dogs, but can perform a variety of duties with mice, rats, sheep, pigs, cattle, monkeys, birds, fish, and frogs. Very few veterinary technologists work in mixed animal practices where they care for both small companion animals and larger, nondomestic animals.

Besides working in private clinics and animal hospitals, veterinary technologists and technicians may work in research facilities, where they administer medications orally or topically, prepare samples for laboratory examinations, and record information on an animal's genealogy, diet, weight, medications, food intake, and clinical signs of pain and distress. Some may sterilize laboratory and surgical equipment and provide routine postoperative care. At research facilities, veterinary technologists typically work under the guidance of Veterinarians or physicians. Some veterinary technologists vaccinate newly admitted animals and occasionally may have to euthanize seriously ill, severely injured, or unwanted animals.

Also Known As

Some veterinary technologists and technicians have job titles that reflect specializations, such as *anesthesia veterinary technicians, intensive care unit veterinary technicians, surgery technicians,* or *X-ray operators.*

Many veterinary technologists and technicians perform diagnostic tests on animals.

Job Fit

Personality Type
Realistic-Investigative

Career Clusters
01 Agriculture, Food, and Natural Resources
08 Health Science

Skills
Science
Mathematics
Equipment Use/Maintenance
Communications
Social Skills
Management
Equipment/Technology Analysis
Thought-Processing
Computer Programming

Work Styles
Social Skills Orientation
Integrity
Stress Tolerance
Self-Control
Concern for Others
Dependability
Attention to Detail
Cooperation

Working Conditions

People who love animals get satisfaction from working with and helping them. However, some of the work may be unpleasant, physically and emotionally demanding, and sometimes dangerous. At times, veterinary technicians must clean cages and lift, hold, or restrain animals, risking exposure to bites or scratches. These workers must take precautions when treating animals with germicides or insecticides. The work setting can be noisy.

In some animal hospitals, research facilities, and animal shelters, a veterinary technician is on duty 24 hours a day, which means that some may work night shifts. Most full-time veterinary technologists and technicians work about 40 hours a week, although some work 50 or more hours a week.

What's Required

There are primarily two levels of education and training for entry to this occupation: a 2-year program for veterinary technicians and a 4-year program for veterinary technologists.

Education and Training

Most entry-level veterinary technicians have a 2-year associate degree from an American Veterinary Medical Association (AVMA)-accredited community college program in veterinary technology in which courses are taught in clinical and laboratory settings using live animals. Currently, about 20 colleges offer veterinary technology programs that are longer and that culminate in a 4-year bachelor's degree in veterinary technology. These 4-year colleges, in addition to some vocational schools, also offer 2-year programs in laboratory animal science. About 10 schools offer distance learning.

In 2009, about 160 veterinary technology programs in 45 states were accredited by the American Veterinary Medical Association (AVMA). Graduation from an AVMA-accredited veterinary technology program allows students to take the credentialing exam in any state in the country.

> ### CONSIDER THIS...
> Several AVMA-accredited colleges offer courses by distance learning so students can learn from home or without relocating from an area where no classroom program is available. These programs allow students to fulfill the clinical training component by learning from a local licensed veterinarian.

Technologists and technicians usually begin work as trainees in routine positions under the direct supervision of a veterinarian. Entry-level workers whose training or educational background encompasses extensive hands-on experience with a variety of laboratory equipment, including diagnostic and medical equipment, usually require a shorter period of on-the-job training.

Each state regulates veterinary technicians and technologists differently; however, all states require them to pass a credentialing exam following coursework. Passing the state exam assures the public that the technician or technologist has sufficient knowledge to work in a veterinary clinic or hospital. Candidates are tested for competency through an examination that includes oral, written, and practical portions and that is regulated by the State Board of Veterinary Examiners or the appropriate state agency. Depending on the state, candidates may become registered, licensed, or certified. Most states, however, use the National Veterinary Technician (NVT) exam. Prospects usually can have their passing scores transferred from one state to another, so long as both states use the same exam.

Employers recommend American Association for Laboratory Animal Science (AALAS) certification for those seeking employment in a research facility. AALAS offers certification for three levels of technician competence, with a focus on three principal areas— animal husbandry, facility management, and animal health and welfare. Those who wish to become certified must satisfy a combination of education and experience requirements prior to taking the AALAS examination. Work experience must be directly related to the maintenance, health, and well-being of laboratory animals and must be gained in a laboratory animal facility as defined by AALAS. Candidates who meet the necessary criteria can begin pursuing the desired certification on the basis of their qualifications. The lowest level of certification is Assistant Laboratory Animal Technician (ALAT), the second level is Laboratory Animal Technician (LAT), and the highest level of certification is Laboratory Animal Technologist (LATG). The AALAS examination consists of multiple-choice questions and is longer and more difficult for higher levels of certification, ranging from 2 hours and 120 multiple choice questions for the ALAT, to 3 hours and 180 multiple choice questions for the LATG.

Postsecondary Program to Consider

- Veterinary/animal health technology/technician and veterinary assistant training

Additional Qualifications

As veterinary technologists and technicians often deal with pet owners, communication skills are very important. In addition, technologists and technicians should be able to work well with others, because teamwork with Veterinarians is common. Organizational ability and the ability to pay attention to detail also are important.

School Subjects to Study

- Algebra
- Biology
- Chemistry
- Computer science
- English
- Geometry
- Trigonometry

Moving Up

As they gain experience, technologists and technicians take on more responsibility and carry out more assignments under only general veterinary supervision. Some eventually may become supervisors.

Employment

Veterinary technologists and technicians held about 79,600 jobs in 2008. About 91 percent worked in veterinary services. The remainder worked in boarding kennels, animal shelters, rescue leagues, and zoos.

Job Prospects

Employment of veterinary technologists and technicians is expected to grow 36 percent over the 10-year projection period ending in 2018, which is much faster than the average for all occupations. Pet owners are becoming more affluent and more willing to pay for advanced veterinary care because many of them consider their pet to be part of the family. This growing affluence and view of pets will continue to increase the demand for veterinary care. The vast majority of veterinary technicians work at private clinical practice under veterinarians. As the number of veterinarians grows to meet the demand for veterinary care, so will the number of veterinary technicians needed to assist them.

The number of pet owners who take advantage of veterinary services for their pets is expected to grow over the projection period, increasing employment opportunities. The availability of advanced veterinary services, such as preventive dental care and surgical procedures, also will provide opportunities for workers specializing in those areas as they will be needed to assist licensed veterinarians. The growing number of cats kept as companion pets is expected to boost the demand for feline medicine and services. Further demand for these workers will stem from the desire to replace veterinary assistants with more highly skilled technicians in animal clinics and hospitals, shelters, boarding kennels, animal control facilities, and humane societies.

Continued support for public health, food and animal safety, and national disease control programs, as well as biomedical research on human health problems, also will contribute to the demand for veterinary technologists, although the number of positions in these areas is fewer than in private practice.

Excellent job opportunities are expected because of the relatively few veterinary technology graduates each year. The number of 2-year programs has recently grown to about 160, but due to small class sizes, fewer than 3,800 graduates are anticipated each year, a number that is not expected to meet demand. Additionally, many veterinary technicians remain in the field less than 10 years, so the need to replace workers who leave the occupation each year also will produce many job opportunities.

Veterinary technologists also will enjoy excellent job opportunities due to the relatively few graduates from 4-year programs—about 500 annually. However, unlike veterinary technicians who usually work in private clinical practice, veterinary technologists will have better opportunities for research jobs in a variety of settings, including biomedical facilities, diagnostic laboratories, wildlife facilities, drug and food manufacturing companies, and food safety inspection facilities.

> **CONSIDER THIS...**
> Keen competition is expected for veterinary technologist and technician jobs in zoos and aquariums due to expected slow growth in facility capacity, low turnover among workers, the limited number of positions, and the fact that the work in zoos and aquariums attracts many candidates.

> **CONSIDER THIS...**
> Employment of veterinary technicians and technologists is relatively stable during periods of economic recession. Layoffs are less likely to occur among veterinary technologists and technicians than in some other occupations because animals will continue to require medical care.

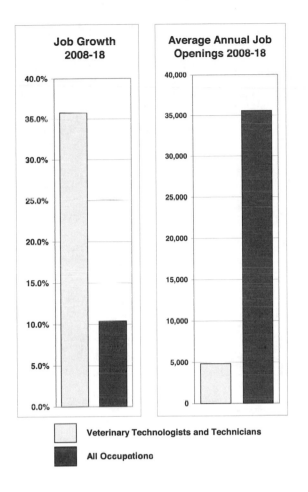

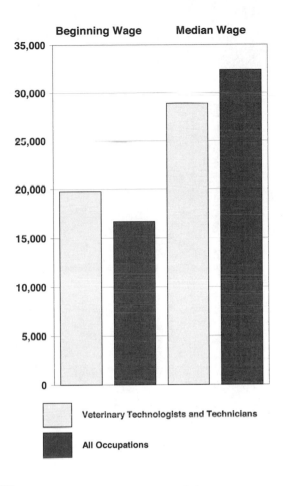

Income

Median annual wages of veterinary technologists and technicians were $28,900 in May 2008. The middle 50 percent earned between $23,580 and $34,960. The bottom 10 percent earned less than $19,770, and the top 10 percent earned more than $41,490. Veterinary technologists in research jobs may earn more than veterinary technicians in other types of jobs.

Related Jobs

- Animal care and service workers
- Laboratory animal caretakers
- Veterinarians
- Veterinary assistants

How to Learn More

For information on certification as a laboratory animal technician or technologist, contact

- American Association for Laboratory Animal Science, 9190 Crestwyn Hills Dr., Memphis, TN 38125. Internet: www.aalas.org

For information on careers in veterinary medicine and a listing of AVMA-accredited veterinary technology programs, contact

- American Veterinary Medical Association, 1931 N. Meacham Rd., Suite 100, Schaumburg, IL 60173-4360. Internet: www.avma.org

Why It's Hot

Excellent job opportunities will stem from the need to replace veterinary technologists and technicians who leave the occupation and from the limited output of qualified veterinary technicians from 2-year programs, which are not expected to meet the demand over the next 10 years.

The Outlook for Industry Employment Through 2018

This appendix illustrates projected employment change from an industry perspective over the 10-year period ending in 2018. Workers are grouped into an industry according to the type of good produced or service provided by the establishment in which they work. Everyone who works in a hospital, for example, is part of the hospital industry, regardless of his or her job duties. The hospital industry includes not only health-care workers, such as doctors and nurses, but also thousands of other workers, such as office managers and janitors.

Industry employment projections are shown in terms of numeric change (growth or decline in the total number of jobs) and percent change (the rate of job growth or decline). Employment totals in this appendix cover only wage-and-salary workers and do not include self-employed or unpaid family workers.

Employment growth for all wage-and-salary workers is projected to average about 11 percent through 2018. This average is shown as a dotted vertical line in two charts. Job growth or decline in some industries affects particular occupations significantly. The number of jobs for registered nurses, for example, is highly dependent on the growth of the hospital industry. Many occupations, however—from human resources managers to computer systems analysts—are found in nearly every industry.

Employment growth in industries depends on industry output (the total amount produced) and worker productivity (how much each worker produces). Labor-saving technologies and methods can increase productivity, limiting employment growth even as output increases. For example, even as agricultural output is projected to increase, employment on farms is projected to decline as advanced methods and machines reduce the number of workers needed to raise crops and livestock.

Likewise, employment in one industry can be affected by changing practices in another. For example, increased use of contractors and consultants has led to greater employment in the management, scientific, and technical consulting services industry. But this practice has led to reduced employment in the many industries that previously hired management and technical analysts as employees.

Industries shown in the charts are defined primarily according to the North American Industry Classification System (NAICS), a system used by the federal government to classify establishments into industry categories. Industries fall into either goods-producing or service-providing sectors.

The goods-producing sectors are as follows:

- **Construction.** Examples of establishments in this sector include electrical contracting firms and construction companies.

- **Manufacturing.** Examples include businesses that make computer chips, machinery, and other goods.

- **Natural resources and mining.** Establishments in this sector include farms, aquaculture companies, and oil and gas extraction companies.

The service-providing sectors are as follows:

- **Educational services.** This sector includes local, state, and private schools and other providers of education.

- **Financial activities.** Included in this sector are finance, insurance, real estate, and rental services organizations.

- **Health care and social assistance.** Health care and social assistance providers—including public and private providers of health care and private providers of social assistance—are part of this sector. Examples include hospitals, doctors' offices, and assisted-living facilities.

- **Information.** This sector includes print, software, and database publishing firms; movie, video, and sound production and distribution establishments; broadcasting and telecommunications providers; and information and data processing providers.

- **Leisure and hospitality.** Examples include hotels, restaurants, sports teams, theme parks, performing arts companies, and arcades.

- **Professional and business services.** Examples include temporary help firms, consulting services, and waste management establishments.

- **Public administration.** This sector consists of government establishments that administer programs and provide for public safety. Federal, state, and local government (except education and hospitals) are classified here.

- **Trade, transportation, and utilities.** Included here are wholesale and retail trade establishments, airports, messenger services, and power plants.

Wage and salary employment by industry type, 2008 and projected 2018

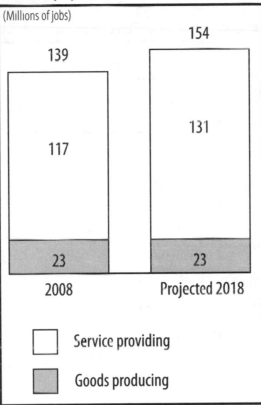

Chart 1

As shown in chart 1, service-providing industries are projected to account for the most job growth through 2018. In goods-producing industries, employment is projected to stay about the same over the decade.

Employment Change

Numeric change in employment of wage and salary workers by industry sector, projected 2008–18

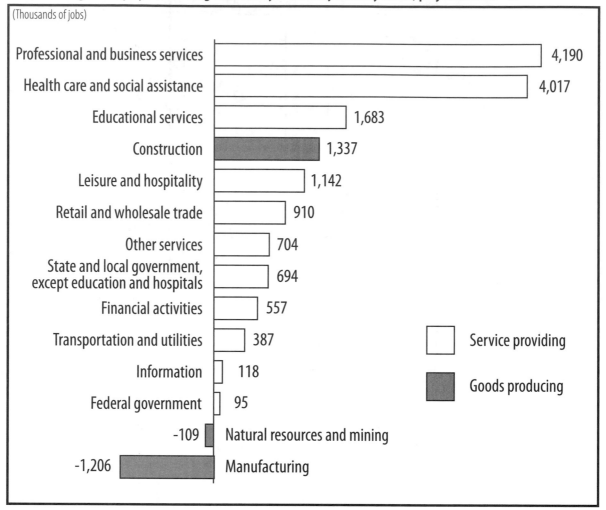

Chart 2

As depicted in chart 2, employment is projected to increase by more than 4 million in both the professional and business services sector and the health care and social assistance sector. Growth in professional and business services is expected to be led by providers of administrative support services and consulting services. Growth in health care and social assistance is expected to be driven by increased demand from an aging population.

Percent change in employment of wage and salary workers by industry sector, projected 2008–18

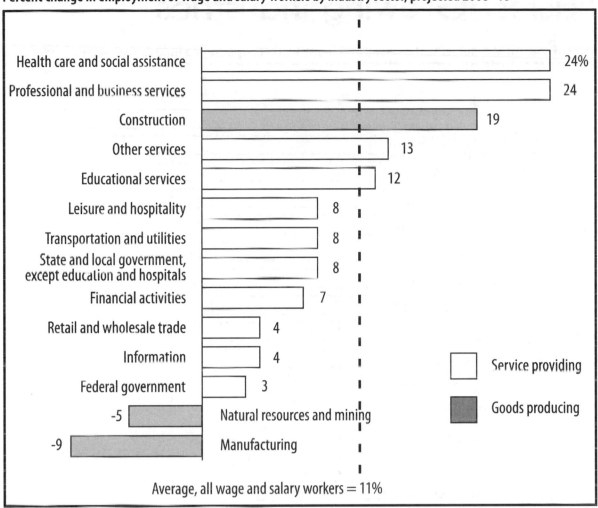

Chart 3

Both the health care and social assistance sector and the professional and business services sector are projected to grow more than twice as fast as the average for all industries through 2018, as shown in chart 3. The average employment growth of 11 percent for all workers through 2018 is shown as a dotted vertical line in chart 3.

Fastest-Growing Industries

Percent growth in employment of wage and salary workers by detailed industry, projected 2008–18

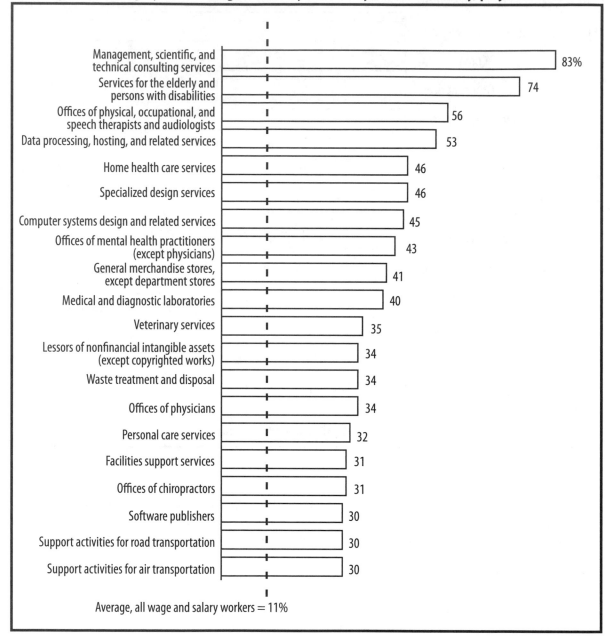

Industry	Percent
Management, scientific, and technical consulting services	83%
Services for the elderly and persons with disabilities	74
Offices of physical, occupational, and speech therapists and audiologists	56
Data processing, hosting, and related services	53
Home health care services	46
Specialized design services	46
Computer systems design and related services	45
Offices of mental health practitioners (except physicians)	43
General merchandise stores, except department stores	41
Medical and diagnostic laboratories	40
Veterinary services	35
Lessors of nonfinancial intangible assets (except copyrighted works)	34
Waste treatment and disposal	34
Offices of physicians	34
Personal care services	32
Facilities support services	31
Offices of chiropractors	31
Software publishers	30
Support activities for road transportation	30
Support activities for air transportation	30

Average, all wage and salary workers = 11%

Chart 4

As charts 4 and 5 show, all of the detailed industries that are expected to have the fastest growth and the most gains in employment between 2008 and 2018 are service-providing ones. The management, scientific, and technical consulting services industry is projected to grow the fastest and to gain the most jobs. Firms in this industry help companies respond to globalization, technological changes, and other business challenges. The average employment growth of 11 percent for all workers through 2018 is shown as a dotted vertical line in chart 4.

Most New Jobs

Numeric growth in employment of wage and salary workers by detailed industry, projected 2008–18

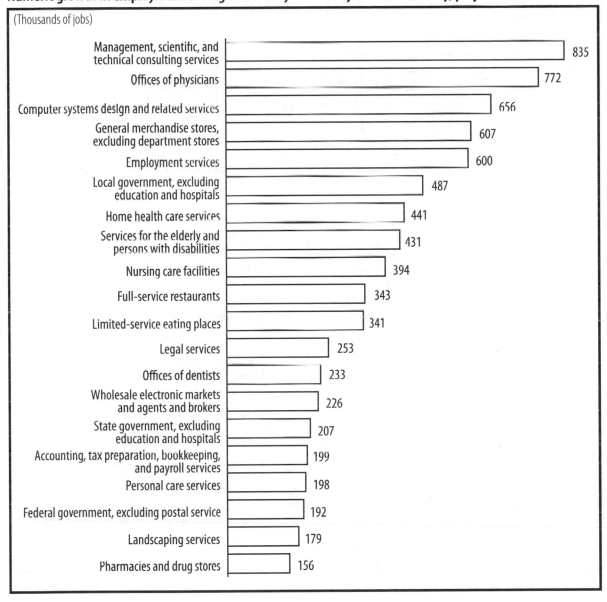

(Thousands of jobs)

Industry	Jobs
Management, scientific, and technical consulting services	835
Offices of physicians	772
Computer systems design and related services	656
General merchandise stores, excluding department stores	607
Employment services	600
Local government, excluding education and hospitals	487
Home health care services	441
Services for the elderly and persons with disabilities	431
Nursing care facilities	394
Full-service restaurants	343
Limited-service eating places	341
Legal services	253
Offices of dentists	233
Wholesale electronic markets and agents and brokers	226
State government, excluding education and hospitals	207
Accounting, tax preparation, bookkeeping, and payroll services	199
Personal care services	198
Federal government, excluding postal service	192
Landscaping services	179
Pharmacies and drug stores	156

Chart 5

Of the 20 industries projected to gain the most jobs, 5 relate to health care, as depicted in chart 5. These industries are offices of physicians, home health care services, services for the elderly and persons with disabilities, nursing care facilities, and offices of dentists. The employment gains in these industries reflect an aging population's increasing demand for services.

Most Job Losses

Numeric decline in employment of wage and salary workers by detailed industry, projected 2008–18

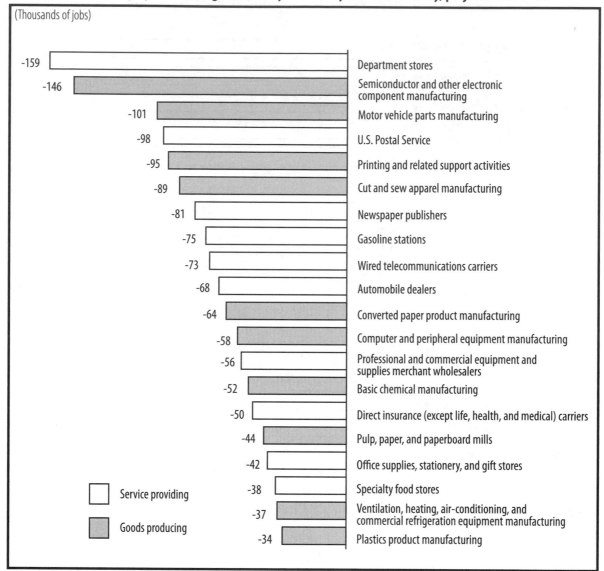

(Thousands of jobs)

-159	Department stores
-146	Semiconductor and other electronic component manufacturing
-101	Motor vehicle parts manufacturing
-98	U.S. Postal Service
-95	Printing and related support activities
-89	Cut and sew apparel manufacturing
-81	Newspaper publishers
-75	Gasoline stations
-73	Wired telecommunications carriers
-68	Automobile dealers
-64	Converted paper product manufacturing
-58	Computer and peripheral equipment manufacturing
-56	Professional and commercial equipment and supplies merchant wholesalers
-52	Basic chemical manufacturing
-50	Direct insurance (except life, health, and medical) carriers
-44	Pulp, paper, and paperboard mills
-42	Office supplies, stationery, and gift stores
-38	Specialty food stores
-37	Ventilation, heating, air-conditioning, and commercial refrigeration equipment manufacturing
-34	Plastics product manufacturing

☐ Service providing
▨ Goods producing

Chart 6

Chart 6 shows the projected job losses through 2018. Declines in industry employment are usually the result of falling demand for specific goods and services, increased imports that reduce domestic production, or the use of technology that increases worker productivity. Declining employment may lead to unfavorable job prospects, but the need to replace workers who leave an industry often creates some job openings.

This appendix was adapted from an article in the Winter 2009–10 edition of the Occupational Outlook Quarterly, *a publication of the U.S. Department of Labor.*

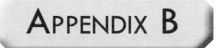

The Outlook for the Overall Economy Through 2018

The economy's need for workers originates in the demand for the goods and services that they provide. So, to project employment, the Bureau of Labor Statistics starts by projecting the gross domestic product (GDP) for 2018. GDP is the value of the final goods produced and services provided in the United States.

Then, BLS estimates the size—in inflation-adjusted dollars—of the five major categories of production. The categories are as follows:

- **Personal consumption expenditures.** This category includes purchases made by individuals, including goods (such as automobiles, clothes, and food) and services (such as education, health care, and rental payments).

- **Gross private domestic investment.** This category includes business investment in equipment and software; the construction of houses, factories, hospitals, and other structures; and changes in business inventories.

- **Government consumption expenditures and gross investment.** This category includes goods and services bought by federal, state, and local governments.

- **Exports.** These are goods and services produced in the United States and purchased in foreign countries.

- **Imports.** Imports are goods and services produced abroad and purchased in the United States. Because GDP measures production in the United States, the value of imports is subtracted from the other four categories of GDP.

Next, BLS breaks down these major categories into more detailed ones, such as the production of automobiles or the provision of medical services.

Changes in the level and composition of production often affect industry employment levels. For example, an increased level of business investment in computer software may increase employment in the computer industry and in all those industries that provide inputs—either products or services—to the computer industry. In turn, employment in occupations in those industries would also grow.

Industry employment levels are also affected by changes in labor productivity—the amount an employee produces per hour of work. Because of technological advances, for example, some industries are able to increase output with fewer employees.

The growth charts in this appendix show annual rates of change instead of the percent change over the entire projections decade through 2018. Annual rates are used here, in part, because they are the measure used for other economic indicators, including inflation.

To show changes in demand more accurately, dollar amounts in these charts are given not in current dollars but in 2000 chain-weighted dollars. This means that amounts have been adjusted for changing prices over time.

GDP in 1988, 1998, 2008, and projected 2018

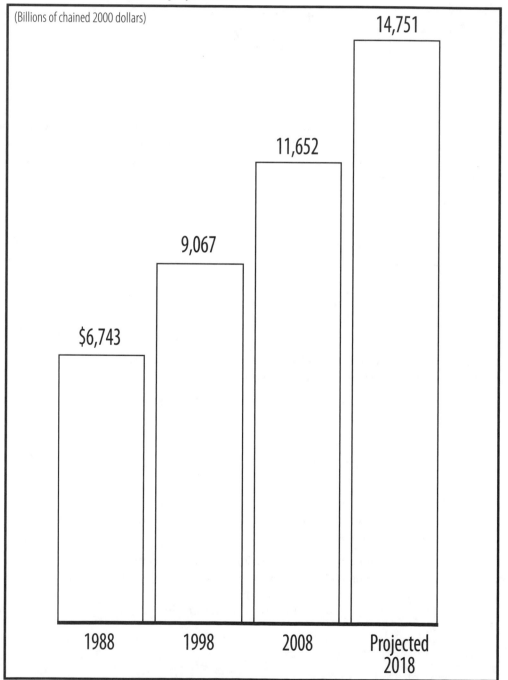

Chart 1

By 2018, the value of goods produced and services provided (gross domestic product, or GDP) in the United States is projected to reach nearly $14.8 trillion, as shown in chart 1.

Average annual percent change in productivity by decade, 1968–2008 and projected 2008–18

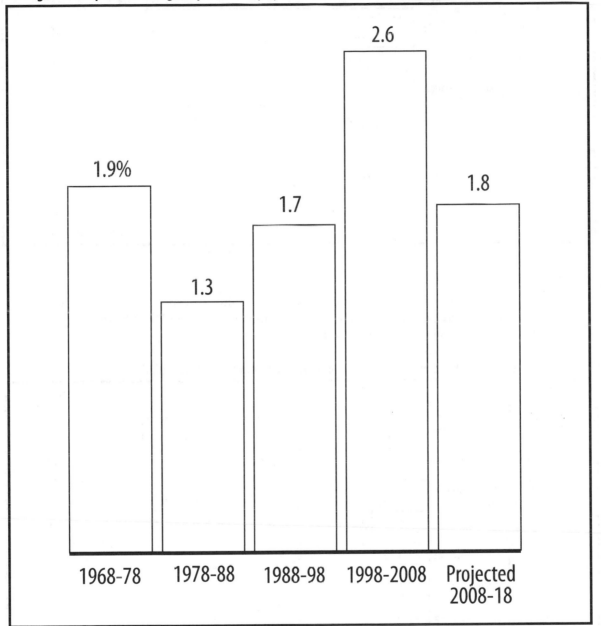

Chart 2

Growth in GDP is due, in part, to increasing productivity. As illustrated in chart 2, productivity is projected to grow 1.8 percent annually over the decade ending in 2018. This rate is slower than the 2.6 percent average rate of growth over the 1998–2008 decade but is in line with growth rates from prior decades.

Growth in goods components of personal consumption expenditures, projected 2008–18

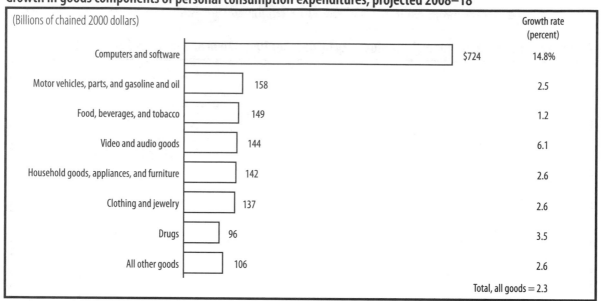

Chart 3

Of all goods components, computers and software expenditures are expected to have the largest and the fastest growth, as shown in chart 3. Contributing to this growth will be the continued expansion of the Internet and ongoing development of mobile technologies.

Growth in services components of personal consumption expenditures, projected 2008–18

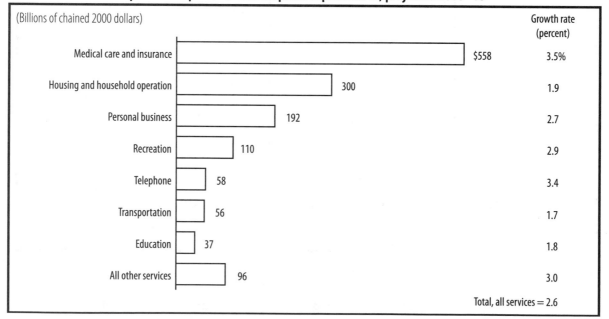

Chart 4

Of the services components, spending on medical care and insurance is expected to have the largest and fastest growth as the population ages, as reflected in chart 4.

This appendix was adapted from an article in the Winter 2009–10 edition of the Occupational Outlook Quarterly, *a publication of the U.S. Department of Labor.*